Gerald Stone is one of Austr... award-winning reporter, founding producer of Nine Network's *60 Minutes* and former editor-in-chief of the *Bulletin* magazine. American-born, he has lived in Sydney since 1962. His previous books include *War Without Honour, Compulsive Viewing* and *Singo: Mates, Wives, Triumphs, Disasters.*

1932

GERALD STONE

MACMILLAN
Pan Macmillan Australia

First published 2005 in Macmillan by Pan Macmillan Australia Pty Limited
This Macmillan edition published 2006 by Pan Macmillan Australia Pty Limited
1 Market Street, Sydney

Copyright © Gerald Stone 2005

Every effort has been made to contact copyright holders of material reproduced in this book. Any person or organisation that may have been overlooked should contact the publisher.

All rights reserved. No part of this book may be reproduced or transmitted in any form or by any means, electronic, mechanical, including photocopying, recording or by any information storage and retrieval system, without prior permission in writing from the publisher.

National Library of Australia
Cataloguing-in-Publication data:

Stone, Gerald (Gerald Louis).
1932.

ISBN-13: 9 78140503 7365.
ISBN-10: 1 40503736 9.

1. Depressions - 1929 - Australia. 2. Australia - History - 1929-1939. 3. Australia - Economic conditions - 1929-1939
4. Australia - Social conditions - 1929-1939. I. Title

994.042

Papers used by Pan Macmillan Australia Pty Ltd are natural, recyclable products made from wood grown in sustainable forests. The manufacturing processes conform to the environmental regulations of the country of origin.

Set in Sabon by Midland Typesetters
Printed in Australia by McPherson's Printing Group

*To my adopted country,
with thanks for all the marvellous
stories it has to tell.*

Contents

Author's note		ix
Prologue: Judgement day		1
1	1931: The prequel	6
2	1932: A leap into the void	23
3	A call to arms	33
4	Faces in the street	44
5	Love in the time of the Great Depression	50
6	Surprise attack	63
7	Flying high	73
8	Blood sport	79
9	The case of the not-so-jolly swagman	88
10	The New Guard bares its teeth	104
11	Off with his head!	113
12	A blue-ribbon occasion: Part I	128
13	A blue-ribbon occasion: Part II	140
14	The Swindell saga: A morality tale	151
15	Getting physical	171

16	Phar Lap: Myth and reality	182
17	The battle of the decrees	189
18	Descent into chaos	202
19	Vested interests	212
20	Dirty tricks: The unmaking of the New Guard	226
21	The power of one	240
22	The longest day of the year	250
23	Legal pornography: Field v Field	258
24	The suicide note	272
25	Game and Lang: The final showdown	281
26	Unanswered questions	292
27	The search for *Atlantis*: Part I	301
28	The big smear	307
29	Radio days: The birth of the ABC	317
30	The last hurrah!	331
31	11 June: The people's verdict	344
32	The search for *Atlantis*: Part II	351
33	1932: A helluva year	372

Epilogue: Winners and losers	384
Endnotes	390
Bibliography	410
Index	415

Author's note

The publication of this book happens to coincide with the 75th anniversary of an event that – more clearly than any other – marked Australia's plunge into the worst of the Great Depression. Economic conditions had been deteriorating for many months, but it was in August 1930 that human folly sealed the country's fate. Panicky political leaders allowed themselves to be stampeded into ill-conceived emergency measures that only served to aggravate the crisis and condemn the population to the world's second highest rate of unemployment. Such a terrible miscalculation was bound to have explosive repercussions, the full force of the backlash erupting at the start of 1932. With the catalytic upheaval to follow, rocking the very foundations of the young Australian federation, it could truly be described as the year that changed a nation.

In trying to do justice to this story I have probably taken more creative liberties than might be considered permissible in a straightforward historical account. All the characters are certainly real and all the events did happen, but to help bridge the inevitable gaps between one known fact and another, I've occasionally ventured a possible scenario for what the participants might have thought, said or done in their unrecorded, private moments. The reader will always be alerted to such speculative passages and can be confident they are supported by available evidence. A case in point is my use of Sydney's notorious sly grog palace, the Fifty-Fifty Club, as a scene in which to postulate conversations built around the main talking points of the day. One can easily imagine what they were just by reading the morning's headlines.

Much of my research has focused on the day-to-day coverage of leading newspapers across the country. Daily press reports can reveal a great deal about the general public mood: the prevailing hopes, fears and prejudices. Unfortunately, they are sometimes tainted by a frustrating melange of conflicting facts, right down to differing versions of a significant quote. In such cases I've extrapolated as best I can. I've also used minor edits – though always within context – to help clarify various documents and textual excerpts. To avoid slowing down the narrative, significant references will receive detailed attribution in the endnotes. However, it might be useful at this point for readers to know the source materials I've relied on most in constructing the chapters that follow.

C. B. Schedvin's *Australia and the Great Depression* is the classic reference in terms of economic analysis. Michael Cannon's *The Human Face of the Great Depression* offers a comprehensive social history of the era. Bede Nairn's *The Big Fella* gives unmatched insights into the political career of Jack Lang. Lang himself wrote several very readable autobiographies: *I Remember*, *The Great Bust* and *The Turbulent Years*. The subversive activities of the New Guard in bringing New South Wales to the verge of civil war are thoroughly documented by Keith Amos in his *The New Guard Movement*

Author's note

1931–1935. New Guard leader Eric Campbell naturally presents a more benign view of his militia's aims, but he couldn't help leaking explosive secrets in his autobiography, *The Rallying Point.* Meanwhile, the wild side of the early thirties, including the illicit carousing at the Fifty-Fifty Club, is well covered in *Razor* by Larry Writer.

The personal letters of Governor Sir Philip Game and his wife, Lady Gwendolen Game, offer precious insights into the tensions of the time. They are held in the manuscript section of the Mitchell Library in Sydney. I am grateful to Mrs Veronica Smith, a granddaughter of the Games, for giving me the family's permission to quote from this material. Bethia Foott's *Dismissal of a Premier: The Philip Game Papers* made my research much easier with its meticulous presentation of all significant correspondence. The staff of the State Library of New South Wales, and of the Mitchell in particular, deserve the highest praise for their courteous assistance. I am also indebted to investment analyst John Hempton of Platinum Asset Management for suggesting a plausible formula to convert 1932 currency into its rough equivalent in today's dollars. The thought of a wealthy socialite of the period splurging £75 on a dress may not mean much to most readers until they realise that's well over $5000.

No author could ask for more encouragement from his publishers. Pan Macmillan's Tom Gilliatt, Karen Penning and their editorial associates – in particular, Karen Ward – guided me calmly but firmly through the minefield of indiscretions that always threaten to blow up in an author's face. My agent, Deborah Callaghan, deserves credit for spotting the glint of a gem buried in my first rather confused and rambling mention of the 1932 concept. My long-time friend and colleague, Peter Luck, offered valuable information and advice. As always, my wife, Irene, has buoyed me with her unshakeable faith and inexhaustible optimism.

Finally, a word of explanation about my dedication. As an American-born migrant with deep affection for my adopted country, I've often wondered what it might have been like growing up here. Writing this book has taken me as close as it's possible to get to reliving the era in which I was born and raised, this time through Australian eyes. In that sense, *1932* has been a grand personal adventure.

Prologue
Judgement day

The Great Depression was born of a great delusion – the Midas myth of a bubble of boundless prosperity that could never burst. Australians, imbued with the hopes of a vibrant young society, would be swept up in the fantasy more than most. By the fateful year of 1929 their recently formed Federation owed more to the financial houses of London than all the governments of Europe, Africa, the Far East, Middle East and South America combined. It ranked as the most credit-addicted, debt-ridden country on earth, next only to Germany; and its small population was destined to be singled out for special punishment come economic judgement day.

A decade earlier prospects could not have appeared brighter, with the end of World War I promising an exciting new era in international trade. After four years of ruinous conflict, Europe clamoured for wheat to feed its ravaged populations and wool to clothe them. Australia had every reason to think of itself as an ascendant force in primary industry just as the United States would emerge as the leading power in manufacturing and investment. So long as primary exports continued to do well it seemed easy enough to service mounting interest bills, but the first months of 1929 showed disaster looming as surely as an iceberg sighted too late to avoid. Wool and wheat receipts nosedived almost simultaneously, partly due to cutthroat foreign competition but also because of the rise of rampant protectionism – the punitive tariffs and other import restrictions that would soon prove so disruptive to the world economy.

British lenders previously could have been counted on to offer temporary assistance until prices came good again. However, events were taking place on the other side of the Atlantic that would plunge Australia into crisis well in advance of most other nations. New York's Wall Street had begun its infamous feeding frenzy, disrupting normal patterns of international investment as all available funds were diverted to high-profit speculation in shares. The market for government securities, especially those of a clearly overstretched borrower like Australia, vanished virtually overnight. The loan-hungry Federation would be left bleating at the bottom of the world like a calf sucking on a dry teat.

What was all that borrowed money being used for? Much of it had been poured into urban development, with a burgeoning new class of city dweller demanding paved suburban streets on which to drive their cars and electricity to run their radios and household appliances. The giant bridge taking shape above Sydney Harbour was the outstanding testament to such unrestrained expenditure – every inch of it another IOU. Other ambitious works programs were under way throughout the nation, perhaps most notably in the newborn city of Canberra. Such projects employed tens of thousands of workers whose incomes were wholly dependent on regular injections of loan money. Their pay packets, in turn, created jobs for many thousands more. When the financial axe fell in London, those necks would be first on the line.

Australia, of course, was hardly the only nation to be brought unstuck by unrealistic expectations. All across the industrialised world, national economies had been steadily undermined by self-indulgent excesses – overproduction, overspending, overborrowing. Instead of scraping away the accumulated rot of inefficient work practices, lazy and incompetent governments merely imposed new protective barriers against outside competition. One unstable economy attempted to prop itself up at the cost of another. The Wall Street crash of October, 1929 was all that was needed to set off an avalanche. Traditional export markets for both primary and manufactured goods would end up buried deepest in the rubble.

The loss of trade income was bound to cause widespread unemployment in Australia under any circumstances but it would be the loans burden above all else that tipped the scales from tough times to a true national calamity. The subsequent cuts to public expenditure would send job losses soaring to the second highest rate recorded in the Great Depression, exceeded – once again – only by Germany. Meanwhile, the crushing debt burden left the federal and six state governments with severely limited options on how to respond to the emergency. As their revenues from taxes, import duties and other sources dipped precariously, the one factor to remain constant was the steady drain from the huge overseas interest bill. That blew out into a critical haemorrhage with the rapidly diminishing value of the Australian pound.

No one political party or government could be blamed for the miscalculations that precipitated the emergency. They were due more to a national mind-set which, like a cracked mirror, distorted the way Australians saw themselves. Many still preferred to think of the island continent not as an independent country but a valuable economic unit within the British Empire, very much like the Middle West corn belt was to the United States. So long as they kept their raw produce flowing northward, they were more than just a tiny population at the bottom of the planet: they formed an indispensable part of a powerful whole.

The illusion of being forever under the protective wing of Britain may well have encouraged the prodigal excess of borrowing. More significantly, though, it blinded the fledgling nation to its own limitations once the endless supply of credit inevitably ran out. A host of other small countries, from Austria to Uruguay, had been quick to appeal for some form of moratorium to suspend debt repayment while they tried to repair their shattered economies. Australia – at least in the eyes of its conservative establishment – was synonymous with British might and majesty and thus far too proud to cry poor.

At the beginning of 1931, however, an imposing figure strode onto the national political stage to turn the loans debacle into the most explosive issue of the Great Depression. Jack Lang, the pugnacious Labor Premier of New South Wales, declared it nothing short of madness to keep paying massive amounts of interest to overseas moneylenders while the families of unemployed Australians were starving.

Lang was popularly known as 'the Big Fella', not so much a comment on his muscular 6 foot 4 inch (193 centimetres) frame as the way he tended to throw his weight around in political forums, purposely setting out to shock and intimidate all who dared oppose him. His rallying cry, *people before money*, would polarise the nation – sparking a wave of passionate confrontations not only between the haves and have-nots, but between those who put their British heritage before all else and those who saw themselves as Australians, first and last. As much as Lang was loved, he was hated even more fiercely –

denounced by his enemies as a mob-provoking demagogue. The political storm stirred up by the Big Fella would reach its peak in the middle of 1932, bringing Australia as close as it ever got to civil war. But to understand the traumatic events of 1932, it is best to begin with 1931, the second most tumultuous year in the life of the nation.

1
1931: The prequel

Nineteen thirty-one was winding up with a bang. Literally. Bang, bang, bang, bang, bang, bang, bang, bang. Eight shots punctuated the usual drone of evening rush-hour traffic streaming along William Street, gateway to Sydney's bustling Kings Cross, three days before the New Year. Flappers in their saucy cloche hats and figure-hugging skirts, mothers wheeling prams, shoppers and office workers on their way home to the eastern suburbs – terrified pedestrians of all description ducked for cover or collided in confusion as they turned to flee. The long line of outward-bound cars, from ubiquitous Fords and sturdy Hudson sedans to elegant Packard saloons and jaunty Rover roadsters, screeched to a halt amid much gnashing of gearbox teeth.

Fred Roberts and James White were too intent on killing each other to notice all the commotion they were causing. In their stylish double-breasted suits and grey fedoras they might have been mistaken as business executives except for the ominous glint of the pistols they waved in each other's direction.

A few paces from White, Irene Carson, a curvaceous brunette with a fetching wisp of hair dangling in the middle of her forehead stood screaming her encouragement like an excited fan at a wrestling match. As she would later tell the court, she had been innocently strolling through the Cross earlier that steamy summer's afternoon when Roberts, a notorious pimp and standover man, jammed a gun in her ribs and demanded that she start selling her body for his benefit. She ran home and complained to her boyfriend White, who immediately set off to avenge her honour.

'Hey, you mongrel,' he shouted on spotting Roberts, 'what do you mean by pulling a gun on this girl?'

'Mind your own business,' the other man snapped back, 'or I'll blow your head off.'

They both drew their revolvers, with White taking cover behind a kerbside rubbish bin. His adversary started backing away to the other side of the street, firing as he went, while motorists manoeuvred frantically to stay clear of his path. Before Roberts reached the opposite kerb, he aimed a final spiteful round in Carson's direction. It missed her by a kiss-curl, shattering the plate glass shop window behind. By then, though, two of White's slugs weighed heavily in his chest.

Fred Roberts slumped slowly to the gutter, coughing blood until his heart could pump no more.

For sheer spectacle the Kings Cross shoot-out topped the list of 128 homicides recorded across Australia during 1931, a worrying upward trend compared to previous years. Yet this was in the midst of the Great Depression when terms like 'crime' and 'violence' had begun to lose all meaning. What could be more 'criminal' than another worker getting robbed of a job every two minutes? What could be more 'violent' than a destitute family being thrown out of their home? For each brutal death like that of Fred Roberts, there were 5000 dead men walking, doomed to tramp endlessly through city streets or country roads with nothing to do and nothing to hope for. In a population of 6.5 million, 650,000 had been reduced to living like refugees in their own land, without adequate food or shelter. Many of them would see in the New Year crammed into one of the sprawling depression-era shanty towns sardonically referred to as Happy Valley. A lot more worrisome things had been happening in 1931 than the odd stray bullet.

Any society would find it difficult to cope with such economic upheaval but Australians, only 30 years into nationhood, faced the very real danger of being torn apart by it. While Anzac bravery had certainly helped to inspire a sense of national pride, Federation remained in many eyes a vague and unwieldy concept. The petulant rivalries that marked the colonial period still bubbled beneath the surface and the advantages to be gained from free trade across state borders were not all that apparent to hard-pressed farmers or manufacturers anxious to protect whatever was left of their local markets. New South Welshmen, Victorians, Queenslanders, South Australians, Western Australians, Tasmanians – if the ordinary citizens of those states felt at all united, it was only by the thinnest thread of an idea. They shared the vision of a classless society, the land of the Fair Go, made possible by one of the world's highest standards of living. The economic crisis would soon expose such an egalitarian dream as a cruel delusion.

Yet there was an ironic flip side to the plight of ordinary Australians in the Great Depression. It was encapsulated by a sensational divorce trial which featured prominently in the Sydney newspapers of 1931. An eastern suburbs socialite named Ivy Field sought alimony of £5000 a year from her estranged husband, Sidney, pointing out that she was accustomed to paying £75 just for a frock to wear at the races. Translated into today's equivalent (at a credible ratio of £1 equalling $70) she was asking for $350,000 a year to support a lifestyle that allowed her to splurge $5250 on a dress. The Field case spilled over into 1932 and will be looked at later in all its lurid detail but the message it broadcast was clear enough. While the crash caused heartache for so many – dragging them from normal, comfortable lives into abject misery – a lucky minority would emerge better off than ever. People from more privileged families, especially those whose incomes were bolstered by inherited wealth, could live rich as third-world rajahs. Their cash reserves allowed them to make great killings on share and property deals and to splurge their profits on luxurious town and country estates manned by platoons of cheap domestic help. Even within the working class a fortunate few would also find themselves better off, so long as they could hold on to their jobs. They benefited from a sharp fall in the cost of food, clothing and other necessities.

The widening gap between the well off and hard done by was to create a volatile atmosphere of divisiveness unknown since the early convict days. Many of the unemployed felt themselves treated like pariahs and their outrage inevitably led to violent protests in every corner of the nation. Grievances varied from state to state, though they flowed from the same scalding cauldron of frustration and despair.

South Australia's worst clash, known as the Beef Riot, saw 2000 demonstrators pitted against baton-wielding police in a protest over substandard food rations. The battle erupted on Friday, 9 January 1931, raging along Adelaide's King William Street for almost twenty minutes, with the more aggressive of the jobless swinging axe handles and hurling rocks before they were finally dispersed. Scores were injured, including seventeen hurt badly enough to require hospital treatment.

Western Australia would follow in March with its Treasury Building Riot, another club-swinging, missile-throwing free-for-all.

'Don't hide our poverty – parade it on the Esplanade to those who are responsible!' the jobless were urged. Again, nearly 2000 marchers converged on government offices in Perth, attempting to break through police barriers to make their case directly to the Premier who, with several of his senior advisers, looked nervously out from the windows above. Roadworks were in progress and the furious protesters hurled clumps of bitumen or ripped up fence posts to wield as clubs before inevitably being beaten into bloody retreat by mounted reinforcements.

In Victoria, house evictions became a common cause of violent protest. The first case of organised resistance was reported in early February, 1931, when 500 demonstrators confronted a bailiff who was attempting to serve a court order for unpaid rent on a family in the Melbourne suburb of West Brunswick. He was badly roughed up and had his car tyres slashed. The following weeks would bring increasingly hostile confrontations, until one incident saw police having to resort to firearms to scatter a threatening mob. Eight officers found themselves set upon by a large group of activists from the Unemployed Workers' Movement who had converged on the Melbourne suburb of Reservoir to try to prevent a family being removed from their home. The constables were punched, kicked and pelted with chairs. One was even struck with a bystander's crutch before the officer in charge fired a warning shot over the attackers' heads to force them to back off.

Queensland's pleasant climate made it a magnet for jobless drifters who became an increasing source of tension throughout 1931, testing the patience of police and local townspeople alike. Their presence would generate a number of skirmishes, culminating in one of the ugliest incidents of the entire depression era – not in terms of casualties but because it raised the spectre of outright class warfare. In this case the tables were turned and the protest involved a vigilante-style attack on 200 itinerants who had set up camp in the Cairns showground. A volunteer force of 4000 'respectable' local citizens – city folk and farmers – armed themselves with clubs and staged a Sunday morning raid to drive the jobless out of town. Some of the showground squatters were toughened swaggies and they attempted to make a stand, fighting back with homemade weapons like tree branches studded with nails or bristling with barbed wire. They were hopelessly outnumbered and those not beaten to the ground quickly vanished into the bush. Later that morning the local hospital took on the appearance of an army field hospital overflowing with casualties, many with broken limbs and gashes wide as bayonet wounds.

Cairns's 'Bloody Sunday' would not occur for some months to come – July, 1932 – but it offered stark proof of how the Great Depression had progressively undermined the very foundations of the Australian way of life. The society seemed to be splitting along discriminatory lines even more insidious than rich versus poor. Every nation had its underclass, whether in the form of a peasantry or unskilled labour force. In contrast, the depression era's poverty-stricken included a sampling from virtually all sections of the population – entrepreneurs, managers, shop owners, salespeople, clerks and artisans, as well as those with lesser qualifications. Among the jobless seeking refuge at the Cairns showground there certainly would have been some who, only a short time earlier, had enjoyed higher wages and status than many of the townspeople who attacked them.

That, indeed, was what made their presence so threatening. The growing army of unemployed could not be easily dismissed as a bunch of deadbeats or no-hopers who deserved their lot and should be grateful for any handout given to them. Instead, they were for the most part as capable and hardworking citizens as any other. Theirs were the haunting faces of victims of a great injustice – not just pitiful to look upon but intimidating as well, since a man who had nothing to lose was capable of anything. Little wonder the solid citizens of Cairns felt compelled to drive them out of sight.

Such flare-ups, though, would prove to be mere sideshows to an all-encompassing confrontation set in motion well before 1931 but rapidly gaining force month by month. In August 1930, Sir Otto Niemeyer, a high-ranking emissary from the Bank of England, met with Australia's political leaders to share his views on the steps needed to pave the way for economic recovery. It was well understood his opinion carried the full weight of the London financial establishment. The portly, homburg-topped Sir Otto couldn't have been received with more deference if he had just descended from Mount Sinai with a flowing white beard and stone tablets under each arm.

Much of the nation's current troubles, Niemeyer opined, could be put down to the 'natural optimism' of Australians – a character trait that tended to blind them to the harsher facts of life. Their standard of living had been allowed to soar much too high, higher even than that of the average British worker, while their productivity was much lower. Commonsense dictated that their main role within the British Empire should be as primary producers – farmers, graziers, miners and hewers of wood; yet they had unwisely attempted to develop a local manufacturing capacity, thus spawning an ever-more-demanding urban work force hungry for modern conveniences and the continual wage rises needed to pay for them.

'Australian credit is at a low ebb, lower than that of any of the other Dominions, not excluding India,' the visiting guru admonished the assembled leaders. 'I assume everyone in this room is in agreement that costs must come down.'

Sir Otto was a banker of the old school, a firm believer in thrift and good management as the answer to most every financial problem, and his prescription for getting out of such a mess could be summed up in just two words: balanced budgets. The first priority must be for federal and state governments to set their own houses in order, eliminating deficits and spending no more than their rapidly shrinking tax revenues allowed. Only then could they hope to restore the business confidence needed to encourage renewed investment. His prescription sounded innocent enough but its likely side effects were horrendous. In the midst of the Great Depression, Australia's political leaders were being urged to impose massive cuts in public works, social services and other government spending, inevitably dumping tens of thousands of more people onto the dole queues. Wages and pensions, too, would have to be drastically reduced, leaving consumers with less to spend, thereby causing further shutdowns of shops and factories. In essence, Niemeyer was advising Australia to make a fresh start, driving all production costs back down to Year Zero.

While such a 'solution' could only be regarded as absurd from today's perspective, it was the prevailing economic wisdom of its era – indeed, one with a persuasive rationale not so different from the popular contemporary slogan extolling the benefits of *short-term pain for long-term gain*. The bitter irony was that Sir Otto had just sailed in from a land whose renowned universities were then abuzz with the radical doctrines of new-wave economists like John Maynard Keynes, urging an exactly opposite approach. In periods of stagnation, Keynes argued, what was needed was more public spending not less: making enough credit available on an emergency basis to pump-prime stalled economies and stimulate employment. Unfortunately, it was one of those revolutionary ideas whose time had not quite come. The assembled leaders promptly fell into line with Niemeyer, drafting a unanimous resolution which pledged in part: 'That the several governments declare their fixed determination to balance their respective budgets in 1930–31 and to maintain a similar balance in future years.'

It should have been obvious to all that as a senior Bank of England representative, Niemeyer had a serious conflict of interests. He was no doubt sincere in wanting to help Australians out of their difficulties but he was also on a mission to protect the hundreds of millions of pounds in British loans accumulated over the years, making sure they continued to return regular dividends until they could be repaid in full. Sir Otto's lecture to the premiers made no mention of the privileged few reaping bonanzas out of the Great Depression through property speculation or share manipulation, nor of the moneylenders delighted to find their annual interest cheques virtually double in value as prices became cheaper and cheaper.

The Niemeyer doctrine, of course, fitted in perfectly with the mind-set of Australia's managerial class, always eager to see less government spending, lower wage rates and troublesome unions brought to heel. Yet, surprisingly, Labor Prime Minister James Scullin, as well as the two Labor premiers of Victoria and South Australia, seemed happy enough to join the conservative-led states in offering their unqualified endorsement of Niemeyer's remedy. It was a decision they would soon regret.

The Melbourne Agreement, as it became known, would pitch the nation into almost two full years of unprecedented upheaval. The suffering thus inflicted was all the more lamentable for the fact that it might well have been avoided but for a curious twist of circumstance. Niemeyer's visit happened to come at a time when the only two public figures in the land who had the foresight, the courage and the stature to challenge him had been temporarily sidelined from the national political arena. One of them was Edward Granville Theodore, Treasurer in the federal Labor government, renowned for his sharp intellect and progressive thinking. Barely a week before Sir Otto's arrival, he had been forced to resign from Cabinet under the shadow of vague corruption allegations dating back to his days as Premier of Queensland.

Of all Australian politicians, Theodore had the best understanding of the exciting new Keynesian theories justifying deficit spending to spur jobs growth. If he had been present at the Melbourne summit he almost certainly would have demanded that the impact of budget cuts be softened with some sort of plan for opening up new sources of credit. In February, 1931, after clearing his name and returning as federal Treasurer, Theodore did, indeed, put forth his bold vision for an emergency employment scheme funded by a special issue of promissory notes, in effect a kind of temporary, depression-era currency. 'Every 100 additional men employed upon productive work would necessitate the employment of at least 200 additional men in the factories, shops and transport services,' he argued forcibly. By then, however, the Scullin Government had been seriously weakened by factional rivalry and was under great pressure from the nation's powerful banking interests to stick strictly to its budget-cutting pledge. The bankers, along with their conservative parliamentary allies, denounced Theodore's far-sighted proposal as a mere ruse for printing phoney money without the gold to back it, a dangerous heresy thought sure to trigger a disastrous wave of runaway inflation.

Jack Lang, leader of the New South Wales Labor Party, may have lacked Theodore's economic expertise but he had two qualities that made him an even more formidable politician: a gift for mesmerising oratory combined with an uncanny ability to sense the public mood. Had he been present at the Niemeyer meeting he could have been counted on to douse the eminent oracle in buckets of acid scorn. 'If lower wages are the cure to our ills,' Lang might have chided in one of his typical lampoons of Sir Otto, 'just imagine what we could save if we paid no wages at all!'

The Big Fella, however, was going through a period in the wilderness after losing an election for his second term as premier in 1927 and had no input whatsoever into the talks. He was left aghast that any Labor government, federal or state, could sign an agreement so detrimental to its blue-collar constituency and rightly predicted the incendiary results – the rage of ordinary workers sweeping fast and hot as a bushfire across the entire country. How else could they react to the prospect of having their hard-won living standards demolished at the snap of an English finger? On 25 October 1930, just two months after Sir Otto cast his spell over the premiers, Lang would be swept back to power on his ringing promise to defy the Melbourne Agreement and defend the nation's cherished lifestyle.

'The issue is very clear,' he declared during a torrid campaign that turned the New South Wales poll into a virtual referendum for or against Niemeyer and the financial interests he represented. 'You are asked to vote for the maintenance of our Australian idealism and our standard of living, or for poverty, unemployment and degradation.'

Lang saw his landslide victory in late 1930 as a popular mandate to push for a radically different approach to recovery. His first opportunity to make his voice heard at a leaders' forum came in early February, 1931. By then even the most ardent Niemeyer admirer had cooled down enough to admit that the balancing of budgets was a goal that could only be achieved in stages over several years. Governments would still be obliged to cut back on public spending and steadily reduce their deficits but the issue to be settled was: by how much per year? Exactly how many more jobs would have to be sacrificed – 20,000? 50,000? 100,000? Such would be the framework of prolonged debate leading to a national recovery strategy known as 'the Premiers' Plan'. It was a debate that, to Lang's mind, ignored the single most important issue of the Great Depression.

As a consummate public speaker, the Big Fella had a talent for breaking down a complex issue into its simplest components. He quickly homed in on a glaring flaw in the budget-cutting pact. If its intention was to stop the haemorrhaging caused by deficit spending, the largest single source of state and federal expenditure was not wages but the interest that had to be paid annually on government borrowings – much of it to British banks and bondholders. Yet, up to that point, the issue of overseas interest had been treated as a sacred cow, almost totally excluded from all official discussions about cost cutting.

Amid the hardships of the depression, many other nations were finding it necessary to delay payment on their borrowings or default on them altogether. Britain itself had persuaded the United States to grant a 40 per cent reduction in the amount due annually on its mountain of war debts. The British, though, did not see fit to offer any such concession to Australia. Their loyal Dominion down-under still paid premium rates on some £90 million – $6.3 billion – in war loans accrued during 1914–1918. Perverse as it may seem, most of that money was borrowed to repay the 'Mother Country' for the expense of billeting, feeding, equipping and transporting the young Australians sent to the killing fields of Gallipoli and France in her defence. More than a decade later, blinded or limbless war veterans remained a painful sight on the streets of every Australian city. How could they possibly be asked to make the further sacrifice of having their meagre pensions slashed while British bondholders got paid every penny in full? Why should hundreds of thousands of Australians go without the necessities of life 'so that that the international money ring shall have its pound of flesh'?

Such were the arguments Jack Lang would use to justify the surprise resolution that he introduced to the Premiers' Conference in Canberra on Monday, 9 February 1931. With his first words, the history of Australia's struggle in the Great Depression changed course irrevocably. Rising to speak in his resonant baritone, the New South Wales Premier proposed: 'That the Governments of Australia decide to pay no further interest to British bondholders until Britain has dealt with the Australian overseas debts in the same manner as she settled her own foreign debt with America.'

At that stage a total of £36 million, over $2.5 billion, poured out of the country each year to meet interest charges – enough to put half the nation's unemployed back to work.

'It is money that was borrowed at inflated prices and must now be repaid during a period of deflation,' Lang went on to plead his case. 'Where two shiploads of wool would have paid a portion of this interest a few years ago, four shiploads are now required to pay the same amount. No Government can continue under such conditions. Surely it is only fair that our British creditors deal with us on the same terms as America dealt with Britain.'

Lang also targeted the large amounts of interest then being paid on government borrowings within Australia, urging legislation to cut the domestic rate by up to half. On the issue of freeing up credit to encourage employment, he went a giant step further than Theodore by advocating an entirely new system of currency. Instead of being tied to the gold standard, the Australian pound note was to be based on a 'goods standard' equal to the net value of all the goods the nation was capable of producing. The concept, dubious as it might be, provided a rationale for printing as much extra money as needed in a period of crisis.

Those last two measures of the 'Lang Plan', while controversial enough, were hardly noticed amid the shock waves created by its first point. In publicly mentioning the taboo subject of overseas interest, the Big Fella had loosed a thunderbolt.

If Lang had chosen to join forces with Theodore, they might well have been able to push through a sensible compromise plan combining a moderate easing of credit with a moderate reduction in interest payments, whether through negotiation or proclaimed unilaterally on the basis of dire need. Such a formula certainly would have helped to ease the strain of essential budget reform. The sad truth, though, was that the two politicians were arch-rivals, ambitious princes manoeuvring for control of the Australian Labor Party and never likely to see eye to eye even at such a critical time. Whether or not professional jealousy played a part, Lang came to the view that Theodore was too ready to give in to the banks and would never win approval for his emergency employment fund. Rather than see the conference stretch on in endless dithering, as he later explained, he decided to put forward the Lang Plan to give heart to a badly demoralised people. He did, however, finish his presentation with this conciliatory gesture to Theodore and the other delegates. 'If any better plan than my Government has submitted can be brought forward, I will gladly agree to it. I am prepared to agree that budgets should be balanced, but not that anyone should tell New South Wales how it is to be done.'

It was too late to stave off the condemnations to follow. The other leaders, Theodore and Scullin among them, rose one by one to denounce the Lang Plan as not only impractical but downright dangerous in terms of its potential to damage Australia's image as a trustworthy trading partner.

'I desire to disassociate myself from every word and every sentiment, uttered by Mr. Lang,' the Premier of Western Australia, Sir James Mitchell, fairly shouted across the room. 'Australia would be discredited in the eyes of the world. It is repudiation. I know the rate of interest is too high, but we have agreed to pay it. We must pay it.'

Outside the conference, a rising young Victorian politician would go even further. 'If Australia is to surmount her troubles by the abandonment of traditional standards of honesty, justice and fair play, it would be far better for Australia that every citizen within her boundaries should die of starvation during the next few months,' Robert Menzies proclaimed to loud applause.

The Big Fella thus emerged from the February conference as a symbol of the deepening social divide that stretched like an earthquake fault line from one end of the continent to the other. In coming weeks depression-era battlers, employed and unemployed alike, would flock to the Lang Plan banner. The federal Labor government was left choking in their dust, riddled with increasing internal strife. In March, five of its right-wing members crossed the floor to vote with the Opposition in protest over what they deemed to be Theodore's wildly inflationary credit schemes. At the same time a clique of five MPs and two senators from New South Wales also defected to form a breakaway party calling itself 'Lang Labor' – in effect splitting the labour movement into two versions of the 'true' ALP.

Scullin and Theodore felt they had no choice but to remain aligned with the Premiers' Plan for national recovery despite its poisonous association with Niemeyer and the inevitable heavy toll in job losses. Their stand sparked widespread rebellion within the unions. Trades Hall officials, who in some states controlled the Labor Party's selection of parliamentary candidates, declared a vote for the Premiers' Plan to be grounds for instant expulsion. Initially, Lang Plan supporters, who held the balance of power in federal parliament, could be counted on to save the Scullin–Theodore administration in critical votes. Towards the end of November, however, they delivered the coup de grâce, joining with the despised conservatives to defeat the government on a motion alleging mishandling of relief funds. Scullin felt he had no choice but to resign, setting the stage for a December election.

Looking back through 1931, the Big Fella could well claim to have become a force to be reckoned with. His constant agitation over interest would bear fruit in the final version of the Premiers' Plan adopted in June. All delegates accepted the urgent need for a significant decrease in the interest rates within Australia, though the downward conversion would be voluntary rather than compulsory as Lang had proposed. Lang also kept the pot boiling on overseas interest by declaring his state unable to pay a £730,000 ($51.1 million) instalment due to two British banks in April. The federal government quickly came up with the amount needed to prevent a default and actually took the New South Wales Government to court before getting back its money. Though Lang had to back down, his action rang alarm bells in London, warning officials there that without a fair-minded renegotiation of Australian loan contracts, more such defaults were likely.

But the Big Fella suffered his setbacks as well. In late April, thousands of families rushed to withdraw their modest deposits from the venerable Government Savings Bank of New South Wales, whipped into a frenzy by constant warnings that under Lang, their money was no longer safe. The savings bank was forced to close temporarily, eventually to be taken over by the Commonwealth Bank. In the meantime many panicky depositors were conned into selling their accounts at a considerable discount to unscrupulous moneylenders. Lang blamed his opponents' scare tactics for the bank's demise but it would be his name that was most closely associated with one of the blackest episodes of the depression.

The most disturbing legacy to be passed on from 1931 was a dangerous skew toward extremism that threatened to send the young society spinning out of control. None of its most important institutions could claim to be immune, not the church, the courts, the professional and business establishments, but least of all the media. From the moment the Big Fella announced his Lang Plan, he would be pilloried in the conservative press as nothing less than a traitor, a closet communist hell-bent on stirring up a civil war.

To answer that perceived threat, tens of thousands of volunteers – many of them combat-trained veterans of World War I – signed up to join a shadowy right-wing militia known as the New Guard. Their leaders insisted the Guardsmen's only aim was to offer police their patriotic assistance in case of general strikes or rioting in the streets. However, ample evidence would soon emerge of their preparedness to remove Lang from office by force if necessary.

By late December, 1931, with the election of a hard-line conservative government in Canberra to replace the Scullin–Theodore administration, all the elements for a bruising showdown had been set in place. The new Prime Minister, Joe Lyons, had made the so-called Lang threat one of the key issues in his campaign, vowing to pull the Big Fella into line. Looming ahead was a political shoot-out to make William Street's look tame by comparison – an epic clash of wills between Lyons and Lang, between the Commonwealth of Australia and its largest state. Before that drama had run its course, it would transform the very nature of the Australian federation, shifting the balance of power between the federal and state governments in a way that could never have been imagined by the founding fathers. Indeed, it would be a change so drastic as to be described as revolutionary, though without the rivers of blood. The blood could easily have flowed as well. All it needed was for the Big Fella to say the word.

If Fred Roberts thought 1931 was a helluva year, he should have seen 1932.

2
1932: A leap into the void

Dancing in the dark ... waltzing in the wonder of why we're here, time hurries by, we're here and gone. For the couples dancing into the dawn of a new year, Sydney's wickedly chic Fifty-Fifty Club must have seemed like a cruise ship, separated from the troubles that beset the rest of Australia by a sea of boozy indifference. History does not record who was there in the first hours of 1932, but then, how could it? Even in the rare instances when police raided the illicit gin palace, no one was ever expected to give their correct names so long as they were prepared to surrender a hefty £2 bail. Assuming the usual mix, the New Year's celebrants most likely included a sprinkling of tuxedo-clad doctors, barristers and businessmen, even a knight or two (the Earl of Jersey with his new Australian bride would show up later in the year): satin-wrapped socialites foxtrotting backwards through the crush in kaleidoscopic bursts of crimson, lime green and ivory; actors, artists and other bohemian types; a few commission salesmen, hustlers or ordinary punters who may have struck it lucky; scar-faced standover men, pimps and cocaine dealers from the gangs whose weapon of choice had turned nearby Darlinghurst into the more commonly known 'Razorhurst'; and invariably, the club's star attraction: as dazzling a display of art deco harlotry as could be found in any port city in the world.

Young women of the time were still referred to as flappers though the look had by then evolved from girlishly low-waisted and knobby-kneed – as it was in the early 1920s – into longer, slinkier silhouettes draped in sheeny fabrics that flowed down the body like hot wax. If nineteen-year-old Dulcie Markham was among the revellers, she would have had the tipsy playboys flocking: an angelic blonde with storm-cloud eyes and a tongue that could melt asbestos. Hollywood vamps like Jean Harlow and Carole Lombard may have been her role models, but Dulcie couldn't have been all that far behind them when it came to earning power. She easily made £50 a night from grateful clients, equivalent to $3500 a night in today's terms, or roughly half a year's salary for a good secretary at the time.

December 31, 1931 fell on a Thursday. By the early hours of the new year, revellers streaming in from private parties, upmarket hotel ballrooms or high-society restaurants would have packed the club solid. A four-piece band kept the adrenaline pumping with rousing American swing numbers like 'Them There Eyes', 'Three Little Words', 'Walkin' My Baby Back Home', 'You're Driving Me Crazy'. Many of the best-loved tunes, though, were languidly sentimental: 'Stardust', 'I Don't Know Why', 'All of Me', 'Dancing in the Dark', 'Goodnight Sweetheart'. A well-chosen medley would have whipped the dancers into a froth as they pranced, strutted, kicked, wiggled or slid their way through a staggering range of styles: foxtrot, waltz, tango, onestep, twostep, charleston, Black Bottom, Lindy Hop. No generation ever had more ways to enjoy themselves on their feet.

Still, the mood at Fifty-Fifty could change in an instant. Its atmosphere was always thick with the scent of underlying menace: a volatile mix of alcohol fumes, telltale whiffs of cocaine and cheap perfume, not to mention the fruity pong of body odour that pervaded all 1930s party scenes in the absence of effective antiperspirants. Inevitably, tempers flared and fights broke out. Patrons occasionally got their pockets picked or purses snatched. There was always the chance of a police raid, though none would be recorded that year until the last week of July, when 127 guests were bundled away in paddy wagons. The club's owner, a prominent gangland figure named Phil 'the Jew' Jeffs, prided himself on knowing how to stay on the right side – namely the hip pocket side – of the law. As it happened, a new superintendent of police with a reputation for absolute incorruptibility was just about to take over the metropolitan force. Fortunately for Jeffs, though, the bull-necked untouchable, William 'Billy' Mackay, would have his hands full in the first months of 1932 dealing with extensive civil unrest. Stopping people from enjoying themselves after hours was the last thing he was worried about.

The Latvian-born Phil the Jew, looking eminently legitimate in his white tie and tails, glided between tables, mixing easily with all levels of his clientele. One moment he could be seen chatting knowledgeably with the upper crust, the next shouting drinks for old mates from his early hoodlum days of mugging drunks in back alleys. Tilly Devine, the reigning Sydney vice queen, could always count on VIP treatment whenever she chose to make a grand entrance with some of her girls. If the feisty former London streetwalker was there that New Year's morning, Jeffs may well have picked up the tab for a round or three of champagne toasts. He could afford to be generous considering even a casual stray-in customer would find it difficult to leave his establishment without having blown 10 shillings ($35) on beer and tips.

For those who had the money to splurge – and plenty did even in the midst of the Great Depression – Fifty-Fifty was merely the wind-up to a long, expensive evening and not necessarily the priciest spot in town. Newspapers covered a good sampling of the celebrations. Romano's, where a champagne feast could cost up to £3 ($210) a head, was reported 'packed to suffocation'. Among the guests there, dashing playboy Berkeley Gordon was said to have stolen the show as he whirled partner after partner around the floor in his ultra-stylish white mess jacket. An exotic touch was added by the presence of the Mexican consul, Don Carlos Salappo, hosting a table of prominent socialites.

Those seeking larger gatherings might go to prestigious hotels like the Australia or Wentworth, whose ballrooms were transformed for the night into fantasylands worthy of a Busby Berkeley screen spectacular. For the civic-minded, there were any number of charity balls. A crowd of 800, paying £1/10 ($105) a ticket, jammed the Town Hall to be bombarded at the stroke of midnight by 'seventeen miles of streamers and three tons of confetti'. The 'Prosperity Fiesta' in the nearby suburb of Darlinghurst also proved a grand attraction. It was held in the Stadium, a sprawling tin-roofed arena better known for its boxing but converted for the occasion into a South Seas paradise. Approaching midnight an enormous cake was wheeled into the centre of the floor. To gasps of delight, a bevy of pretty young ladies burst forth, dressed to look like dancing doughnuts. Palm readers circulated among the crowd predicting good fortune for all in 1932. They should have bitten their tongues.

At this time of year, of course, many of the Sydney elite preferred to travel to their holiday retreats at Palm Beach or relax in the bucolic comfort of the southern highlands, where the Governor of New South Wales, Sir Philip Game, took refuge.

However, for the city stay-puts there was no shortage of lavish house parties like that thrown by Ernest Watts, inviting his select group of friends to enjoy dancing and a moonlight dip at his home in Darling Point.

What did people talk most about on that portentous New Year's morning? At any venue in Sydney – let alone the Fifty-Fifty – the hottest topic was almost certainly the sensational William Street shoot-out that had paralysed the city just three days before. Phil Jeffs and his underworld mates no doubt spent the wee hours debating whether the slain gangster, Fred Roberts, finally got what he deserved. He was known as a wild card – an undisciplined loner who gave extortion and pimping a bad name. Further east at Darling Point, though, the guests at Ernest Watts's poolside party may well have made a joke of the shooting, linking it to the next most popular topic of the night. What a pity that instead of a petty criminal like Roberts bleeding in the gutter, it couldn't have been that even more vile thug, Jack Lang.

Among the more comfortably well off – managers, professionals and the like – the New South Wales Premier was by then so despised that people talked openly of the need to be rid of him one way or another. Almost anyone connected with the Darling Point set would have been a strong admirer of the New Guard, if not an outright member. The Guard drew a number of its recruits from the wealthier families of Sydney's eastern suburbs and the north shore and was widely praised for the mounting pressure it had been putting on Governor Game to dismiss the Premier. Its argument – put forward at various patriotic rallies – was that the Big Fella had lost the public's confidence. Sir Philip's steadfast refusal to act on the strength of such a dubious premise led to whispers of the Guardsmen preparing an outright coup in the new year, perhaps timed to coincide with the gala opening of the Sydney Harbour Bridge in

March. A comment about Lang lying bleeding in the gutter wouldn't have been made entirely in jest.

Yet, the Big Fella had his own supporters – Langites as they were known – every bit as fervent and even fanatical. For them, his stand on suspending loan repayments in a time of economic crisis was the clarion cry of a true patriot. While most Langites were blue-collar workers or from the lowlier ranks of the civil service, they also could be found within intellectual circles and even among the eclectic mix of patrons at Fifty-Fifty. Their campaign slogan, *people before money*, certainly struck a responsive chord with Tilly Devine. She would have a chance to express her feelings later in the year in rather sensational circumstances.

Though politics was a major preoccupation at the start of 1932, no gathering of Australians in any context could go for very long without the conversation turning to sport. On that very New Year's Eve Thursday, Australia had got off to a disastrous start in its third test against South Africa at the Sydney Cricket Ground; all out for 198. The really devastating news, though, was that Donald Bradman had scored only two. Bradman, of course, would later be remembered as an indestructible run machine whose rare failures at the bat were mere specks of dust on perfection. That's hardly how he was seen at the age of 23, just three years into his international career. Cricket lovers knew they were watching a miracle in the making but were also keenly aware of the many pitfalls that could bring the phenomenal batsman unstuck: injury, conflicts with dictatorial administrators, or – far more worrying in Bradman's case – lucrative offers to leave Australia to play in England. In a period when the social fabric was torn by deep division, willing Donald Bradman to greatness was the one thing all Australians could agree on. A bad day for the young cricketer was thus a calamity for his fans. His miserable two runs would have sent shudders through New Year's gatherings everywhere, from the wealthiest to the poorest, including those in the makeshift Happy Valley settlements spreading like a noisome stain on the fringes of every capital city.

At least there was also a bit of good news on the sporting front to help cheer everyone up. Phar Lap was reported to be safe and well aboard the steamer *Monowai* taking the beloved Australian champion to race in America.

Meanwhile, one of the racing world's most colourful and controversial figures may well have dropped into the Fifty-Fifty that New Year's, hosting a table of investors who would have been in very high spirits indeed. Frederick Shaver Swindell, known as 'Judge' Swindell back in Dixie, where he supposedly came from, had just struck it fabulously rich. The immaculately dressed American with his booming voice and convivial Y'all southern drawl had somehow persuaded the Lang Government to approve a licence to stage greyhound racing under lights at Harold Park. The venture had been launched in late December and proved an immediate success, with crowds of more than 20,000 turning up to bet on the 'tin hares' as the new form of mechanical coursing was dubbed. Swindell's personal worth in terms of shares and percentage of profits had blown out overnight from zero to perhaps £200,000 – $14 million. Rumours of bribery were rife and his remarkable influence within the Lang Government would later be the subject of a headline-making royal commission. For the moment, though, he was king of the tin hares, the hottest new business venture in the state of New South Wales.

Of all the 6,525,918 people seeing in the New Year downunder, Frederick Swindell certainly appeared to have the brightest prospects for 1932. Who had the dimmest? Any one of more than two million Australians then jobless or otherwise impoverished might qualify for that sad distinction. No one particular class was involved. The Great Depression struck at all levels of society in a way that made nonsense of glib generalities such as 'greedy landlords' exploiting 'destitute tenants'.

'May I ask you to insert this letter on behalf of the so-called Shylocks, the blood-suckers,' one property investor wrote to the papers, pleading for understanding. 'Take my case, for instance: a woman partly crippled and alone, with all my life's savings from hard work and self denial invested in first mortgages in the hope of peace and security in my old age. So much for my dreams. At present I am living in one small room on one and a half meals a day whilst the principal mortgagor, who has borrowed two thirds of my savings, resides in a beautiful home, runs a good car and owes me one year's interest with no intention of paying anything in the future. Two other mortgagors pay when and how they like. So much for a bloodsucking mortgagee. My future looks black as the Gap. For charity I loathe and to beg I am ashamed.'

The letter was signed, appropriately enough, *Desperandum*. Every day, in cases much like hers, the courts were called on to intervene in applications for eviction or foreclosure based on comparisons of the relative hardships faced by mortgagee/landlord or borrower/tenant. The difference in degrees of desperation sometimes proved so minute as to defy rational judgement. How was one to decide, for example, between two good-hearted, conscientious family men like Harold Furner and Julius Monty? Monty, a year out of work and no longer able to pay his rent, pleaded with a magistrate for a three-month delay in an eviction in order to stop his wife and children being thrown onto the streets. His landlord, Furner, though, was also in dire straits. A successful master builder, he had invested every cent he had in a suburban block of flats just before the crash. Not only was the value of his property immediately slashed by half but he himself was now unemployed, yet still had a £3500 ($245,000) mortgage hanging over his head. He faced immediate bankruptcy unless the court gave him permission to replace the Monty family with a paying tenant.

The magistrate had been forced to deal with many such cases, but this one touched him more than most. 'Both you men are honest and your plight affects me acutely,' he told them. 'Through no fault of your own you are victims of the depression and it has not been an easy matter to arrive at a fair and just decision.' His verdict: to give the tenant one more month before his family was thrown out instead of the three months he had pleaded for.

Yet as Australians headed into 1932, there was one hard luck story that stood out from all the rest – not because it was the most tragic, it was far from that. Rather, it seemed to symbolise the chaotic randomness with which the Great Depression plucked one victim after another from a normal existence and hurled them into the abyss.

On New Year's Day Albert Jacka lay dying, floating in and out of consciousness, in a Melbourne hospital. He was the nation's most celebrated hero, the first Australian soldier to be awarded a Victoria Cross in World War I when he single-handedly wiped out a trench full of Turks at Gallipoli. That, however, would turn out to be the least amazing of his audacious deeds. At Pozieres in France he led a handful of diggers in a brazen counterattack against scores of Germans who had overrun their positions, routing the enemy though he was wounded seven times, including a shot through the neck. The deed was later described as 'the most dramatic and effective act of individual audacity in the history of the AIF'.

Jacka returned from the front to great fanfare, going on to open an electrical goods shop and for a time to serve as mayor of the Melbourne beachside suburb of St Kilda. The depression suddenly brought his world crashing down around him, his once thriving business driven into bankruptcy when customers could no longer afford the prohibitive cost of imported goods. He spent the next twelve months in a demoralising search for work before he finally managed to get a job selling soap products. By then, his wife, Vera, had walked out of their marriage. In mid-December 1931 he fell seriously ill. Doctors diagnosed a kidney ailment and his old war injuries – he had been wounded in three separate engagements and also heavily gassed – no doubt took their toll. But those closest to him insisted he was really suffering from a crushed spirit, realising that all his brave deeds in defence of his country counted for nothing in the midst of economic depression.

In one of his rare moments of consciousness he was reported to have opened his eyes long enough to tell his father: 'I'm still fighting, Dad.'

By 17 January, however, Albert Jacka was dead.

3
A call to arms

On the day of Captain Albert Jacka's funeral a searing northwesterly swirled like dragon's breath through Melbourne's CBD. The temperature that Tuesday, 19 January hit a near-record 108.9 degrees Fahrenheit, nearly 43 degrees centigrade. Yet 30,000 mourners stood shoulder to shoulder in silent vigil as the horse-drawn gun carriage bearing the dead hero – his sword and slouch hat atop the casket – proceeded slowly across Princes Bridge on its way to St Kilda Cemetery. An honour guard of eight other Victoria Cross recipients walked close behind and after them, marching four abreast, an endless column of World War I diggers, the sweat streaming from under their grey felt hats, their medals glinting almost too hot to touch in the oppressive mid-afternoon sun. It was as if Anzac Day had come early just to say goodbye to Bert. And no wonder, when the enduring legend of the tall, bronzed Anzacs with their fierce fighting spirit quite literally began with him.

One can picture the scene – the tall young Colonial, his

face bronzed with the suns of three continents, his eyes flashing, his strong arm ready with rifle either to shoot or thrust . . .

Thus did a widely read British account, published in 1916, introduce the story of Jacka's gallant one-man stand against the Turks at Gallipoli. Albert Jacka was in reality a little over 5 foot 6 inches tall; but his fellow Australians were more than happy to bask in the glow of the hyperbole that radiated from his every deed.

When the cortege reached St Kilda junction, the mourners were joined by another 300 returned servicemen, former comrades who had been too ashamed of their reduced circumstances to think of marching through the city. Their suits – if they owned one – were soiled and frayed; the soles of their boots tramped paper-thin. Whatever medals they might have earned had long since been pawned. They were drawn from among the ragged legions of Victoria's unemployed. As mayor of St Kilda, Jacka – while without a job himself – had spent almost every waking hour raising funds to help feed and clothe such down-at-heel veterans. He might well have blamed himself for their plight since he was, after all, the role model who had encouraged so many to leave secure occupations for the stygian horrors of the Western Front. They rushed to enlist, inspired by Bert Jacka's image on recruitment posters and the stirring tale of how a shy Victorian farm boy with a primary school education fought his way to glory. 'Show the enemy what Australian sporting men can do', the Jacka posters urged. Two in every five of those good sports would be killed in action or permanently crippled. The able-bodied survivors had only a few years to try to re-establish themselves in civilian life before they were caught up in the change of tides between boom and bust. As if the revered Anzacs hadn't been through enough at Gallipoli, they would suffer far more than their share of hardship and heartbreak in the throes of the Great Depression.

Jacka was just 39 when he died. Most of those marching at his funeral would have been in that general age group, between 35 and 45 – prime years which should have seen them advancing toward the upper levels of their chosen careers. Instead, the time the volunteers spent abroad in war service often counted against them when they attempted to rejoin the work force. In theory, every soldier had a right to his old job back but that could merely mean having to start all over again as a junior clerk or general factory hand after four years in the trenches. If a veteran's place had been filled while he was gone, his former employer faced a Solomon-like decision of whether to sack or demote a loyal staff member to make room for his return. Not a few bosses were deadset against hiring a war veteran in any circumstances, doubtful about their ability to settle back down to daily routine or perhaps, even secretly fearful of having their authority challenged by a brash young man with a row of decorations on his chest. The ex-diggers, for their part, often couldn't stomach taking orders from some pot-bellied, stay-at-home martinet who had no inkling of what they had endured in the front lines. Like Jacka, many preferred to risk striking out on their own, borrowing heavily to set up a small business or carve out a soldier-settler farm. Their failure rate would prove ruinously high no matter what path they chose. As times grew tougher it was natural for the war veterans to close ranks and stick together for support, considering themselves unappreciated and misunderstood by the wider community. Even the more successful among them, however, were often plagued by a sense of alienation: bored with the suffocating complacency of civilian life. It was as if their spirit, forged anew in the white heat of combat, shined too bright in the dullness that surrounded them.

So it was that two powerful 'citizens' armies' would emerge in the turmoil of the Great Depression, first in Victoria and then New South Wales, to harness the restless energy of tens of thousands of disgruntled war veterans. Both trained their eager volunteers in the special tactics of street fighting. Both took upon themselves the mission of assisting police to suppress any outbreak of general strikes or rioting that might be the prelude to an attempted communist takeover. The Victorian group, known as the League of National Security, or 'White Army', was more secretive than its New South Wales counterpart – its numbers unknown and its leadership only whispered about, though it was said to include no less a figure than General Thomas Blamey, a renowned wartime commander. As the state's hard-line police commissioner he had previously shown no hesitation in allowing his constabulary to fire on unruly demonstrators. The League enjoyed strong financial backing from the Melbourne business establishment but was prepared to maintain a low profile so long as local unionists distanced themselves from the more militant antics of their counterparts across the border.

The New Guard of New South Wales was formed in early 1931, a year after the League of National Security, with the same stated intentions of helping police; but from its very inception it seemed a far more sinister organisation. By the start of 1932, it could claim an astounding 100,000 members, one in four of them with combat experience and led by an impressive cadre of retired officers up to the rank of Brigadier General. It was undoubtedly among the largest paramilitary forces ever assembled within the framework of a democratic society.

The militiamen wore no special uniform though they did have armbands to signify their rank and unit and a straight-armed salute to match their bellicose anthem.

We of the New Guard
Are always at the ready
In the case of danger in our midst
We'll all be firm and steady . . .

The rigid salute and patriotic fervour were eerily familiar. Newsreels of the day depicted similar martial sentiments echoing throughout the streets and meeting halls of Europe. The end of World War I had seen the Continent infected by a virulent ideological fever: hard-line fascist groups springing up everywhere to counter the spread of radical workers' movements spawned by the Russian Revolution. The threat of further uprisings was hardly theoretical. The peace treaty had barely been signed before Germany erupted in revolutionary ferment, with vast crowds in Berlin raising the Red Flag and occupying public buildings only to be slaughtered en masse by machine guns and heavy artillery. In Munich, to the south, a newly proclaimed 'Bavarian Soviet Republic' held power for 24 days, finally to be crushed by a hastily formed band of citizen soldiers known as the Freikorps. Hungary followed with a 'Socialist Federated Soviet Republic' lasting 133 days until its overthrow by the right. During their brief tenure, the Hungarian communists had sent agents to try to seize control in Austria, their assault on police headquarters in Vienna put down in a bloodbath.

In cases where leftist coalitions did succeed in gaining government, their history was predictably short and violent – marked by right-wing coups in Bulgaria and Spain in 1923, Albania in 1924, Greece in 1925, Poland and Portugal 1926, and Yugoslavia's descent into dictatorship in 1929. The new regime in Portugal was particularly ruthless in putting down protesting workers, sending planes to bomb them in the streets of Lisbon a decade before Guernica; but all such episodes were rife with assassinations, summary executions and cruel reprisals. Much of that relentless colour-coded strife – reds versus whites versus brownshirts, blackshirts and greenshirts – would be wiped from memory by the sheer shock of the great war to follow. But for those who actually watched it unfolding year by year, Australians included, it transformed the vague term 'red menace' into a tangible and frightening reality.

The New Guard's founder and supreme commander, Eric Campbell, was one of those who saw a disturbing parallel between the ideological struggles unfolding in Europe and the increasingly aggressive tactics of radical unionists in Australia. A prominent Sydney lawyer, he made no attempt to conceal his personal admiration for Italy's fascist dictator Benito Mussolini and even for Germany's fast-rising Nazi leader, Adolf Hitler. He insisted, however, that his Guardsmen – despite their straight-arm salutes – were an entirely home-grown creation, having no affiliation with overseas groups such as Sir Oswald Mosley's British Union of Fascists.

Campbell fought on the Western Front, reaching the rank of Lieutenant Colonel by the age of only 25. Like many of his fellow officers, he had come to feel increasing disdain for the politicians who seemed incapable of providing Australia with the decisive leadership needed at such a critical phase of its history. As he saw it, their futile wrangling made it all the easier for left-wing agitators to exploit the depression for their own revolutionary ends. If the New Guard and White Army shared a paranoid fear of communism, they did appear to have more than a grain of justification. In New South Wales and Victoria, where Labor governments presided, delegates to ALP and Trades Hall conferences seriously debated the pros and cons of imposing an immediate dictatorship of the proletariat, nationalising all means of production from banks to factories, mines and farms.

'We have been fooled long enough,' one steamed-up member of the Boilermakers' Union cajoled his colleagues. 'Instead of trying to knock capitalism over the precipice immediately, you will be asked to wait. You can gain control only by revolutionary action. Why not now?'

Ironically, Jack Lang was one of the few parliamentarians Campbell respected – 'an astute politician of no mean calibre,' as he was happy to admit. The Big Fella clearly outshone any other political figure in the land in his ability to inspire people and his call to 'put Australia first' no doubt had wide appeal for many a war veteran. But that only made it all the more urgent to get rid of him. Campbell regarded Lang as the key to the far left's revolutionary ambitions: if not an ideologue himself, then a pliable figurehead who could be used to rally the masses to the point where they were easy prey for manipulation. More than any other event, it was the announcement of the Lang Plan that spurred Campbell into action, with the New Guard holding its formal inaugural meeting a month later in March, 1931. He instantly recognised the issue of overseas interest as the perfect torch to light the flames of insurrection.

In those first few months of 1931, applications for membership poured in at the extraordinary rate of 2000 to 3000 a week. Apart from the returned servicemen, there was a solid sampling of middle-class folk – bank managers, shop owners, accountants, public servants and skilled tradesmen. If the balance swung toward the more privileged end of the social spectrum, the Guard also claimed a sizeable share of blue-collar workers, both employed and unemployed, opposed to the growing influence of pro-Soviet propaganda in union affairs. As the fame of the organisation spread, donations flowed in from numerous sources, including insurance companies and large retailers which saw their contributions as having good public relations value. The Guard even put its own official 'bond certificates' on sale to the public, priced from 2 shillings to a pound.

Like any field commander surveying the battle lines, Campbell tried to anticipate the tactics the enemy was most likely to use to bring down the capitalist system. He assumed the radical offensive would begin with a prolonged general strike designed to paralyse all of Sydney's essential services. The resulting chaos would serve as an excuse for Lang – sooled on by the firebrands in his party – to issue a flurry of emergency decrees transforming New South Wales into a socialist police state. In this kind of all-out industrial warfare, the most important targets would be where militant unions were already solidly entrenched: the power station, gasworks, water and sewerage plants, road transport, rail and tram depots. The New Guard was therefore determined to protect all such facilities from seizure and to operate them as long as necessary until the police were in a position to restore order. The entire New South Wales police force numbered only 3600. The New Guard, on less than 24 hours' notice, could dispatch ten times that many militiamen to their pre-assigned duty stations.

Campbell had made his mark as a staff officer renowned for his meticulous attention to detail. His master plan for the militia called for a sprawling network of commando-like units, each operating independently within its given 'Locality' but capable of joining forces with other elements anywhere in the state. Several neighbouring localities formed a division and several divisions, in turn, came under the supervision of one of four zones. At the top of this command structure was a mysterious 'Council of Action' whose secret meetings decided when and how the main force of the Guard might be mobilised for united action. The council was tightly controlled by an inner clique of former front-line officers and ordinary members were kept largely in the dark about its machinations. On Campbell's instructions the incoming volunteers were to be classified into three categories:

A class – The physically vigorous . . .
B class – Those technically qualified to assist in maintaining essential services: water, gas, electricity, transport, etc.
C class – Those whose age or inclination confined them to tasks within the Locality.

The term 'physically vigorous' was a euphemism for men willing and able to fight the Reds with whatever degree of force was required. Campbell calculated that in the early stages of a crisis, fists and axe handles would probably be enough to break through picket lines or disperse leftist demonstrations. Come a full-scale showdown, however, weapons would almost certainly be needed and the New Guard quietly set out to equip selected A-class units with firearms. Campbell referred to this inner hard core as his 'Ironsides' and put their number at 20,000 – an elite to be assigned the most secret of missions.

The militia as a whole was highly mobile, able at short notice to assemble convoys of 120 cars or more. It even drew up plans for its own version of a tank company. Senior officers gave lectures on how to fit a vehicle with steel plates, put a machine gun inside and rush it 'into the thick of any hard fighting with a very demoralising effect upon rioting mobs'. Incredibly, there was also a New Guard air wing of perhaps a dozen planes whose pilots had volunteered their services.

In the first months after its founding, the Guard devoted its energies to training exercises and organising patriotic rallies to attract further public support. For many of its recruits the nightly drills and lectures added a sense of purpose that hitherto had been sadly lacking in their lives. The truth was, though, that while they prepared themselves for the coming revolution, there really wasn't all that much to do. The Guard's A-class patrols roamed the city breaking up left-wing meetings, heckling speakers and sometimes pulling their podiums out from under them. They also stood watch at conservative functions, frightening off potential troublemakers. Such activities hardly seemed to justify the creation of so large and sophisticated an organisation.

In the first weeks of 1932, however, operations turned distinctly more aggressive. Campbell had obviously decided it was time for his New Guard to start flexing its considerable muscle. He himself set the tone in a fiery speech at Lane Cove in mid-January when he denounced Lang as a 'tyrant and scoundrel' and pledged that the New Guard would not allow him to open the Sydney Harbour Bridge on 19 March.

'We will not have Lang to open the bridge,' he told wildly cheering supporters. 'We want some person or prince of the royal blood. We don't want this man who is masquerading as a premier.'

Soon after, the Guardsmen were involved in a series of incidents clearly intended as a show of force. One Saturday afternoon two battalions smartly outfitted with armbands and badges converged on suburban Belmore Park in a convoy of 73 cars and proceeded to go through a snappy display of close-order drill. Another mobile force of 200 men staged a lightning raid to break up a communist meeting in Bankstown, only to find themselves overwhelmed by a large and angry crowd of unionists who happened to be attending a nearby Labor picnic. The running brawl that ensued attracted headlines across the nation.

Campbell, meanwhile, kept the pot boiling with provocatively cryptic messages that became more menacing as Sydney prepared for one of the most exciting occasions in its history. 'Hold yourself in readiness,' he advised his Guardsmen in advance of the Harbour Bridge opening. 'Important events will take place within three weeks.' An admiring media as well as large sections of the public treated such pronouncements as a welcome ray of hope that rescue from Lang and his extremist cronies must surely be on the way. The Big Fella's more ardent supporters, for their part, were whipped into a fury, denouncing Campbell and his Guardsmen as fascist bullyboys.

'I did not mind a little sabre rattling,' Campbell would later acknowledge. 'It gave Mr. Lang's mates at the Trades Hall a sinking feeling.'

But someone else was taking careful note of the New Guard leader's every word – a giant Scotsman with fists like demolition balls and a mouthful of teeth so rotten it looked as if he had just bitten into a tree trunk. Detective Superintendent Billy Mackay had a reputation to match his looks, known to the underworld as a ruthless operator who could walk alone into a pub packed with standover men and leave them begging to get to their cells. He was undoubtedly Jack Lang's kind of cop and the Big Fella had personally selected him at the start of 1932 for a very special assignment.

'Do you want to be commissioner?' the Premier had asked him. 'If I put you in temporary charge of the force, do you think you could handle the New Guard?' The Glasgow-born Mackay, twenty years on the New South Wales force, didn't hesitate.

'You give me the job and the responsibility and I will show you how it can be done,' the burly cop assured him.

'Right, then sort out these New Guard bastards for me!'

Billy Mackay needed no further instruction. Lang's order had been as sweet to his taste as a wee dram of whisky.

4

Faces in the street

'Jack Lang's coming up the street!'

The shout was enough to empty a nearby pub, sending several dozen people rushing out to gawk at 'the Big Fella' lumbering along a Melbourne footpath like a bronze statue come to life. The New South Wales Premier was on his way to a conference called in late January to meet with the newly elected Prime Minister, Joe Lyons, and the five other state premiers. Lang, a reporter noted, was the only one to attract attention wherever he went.

'I just want to touch him,' a flapper giggled, though she settled for a wink and a gracious smile that spread beneath his bushy black moustache flecked with grey.

When a journalist tried to approach, though, the lips tightened and the jaw tilted pugnaciously.

'Well, I suppose you expect to find my hands red with the blood of innocent babies,' Lang chided.

Charming or challenging, Lang knew instinctively how to plug into any crowd, reading faces perfectly, sensing the vibrations, drawing even the shy or sceptical to him with sheer magnetic force. Within the political arena he was regarded by allies and foes alike as arrogant and aloof – the classic dark and brooding loner – but he felt a special bond with the people he referred to as his 'children', the common folk. He, too, had endured the hardships of being a 'battler', though from the unique perspective of someone born into middle-class comfort only to descend into absolute poverty. His father, a prosperous jewellery shop owner, lost everything after suffering a crippling illness. The young John Thomas Lang was left to fight his way up like any slum kid. From the age of seven he walked the streets barefooted selling newspapers from a billycart, using his fists to defend his territory from would-be usurpers, including much older and bigger lads. The experience established a mind-set that stayed with him all his life. Other kids had friends – young Jack had only rivals.

A particularly painful memory from that period would remain aglow in his consciousness like a half-buried ember. One of the few confidants he later mentioned it to felt it had a profound effect – giving him a 'grouse against society' – and it is easy to see why. Returning home from selling papers one afternoon, cold, tired and hungry, he heard a buggy clattering up the street from behind him. Without warning, the driver purposely cracked a whip over Lang's head, forcing him to drop to the gutter, much to the amusement of the passengers in the buggy. Their raucous laughter stung far more than any whip. Not long after that incident, the boy was peddling his papers along one of the city's busy cross streets between Market and King, when he suffered some kind of mental breakdown. He crumpled into a pitiful heap on the footpath, lying there whimpering until kindly bystanders carried him off to hospital.

Lang rarely discussed what might have happened to him that morning, perhaps because he really didn't want to know. He was a fighter by nature, prepared to shrug off a bloodied nose or two; but the humiliation of being treated as if he didn't matter may well have been more than he could bear. That buggy whip from nowhere, it seems clear enough, laid bare the kind of chink in his armour that would come back to haunt him during the biggest crisis of his career.

His early struggle made him naturally sympathetic to the ideals of the Labor Party. Lang entered politics with Henry Lawson's poem, 'Faces in the Street', the perfect expression of all he hoped to achieve: exposing the hidden injustices in Australian life, providing relief for those in most desperate need. The poem read in part:

> They lie, the men who tell us for reasons of their own
> That want is here a stranger, and that misery's unknown;
> For where the nearest suburb and the city proper meet
> My window-sill is level with the faces in the street –
>   Drifting past, drifting past,
>   To the beat of weary feet –
> While I sorrow for the owners of those faces in the street.
>
> And cause I have to sorrow, in a land so young and fair,
> To see upon those faces stamped the marks of Want and Care;
> I look in vain for traces of the fresh and fair and sweet
> In sallow, sunken faces that are drifting through the street –
>   Drifting on, drifting on,
>   To the scrape of restless feet;
> I can sorrow for the owners of the faces in the street.
> . . .
>
> I wonder would the apathy of wealthy men endure
> Were all their windows level with the faces of the Poor?
> . . .
>
>   Henry Lawson, July, 1888

By a quirk of fate, Lang was to become Henry Lawson's brother-in-law. In 1896, at the age of just nineteen, he married seventeen-year-old Hilda Bredt, the youngest daughter of Bertha Bredt, a radical feminist and shining light in the early labour movement. A month later Lawson married Hilda's older sister. The two men obviously hit it off. Lang would later tell the story of how he once had to rescue the famous poet from one of his frequent drinking sprees, bundling him into a hansom cab to take him home after discovering him drunk on a city street corner.

'Harry decided that the driver was too slow. So he started letting him have it in good ripe Australian bush oaths,' Lang recounted. 'The driver said he wouldn't go any further. I took out a huge bandanna handkerchief and gagged Harry for the rest of the journey. On arrival we thought he was dead. He was only dead drunk.'

Both brothers-in-law soon became disenchanted with their wives and it is not unreasonable to assume that their mateship led to some lively escapades together. Lang never gave much away about his personal life, even in three later autobiographies. There was one emotional entanglement, however, that seems to have profoundly changed him and may help explain why he went on to become such a hard man of politics, prepared, time and time again, to risk all rather than compromise.

In his early thirties Lang left his wife and four children to live with a mistress, Nellie Louisa Anderson. Hilda filed for a legal separation at one point, citing her husband's adultery, but withdrew her petition only three days later, presumably on his promise to return to the matrimonial home. Still, the relationship continued, with Nellie giving birth to a son by Lang in 1910. Whether influenced by his Catholic upbringing or simply through a sense of responsibility to his lawful wife, Lang made repeated attempts to end the affair but couldn't summon the strength to break off completely with the woman who had obviously become the great love of his life. The choice was cruelly taken out of his hands when Anderson suddenly died in September, 1911 at the age of only 28. Her death certificate suggests she contracted a fatal infection after suffering a miscarriage of what would have been their second child. Lang was shattered by her loss, overcome by much the same sense of helpless rage that had pushed him to the edge during his childhood. He was no doubt torn by guilt as well, knowing the tragic consequences of his ambivalence. It was almost as if his very soul shrank in bitter regret. Whatever kind of man he had been before, he would never again allow himself to become so vulnerable.

Lang by then was well established in the real estate business and had made his mark in local government, becoming mayor of Auburn. With Nellie gone from his life, he channelled all of his passion into politics. Hilda, indifferent about her looks and intensely intellectual, would not have been an easy woman to live with but her strong-willed mother had obviously instilled her with a solid sense of right and wrong and utter disdain for the prevailing social pretentions. She soon found it in her heart to come to terms with her husband's double life, for she embraced Nellie's son, James Christian, as her own. When she later gave birth to a daughter – exactly two years after Anderson's death – she generously christened her Nellie Louisa in memory of the dead mistress.

An astute political observer in her own right, Hilda put all her heart into campaigning for her husband's election as New South Wales Premier in June, 1925 and again – after his period in Opposition – for his return to office in October, 1931. She remained loyally at Jack Lang's side through the tumultuous events that would lead to both his proudest moment and his most humiliating defeat. The summit conference he was about to attend in Melbourne, starting Thursday 28 January, would mark a dramatic turning point in his fortunes. But the Big Fella was hardly alone at the start of 1932 in facing the biggest crisis of his life – and Hilda was hardly the only long-suffering wife.

5

Love in the time of the Great Depression

Saturday night theatregoers in Brisbane took little notice of the Raggedy Ann who had just put down her begging bowl close by the Tivoli. She was in her mid-thirties, pale-faced and cardboard-thin, wearing an unstylish black hat and tattered pink dress, its collar pulled protectively high up over her neck to ward off the occasional speck of rain. Next to the bowl was a battered violin case, tilted against a wall in such a way as to keep the rain off the certificate she had carefully placed beneath it. It was a police department permit for 'Itinerant Musicians' made out in the name of Winifred Donnier. Buskers were rife in every capital city, most of them doing little more than waving an instrument about to distinguish themselves from common panhandlers. The few pennies they managed to earn, rather than being tokens of appreciation, were just as likely to have been offered in hopes of discouraging them from playing further.

Winifred Donnier proved to be in a category all to herself. As she raised bow to string, her right hand trembled so noticeably that it seemed she might not be able to carry on. After only a moment's hesitation, however, she followed through, upstroke and down, creating a sound as mellow as candlelight – yet of such vibrancy as to stop passers-by in mid-stride. Among the audience gathering around her, few would have had the slightest clue what she was playing, though it was clear from the start that this would be no usual fiddler's medley of Scottish reels and sentimental favourites. With her eyes shut tight and lips aquiver in sympathy with the chords, the violinist let herself be whisked away to a more compassionate world where Paganini, Bach and Mozart reigned supreme.

If any of her listeners had bothered to look more closely, they would have seen a second piece of paper under the violin case, next to Donnier's police permit. It was dated 10 April, 1919, and bore the distinctive seal of Buckingham Palace. It was addressed to Winifred Pare, Donnier's maiden name, and it read in part: 'Her Majesty wishes me to tell you that she much enjoyed your playing on the violin on Monday last.' It was signed by Queen Mary's private secretary.

English-born, Winifred was the great-great-granddaughter of the early nineteenth-century composer Sir Henry Rowley Bishop. As a young virtuoso she studied music at Trinity College and earned such glowing reviews that she was soon invited to the Palace for a private recital. She would go on to marry Emil Donnier, an internationally renowned horticulturist, who persuaded her to migrate to Queensland in 1929 with prospects of starting up a flourishing export trade in seeds from his own hybridised strain of tomato. That dream disintegrated with the Wall Street crash, sending Emil heavily into debt and inevitably into a downward spiral of despondency and self-loathing. His wife tried to help but amid the havoc of the sudden downturn, no one was interested in taking violin lessons.

Winifred's impromptu performance that evening was interrupted only by the cheerful clink of coins thrown into her collection bowl. They added up to an extraordinary 30 shillings, more money than she had seen in months. Near nine o'clock, as her permit was about to expire, she decided to repay the generosity of appreciative onlookers by treating them to the more familiar melody of 'Home, Sweet Home'. It was always a sure crowd-pleaser, touchingly nostalgic, but her haunting rendition imbued it with the added poignancy of a heartfelt lament. Upon the final note, she stooped to pack up her precious violin – the work of the Italian master, Gianfrancesco Pressenda – and then hurried off into the darkness, struggling not to cry in front of strangers.

'Home, Sweet Home' had actually been composed by Winifred's famous ancestor, Henry Rowley Bishop, the one melody for which he is most fondly remembered. For Winifred, though, there was no longer any home to go back to. A few weeks earlier her husband, Emil, with no more will to struggle on, had succumbed to a lingering illness, leaving her so destitute she could not even afford to pay off his funeral expenses. She might easily have been thrown onto the streets if it wasn't for kind neighbours allowing her the shelter of a tiny shed at the back of their house. They also loaned her the two shillings and sixpence needed to obtain her Itinerant Musician's licence, probably thinking they had little chance of ever getting their money back.

Winifred Donnier, however, had earned enough from a few hours' busking not only to repay them but everything she still owed for Emil's burial. That night, retiring to a bedroom not much larger than a closet, she looked once again at the two documents that so perfectly summed up what had become of her life: one from Buckingham Palace, the other from the Brisbane police department. While her eyes flitted from one to the other, she replayed in her mind the glorious four minutes or so of the Paganini 'Caprice' that had opened her brilliant recital on that wind-swept Brisbane Street. The renowned variations led her once again through every byway of human emotion: flirtatious, excited, petulant, passionate, mournful, hysterical, exquisitely erotic and joyously free.

And then she wept herself to sleep.

～⋄～

The Great War was fought by men, but women were the front-line troops of the Great Depression in Australia. Their heroism, though largely unsung, revealed itself in countless ways. Throughout the land it was the women – wives and mothers – who would be called on to make the biggest sacrifice in the day-to-day battle for survival; skimping on their own meals to ensure their families had more to eat, working themselves into a twilight state of perpetual exhaustion to compensate for what their idle menfolk could no longer provide.

Early widowhood, like that suffered by Winifred Donnier, was not necessarily the cruellest of ordeals confronting a woman of that period. During the war, a wife had to get by for years without the man she loved. In the Great Depression she often had to battle on *despite* him. Of all the trials she would be forced to suffer through, none could be more heartbreaking than watching an unemployed husband coming home with another day's failure etched in his face, the last vestiges of his spirit steadily draining away. It was as if his soul's blood was seeping through some secret wound, silently, invisibly, with nothing she could do to stem the flow.

Simply trying to keep a marriage together in such demoralising circumstances was difficult enough but there were many more challenges ahead. The women of 1932 learned to move like nomads from one traumatic eviction to the next, doing what they could to turn a filthy hovel into the semblance of a home. On top of their own arduous domestic chores, many looked after other people's children or took in washing to earn extra money. Some made preserves and sandwiches or collected bits and pieces – soap, pins, coathangers, shoelaces – to sell door to door. Not a few were prepared to barter their bodies, putting up with a minute or two of clumsy pawing in exchange for a basket of fresh fruit or to persuade some sleazy dole inspector to ignore a petty infraction. As colder weather set in, they did what they could to patch tattered jumpers or line one threadbare frock with scraps from another. When a child fell ill and there were already too many doctor's bills left unpaid, they even prepared their own poultices and herbal remedies.

No feat was beyond their ingenuity nor physical strain too much to bear – a resilience all the more remarkable considering a goodly proportion of these wives and mothers came from comfortable middle- or lower middle-class backgrounds and had until then never known real poverty in their lives. Their husbands, perhaps only a year or so before, might have been earning substantial salaries as managers, salesmen, clerks or skilled tradesmen. For such men a sudden sacking could hit with all the shock of a serious road smash – taking them months to recover enough to carry on. While it would be too much of a generality to suggest that women were stronger in times of domestic crisis, they certainly tended to be more pragmatic and adaptable. Theirs was the delicate task of replacing the man of the house in the dominant protective role without causing further irreparable damage to his ego – encouraging him to try harder without appearing to blame or nag.

In a perverse way, it might have been a lot easier to be married to some drunken ne'er-do-well. At least then they could justify exploding in anger and contempt – even opting to make a clean break. Instead, many a Great Depression wife learned to bite her lip and guard her every word, telling herself over and over that no matter how long her husband remained out of a job, it was not his fault.

They only had to look a few doors down the street to see other husbands leaving for work every morning, their kids well dressed and fed. For the four in every ten families dumped at random on the economic scrapheap, it was all the more humiliating to watch the rest of society getting by relatively unscathed, even thriving. It is not hard to imagine how such hard-pressed wives must have felt when they read about some prominent socialite showing up at a charity ball in a gown costing more than a year's worth of dole money.

For every such society hostess, of course, there were a thousand impoverished Winifred Donniers; and sad as Donnier's situation might seem, it didn't come close to matching the calamitous plight of women living in hard-hit rural areas.

A farm wife's burden was likely to be close to unbearable in any circumstances. Even without the collapse in primary exports, the soldier-settler or migrant-settler schemes adopted by various states were doomed from the start with blocks far too small to support profitable agriculture of any description. The eager couples who flocked to take part in such ventures were driven by the most seductive of all delusions: to re-create their own private Eden from the sweat of their brow and their boundless devotion. Their willingness to labour on together, day after day, month after month, was the most heart-wrenching part of the tragic endings in store for almost all of them.

If a hardworking city couple ran into trouble trying to operate a fruit and vegetable shop, they had little choice about how much longer to continue. Their creditors soon stepped in to lock the doors. Meanwhile, though, a dedicated farming couple could keep struggling year after year, getting deeper into debt, until they virtually buried themselves alive. They were like gambling addicts, throwing good money after bad, unable to face the fact that all their previous hard work had been in vain. Banks, especially as the depression set in, delayed foreclosure knowing there was little chance of reselling the property. Governments, meanwhile, were reluctant to evict a defaulting family from a failed settlement scheme for fear of admitting the atrocious blunder that was leading to so many ruined lives.

Either way, patience was definitely no virtue – merely a prolonging of sheer torment, as demonstrated by the harrowing case of Ethel Jane Anderson, wife of a West Australian wheat farmer living in a remote district 250 kilometres north-east of Perth.

The mother of five children aged from thirteen to two, Anderson appeared in Perth Criminal Court accused of arson and malicious damage, charges serious enough to carry a lengthy prison sentence. In the early hours of Sunday morning, 24 January, neighbours reported seeing flames sprouting up from various locations around the Anderson farm. When they rushed over to help, they found Ethel herself setting alight haystacks and ramshackle outbuildings, including stables and a blacksmith's shed. Her husband tried to calm her but she was in a hysterical state. Police arriving from the nearby town of Dalwallinu had no choice but to lay charges.

As the story emerged at Ethel's trial, the family had bought the farm five years earlier but soon ran into trouble paying off interest on their mortgage and had to surrender the title. For the past two years they had been living there as virtual sharecroppers, working the land for free in return for being allowed to remain in the homestead they had built with their own hands. All they could look forward to was a small share of any profit from the wheat crop, as unlikely as that might be in the middle of a worldwide slump. That Friday, however, their mortgagee had suddenly ordered them to pack up and clear out over the weekend, adding insult to injury by seizing the few pieces of furniture of any value in lieu of money still owed.

At first, Ethel appeared to take the distressing news stoically enough, sticking to the same routine she had followed slavishly almost every day over the last five years. On Saturday she worked through the daylight hours, washing clothes in a narrow stream a kilometre from the farm house and then toting buckets of water back to bathe the children. That evening after her husband and the five little ones fell asleep, she carried a hurricane lamp out into the night so as not to disturb them and stayed up stacking hay for an hour or two before settling down in the blacksmith's shed to stitch up a pile of hessian bags and then do the family sewing. Towards midnight, though, something snapped inside her – perhaps when she took a closer look at the faded blouse she was trying to salvage for her youngest daughter and realised it was no longer fit to be used as the meanest rag. She had long ago forgotten what colour it used to be when she herself first proudly wore it as her 'Sunday best', arriving in Dalwallinu to begin the family's exciting new adventure. Now, in her troubled state, her last shreds of hope somehow seemed to become interwoven with this one piteous fragment of cloth.

Ethel's husband had been a police constable for thirteen years, earning a good, steady income. His work, though, brought him into contact with the seamy side of city life and showed him the evil things that could happen to families as they fell apart under the pressures of urban living. He and Ethel talked constantly of giving their children a healthier lifestyle. Wheat was booming – why not take the £1000 ($70,000) they had saved and trust their future to an export market that could only grow stronger? That was in 1927. They had barely reaped their first crops before wheat prices the world over fell to less than the cost of planting.

When Ethel Anderson impetuously swung her lantern against the first heap of straw it wasn't someone else's property she was setting aflame. Instead, it was her own withered Eden – the elusive dream that had sentenced her and her loved ones to five years of hell. The real owner could hardly be expected to see it that way and demanded that she be prosecuted to the fullest extent of the law. In response Ethel's defence lawyer was only able to offer a few stark facts in hopes of a lighter sentence.

'The circumstances in which she lived were almost unbelievable,' he began, 'and while they do not excuse her crime, explain the state of mind that caused it. This family has existed on bare sustenance for two years, without meat, butter or vegetables. In the whole of those two years they have not handled more than £2 [$140] in cash. Mrs. Anderson had only one light dress, no underwear or stockings. Her only footwear was a pair of number 10 canvas boots found at a railway siding. The children themselves had no shoes, nor hardly ever enough to eat – and their state preyed heavily on their mother's mind. Two years ago she was still a healthy woman weighing eight stone [51 kilograms]. At the time of the offence, her weight had dropped to six and a half stone [41 kilograms] . . .'

When he finished, a hush fell over the courtroom. Finally, the crown prosecutor rose to speak, goaded into action by the judge's steely gaze.

'I believe the facts have been correctly stated by the defence counsel,' he confirmed, coughing and clearing his throat, sick at the thought that he should have added to this poor woman's misery.

Ethel Jane Anderson was immediately set free on a good behaviour bond. Every eye turned to see her reaction as she left the dock but she was long beyond all caring.

A family can be sorely tested by such extreme hardship at any point in time but the Great Depression's impact on married life was so widespread and sustained as to transform the attitudes of an entire generation. Against the backdrop of bare survival, it was almost inevitable that a woman began to ration her feelings in a way that made her seem relatively brittle or 'pinched' – her tenderness marred by prickly knots of emotional scarring, her natural affection stretched too taut to spare another atom more. Among the thousands of husbands who left home during the depression years, it is impossible to know how many were propelled not so much by the hope of finding work as by a gnawing sense of rejection or shame. If an itinerant spouse joined a government-supported labour camp he might remember to send a few spare shillings home every month. In many cases, though, it was understood the wife and kids would be better off consigning themselves into the care of relatives or friends. Although official divorce rates actually dropped, largely because of the cost, countless marriages would wind up for all practical purposes in de facto separation.

Even when the husband remained at home, however, many relationships tended to fall into a state of suspended animation. Fear of an unwanted pregnancy was as thick in the air as the pungent smell of 'Collingwood coke', the fires made from discarded leather offcuts gathered by families too poor to afford coal or firewood. Childbirth not only meant another mouth to feed but the impairment of a mother's capacity to contribute to the family's welfare. Contraceptives were still considered a taboo subject in many households, not just among Catholics. The more reliable devices such as diaphragms, known as Dutch caps, or spermicidal pessaries were not widely available, with many Catholic chemists flatly refusing to stock them. When they could be obtained, they were well beyond the budgets of most unemployed. For both married and unmarried women, the most common method of protection, when it could be enforced, was jokingly referred to in Sydney slang as 'getting off at Redfern' – interrupting the journey a stop before reaching Central Station. The hit-or-miss results of coitus interruptus, unfortunately, too often turned out to be no laughing matter. Depression-era hospitals were notorious for women's wards filled with patients suffering the tragic consequences of botched backyard abortions.

From the very start of the economic crash, Catholic families tended to fare the worst, their incomes already lower on average compared to Protestants and often with twice the number of children to support. Even if a mother was prepared to defy the teachings of her church, she faced a frightening barrage of warnings against the supposed medical hazards of birth control – pseudoscientific nonsense which seemed to flourish in the hothouse atmosphere of the 1930s alongside Ouija boards and ectoplasmic ooze. As one Melbourne writer assured his readers in a pamphlet entitled *The Dangers of Birth Control*: 'Today, the bursting walls of the insane asylums can trace the larger number of their inmates to the untoward conduct of arresting the normal results of sexual intercourse.' Not to mention 'the extraordinary prevalence of tumours, fibroids and cancers, every one of them almost exclusively confined to those portions of the body most intimately associated with child bearing.'

The sad truth was just the opposite: women worried themselves sick over the risks of unprotected sex. Even the most loving relationship could be destroyed by anxiety about an unwanted pregnancy in such uncertain economic times, as one Sydney housewife noted about her next-door neighbours.

'They would have been an ideal family if only the awful burden of fear had been removed,' wrote Daisy McWilliams in her personal memoir of the depression years. 'Her husband had a part-time job that threatened to end any day. The wife's fear was what so many of the women of Australia suffer from and is affecting their health – the fear of having more children when there is no way of keeping them.'

Whatever technique they turned to – whether it was the Dutch cap, condoms, quinine pessaries, vinegar douche, rhythm method, Redfern method, or plain old Cold Shoulder – women across Australia somehow succeeded in reducing the national birth rate to an all-time low in 1932, a mere fraction of what it had been in the previous century. One of the immediate side benefits was a remarkable decline in infant mortality, cutting the toll of such baby-killing diseases as diarrhoea and enteritis by up to 70 per cent.

Perhaps the most notable change in attitudes toward love and marriage to come out of the depression was the major rethink it caused among couples preparing to tie the knot. The number of weddings slumped by a drastic 25 per cent. Obviously, some of those deciding to postpone their plans were worried about their economic prospects or hesitant about starting a family in such an unstable period. A more compelling reason, though, was left largely unspoken. Since the beginning of the downturn women had begun entering the work force in increasing numbers, replacing males on the basis of their willingness to accept wages well below the official rates. By 1932, however, a severe backlash brought widespread agitation against married women holding down jobs that might otherwise go to men, a sentiment that in some cases was backed up by law. Schoolteachers and other females in the civil service risked immediate dismissal if word got out that they had wed. The mores of the day were a powerful dissuader against couples living together outside of marriage, although it is likely that some still found a way, occasionally aided by understanding parents prepared to turn a blind eye. On the other hand, the long years of austerity also produced an unusually large crop of spinsters unwilling to sacrifice a regular fortnightly pay cheque for the uncertainties of love in the time of the Great Depression.

∽∾∾

Many depression-era women had a secret soft spot in their hearts for the Big Fella – secret if they suspected it would make their husbands apoplectic to hear of it. Jack Lang's rugged persona held a natural appeal for females of all ages, to some as a forceful but empathetic father figure, to others as a classic role model for the masculine qualities they might hope for in a spouse or son. During his first term as New South Wales Premier he had also endeared himself to female voters by championing two welcome reforms to give them more financial security: the nation's first widow's pension and a special family endowment for each new child, with the money paid directly to the mother.

Lang's return to office in his remarkable landslide victory of 25 October 1930 could be credited in no small part to the women who felt more secure having such a strong leader in the driver's seat. They could hardly have imagined the wild ride they were in for next.

6

Surprise attack

The leaders of the seven governments and their entourages filed up the steps of the Victorian Parliament in the same stifling heatwave that had gripped Melbourne during Albert Jacka's funeral. Within the next week, in fact, much of the Gippsland area to the south-east would be engulfed in flames – ravaged by some of the worst bushfires the state had ever seen, taking a toll of nine dead in just one night. The torrid conditions could almost be a metaphor for the tinderbox atmosphere inside the conference room as the main protagonists fixed each other in their sights.

'I may express views in which some of you do not concur,' the new Prime Minister began. 'I wish to emphasise, however, that I am speaking as the leader of the Federal Government, free from any party political prejudice. The times are too serious for anything of such a character.'

Jack Lang would have found it hard to keep from laughing aloud at the sanctimonious tone. No party prejudice? In a speech only a few days before, Joe Lyons had denounced him as an 'incubus' that had to be destroyed to make way for Australia's economic recovery.

The leaders' summit, the first of 1932, had been called to review the progress of the federal and state governments in meeting their financial targets for economic recovery as set by the Premiers' Plan the previous June. Lang had reluctantly added his signature to the pact along with the other leaders in a morale-boosting show of national unity. His every instinct, though, told him it was an unworkable sham. Apart from its punishing impact on working-class Australians, the agreement went against everything he believed in as a staunch defender of his state's sovereign rights. Compared to the rest of the Australian states, New South Wales was far more populous and industrially advanced. Its citizens, under his leadership, received higher wages for a 44-hour week than others could earn for 48; and in return, they paid a greater share of taxes to support pioneering social reforms. How could this dynamic mother colony of Australia possibly be treated as if it was on the same level as a bucolic Tasmania or South Australia? Why should its vote count as merely one in seven in a crucial debate affecting the largest and most cosmopolitan work force in the land? In the three decades since Federation, the relationship between the federal and state governments had largely remained a grey area of untested assumptions but in Lang's eyes the distinctions were clear enough. The federal government's role was restricted to taking charge of certain essential coordinating functions; each state government was to be left free to take care of its own people in its own way.

These national summits took place within two different forums. The Premiers' Conferences determined broad policy initiatives for the nation as a whole. The Loan Council, with a high input from treasury officials and economic experts, focused on the specific amounts of funding to be distributed among the seven governments. The Loan Council had been established well before the onset of the depression to coordinate borrowing and prevent the various governments from competing against each other with bond issues. In the worsening economic conditions, however, the body began to assume more of a supervisory role, with the federal government using it to keep watch over state budgets, discouraging inefficient expenditure. It was within the framework of the Loan Council that Lang and Lyons began playing a game of political chess which could only lead to the fall of one king or the other. Stalemate was not a possibility.

Lyons, with his leprechaunish looks and remarkable brood of eleven children, hardly fitted the image of a political assassin, but that was the role he – more than anyone else – had played in the downfall of James Scullin. He had been an influential figure in the Scullin Cabinet, taking over as temporary Treasurer when Theodore was forced to step aside. As conservative-minded as it was possible to be within the Labor Party spectrum, he promptly convinced Scullin to accept Niemeyer's budget-cutting formula, for all its divisive implications. Yet, almost immediately after putting his Prime Minister in such a precarious situation, he then resigned in a huff when Theodore was reappointed Treasurer. Accusing his former cabinet colleagues of being puppets in the hands of the radical unions, he soon quit the ALP altogether. The delighted Opposition immediately claimed him as their own, persuading him to lead a newly formed United Australia Party (UAP). He was thus, in Labor vernacular, a 'rat' though Jack Lang – considering his own split with the federal ALP – was hardly in a position to call names.

Lyons had started off as a schoolteacher in Tasmania and still tended to act the pedant, ponderously spelling out every small detail as if he were speaking to children. The main thrust of his lesson for the day was on the failure of New South Wales to meet its targets under the Premiers' Plan. He even whipped out a chart to prove it.

'The wide disparity in rates of wages and hours of labour between New South Wales and her neighbours is matched by a heavier percentage of unemployed in New South Wales, despite her great resources,' he scolded. 'The remedy for unemployment, jobs that will last, can be found only by sound economy.'

Lyons went on to note with obvious distaste that New South Wales alone had a system of family endowment, paying a fortnightly benefit for each child. It was also the only state to provide a widow's pension. The Lang Government had done virtually nothing to cut back on such welfare programs and as a consequence it was lagging well behind the other states in meeting the agreed 20 per cent reduction to its budget. Its projected deficit for the year, in fact, would be as much as the deficits of all the other governments put together.

'This is an alarming situation,' he told the delegates. 'To falter now and depart from the Plan would mean the loss of all that we have gained. The alternative to the Plan is default or inflation, either of which would destroy Australia's credit and have calamitous effects.'

The leader of the most powerful state in the Commonwealth of Australia sat quietly fuming. Of all his accomplishments in political life, the widow's pensions and family endowment were Lang's greatest source of pride; but to this dreary country schoolmaster lecturing to him now, they were merely an extravagance the nation could ill afford.

'Not even the most soulless bondholder would snatch his interest out of the mouths of undernourished children,' the Big Fella rebuked the Prime Minister when he got his chance to speak. However, nothing that Jack Lang had to say at the conference that Thursday, 28 January, would come close to matching the shock waves from the official memorandum he sent to Lyons later that night. The New South Wales Government, it announced, would be unable to meet the full instalment of overseas interest which was due the following Monday. The bill amounted to almost £1 million ($70 million) owed mostly to British but also to US lenders. New South Wales was prepared to pay just under half of it if the Commonwealth came up with the rest. Otherwise New South Wales would have no choice but to default.

The Big Fella, with a showman's flair, failed to appear for the Friday morning session claiming to have been unexpectedly tied up. It was left to Joe Lyons to inform the other delegates of Lang's bombshell disclosure. The unexpected news threw the national summit into disarray. No Loan Council had ever been faced with such a large-scale emergency, let alone on such short notice.

The previous year, when the New South Wales Premier had first failed to meet an interest instalment, he had at least given ample warning of the state's difficult financial position. The Scullin Government quickly stepped in to make the payment, and was soon reimbursed from the New South Wales Treasury, albeit under threat of court action. Then, however, it was a case of one Labor government dealing with another, whatever tensions existed between them. Joe Lyons was a more cunning and ruthless politician than James Scullin. Not only was he the leader of a brand new conservative alliance, he was from the smallest Australian state and strongly resented the idea of being bullied around by New South Wales. So, too, it appeared, did all the other states. One after another the other Loan Council delegates proceeded to issue vehement denunciations of Lang before unanimously rejecting his request to borrow the £500,000 he needed to avoid default.

While the federal government had ultimate responsibility for making sure all debts incurred within the framework of the Loan Council were duly honoured, there were any number of options it could choose for forcing a state to repay what it owed. It could sue in court, as any company might sue a defaulting customer, or it might even move to put a state government into receivership. All eyes fell on the Prime Minister to announce his government's next step in the crisis. His decision on the following Saturday morning stunned even the most hard-line elements among his own supporters. It was to do nothing at all.

'The Commonwealth Government,' Lyons explained, 'has been forced to the conclusion that Mr. Lang will ignore any undertaking he has given whenever it suits him so long as the Commonwealth is prepared to shoulder the responsibilities of the Government of New South Wales. It would be useless to advance the money because it would merely amount to postponing the day of reckoning. In a month or so there would be further default and so it would go on. The decision means that unless the New South Wales Government itself can find the money in time, there will be, for the first time, nominal default on the part of an Australian government abroad.'

In plainer language the federal government's response to the loans emergency boiled down to this. Lang's head was in a noose of his own making. Let him hang by it.

The Big Fella abruptly left the summit and returned to Sydney without bothering to say goodbye.

'I had the door shut on me and the key was turned,' he told a reporter. 'They are treating New South Wales as an enemy country.'

At dusk, a gangling young red retriever bounded from a duck pond in the Botanic Gardens, shaking the muddy water from its coat as it raced to the call of its master.

'Here, Micky!'

Sir Philip Game frequently walked his dog at sunset across the lush parklands bordering Government House. It was far more enjoyable therapy for the debilitating headaches he had been suffering recently than the injections his doctor persisted with. Even in the dimming light Game was easy to pick out from among other strollers because of his decided limp, the legacy of an old ice-skating injury. When he reached the Domain, he invariably stopped to chat with the unemployed men camped there under rock ledges or in makeshift tents while Micky sniffed at their ragged clothing. Sometimes he would give them a few coins or remind them that they were welcome to a free feed from Mrs Musson, the Government House cook. Under Game's instructions, she whipped up triple quantities of everything she served in the front rooms so as to make sure there was always enough to hand out at the back door.

Confronting the plight of the homeless helped Sir Philip to keep his own troubles in perspective. On that first day of February, though, his worries were not so easily set aside. The news of Lang's default had caused consternation in London financial circles. The Australian press was filled with new demands for the Governor to exercise his prerogative and dismiss the Premier from office. A formidable array of the most eminent constitutional authorities was quoted offering countless cogent reasons why he must act. The problem was, the Governor himself didn't agree with any of them.

Game was a perfect slice from the English upper crust, of impeccable manners and dress, with a soft voice and eyes that twinkled with goodwill. He stood medium-tall and ramrod straight, as to be expected of a former professional military man; but he was also so thin and slightly built that two of him might well have fitted into one Jack Lang. They happened to be the same age, perhaps the only thing they had in common apart from their iron wills. Lang was from a darker world where suspicion flourished and resentments bubbled everywhere in volcanic pools of spite. Game, who had risen to the rank of Air Vice-Marshal, was strictly stiff upper lip and cheerfully make do. Unlike Lang, after all, he had actually been shot at with real bullets but held no ill will toward his adversaries. If naive about the intricacies of back-room politics, he had an unerring instinct for doing all that was required in his role as umpire. From a historical viewpoint the destinies of the two could not have been more entwined had they been born Siamese twins.

Game arrived to take up the role of Governor of New South Wales only six months before Lang won his second term in office. Their clashes had been sharp and frequent, mainly involving the Premier's attempts to reform the notoriously troublesome Upper House of parliament, known as the Legislative Council. Its members, at that stage, were appointed rather than elected and Lang had inherited a hotbed of arch-conservatives who stubbornly persisted in blocking his most important pieces of legislation. Lang's solution was to flood the Council with his own Labor appointees but for that he needed Game's approval and the Governor was extremely reluctant to undermine the Upper chamber's constitutional role as a house of review. Sir Philip's headaches were a measure of the increasing tension, though relations between the two at all times remained well mannered. Toward the end of 1931, however, the Governor had found himself under attack from an entirely different direction. Those who might normally be counted as his loyal constituents – the upper echelons of business and professional life, the squattocracy, the social elite – had gone out of their way to demonstrate their disgust at Game's refusal to sack the despised Premier. While attending the Boxing Day races at Randwick, Sir Philip had been openly snubbed by AJC members. At Sydney's prestigious Union Club – frequented by the wealthiest businessmen and graziers – the bunyip aristocracy quite literally turned their backs on him.

Sir Philip, a highly decorated veteran of numerous campaigns, was well able to handle the personal insults but he could not bear to see his wife Gwendolen so unfairly treated. It was she who had to deal with much of the day-to-day correspondence. 'Will you please ask your hubby how much Lang pays him on the quiet to keep him in power?' read one letter. And another: 'Suggest your hubby should change his name from Game to Coward, it would be more suitable for his stamp. Ask him to pack his trunks and go back to where he comes from. He is not wanted in Australia; if not he will be tarred and feathered.'

Some of this hate mail, though perhaps not so crudely worded, came from people the Games had come to regard as friends. They wrote to have their names deleted from the Government House visitors' book or even to decline dinner invitations previously accepted. Lady Game, the mother of a son of university age and two younger children, had no experience to prepare her for such intense hostility. Though she fell immediately in love with Sydney and did all she could to fit in, she found herself slighted even by those royalty-mad loyalists who would normally have fawned all over her. In one notable snub, the New South Wales Country Women's Association pointedly withheld the invitation traditionally sent to the Governor's wife to open its annual meeting.

Perhaps Gwendolen's most hurtful single moment, however, came while attending a charity function. She spotted a woman she knew well who happened to be standing by herself in the middle of the room. Lady Game, hoping to make her feel more comfortable, walked across to speak to her but the woman abruptly turned her back. The Governor's wife was then herself left stranded and alone, for all to stare at, struggling to hold back her tears at such calculated rudeness.

'She refused, very curtly and pointedly, in front of quite a lot of people,' Gwendolen would later lament in a letter to a friend back in England.

For Sir Philip, though, the stress of being subjected to so much public abuse was nothing compared to the pressures put on him by Lang in his persistent nagging about the Upper House. Here history fails to give credit where credit was due, but Micky, the Game family's beloved pet, would come to play an important advisory role in his master's many clashes with the Big Fella. Game explained why one afternoon when he limped back from his office to the comfort of his living room and plopped himself down on a chair, his stiff leg out before him, Micky settling at his feet.

'I've just been seeing Lang,' he announced. 'I was glad Micky was in the room with me. You know, Lang really has got some hypnotic power, I'm sure he has. But whenever I feel myself becoming mesmerised, I stoop down and give Mick's ear a tweak; he waffles and licks my hand – and the spell is broken.'

Whatever the Governor and his family had been through so far, though, it paled in comparison to the tensions to come. Jack Lang's defiant stand on overseas interest was about to trigger a showdown of historic proportions between the Commonwealth and its most rambunctious state.

Sir Philip Game would inevitably end up in the middle, a refined English gentleman caught in the no-man's-land of Australian-style party politics at its vitriolic worst.

7

Flying high

The Fifty-Fifty Club's thirsty clientele had a lot more to talk about than deficits and defaults. The last days of January had been packed with heroic exploits: Donald Bradman with his unrivalled fifteenth double century scored in the fourth test against South Africa; billiard champion Walter Lindrum chalking up the highest ever break of 4137 during a tournament in London; motor racing's Norman 'Wizard' Smith reaching speeds of up to 200 mph in his Australian-designed 12-cylinder *Enterprise* to set the world record over ten miles on New Zealand's Ninety Mile Beach.

The most exciting deed of all, however, had nothing to do with sport, though everything to do with courage and the will to succeed – the competitive spirit which Australians liked to think of as being so much a part of their national character. Charles Kingsford Smith flew into Sydney just on nightfall, Thursday, 21 January, after a gruelling round trip to London and back. It was a flight he never should have been asked to make since he was still ill from the effects of carbon monoxide poisoning suffered during a failed long distance record attempt the year before. Instead, he had been called in as an emergency replacement after another pilot from his aviation company, ANA, was involved in a serious crash in Malaya. When Smithy finally stepped down from the cockpit, he looked haggard and totally drained.

'Where's the missus?' he called to the hundreds pressing around.

His wife Mary stepped forward to give him a hug. It was as much a matter of falling into her arms from exhaustion as an embrace. The reason for all the urgency surrounding the flight revealed itself when eight bags were quickly unloaded from the cargo bay and rushed to a waiting postal van. They were filled with Christmas mail and New Year's greetings from Britain. Kingsford Smith and his ANA colleagues had been carried away by a dream: that this moment could mark the beginning of a regular airmail service between Australia and the Mother Country. For 11,172 lucky Australians it meant the first chance to read a letter from 'Home' within the same month it was mailed.

Smithy was already the most admired figure in the nation. His landing at Mascot that Thursday evening was met by only a modest crowd; but it still brought back memories of the glorious welcome he had received there four years earlier, in May, 1928, when 300,000 massed on the aerodrome that would one day bear his name. He had just completed a feat considered far more daring and significant than Charles Lindbergh's: the first flight across the Pacific from the United States. With Charles Ulm as his co-pilot and two other crew, he had guided the three-engine *Southern Cross* through storms and darkness across intimidating expanses of ocean from one tiny dot of land to the next. The trip had been considered so hazardous that the federal government even threatened to pass a law prohibiting him from attempting it on grounds a tragic accident could set back the development of civil aviation in Australia for years to come. 'Efforts to promote the development of civil aviation would be neutralised as a result of tragedies caused by long overseas flights in aircraft not suitable to that purpose,' warned Stanley Bruce, the prime minister at the time.

The southern continent, more than any place on earth, had its future tied to the skies. Its remoteness made it a magnet for the best and bravest of pilots, those eager to push the new technology to its outer limits. In 1919 Adelaide brothers Ross and Keith Smith had flown the first aircraft ever to land in Australia from overseas, taking 27 days and 20 hours. By October, 1930, Smithy had set a new speed record between England and Australia of 9 days, 21 hours, 40 minutes. That was quickly whittled down hour by hour in spirited competition between Australian and British aviators. A few months into 1932, it would be reduced to less than nine days, five times faster than a passenger ship.

Such rapid progress in aviation, however, only came at a heavy cost. ANA claimed to have made a small profit from that first overseas airmail run but in practical terms – with the crash in Malaya and several other minor mishaps – it proved to be a commercial disaster. The federal government refused to grant the subsidies needed to keep the service going. By the end of the month, ANA had been hauled into the bankruptcy court over unpaid debts. Smithy himself would eventually be reduced to scratching out a living by taking people on joy-flights.

Yet, what he accomplished in bringing home the mail in the depths of the Great Depression could never be measured in dollar value. Each letter in itself would have been regarded as a precious gem aglow with its own sentiments – the pleasures of family life, the anxiety of separation, perhaps even a marriage proposal or two. Together in the thousands, though, they conveyed a single message to an isolated population struggling to survive in desperate times. The distance separating Australia from the wider world had just shrunk beyond belief.

The envelopes, with their specially designed airmail imprints, were soon shown off around the town like prized collector's items. Perhaps a few even circulated at the Fifty-Fifty, bringing a slap on the back and a drink on the house from the club's boss, Phil Jeffs. For him and his underworld cronies, however, one sensational event in late January would almost certainly have outshone the rest.

Jeffs's favourite customer, Tilly Devine, had staged one of her most disruptive appearances ever at Sydney's Central Court. Her whorehouses were still doing a thriving trade despite the sultry summer heat and shrinking pay packets of her customers; that was not what brought the boisterous madam unstuck. She had been arrested for using indecent language at a popular inner city cafe during a row over a crayfish she claimed smelled off. Tilly decided to teach the law a lesson by hiding the offending crustacean in a suitcase and taking it along to court as her Exhibit A for the defence. The stench had onlookers feeling faint before police discovered the source. The magistrate, after gathering his composure, went on to hear the non-olfactory part of the evidence. Witnesses proceeded to recount how Devine had confronted the proprietor in a volcanic rage, spewing obscenities torrid enough to turn the court transcripts to ash.

'The worst language I have ever heard,' agreed the magistrate, fining her £5 ($350), double the usual amount. Considering his extensive experience with drunken sailors from every corner of the globe his judgement could only have been taken as a tribute, perhaps even official recognition of another world record of sorts. One might imagine Phil Jeffs – gracious host that he was – proposing a toast to it, clinking glasses with the brothel queen and her girls.

'To Tilly Devine, the Bradman of the four-letter word!'

Such was the stuff that kept the pubs abuzz while political leaders debated weightier matters. Amidst the economic plague that swept down upon it from the Northern Hemisphere, Australia's passion for competitive sport, in all its variations, never skipped a beat. Just the opposite: cricket and rugby league would both attract world-record attendances in 1932. As for devoted fans of Australian Rules Football, the unique game was frequently cited as the only thing that made the hard times liveable. It is no coincidence that the Richmond Club, smack in the middle of one of Melbourne's heaviest areas of unemployment, would look back on the Great Depression era as its proudest time.

As for Charles Kingsford Smith, six months after his abortive attempt to launch a regular overseas airmail service he would be awarded a knighthood. Yet he was never granted the continuing subsidies required to further his pioneering efforts, nor even a job to help administer the blossoming aviation industry. Only one political leader had been prepared to stick his neck out enough to offer the pioneer aviator a hefty sum of cash when he really needed it. In 1927 the Big Fella met Smithy for the first time while presiding at an official ceremony to welcome him back to Sydney from a ten-day around-Australia flight. The aviator wasted no time telling the premier about his hopes of making the first trans-Pacific crossing from California. Lang was so taken with the young pilot's enthusiasm that he approved a New South Wales Government grant of £3500 ($245,000) to help cover expenses. Only part of that would actually be paid because Lang lost a subsequent election and his conservative successor, Tom Bavin, refused to honour the full pledge.

The Big Fella would later describe his decision to back the flight as one of the most satisfying of his career.

'They certainly took risks,' he said of Smithy and Ulm. 'But those risks were taken because they were good Australians and were inspired by the thought that they were pioneers whose work would be remembered by this country. Of course they gambled. If they hadn't there would have been no flight.'

When Kingsford Smith completed his historic mission, one of the first things he did was to invite the ex-premier to fly over Sydney with him in the celebrated *Southern Cross*. Lang declined because he didn't want to be seen to be making political capital out of his connection with the aviation hero.

Four years later, however, whatever gratitude Smithy felt he owed to the Big Fella had obviously vanished. In 1932 Sir Charles Kingsford Smith was one of the most prestigious names to be counted in support of the New Guard, the organisation pledged to destroy Jack Lang by any means.

8
Blood sport

Jack Lang, in full oratorical flight, was a study of power in motion – his right fist raised high as an avenging angel's, his gritty baritone rippling with enough muscle to lift his audiences almost bodily from their seats. So it was at the Paddington Town Hall on the evening of Wednesday, 3 February – the Big Fella's first chance to publicly vent his anger at the federal government's stand on the interest issue. The long, narrow room was filled to overflowing an hour before he was due to appear and thousands more gathered on the streets outside to listen through loudspeakers. To wild cheering he was introduced as 'the great big Australian, the gentleman who is going to open the North Shore Bridge' and it was some minutes before he could be sure of being heard above the din.

'Make no mistake about what is before you, people,' he finally began. 'This is not an academic argument about the ethics of paying or not paying interest. It is a bread and butter problem, not only for the man who relies upon manual labour but for every one of you – clerk, shopkeeper, professional man.

The question that faces Australia is whether she will feed her people or pay her overseas interest. I say a government's first duty is to feed its people.'

Lang rarely spoke in abstract terms. He preferred to put a face to every point of debate and then smash it to smithereens. The visage he invoked on this night was that of the imperious Stanley Bruce, a wealthy Cambridge-educated Melburnian who had served for six years as prime minister. Bruce was the perfect symbol of everything the labour movement detested, a top-hatted, pinstriped Croesus who had cynically exploited the Red scare to try to break the back of the unions. The defeat of his government in 1929 was so overwhelming as to see him lose his own seat, the only incumbent prime minister ever to do so. Lyons later encouraged him to return to politics to bolster the image of the newly formed United Australia Party, though in the relatively minor role of assistant treasurer. Lang, however, saw advantage in portraying the ex-prime minister as the true power behind the throne, hell-bent on slashing wages. Just the mention of the name Bruce was enough to unleash a gale of hisses, but Lang then worked his audience into a lather by revealing details of the secret discussions that had taken place among the leaders in Melbourne.

Mr. Bruce – who is in fact the Prime Minister of Australia, though he permits Mr. Lyons to adopt the title – said that public works must stop. These words are as nearly as exact as it is possible for a person to remember. Mr. Bruce said: 'We must adopt a policy of tapering; that is, instead of putting off, say, 20,000 men all at once, put them off at the rate, say, of so many thousands a month. In this way the people will become accustomed to unemployment.

The Premier stood silent a moment to allow his audience to give full vent to their gasps of horror and scornful guffaws.

'Those are not my words,' he finally went on, 'they are the words of Mr. Bruce, the actual leader of the Nationalist Federal Government. Can you people see where you are going? Do you realise that in charge of this nation there is a Government whose expressed objective is to teach the people to become accustomed to unemployment so that they may pay their interest?'

Then, the masterful punchline.

'Don't you think you can become accustomed to unemployment on your own account without any particular assistance from the Government?'

The speech marked the last week of campaigning in a by-election widely seen as an important test of public opinion on the Lang versus Lyons confrontation. The federal electorate of East Sydney was a traditional Labor stronghold but that long-term loyalty had been badly shaken in December's general election amid the confusion of the Scullin Government's sudden collapse. Bewildered voters, faced with choosing between two rival ALP factions, each claiming to represent the true Labor Party, cast a plague on both houses and switched sides to Joe Lyons's conservative coalition. The ALP incumbent, Eddie Ward, was defeated, though by just 1300 votes, a relatively narrow margin compared to the overall landslide.

Then, however, fate stepped into the equation. The sudden death of his UAP successor, John Clasby, only a month later gave Ward the chance to win back his seat. There would still be two ALP factions on the by-election ballot paper, the Lang Labor Party of New South Wales and the federal Labor Party, represented by Lucien Cunningham, a former minister in the Scullin Government. This time around, however, the average voter would have a much clearer idea of exactly who stood for what. Ward had the advantage of a simple message: putting the welfare of the Australian worker first. A tick for Cunningham, on the other hand, seemed virtually the same as voting for the conservatives since both backed the Premiers' Plan with its bitter medicine of lower incomes and further job losses.

The federal Labor Party had little popular support in New South Wales at this stage. It relied heavily on its best campaign speaker, Ted (E.G.) Theodore, to drum up the votes for Cunningham's East Sydney bid. The former treasurer was the one figure in the labour movement who could come close to matching Jack Lang in charismatic appeal – and he had plenty of reason to want to even the score with the Big Fella. In December Theodore had been cast out of his own seat of Dalley in Sydney's inner west – a defeat all the more humiliating because it was inflicted not by a UAP candidate but a Lang Party nominee, with Lang himself using all his influence to achieve his arch-rival's defeat. The by-election campaign now gave the ex-treasurer his first opportunity to hit back at his tormentor, and hit back he did, unleashing the full fury of his scorn at a tumultuous open-air rally in Darlinghurst.

'Lang! This giant with the wonderful brain, this great idol with feet of clay, the old man of the sea who has broken the labour movement,' Theodore boomed, his voice rising above the protesting jeers of Langites strategically positioned in the crowd. 'The principal charge I make against Mr. Lang is that he frustrated all opportunity of unity among Labor forces. He was jealous that the Federal Labor Government might take a little of his limelight. He will never find work for the unemployed. While he remains in office you will always have misery and destitution.'

'Go to China!' an interjector screamed. Others began chanting the time count used in boxing matches to declare a pugilist out: 'One ... two ... three ...'

Election meetings of the period featured all the lurid fascination of a blood sport, perhaps a variation on a bullfight in which many a speaker proudly entered the ring as matador only to discover himself wearing the horns and poked at by picadors. Hecklers managed to infiltrate even the best organised of gatherings. Fist fights continually broke out on the fringes among drunks or thugs from various union factions. The New Guard – dubbed the Boo Guard by its detractors – was always a threat at left-wing functions, its storm troopers sometimes pushing through to the podium like a rugby pack to grab away the microphone. Federal Labor, because of its support of the Premiers' Plan, was an unlikely target of the Guardsmen but agitators from the pro-Lang Trades Hall were just as capable of wreaking havoc.

Their furious interjections, however, only inspired Theodore to hit back all the harder. In contrast to Lang, who had no real union background, he had honed his skills as a scrappy young labour organiser in the bush able to put down any opponent with an instant retort or a sharp right hook; both, if the occasion demanded. He had even earned the nickname 'Red Ted' in recognition of his belligerent style. The passing years, though, had channelled much of that natural aggression into a passion for learning and Theodore was recognised as one of the more widely read and cultivated figures in politics. Still, his basic survival instincts tended to take over in hostile arenas like this.

'The labour movement in New South Wales is not a thinking movement,' he goaded his harassers. 'It is a movement that has been duped by unscrupulous manipulators.'

'We asked for bread and you gave us stones,' someone challenged.

'You asked Mr. Lang for bread and he gave you tin hares,' Theodore shot back, referring to the scandal then brewing over the New South Wales Government's dealings with Judge Swindell, the shady greyhound racing magnate. Unfortunately for Theodore, he himself had never quite managed to shake off the mud from unproved but persistent accusations of illegal profiteering in connection with Queensland's Mungana Mines. It was not something an unruly audience was about to let him forget.

'What about Mungana?' he was challenged.

'The fact that a bunch of leather-lunged lowbrows are prepared to throw dirty insults is a true sign of the decadence of the workers of New South Wales,' he persisted, returning with even more vehemence to the Lang Plan. 'While ever that foolish policy Jack Lang promulgated is being advocated here, you must always have business drifting out of this state and confidence lost. It is the policy of lunatics and hobos, of ultimate ruin . . .'

Theodore was at his scathing best in debunking the Lang Plan, citing statistic after statistic to try to prove that the interest issue was merely a smokescreen to hide the Premier's poor record of administration. New South Wales, under Lang, imposed the highest tax rates in the land, almost half as much again as in Victoria. Its railway system was the least efficient of any of the states, employing more workers per track mile, with annual losses far in excess of all the rest. Its civil service payroll, even after paring down, was still notoriously inflated with political appointees, including scores of Trades Hall officials given plum jobs as dole inspectors or industrial commissioners.

One statistic, though, stood out more than all the rest as a tangible measure of the damage done in the year since Lang had first started talking about loan defaults. New South Wales had suffered a sharp drop in bank deposits, with almost all of that money showing up in Victoria. It amounted to nearly £900,000 ($630 million) in lost investment opportunities – most of that attributable to people's fears that their savings could be frozen indefinitely under a Lang Government or even confiscated. As Theodore contended during his fiery exchanges with interjectors, Lang's favourite slogan was nothing more than a cruel deception. The question was not whether a government's first duty should be to feed its people or pay its interest. A government's first duty was to get its stalled economy moving again in order to let the people feed themselves.

Prime Minister Joe Lyons was well aware of the by-election's potential impact on his continuing confrontation with the New South Wales Premier. A second win for the United Australia Party in such a solid working-class seat could well spark a panic in the Lang camp, causing his more reasonable advisers to urge him to tone down his rhetoric. Then again, Lyons also had to prepare for a worst-case scenario. Eddie Ward had the best of blue-collar credentials and a big personal following in the area. A win for Ward was bound to be portrayed as a surge of popular support for the Big Fella in his defiant stand against the new federal government and the Premiers' Plan.

Lyons, though an experienced politician, was hardly used to the blowtorch intensity of an inner-city election. His own campaigning style, suited to the gentler atmosphere of Tasmanian politics, could only be described as more ho-hum than harangue. If he was pedantic in his dealings with his peers, he tended to speak to voters as if they were intellectually impaired, breaking every proposition down to the simplest of apples and oranges analogies.

So uneasy was he at the thought of ever having to cope with a heckler that his advisers secretly arranged for New Guard commander Eric Campbell to fill the Sydney Town Hall with 5000 of his men for Lyons's UAP policy speech leading into the December election. They made sure to take their seats earlier than the advertised opening of the auditorium so that any 'undesirable characters' – not to mention ordinary members of the general public – would have to be turned away by police. Apart from the New Guard, the only other guests allowed in that night were white-ticketed VIPs sitting in the first few rows.

'And what a grand meeting it was,' Campbell recalled in his later memoir. 'The policy speech was good and well delivered and the audience rose to the occasion. Their applause was thunderous and heart-warming. There was not one discordant voice.'

Lyons would later deny requesting any such assistance, though the giant banner stretched high up across the width of the Town Hall seemed in perfect harmony with New Guard philosophy. It read: 'Smash the Red Wrecker'.

The Prime Minister, needless to say, found himself too busy to visit the working-class district to speak on behalf of the UAP's candidate in the by-election, W. V. McCall, an executive in the wool trade. He did, however, issue a statement from Melbourne appealing to the electorate to vote for the UAP as they had done the previous December. His words almost fell asleep across the page.

> That party which I have the honour to lead is asking your votes tomorrow for Mr. W. V. McCall, in whom, I believe, East Sydney will find a worthy representative in Parliament. The issues upon which the election was fought in December last have not changed. They are, if anything, intensified today.

Stanley Bruce, meanwhile, indignantly denied Lang's damaging allegations about his secretly proposing to 'taper' job losses to teach people to accept unemployment.

'Mr. Lang's references to myself and to the Commonwealth Government are utter nonsense – a tissue of lies and misrepresentation,' Bruce told reporters at a hastily called Melbourne press conference. 'His object in venting his spleen upon me is to try to mislead the people by suggesting that there is a great conspiracy afoot to attack the workers in Australia. The people of

Australia know only too well that Mr. Lyons would not be a party to such a conspiracy even if I would dream of setting it afoot.'

***

The Lang Labor candidate, Eddie Ward, would go on to win the election from his UAP rival by less than 250 votes from the 38,063 ballots counted. Either side could – and did – claim the close results as a victory. For Lang Labor it added a fifth MP to the small but vocal Langite chorus in the federal House of Representatives. Joe Lyons, on the other hand, could rightly tell himself that the narrow win actually spelled trouble for Jack Lang. For the conservatives to continue to pick up so many votes in a once safe Labor seat was a signal that ordinary people might well be turning against the demagogue who claimed to speak on their behalf.

Yet Lyons was far too crafty a politician to let the matter rest there. Lang had given him a nasty surprise at the Melbourne summit. He intended to return the favour, and then some, when federal parliament resumed later in February.

Meanwhile, the by-election's one certain loser was the once great party to which Joe Lyons and Jack Lang had both belonged only a year before. The federal Labor Party's candidate, Cunningham, won so few votes he lost his deposit. As for Ted Theodore – the only politician of the period who had the will and the wile to match Jack Lang's – it was the end of the political road. He would go on to outstanding success in the business world, while always regretting his failure to destroy his nemesis.

Instead he would have to settle for second-best: watching the Big Fella destroy himself.

9
The case of the not-so-jolly swagman

Mary Barrie hobbled stiffly down the hall from her kitchen to answer the unexpected knock at her front door. Her husband Alex was in the living room, much closer, but it was no good expecting him to answer. He could barely see any more. He was 85. She was 80.

'Good morning, we're from the gas company,' said a tall, thin man standing at the step. He was wearing a grey salt-and-pepper suit and appeared respectable enough. Behind him was a short, pot-bellied young man who for some reason kept glancing up and down the street. Mary noticed his beady black eyes and didn't like the cut of him at all.

'We need to look at your stove,' the tall man persisted.

'There's nothing wrong with the stove but come see for yourself,' Mary said a bit grumpily. She had been making Alex an egg flip for his mid-morning treat and he didn't like to be kept waiting.

The tall man stepped forward and brushed past her. No sooner had she followed him into the kitchen than he turned and seized her by the shoulders, spinning her frail frame around and throwing her backwards to the floor. He fell upon her, digging his knee into her throat while he set about tying her hands to the legs of the stove.

'Where's the money?' he demanded. On the street where the Barries lived in the Sydney suburb of Paddington, it had not gone unnoticed that the old couple seemed to have none of the financial problems of their neighbours – no angry landlords demanding rent or bailiffs come for the furniture. Down at the corner pub there were even whispers about them living off a fabulous hoard of golden sovereigns.

'*Where's the money?*' her attacker screamed again, pressing his knee into her even harder. Trembling to the core and with his weight crushing her chest, she could barely get the words out.

'Upstairs . . . in a box . . . in the back bedroom,' she managed to gasp.

With that he cracked a hose pipe against her skull, splitting her scalp and spattering her silver hair with crimson. The blow left her mouth agape in shock. Her assailant stuffed a rag between her lips before rushing off to the stairs. As he did, he glanced into the living room to see his mate repeatedly smashing Alex over the head with the butt of a revolver. When the old man finally slumped to the floor, the short one shoved a gag in his mouth and stayed in the room to get some extra cord from a venetian blind to tie him up with. The taller man raced up to the bedroom to search for the money. He found seven single pound notes in the box the old lady had mentioned and two sovereigns hidden on the porch.

Returning to the kitchen, he noticed Mary bleeding more heavily than before. His accomplice had gone to wash his hands and decided to smack her over the head a couple of times more because she was making too much noise. The tall man was at least considerate enough to remove the gag from her mouth and slightly loosen the ropes around her wrists before they left. It was, after all, the season for kindness – just eleven days before Christmas, 14 December 1931. They hadn't bothered to try to make Alex Barrie more comfortable, though. They already knew he was dead.

'I'd give a thousand pounds to get out of this,' the tall man muttered as the two house-raiders split the loot and walked off in different directions.

From where Mary lay, in a semiconscious daze, she could see her husband's egg flip sitting on a bench, coagulating in the summer heat.

When Superintendent Billy Mackay heard the full details from his detectives, his voice must surely have turned as cold and dark as the bottom of Loch Ness. 'We will get those mad dog bastards, whatever it takes.'

The manhunt that followed would lead an enterprising detective on an extraordinary journey into the Great Depression's equivalent of the heart of darkness: a hidden world of swaggies and bagmen, sundowners and train jockeys who made up the floating legions of Australia's itinerant unemployed. Court transcripts set out the key points of the story. It requires only a small stretch of the imagination to fill in the gaps.

Mackay's investigating task force started off with only the tiniest of clues. They found a small knife near the window with the venetian blind. The handle and blade had been wiped clean of fingerprints except for a partial impression at the very tip. Someone had obviously held it there while trying to remove any incriminating evidence. With barely a microscopic quarter-moon to work with, forensic experts still managed to find nine different sets of prints on file that could be a possible match. All but one of these potential suspects were quickly tracked down and questioned. All had airtight alibis. The one who couldn't be found had only a single recorded conviction, caught riding a freight train – 'jumping a rattler', as the practice was commonly known. Thousands were doing that every day; it was hardly the sign of a criminal mind. Still, detectives at least had another name to check out and a face to put to it. Mary Barrie had barely survived the attack and was far too ill to try to identify the blurry police photo but others who recognised 26-year-old William Morton were able to show detectives where he lived. Morton's landlady told them her tenant had been gone for some days and was frequently away in the country for weeks at a time. They found his wardrobe filled with expensive suits, immaculately clean and pressed, yet there was also a pile of threadbare clothing stacked up in a corner along with the odds and ends of camping gear.

At the Fifty-Fifty Club Phil Jeffs would have been more than happy to keep police onside by helping them in a murder inquiry, looking at the photo and telling all he knew. The homicide blokes couldn't care less what went on at the sly grog palace so long as they got a useful tip or two and Morton was the kind of wild young punk who had no claim to the underworld code of secrecy. Jeffs's account no doubt reinforced the picture of Morton as a weird loner. He didn't drop in to the club all that often but any night that he showed up, it was a sure sign someone had just been mugged or had his pocket picked. When he was in the money he liked to dress up in snazzy sharkskin suits and try to big-note himself among the flappers. The best sorts, like Dulcie Markham, stayed well clear, sensing he was some sort of creep. The last time he was in the club, though, he seemed twitchy and kept to himself, bolting down a couple of whiskies before hurrying off. Jeffs couldn't remember the exact date but it was a couple of weeks before Christmas – it could well have been the night of 14 December.

Mackay's men, by early January, had put together the profile of a man with a double life: a city dandy and a country drifter. Perhaps he found hiding out among the anonymous travellers a good way to escape the heat after committing a violent robbery. Possibly he picked up a little extra pocket money by preying upon isolated farmers or rural storekeepers. Maybe he even got some kind of sick thrill going off to play the tramp, mixing in with the tough, single men who wandered in droves through the countryside always looking for an extra quid and with no shred of dignity left to lose.

While police kept a 24-hour watch on the house where Morton lived, Mackay picked out a newly promoted detective for special assignment. Constable first class Gilbert Leary had just arrived in Sydney from Marulan in southern New South Wales. Despite his lack of experience in criminal investigation he had something more valuable to offer: the leathered skin and lean, hard looks of someone who had grown up in the bush, a woodcutter and fencer who was used to spending days out in the open, living off the land. Leary's job was to pack his swag and a billycan and head off to walk the roads and jump the rattlers, joining with different bands of wanderers until he finally picked up the trail of William Morton.

～⌒～

By 1932 perhaps as many as 100,000 dispossessed men roamed the countryside, trying to scratch out a living chopping wood, clearing or fencing paddocks, panning for gold, trapping rabbits. When all else failed they joined the long march to nowhere, mindlessly journeying back and forth from one town to another to qualify for a weekly dole chit that allowed them a few basic groceries. Some had left wives and children back in the capital cities, either in hopes of being able to send home any money they earned or simply because they no longer had the heart to face them, watching the light slowly fade from their eyes. In most cases, though, married men got the first crack at any job on offer in the cities so by far the biggest proportion of itinerants were single, in their twenties or early thirties. Not all of them set off on their own accord. In Western Australia and South Australia, especially, nervous governments made a point of steering them away from the metropolitan areas to prevent them causing political unrest or just plain mischief. Many were assigned to remote labour camps to clear land or dig irrigation canals. Those two states, along with Victoria, also offered to equip unemployed young men as fossickers to go bush searching for gold. It was as if they could be fed on hope alone. For every amateur prospector who discovered a promising speck of colour there were hundreds barely subsisting on cold porridge and water.

The bureaucrats of New South Wales and Queensland hit upon more convoluted ways to keep the drifters moving and prevent them congregating in any one provincial centre. Regulations for collecting meal rations provided that a traveller couldn't remain in the same town from one week to the next. If his dole book showed him in Toowoomba on one Tuesday he had to be at least 80 kilometres away, perhaps in Kingaroy or Dalby, to be eligible to buy food again the following Tuesday. The prescribed time for check-in at the local police station was between nine and twelve and any unfortunate missing the deadline by a minute risked having to go hungry for another week. Queensland's weather, cane fields and orchards made it an especially attractive drawcard for unemployed drifters from other states but its rigid dole registration requirements posed a trap for the unwary.

'When I entered the town, I made for the police station,' a weary veteran of the long march, Bill Kidman, recalled. 'A hard-faced constable met me at the gate [and] told me that the first step was to register myself as unemployed. "All right, I'll do so." "This is the wrong day," he growled. "Go to wherever you're heading and be there on Tuesday to register. Then you'll be able to draw your rations at another town on the next Tuesday."'

Kidman tried to point out that that would be a long time to wait around on an empty belly.

'You'll survive till then,' he was told and then motioned to be on his way.

The tricks of survival were well known to the full-time swagmen and seasonal workers who had been tramping country roads long before the depression set in. City lads picked them up at a painful price. Not a few set off into the bush loaded down with too much gear or squandered their first dole chits on fresh meat that was sure to be flyblown and rotten within a day or two. If they were lucky enough to team up with a bush-wise swaggie like Kidman they had a chance to get by without food poisoning, pneumonia or snakebite until they learned a few basic rules of living rough. The ideal swag consisted of no more than two blankets and an oiled groundsheet, a towel that could be used as a carrying strap, a waterbag and a sugarbag for storing tucker, a pannikin and billy, a spare shirt and possibly a change of socks and underwear depending on the traveller's level of prosperity. Corned beef or bacon bones were the obvious choice for rations to last the week and flour for damper was far preferable to loaves of bread that quickly became stale and barely edible. A sheet of gum bark placed atop four stakes kept the fire from going out in the rain. Water from a waterhole with a dead cow bogged in it could still be fit to drink if it was boiled in a billy with ashes thrown in, then left to cool and the scum scraped off the top. When jumping a rattler, an experienced tramp never chose the wagon next to the engine tender because that meant getting smothered in coal dust and cinders.

Trying to clamber aboard a moving train with a 20-kilogram swag was hazardous work, hard enough for those who were physically fit. After several months on bare rations, however, most of the men were well below their peak. The calories they consumed never quite made up for the energy they expended in their endless trek, so their strength was slowly drained day by day. When they could get away with it, without the train guards or police coming to disperse them, they tried to set up shanty towns close to the railheads or refuelling depots. That was where the goods trains had to stop or at least slow down; and that was where the travellers had their easiest and safest chance to jump a rattler.

Such railside camps were a prime target for Gil Leary as he made his way to the Queensland border, looking for his short, fat mate, Bill Morton. As much as the undercover detective needed to fit in with the other travellers, he also wanted to stand out just enough to attract favourable attention from any criminal elements among them. The travellers were generally a law-abiding bunch, going astray only by hopping free rides or cheating on the dole regulations by doing the odd job to earn a few extra shillings. Inevitably, though, there were some among them eager to get away with whatever they could: shoplifting, cattle stealing, even the occasional armed robbery.

Whatever crowd Leary mixed with, he took a lead in acting the larrikin, talking back to local cops, being first to board a goods car under the very noses of the train guards, even pinching a bicycle. He wanted to make sure that if Morton or his mates were in the vicinity, he would come to their notice as a willing and able accomplice. For all his bush nous, though, Leary almost came unstuck in trying to weave his way through the maze of dole card regulations. At the Queensland border, a zealous constable threatened to arrest him for failing to have the proper forms. He only just managed to talk his way free from a week in the lockup, inventing a hard luck story to melt the heart of the toughest copper short of Billy Mackay.

Mackay and his task force made the educated guess that the suspect was headed north; but which way north? The only reason for a man to choose a direct route was if he had some place to go. For the homeless and unemployed, one destination was no better or worse than another. Instead of being guided by dots on the map, they tended to set their course from one bit of bush gossip to the next. This town had a storekeeper willing to slip in some tobacco on the dole chit; that rail section had a train guard prepared to look the other way; good rains had brought an early crop further west and farmers there were looking for extra hands. The zigzag was a perfect symbol of their purposeless lives: heading from Sydney north-west to Walgett, possibly with a diversion to the opal fields of Lightning Ridge, turning east to pick up the rail line to Wee Waa and Narrabri, then north again to Moree, east to Glen Innes, north to Tenterfield or Warwick in Queensland, then up to the cane fields or east for some fishing and a good wash in the sea.

Leary – walking, hitchhiking or riding trains – got as far west as Walgett, then cut back to the Queensland coast. He would be on the road almost two full months, save for two brief breaks back in Sydney to confer with his colleagues. In discussing Morton with the men he befriended, he couldn't afford to be too specific for fear someone would smell a cop. Swaggies were a taciturn lot at the best of times, wary of personal questions, most of their conversations limited to daily necessities like throwing together a decent stew out of one man's potatoes and another's slab of corned beef. If Leary saw the right opportunity, sitting around the fire at night after a rough day cooped up in a goods wagon, he might put out a feeler like this.

'I'll tell you the funniest bloke I ever did see jump a rattler. He had to throw his belly on first before his swag, it was that heavy. Went by the name of . . . Morton, I think it was, Bill or Billy Morton.'

If he spotted the slightest glimmer of recognition, the nod of a head or even a blink, he might risk one more try.

'Claimed he could get any sheila he wanted back in Sydney, always had a fiver or two to wave in their face. You wouldn't credit it, he was a short bugger, but he always seemed to know where the action was . . .'

In the first few weeks he put in a lot of hard miles for little useful information. A few people thought they had run into such a man, though none could say if he was headed in any particular direction. At a drifters' camp outside Coolangatta, however, Leary picked up his first solid lead. Someone fitting Morton's description had passed through the week before. He seemed to be travelling with a couple of mates, big bruisers who towered over him. When the mates went off to the pub at night, though, he stuck to his tent doing crossword puzzles from the newspapers. Leary's fellow detectives back in Sydney had found a pile of used crosswords in Morton's rented room, notable for the fact that the answers were printed out in block letters except for the letters M and A, as in mammal, which were always in script.

When Leary made one of his rare phone calls back to headquarters to report his progress, he received even more promising news in return. A few days earlier a car driver had been held up by a short, heavyset hitchhiker on the New South Wales coast. It meant backtracking toward Sydney but it was the most positive break since the murder of Alex Barrie and the brutal bashing of his wife.

The Barries were old enough to have lived through a previous Great Depression. A disastrous financial crash in 1893 saw the sudden collapse of scores of banks and building societies, robbing hundreds of thousands of hardworking families of their life's savings. In those pre-Federation days banks issued their own pound notes, promising that each could be exchanged on demand for a golden sovereign. Few depositors managed to get back even a fraction of their savings in the form of gold coinage. The bar-room rumour about the Barries keeping a stash of gold sovereigns – the actual figure overheard by their assailants was 300 – may not have been so far-fetched after all. Many a family that suffered through the previous depression thought it safer from then on to hide their savings under the bed. That was hardly the only wrong lesson learned from 1893. The period had been notable for its bloody clashes pitting unemployed demonstrators against police. Politicians of the 1930s kept those violent images in mind as they set up hopelessly complicated dole systems that seemed designed as much to break a man's spirit as put food in his belly.

For all the indignities endured by the swaggies walking the treadmill from one week's ration to the next, the thousands of men sent from the cities to live in sprawling work camps may have suffered even worse. Every state had its variation, either run directly by the government or by government contractors who agreed to offer jobless applicants at least two days' labour a week at wages better than the dole. Those who signed up certainly had the security of a permanent camp site and a regular income, less the money they had to pay for their meals and sanitation services. The cost to their self-respect, however, could be considerable. Near the town of Harvey, south of Perth, 2500 unemployed men were put to work with pick and shovel digging a 22-kilometre channel to the sea. Some 1500 of them were assigned to Myalup camp where they lived in row upon row of two-man tents, without ready access to showers and constantly enveloped in clouds of black dust.

'To visit the camp is an unforgettable experience,' a 1932 newspaper report began. 'The men are a strange community. There are cultured professional men and professional gamblers, multi-linguists and men of very limited and lurid vocabulary, old bushmen, navvies and city clerks, ex-servicemen, and migrants of varying types, teetotallers and drunkards, men with blameless pasts and men with criminal records, and indiscriminately mixed with them, a large number of susceptible youths.'

> 'There is a vacancy in No. ___ tent,' I was told, after going through the usual procedure; and on entering this tent, picked at random from 700, came upon a nauseating sight. Where there might have been some form of flooring was the original black sand littered with rubbish and filth. A rough table in the corner had apparently never been washed. On it were bags of flour and sugar, open to the flies and a dish and cutlery which bore encrusted remnants of at least one previous meal.

The back-breaking work of shifting megatons of clay-clogged soil could have been accomplished much more efficiently with earthmoving machinery. However, the West Australian Government considered it was doing the Myalup residents a favour by providing jobs for them for at least two days of the week. The definition of favour, though, stretches only so far. The men had to perform to ironclad specifications that required so many shovelfuls to be loaded into each barrow and then the barrows to be pushed up planks from pits as deep as 5 metres. The daily routine even produced its own medical condition known as 'clay-shoveller's fracture,' an injury to the lower back.

'The history of the accident is the same in practically all cases,' reported one doctor. 'The labourer throws up a shovelful of clay; the clay sticks to the shovel; and the worker feels a sudden stab of pain and sometimes hears a crack, and is unable to continue working. The majority of these men were physically below normal standards. No special selection of them was made for this work, and practically all were out of training as well owing to periods of idleness.'

Even at that, there were worse hardships to cope with at Myalup. For many of the single men, particularly the younger ones, the real ordeal began when their two days of labour finished and they were faced with the long, demoralising hours of unrelieved boredom at a lonely bush site far from home. As tough as their work was, they pleaded for an extra day of it but authorities turned them down cold.

As 1932 progressed, governments in all states would find themselves confronted with exactly the kinds of sporadic outbreaks they had sought to avoid: angry bands of swaggies clashing with police trying to remove them from their camp sites, strikers from the labour gangs pouring back down from the bush to march on parliament, just as in 1893. Australia's diaspora of the unemployed was one of the most remarkable occurrences to come out of the Great Depression. In the very midst of it, 38-year-old Detective Gil Leary finally succeeded in tracking down his man.

After hearing about the hold-up of a car driver, Mackay approved a change of tactics. Leary would be a given a battered old Ford to drive along the coastal highway to pick up swaggies who may have run into Morton, or better yet, to serve as bait for another attack. Meanwhile, though, police had made an important breakthrough on another front: the search for

Morton's accomplice. By late February Mary Barrie had recovered enough to offer detectives a much clearer account of the attack. Her description of the tall, thin man – politely spoken, well dressed, but exceedingly brutal – led to the arrest of Leslie Skeen, a well-known criminal with a long record of hold-ups and break-and-enters. In hopes of a lighter sentence, Skeen eventually made a full confession, stressing that Morton alone had pistol-whipped the old man and shoved the gag in his mouth, causing him to drown in his own blood. He told detectives that before the two parted, Morton had mentioned he was planning to lie low for a while. Before he returned to Sydney, he was hoping to join up with a couple of his swaggie mates and pull off a payroll robbery at a mining company somewhere in the Newcastle area.

With his creaky Ford fitted out as disreputably as possible, a swag and pans dangling from the sides, Leary slowly headed back toward Sydney. At Taree the detective took up a publican's offer of a free room for the night in exchange for sharpening an axe and some kitchen knives. When he left early next morning, he noticed a guest register entry from the previous day. It was in the name of William Martin. The M and the A were in script followed by block letters, just as in the crossword puzzles.

Just north of Newcastle the detective stopped for lunch at a small swaggie's camp set up near a rail siding. In exchange for a roasted sausage or two he shared around some meat pies the publican had given him and, with the help of some cheap sherry to wet the lips, started swapping tales about jumping the rattlers.

'I'll tell you the funniest bloke I ever did see jump a rattler . . .' he started off one more time. He didn't even have to finish the routine.

'That would be Bill Morton,' one the swaggies ventured. 'Ran into him yesterday. Said he was on his way back to Sydney.'

'That's a shame,' Leary said, with more feeling than he may have intended. 'I could have given him a lift. I just won this old buggy in a card game up in Coolangatta.'

'It's not too late,' the man told him, taking another swig of sherry. 'He said he was stopping off in Catherine Hill Bay to have a swim and see some mates about a job.'

Leary wasted no time getting to a phone and alerting the task force to have a fast car ready to send north in case he got lucky. Catherine Hill Bay was a tiny mining community a few kilometres south of Newcastle. Leary wasn't there long before he spotted William Morton walking through the scrub from the beach, rubbing his back dry with a tattered towel. They got to talking, as travellers do, about not much at all. Leary mentioned that he was heading back to Sydney. Morton said the job prospect he had been looking into had just fallen through and he wouldn't mind catching a lift back. They camped out in the open in their swags that night. The next morning, as Morton went for a last swim, Leary strolled over to a public phone and called his colleagues, telling them of a roadside picnic spot just north of Gosford where he would stop off for lunch and they could make their arrest.

A few hours later Morton was sitting on a rock munching a cold sausage when a high-powered Packard veered off the highway and screeched to a halt so close to his feet the wheels sprayed dirt in his eyes. He didn't have time to blink twice before two detectives had his arms pinned back and his hands in iron cuffs. He looked over to the Ford where Leary had gone just a moment before, saying he needed to get a billy for tea. He was standing there talking to another plainclothes cop. Morton breathed a little easier, suddenly realising what this was all about. He had never really believed Leary's story about winning his old jalopy in a card game. Obviously, he was wanted for car theft.

Only when Morton was escorted into police headquarters on the evening of Tuesday, 8 March 1932 – thirteen weeks after the death of Alex Barrie – did he find Superintendent Mackay waiting to give him a warm reception and set him straight.

By the end of the month the short fat man with the beady eyes, the expensive suits and a hobo's wanderlust had been found guilty of murder and sentenced to death, though that would later be commuted to life imprisonment. Mary Barrie was in court to wave her tiny fist at him as they took him away.

Detective Gilbert Leary was there, too, with a satisfied smile on his sunburnt face.

10

The New Guard bares its teeth

Superintendent Billy Mackay had a lot more than murder on his mind during the first months of 1932. The Big Fella had told him to 'sort out those New Guard bastards' and he was doing exactly that, starting from the inside out. As he had shown with the manhunt for Alex Barrie's killer, the tough cop had a streak of rat cunning to match his brawn. Unknown to Lang or any of his direct superiors for that matter, Mackay had set out to infiltrate the right-wing militia with his own undercover agents. Those seeds soon bore fruit – a revelation almost too shocking to believe. In late February, the superintendent's spies began picking up the first whispers of a plot to kidnap the Premier of New South Wales.

The New Guard leader, Eric Campbell, had publicly vowed that Jack Lang would not be allowed to open the Sydney Harbour Bridge but were the militiamen really willing to go so far? According to the information reaching Mackay, at least a hard core of extremists obviously were. The mission was to be undertaken by a crack team of 'Ironside' commandos who planned to snatch the Big Fella on his way to or from Parliament House. If at all possible, he was not to be physically harmed. Instead, he would be whisked away to a secret location, along with several key cabinet ministers also marked for abduction. They would be held out of reach until the Governor, Sir Philip Game, felt he had no choice but to appoint an emergency caretaker government pending a new election. To keep up the pressure on Game, the plotters even considered seizing Parliament House itself and barricading themselves inside until the Lang regime fell.

Mackay immediately assigned extra plainclothesmen to keep watch over the Premier, but their task was never going to be easy. The Big Fella was a man of such firmly set habits as to be a kidnapper's dream. At lunchtime each day of the working week he and his private secretary, Harold McCauley, could always be found eating at the same restaurant, Pearson's Fish Cafe on Pitt Street near the General Post Office. After work, his driver, Arthur Fitzsimmons, picked him up either at Parliament House or the Premier's Office on Macquarie Street and always took him home to Auburn along the same route up Parramatta Road. Only for one day did he finally agree to break his routine – the day that was actually set for the snatch, according to an urgent warning from Mackay's informants. Even then, instead of accepting a police escort, Lang typically decided to do things his way.

'When I finished work for the day, I sent for Fitzsimmons and told him that his services were no longer required as I had brought my own car into the city and would be driving myself,' Lang would later recount.

The New Guard plan was to station key members of the organisation along Parramatta Road with instructions to watch for my official car and at a given signal, to drive their cars across the road to block it and then seize me. As I drove through Burwood, Strathfield, Homebush and Flemington, I noticed a large number of cars parked on the side of the road without lights and an unusually large number of cars parked in side streets. I was a very careful driver and proceeded slowly on my way. I was concerned only that some of them might recognise me at the wheel and act on their own initiative. But they were too intent on looking for the official Premier's car to be worried about just another old limousine travelling at a leisurely pace along the road. So I reached my home without challenge of any kind, had my dinner and retired to bed where I had a very sound sleep.

Lang never pinpointed the date of that tense drive home, but it appears to have been about two to three weeks before the 19 March bridge opening. In order to protect his sources, Mackay insisted on tight secrecy at the time of the foiled abduction plan, so there would be no official statement about a kidnap plot for several months to come. The Guardsmen, for their part, must have suspected that their plans had been compromised by an inside leak because they appeared to back off – temporarily at least – from any further talk of such aggressive tactics. Mackay had no tangible evidence which would allow him to start making arrests, but he was hardly prepared to let the matter rest there. He made his feelings known in a memorable set-to with one of the New Guard's most senior officers who had come to complain about police harassment whenever the Guardsmen attempted to drill in public parks.

'I know why you are drilling,' the Superintendent snarled, 'but we are ready for you. And I tell you that if the New Guard takes Parliament House, even if you have 5000 men armed with rifles, I will put you out with 500 police.'

'And may I ask,' the Guardsman coolly responded, 'suppose we did take the place – how would you, who never saw a war, defeat 5000 returned soldiers with rifles?'

'With howitzers,' Mackay snapped back. 'We can get them and bombs also.'

The man he confronted would turn out to be the most famous of all the New Guard's 100,000 militiamen – the only name among them to leave its mark on history. Francis de Groot, an antiques dealer by trade but one of the New Guard's most zealous supporters, merely shrugged off his adversary's rude remarks and strode out of police headquarters to go about his business.

The New Guard had started off portraying itself as a patriotic auxiliary force formed to help beleaguered police control disloyal and riotous mobs. Many of Eric Campbell's active Guardsmen were devout churchgoers, hardly the type to knowingly break the law, let alone be party to sedition. If they were called upon by their leadership to take up arms, they naturally assumed it would be with the tacit blessing of both the federal government and the loyal majority of New South Wales police. Campbell did all he could in his public statements to encourage that belief but he privately felt fully justified in taking whatever action might be necessary to accomplish his mission, with or without official sanction. Only when he came to write his memoirs more than 30 years later did he finally admit where he really stood.

'It is true that had Communism been introduced into New South Wales, either by Act of Parliament or otherwise, we would have crushed it, if necessary by force,' he acknowledged, adding this chilling footnote: 'Had the police, outnumbered 60 to one, been so unwise as to be unpleasant, we might have been reluctantly obliged to politely detain them in their own lockups.'

Naturally enough, during his time as New Guard commander, Campbell would persistently deny the existence of any plot to kidnap Lang or seize parliament. He spoke only in the vaguest of terms of having a contingency plan for 'a week of peaceful civil disobedience' to pressure Governor Game into Lang's dismissal. Peaceful? Whatever move he might have had in mind, he was obviously prepared to carry it out in defiance of the law. It is hard to believe that a responsible lawyer could envisage any situation in which ordinary citizens, no matter how well-meaning, assumed the right to arrest policemen. Even more extraordinary is the blithe assumption that the constables would simply yield without a fight.

If the New Guard leadership was, indeed, planning some sort of coup, the ordinary rank-and-file members would have been the last to hear about it, so secret were the deliberations of the organisation's inner sanctum. Yet clear evidence did emerge of a power struggle unfolding at the very top level over the switch to more militant tactics. One of Campbell's closest associates, his then deputy commander, Major G. D. Treloar, became so disillusioned at what he had seen happening that he broke ranks to alert police. The New Guard had strayed from its original patriotic goals, Treloar warned, to the point where its secret intention had become nothing less than 'to overthrow the present government by force'.

How could Campbell possibly have justified overthrowing an elected premier? He had certainly given the matter great thought.

'This is how I saw the situation,' he would later explain.

Mr. Lang was head and shoulders above any of his colleagues in the government and what he said went. The

Opposition was inert, powerless and hopeless. The more the deflationists sought to put the screw on Mr. Lang by drying up his sources of credit, the more they drove him into the arms of the Trades Hall. The Trades Hall officials were advanced Socialists and Communist-inspired. They saw the chance of realising the Labor plank of nationalisation, and this was the price of their support. This is why I had to keep the movement on its toes.

It was all the more bizarre to hear the New Guard leader singing the praises of the man he wanted to get rid of when he also confessed to having nothing but contempt for the clique of wealthy moguls behind the anti-Lang alliance. He regarded most of them as 'very small-minded men' and it was easy to understand why from his encounter with an elderly banking executive he ran into at lunch one day.

'Look, Campbell,' the man reproached him, 'you and your New Guard keep out of this argument with Lang – we can handle it without your interfering.'

'How are you going to do that?' asked the bemused Colonel.

'Starve him out.'

'Won't that cause the bulk of the people unnecessary suffering?'

'Well, if it does, it's their own fault for putting Lang into power.'

Yet the New Guard chief was not about to allow such pig-headed old fogies distract him from his mission.

With the Harbour Bridge ceremony fast approaching, Billy Mackay kept hounding the Premier to take more care. The Big Fella, though, was soon back to enjoying his daily lunches at Pearson's Fish Cafe. As it turned out, kidnapping would be the least of his worries.

In mid-February, Joe Lyons had a sudden change of heart. He reversed his decision not to pay the Lang Government's interest bills in London and New York and made arrangements for the federal government to transfer the overdue funds abroad immediately. It is possible that the Prime Minister was goaded into action by the mixed results of the East Sydney by-election, when the Lang candidate slipped through by only a narrow margin. Some voters may well have been confused by the Prime Minister's refusal to intervene in the crisis, thus allowing New South Wales to taint Australia with the stain of default. In any case, Lyons's gut instinct told him the time had come to exploit the default issue for all it was worth: Jack Lang, the red menace, versus the decent, law-abiding citizens of Australia.

If he followed the procedures established the year before by the Scullin Government, Lyons simply would have paid the New South Wales debt and then sought a court order for reimbursement. However, he and his advisers had hit upon a far more radical strategy designed not only to recover the money but to publicly humiliate the Big Fella in a most dramatic way. There would be no tedious, plodding court case taking months for a verdict. Instead the issue would be settled by an instant act of federal parliament.

Lyons's new legislation would grant the federal government the extraordinary power to confiscate all revenues of Australia's largest state. Income taxes, train and tram fares, fees paid by racing clubs and bookmakers – with few exceptions, no revenue source was to be immune and the order was to stand until such time as outstanding interest payments were fully reimbursed. The implications in terms of federal–state relations were staggering, giving Canberra the right to tap directly into the cash flow of a disobedient state. In the case of New South Wales that amounted to some £3.5 million ($245 million) each month.

'It is a new action and of a type never before contemplated,' the Prime Minister acknowledged in introducing his proposal to a shocked House. 'But that's because it was believed every government in Australia could be relied on to live up to its obligations. At any time a dishonourable Government could bring disaster upon a state. In the interest of the whole of the people of Australia it is desirable that this should be obviated.'

Lyons reviewed the relatively brief history of the various financial arrangements entered into by the seven governments since Federation. None of them involved any specific provision for penalties should one party or another fail to fulfil its written undertakings. As he argued, though, federal authorities surely had the implied right to enforce each and every agreement under the law. Hence the name of the single most divisive piece of legislation since the founding of modern Australia: the Financial Agreements Enforcement Bill.

'The whole basis of the financial structure will be undermined if it is possible for a State to refuse to meet the obligations it has solemnly entered into,' Lyons insisted. 'It is vital, both in the interests of the Commonwealth and the States, that the possibility of a repetition of what Mr. Lang has done should be rendered impossible.'

Lang could hardly believe his ears when his supporters in Canberra reported back on Lyons's proposal. He ordered his Attorney-General to mount an immediate challenge in the High Court, certain the bill would be found to have no constitutional basis. Even if it did, how would the federal government ever hope to carry out such intrusive measures? Putting armed agents on trams and trains to confiscate the fares? Sending collectors around house by house, asking what the owner normally paid in state income tax and demanding the instalment there and then? If Lyons tried playing such games, the New South Wales police would be ordered to arrest his collecting agents on the spot, just as they would a common thief. The Big Fella may have even allowed himself a chuckle at the thought of some Commonwealth lackey having to confront the likes of Billy Mackay.

'If it is war they want, they will get it!' Lang declared, using a speech in the New South Wales Parliament to deliver his defiant reply.

And war it would be.

11

Off with his head!

As if the Big Fella wasn't causing him enough headaches, Sir Philip Game suddenly had to cope with the fury of an insulted King. Frantic cables from London warned of George V's right royal displeasure upon hearing of arrangements for the opening of the Sydney Harbour Bridge. How had it come to pass that a disreputable rabblerouser like Jack Lang should have the honour of inaugurating one of the most glorious engineering feats in the history of the British Empire? Clearly it was a task fit only for the monarch himself – or at the very least, the monarch's official representative.

Gwendolen Game rarely meddled in her husband's business, but on this crucial issue she was prepared to nag him as tirelessly as any fishwife.

'Philip is having dreadful worries over the bridge opening,' Lady Game confided in early February in one of her letters home. 'The King is intensely annoyed at the Premier opening it instead of Philip. There are all sorts of complications, but I persuaded Philip into trying to get it arranged that he does it after all. I simply hate to interfere, but it seems disastrous to let His Majesty be so angry. Now we are on tenterhooks and I really dread the next few days. You are no sooner out of one awful impasse than another far worse crops up.'

The Governor, with his more pressing worries, had obviously underestimated the importance of the social pecking order – the Realpolitik of who takes precedence over whom. He had been impressed with Lang's desire to keep expenses for the bridge ceremony down to a minimum in recognition of the plight of so many unemployed. That meant avoiding the added frills that went with a full-blown royal occasion. Sir Philip certainly could have insisted on his right to cut the ribbon but he had been happy to give way to the Premier considering all the other problems he was causing him. He may well have hoped that Lang would take his acquiescence as a sign of goodwill. Now, at the eleventh hour, Game was extremely reluctant to have to go back on his word but he knew Gwendolen was right. A disappointed premier was nothing compared to a jealous king.

With sinking heart Sir Philip asked Lang to drop over to Government House late one afternoon towards the end of February to break the bad news. As he paced back and forth in his study bracing himself for the ugly row to come, he might well have called to mind all the other disagreements the two men had had over the past sixteen months. Every time he thought he had managed to win Lang's trust, the cantankerous Premier turned face about and issued some inflammatory statement to harass and undermine him.

Lang's outbursts were invariably triggered by the Governor's persistent refusal to allow him to flood the Upper House with new Labor appointees. Only a few months into 1931 the Premier threatened to send a telegram direct to King George seeking Game's recall. Though he never did, he had parliament pass a formal resolution of protest, in effect asking the

Dominions Office in London to reprimand the Governor for exceeding his constitutional authority.

Game had no real confidence of his stand being upheld and the prospect of his sudden recall was upsetting for the entire family. Government House, for all its historic grandness, was still home to them in every sense and Gwendolen dreaded the thought of their three children being uprooted just when they seemed to be settling in so well. In fact, she was fully prepared to stay on in the ordinary role of a Sydney housewife rather than return immediately to England.

'Some bust-up must come soon,' she forewarned in a letter to her mother. 'Whatever it is, don't worry. If the Dominions Office pronounced that Philip must give way, I think he will want to resign. He knows I don't mind one little atom, and we have spoken of taking a house and staying on here for a time till the boys have finished this stage of their education.'

Their eldest son, formally christened Malcolm Philip but always referred to as Bill, had just turned twenty at the time and was studying geology at Sydney University. The younger boy, David, seventeen, was enrolled at Cranbrook in Bellevue Hill and pre-teen Rosemary attended the Doone school run by a doting Miss Cheriton in nearby Double Bay. If her mother seemed more concerned about disrupting the sons' education, it was actually little Rosemary who would have had every reason to be heartbroken at the prospect of a premature departure. She had been chosen to play the starring role of Alice in her class production of *Alice in Wonderland*.

'Whatever happens, we have both done our best and I shall never regret coming,' Gwendolen concluded, reiterating a constant theme of her letters home. 'I shall always feel the wonderful glamour and romance of this beautiful, beloved Sydney. No place will ever quite be the same to me.'

The Dominions Office eventually came down in Sir Philip's

favour, confirming the duty of a governor to preserve the constitutional rights of an upper chamber of parliament even if that meant overruling the advice of his elected ministers. Lang merely intensified his long-running campaign of psychological warfare to weaken Game's resistance. In the winter of 1931, he organised a Sunday rally at the Domain to put his case directly to a crowd estimated at up to 100,000 people.

Lady Game had toyed with the idea of disguising herself and slipping in among the spectators to hear first-hand what the Premier would have to say about her husband. She quickly thought better of it. 'As the house was guarded by policemen all around, it would have been difficult to get out without being recognised,' she conceded. Instead, she sent Turner, the unflappable Government House butler, to report back. His indignant account suggested the Premier had pushed to within a hair's breadth of outright treason by depicting Sir Philip as a petty tyrant.

'Vested interests are not above attempting to use the King's representative as a tool,' Lang proclaimed, to a chorus of boos. 'They have advanced the amazing and unheard of argument that the Governor has a greater power than His Majesty the King . . .' he continued, triggering more catcalls, 'and would do what His Majesty would never dream of doing. Not for many years has a British King refused to take the advice of his elected Ministers. The Governor has torn the charter of democracy in two and the people do not count. Either you decide that your elected representatives in Parliament shall govern you, or you accept the position that a nominee Governor can come out here and rule you.'

'Send him home!' screamed a heckler, to much approving laughter and applause.

Game found such personal attacks all the more distressing knowing his status would not allow him to give vent to his martial nature by issuing a spirited reply. His bottled up adrenaline presumably went a long way to explaining the headaches that constantly stabbed at him like needles in the brain. Yet whatever stress Sir Philip was under, he also sympathised with the pressure Lang must have been feeling. His government was being increasingly frustrated by the spoiling tactics of the opposition parties and their big-business allies: the banks refusing to grant advances while the Upper House rejected or delayed measures designed to raise new sources of revenue. Sir Philip recognised that if the Legislative Council continued to prevent the elected government from carrying out its proper functions he would have to intervene at some point, either by dissolving the parliament or allowing the recalcitrant chamber to be filled with Lang supporters. His every instinct cried out against subjecting the state to the expense of an early election when the depression was already taking such a heavy toll. At the same time he was appalled at the idea of turning the Legislative Council into a rubber stamp, thus allowing the strong-willed and impetuous Labor Premier to rule as a virtual dictator.

The dispute threatened to run out of control when the Council rejected Lang's most drastic plan yet to raise desperately needed revenue: an emergency tax surcharge of a whopping 25 per cent on every family earning more than twice the basic wage. In a bold attempt to break the deadlock between the two Houses, the Governor approached the Premier with an extraordinary proposal. He offered to mediate at a round-table conference bringing together the opposing political leaders in hopes of finding an honourable compromise.

'I know full well I am asking you a very great deal,' he wrote to Lang on 29 June 1931. 'I am only emboldened to do so because I am entirely satisfied that your one concern is the great interest of this State and its people. Cannot we make the supreme effort to divest ourselves of our pride and prejudices to reach a solution which could be carried out wholeheartedly by all who place country before party? Admittedly such a conference might fail, but would the position be worse if it did fail?'

It was a sincere attempt to try to cut through the destructive entanglements of traditional parliamentary rivalry in a time of extreme economic crisis. Well-intended as his suggestion may have been, though, it was highly unwise for a King's representative to wear his heart on his sleeve in such a way – especially to a politician as obsessively devoted to the pursuit and application of power as Jack Lang.

'I appreciate the assurance of Your Excellency that you are entirely satisfied that my one concern is the interest of this great State and its people,' Lang replied with enough acid sarcasm to burn a hole in the page, 'but I am not able to appreciate the position which Your Excellency has taken up.'

As Lang chose to interpret it, the Governor's proposal was effectively asking the Labor Party 'to give sanction to a coalition with the Opposition'. He scornfully dismissed such a proposition out of hand. 'I am not able to hope for any beneficial results from an alliance with those whom the people, by their verdict last October, regard as the enemies of peace, order and good government.'

Sir Philip was shocked that his words could be twisted in such a way. 'The possibility of a coalition government never even crossed my mind,' he responded in a second letter. 'Even had it done so I should certainly not have considered it within my province to make such a suggestion to you.' The Governor, however, was well aware that he had entered dangerous territory by involving himself so deeply in Australia's bare-knuckle party politics. He had already alerted authorities in London, advising that they should not hesitate to sacrifice him if his round-table proposal caused too much of a furore.

Yet as far as the Governor was concerned, no single action

on Lang's part had caused him more personal embarrassment than an episode that might well be entitled *The Knights who never saw the light of day*. The roots of the contretemps could be traced back to mid-December, 1930, just after the Big Fella's return to office. Sir Philip wrote to the new Premier asking if he would agree to approve the New Year's honours list prepared by his conservative predecessor, Tom Bavin, before his election defeat.

> Dear Mr. Lang,
> It is really not fair to bother you to come down here [to Government House] at the end of a very busy day on a matter which is not at all of primary importance; so perhaps you would be good enough to send me a letter on the back of this. I have had a wire [from London] asking whether you will endorse the Honours List I sent home while Mr. Bavin was Premier. I enclose the list and hope you will feel able to endorse it. If you feel unable actually to endorse the List (I know, of course, that Honours are not favoured by the Party in Australia), can I go as far as to say that you have no objection to the recommendations being considered in the ordinary way, as Mr. Bavin's recommendations? Perhaps I ought to tell you the three names I specially brought to notice.

The Governor then included a minute entitled 'Secret Honours'. It listed eight nominations for the New South Wales honours list on New Year's Day. Lang's mood would hardly have been improved by spotting the despised names of two senior conservative parliamentarians, including a former cabinet minister, apparently to be rewarded with knighthoods for nothing more than their disservice to the labour movement. He replied in writing the next day, rejecting the list out of hand.

Dear Sir Philip,

Your letter and the enclosure, disclosing eight recommendations for Honours (three of which you specifically brought to notice) disturbs me. I could not endorse any of them. To me the idea of Honours is repellent, to my party abhorrent, and some of the nominations are distinctly objectionable. My duty to you is to protest against any countenance being given at any time, or in any manner, to such recommendations. In the difficulties which encompass me, such things as recommendations for Honours can only receive scant consideration.

Game did not pursue the issue, no doubt putting it down to the peculiar egalitarian sensitivities of working-class Australians. To Lang though, the Governor's letter was like a time bomb to set ticking when and where he chose. He waited another six months, until his squabbling with Sir Philip over the Upper House issue had driven him into the blackest of sulks. Then he purposely set out to lure the obstinate Governor into a trap of Machiavellian dimensions.

The first step in the devious plot seemed innocent enough. Lang politely requested Sir Philip's approval to have their recent correspondence tabled in Parliament and thus be made available to the press for publication. Game readily agreed. As far as he was able to see, it could only be a great help for ordinary citizens to know how he had been attempting to make peace between the warring parties. Instead, the Governor of New South Wales was to be turned into an instant laughing stock. Among the letters Lang tabled on the afternoon of Wednesday, 1 July 1931 was the secret memorandum that revealed the names of those proposed for the previous government's New Year's honours list.

(Secret Honours)
Minute for His Excellency the Governor
The Premier begs to submit to His Excellency the Governor, for favour of transmission to the Right Honourable the Secretary of State for Dominion Affairs, the following names of New South Wales Citizens for the bestowal of Honours in connection with the list issued on New Year's Day:

K.B.E.
The Honourable Richard Thomas Bell, M.L.A.
Knight Bachelor
Cecil Purser, Esq., B.A., M.B., Ch. M.
The Honourable Arthur King Trethowan, M.L.C.
C.M.G.
John Galik, Esq.
C.B.E.
William James Kessel, Esq.
William Arundel Orchard, Esq., Mus. Bac.
L.S.O.
George Percy Darnell-Smith, D.Sc., F.I.C., F.C.S.
O.B.E.
Grant Hanlon, Esq.

Full biographical notes in regard to each of the gentlemen are transmitted herewith for the information of His Excellency, the Governor and of His Majesty's Government.

T. R. Bavin, Premier.

The Premier knew perfectly well what a scandal it would cause to violate royal protocol in so dramatic a fashion. How, then, could he possibly justify including such a seemingly irrelevant matter as the honours list among documents dealing with the far more serious issue of Sir Philip's refusal to clear a legislative roadblock? To Lang it was obviously a matter of smart politics. His supporters could now see first-hand the haywire priorities of the conservative upper classes: more concerned with knighthoods than allowing him to provide proper relief for the unemployed. Meanwhile, his stubborn adversary at Government House would find his own position seriously undermined by being party to such an inexcusable indiscretion. Let him squirm, disgraced in the eyes of all the pot-bellied moguls of the Union Club, if not Buckingham Palace itself.

As Gwendolen Game ruefully summed up the situation for her anxious mother:

> Mr. Lang asked for permission to publish the letters that had passed between them when they were discussing the taxation bill and naturally Philip gave it, and to his horror was rung up by Mr. Bavin that very evening to tell him that his honours list was on the table of the House and would be in the papers next morning. It was too late to stop it then, although Philip made an attempt, and got through to Lang himself, who only said it was out of his power to do anything. One can't see what it was done for, unless to get Philip into trouble with the Home Government, who must of course have been intensely annoyed. Philip sent them a long cable, regretting his carelessness intensely and explaining how the thing had happened. The poor old boy is really having a bad time with them.

As upset as Sir Philip had been at the time, there was one lighter moment to help him keep his predicament in perspective. After discovering how the politician had tricked him he had rushed to phone the Premier's office, demanding to be put through to Lang immediately.

'The Governor speaking,' he barked at the person on the receiving end. 'I want to speak to Mr. Lang at once.'

'He dropped dead five minutes ago!' a languid Aussie voice announced, before slamming down the phone.

For a split second Game almost believed it to be true. Perhaps he even hoped it to be true. Then he realised his call had been treated as a practical joke. In the few more minutes it took for one of his aides to re-establish the connection, the Governor was able to recover his normal aplomb. He managed to listen calmly to Lang's implausible explanation that his actions were merely due to a misunderstanding. From that point on Game must have felt it had been safer exchanging shots with the Hun than letters with Jack Lang but he was not the kind of man who would ever blame others for taking advantage of his own mistakes. As a mark of his sense of fairness, he followed up his phone call to the Premier with a brief note absolving him of any charge that he published the secret memorandum without authorisation.

> On thinking the matter over, I realised that you are entitled to claim that I had done so [given permission]. I will only add that I did so quite unwittingly. If I had understood your request to publish anything except our recent correspondence on the subject of a conference, I should most certainly have withheld my approval to the publication of any documents dealing with honours.

Sir Philip somehow managed to survive the corrosive blasts of ridicule that swept down upon him like a desert storm. What may well have saved him in the end was the very fact that the state was seething with so much civil unrest. The King's advisers could only assume that replacing him at such a critical time would be too risky. One of Gwendolen's letters home revealed the strain he must have been under.

> I feel that Philip was almost at the end of his tether this week. It is this dreadful decision he has to face – to give, or not to give. To risk running the country into a crash, with no money and an election, and possible riots, or to countenance a man like Lang in any methods he may choose to employ to get money. We have talked and talked, and tried to see it all from every side, and it is a great comfort to me that he tells me everything, and all he is thinking. I cannot help him much, but I think it helps him to talk it out.

If there was one factor above all that encouraged Game through his prolonged ordeal, it was his contact with those in situations far worse than his own; the jobless men he encountered almost every day. On one of his walks, not long after the embarrassment of the honours list fiasco, he ran into a broken-down tramp who seemed vaguely familiar despite the scraggly beard and torn clothing. The man turned out to be a junior officer who had served under him in the 4th Corps in France. Sir Philip promptly arranged to get the battered veteran cleaned up and dressed in a new suit, with some cash in his pocket to make a fresh start. The Games even invited him to spend the next Christmas holidays at their southern highlands retreat in Sutton Forest. Not until long after Sir Philip and Lady Game left Australia did stories start to emerge about the down-and-outs they helped with lifelong pensions provided out of their personal income. Game was also the first 'fat cat' official to volunteer a cut of 25 per cent on his salary.

'I am anxious to take my small part in securing economy of public expenditure,' he wrote to Lang in the same month that his round-table proposal caused such a stir. The Governor-General, Sir Isaac Isaacs, soon followed by making a similar sacrifice and nine judges of the New South Wales Supreme Court then agreed to take a 22 per cent reduction.

It was only toward the end of 1931 that the gruelling war of nerves between the Governor and the Big Fella ever looked like easing up. The day came – as Sir Philip knew it must – when he felt he had no more room to manoeuvre on the issue of Upper House obstruction. Either he had to dismiss the lawfully elected Labor Government or give way to its demands. He ended up allowing Lang to make far fewer appointments than he originally asked for but enough to break the logjam on several key pieces of legislation. Before he did, though, he had called his two sons, Bill and David, into his study to warn them to prepare for all hell to break loose in the form of taunts and bullying from their classmates.

'There'll be a public outcry,' their father told them. 'I don't mind for myself but I do mind, terribly, for your mother and for you boys. I don't think it will affect Rosemary, she's too young. I'm afraid it may be hard for you at the University, Bill, and for you David at school. I want you to know that I do realise this. But my Premier has a majority vote, and I think the only fair and honourable thing for me to do is to give him what he asks. Goodness knows I held off as long as I could.'

The Governor's concession did indeed allow him a short-lived truce with the Big Fella but it came at a terrible personal price – almost burying Government House under the fallout of the public outcry. Even among avowed loyalists like the New Guard he was mocked as 'Red Game' or the 'Mis-Governor'. To humiliate him further, the militiamen began collecting names for a formal petition to George V beseeching his intervention to order Lang's dismissal. The coming months would see them accumulate the remarkable total of 400,000 signatures.

Thinking of all the grief Jack Lang had caused him in the previous year, Sir Philip might well have looked forward to a showdown over the Harbour Bridge ribbon-cutting ceremony. The King had all but demanded that he do the honours and it might be sweet vengeance to see the look of shock, for once, on the Premier's normally arrogant face. As the Big Fella finally appeared at the study door, though, Game felt nothing but sympathy for him. No matter what had happened between them in the past, he didn't deserve such hurt. He asked the Premier to sit down and set out to explain the changed circumstances of the bridge opening as gently as he could.

Never in Lang's turbulent career had he wanted anything more than this single, historic honour. The thought of being deprived of it would have drained him white in utter disbelief, perhaps even with the same sickening sense of loss he felt after the death of his beloved Nellie Louisa. Still, he had enough composure to realise that his only hope of persuading Game to change his mind was in remaining calm – anger was only likely to make him more adamant. While no record exists of what he said, he obviously spoke with enough logical force to sweep away all objections in his path. Passions were already threatening to boil over. A last-minute switch in the ceremony could only be seen as a surrender to the intimidatory tactics of the New Guard. If ordinary citizens – already so hard done by – suspected for a moment that Government House had taken the side of the fascists in preventing their elected leader from opening the bridge, Lang could not be held responsible for their actions.

In whatever way the Premier put his case, he did it well enough to persuade the Governor to risk defying his Monarch. Sir Philip cabled London that afternoon to advise that the opening ceremony could not be changed.

Having to next face up to Gwendolen might well have been as daunting for Game as his earlier meeting with the Premier, but she understood the decision and accepted it with no further second-guessing. She could only hold her breath waiting for the reaction from Buckingham Palace.

'I am so thankful to tell you that shoals of telegrams have arrived from Home for Philip and that he is allowed to leave things as they were,' Gwendolen would soon rejoice. 'His Majesty has sent a personal message that it was all right. So we feel very relieved and thankful and hope he has forgiven Philip.'

Even the most honourable and fair-minded man, though, has his limits. Sir Philip Game had no intention of giving in to Lang again.

12

A blue-ribbon occasion: Part I

Bob McWilliams left home at 4 am struggling with two large boxes filled with the sandwiches his wife Daisy had cut up for him the night before. He made sure not to wake her. He didn't want her to see how nervous he was. So many things had gone wrong for him in the past couple of years – it was almost as if this was his last chance to make it up to her, to win back her respect. Not that Daisy had ever spoken a word of criticism. He almost wished she had. Instead she kept going along with every crazy venture he ever thought of, putting all her heart into making a success of it, only to see it fail.

After he lost his job, Bob persuaded Daisy to use their savings to set up a fruit and vegetable business. The shop on Botany Road was easy enough to come by – so many of them had gone bust that rents were at rock bottom. But then he came up with the brilliant twist that was sure to double their profits. Daisy could run the shop while he went around the neighbourhood selling extra produce from a horse and cart. He looked in the newspaper ads for a second-hand rig and allowed himself to be totally duped by the fast-talking salesman. The dray he bought was far too heavy for any one horse to pull, let alone the one he ended up with. The salesman claimed it was a young animal in prime condition. Only later did Bob find out the surly nag used to be owned by a milk vendor who got rid of it when it turned too old and feeble for the job.

Daisy was almost ill when she heard the price he paid – equivalent to a good month's solid wages. Instead of making double profits, his shop and cart folly soon buried them in double losses. There wasn't one week when he sold enough to pay for the horse's feed. Daisy began to build up some regular customers for the shop but most of them could only ever afford to buy a few pennies' worth and some just came in at closing time to beg for any piece of fruit that was going rotten.

Within a few months they fell behind in the rent, cheap as it was, and the landlord threatened them with eviction. They were forced to start closing early to save on the light bill. That, of course, only further reduced what little sales they had. Each time Bob went to the market, he had less and less money to spend buying produce. They whitewashed half of their shop window so their display wouldn't look so bare. Eventually, though, they were reduced to selling just onions. Meanwhile, their horse was stolen – presumably by someone with an even worse eye for horseflesh than Bob – and he could only manage to get rid of the cart for a tenth of what he paid for it.

When they were finally kicked out of the shop, Bob signed up for the food dole, to make sure the children still had something to eat. Like many other proud men during the depression, though, he continued to describe himself as self-employed rather than unemployed. The twelve dozen sandwiches he was lugging around were proof enough of that. He had figured his potential earnings down to the penny. He'd sell the sandwiches, sliced into halves, at three pence each. The six loaves of bread, cold meats and the rest of the makings figured out to a cost of just under two pence each. He expected to finish up with a nice little profit of 25 shillings, or $87.50, for the day.

It had been a long time since he and Daisy had anything to smile about. Mostly they seemed headed in only one direction, a downhill run from bad to worse. Some of the low points came to mind as he walked the 6 kilometres into town, the streets deserted, the darkness relieved only by the pale yellow glow of the occasional lamppost with a working bulb. He still felt rotten about coaxing Daisy into moving house from Redfern further south to Rosebery to save on rent. Instead, they ended up spending the difference on rat traps and disinfectants. The place was really only a shed and crawling with pests. He had thought he'd move on the cheap by hiring his own cart and shifting the furniture himself. It poured down rain all day and he caught the flu, having to stay home and losing two days' wages. Still, when the firm had to let him go soon afterward, the boss was very good about it, writing him out a fine reference. He carried the piece of paper around with him until it got too worn to read; but that hardly mattered since none of the people he applied to ever bothered to look.

He and Daisy really did need a good break for once and he hoped this trip into the city on such an important day might do the trick. Otherwise, they'd be in real trouble because he had had to borrow the money for the sandwich makings.

From what Bob McWilliams read in the paper he knew the floats and the marching bands would be assembling in Macquarie Street below Queen's Square on the north-east corner of Hyde Park. He thought that would be the best place for him to start rather than any of the vantage points along the parade route where the crowds would be congregating.

Those participating in the pageant would have been up by daybreak getting into their costumes or putting the finishing touches on their displays – hopefully working up an appetite. His own stomach was rumbling a bit but he wasn't about to give in to his hunger and gobble any of the profits. His walk from Rosebery hadn't been all that long but the boxes were awkward to carry. He put a rope around one to make into a kind of shoulder strap and it chafed against his neck. He carried the other box balanced against his left hip and the edge dug into his skin. By the time he reached Macquarie Street he was already perspiring heavily though the sun was only just rising. He straightened his white shirt and tried to look snappy as he strode past the floats manoeuvring into their positions.

Most of the displays were drawn by teams of horses that stomped and whinnied impatiently amid the general bustle. Workmen aboard the *Federation of Australian States* were still hammering shields and emblems into place while excited young ladies fussed about nearby adjusting their Union Jack blouses and their Australian flag skirts. *The Future of Australia* seemed to be in a bit of bother, its designers struggling to straighten a towering plaster figure of Mother Australia, her papier-mâché baby delicately balanced in her outstretched hands along with a cornucopia of national treasures. In keeping with modern times a few of the more elaborate floral tableaux were cleverly mounted atop motor vehicles to look as if they were simply gliding along. Bob spotted Captain Cook tinkering with the engine of his square-rigged *Endeavour*, sculpted from what must have been fields and fields of flowers. He was especially taken with another car float from the St George District – not so much its petalled dragon as the escort lining up to march in front of it, 21 sturdy women in bathing costume from the Brighton le Sands lady surf lifesavers club.

At first the sandwich vendor was a little embarrassed to appeal aloud for trade but his voice gained strength as he realised he had already gone halfway down the busy street virtually unnoticed. The troop of painted Aborigines, sitting on the kerb practising the popular tunes they were to play on their gum leaves, hardly gave him a second glance. The school children, the bandsmen, the pretty girls dressed as early settlers, dairy maids and luscious fruit – none showed the slightest hint of interest in his wares. They were all far too preoccupied, waiting for the signal to begin their triumphal march across the Sydney Harbour Bridge.

'Sandwiches!' Bob shouted. 'Delicious sandwiches. Only a threepence.'

☙

Despite Lady Game's worries about upsetting the King, Government House had never echoed with more laughter than during the lead-up to the bridge ceremony.

'I can hardly describe to you the fuss and the difficulties and the explosions that are already occurring over the ceremony, and over everyone's position in it,' Gwendolen wrote to an aunt. 'It would really be irritating if it weren't so funny.'

Much of the mirth could be traced to an officious private secretary of the Governor-General who seemed to want to turn the ceremony into another battle of the Somme. He phoned one day to dictate the various royal salutes to be fired according to protocol: twenty-one guns upon the arrival of Sir Isaac Isaacs, seventeen guns for Sir Philip, another twenty-one for His Majesty after the reading of the King's speech. And of course, there were also the visiting Governor of South Australia and the Lieutenant Governor of Victoria to consider. Blanks or no, the barrages would have been noisy enough to bring the bridge

The Sydney Harbour Bridge sends spirits soaring when it opens in the midst of the Great Depression on Saturday, 19 March 1932. An isolated population of 6,500,000 see the impressive span as an inspiring symbol of their young nation's ability to rise above all obstacles. (NewsPix)

Forever Australia's pride and joy: the bright faces of its children, like these carefree youngsters frolicking at Bondi. (Hood Collection, State Library of New South Wales)

1932's flipside: more and more kids are to be found lining up at soup kitchens for their only decent meal of the day. (Hood Collection, State Library of New South Wales)

One in ten families are reduced to living like refugees in their own land – some moving into sprawling shanty towns known sardonically as Happy Valley. (NewsPix)

The not-so-jolly swagmen: tens of thousands of unemployed opt to go bush, wandering aimlessly from one weekly dole ration to the next.

A job lost every two minutes: Australia's unemployment rate became the world's second highest, next only to Germany. (NewsPix)

Shoes speak louder than words, testament to the endless search for work. (NewsPix)

Some, like this Brisbane pencil seller, prefer to describe themselves as self-employed. (John Oxley Library, State Library of Queensland)

Relief work is scarce – and backbreaking. (NewsPix)

Inevitably, tensions rise and violence flares – here militants flee after clashing with police in Newcastle. Their complaint was against forcible evictions of penniless families. (NewsPix)

In January, 1931, Adelaide's 'Beef Riots' – a protest over poor quality dole rations – saw as many as 2000 demonstrators stage a twenty-minute running battle with police along King William Street. (NewsPix)

Scores were injured in the 'Beef Riots', including seventeen requiring hospital treatment. The outbreak would be followed by similar clashes across the nation. (NewsPix)

A scene from a march on Perth's Treasury Building. (*West Australian*)

Visionary or demagogue? So long as Australian children go hungry, Jack Lang demands a halt to massive interest payments on British loans. His slogan, 'people before money', divides the young society like a fault line. (Hood Collection, State Library of New South Wales)

They call him 'the Big Fella'. Lang, Premier of New South Wales, takes centre stage as champion of the depression era's dispossessed. (NewsPix)

Sir Philip Game, Governor of New South Wales, will come under increasing pressure from Lang's enemies to dismiss him from office. Their relationship is polite but strained.

In reality, Game listens carefully to popular opinion – here he speaks to an outback miner – but insists on following his own conscience, wherever it might lead.

Gwendolen Game is deeply hurt by so much public abuse – women turn their backs on her at society functions. One hate letter read: 'Suggest your hubby should change his name from Game to Coward.' (Courtesy Mrs Veronica Smith)

Even the Games's children feel the heat. Rosemary (centre) would hate to have to go back to London 'in disgrace' – she's just won the part of Alice in her school play. (Courtesy Mrs Veronica Smith)

Off with his head! King George V is furious when he learns that Lang – not his appointed Governor – will open the Sydney Harbour Bridge. (Photolibrary.com)

The smug face of greed: visiting British banker Sir Otto Niemeyer is made the bogeyman by Lang supporters. He demands wage cuts before interest cuts.

This pro-Lang cartoon presses emotional buttons. A sizeable chunk of interest debt is due on war loans needed to send Australian soldiers to the defence of Britain in the killing fields of Gallipoli and France. (*Australian Worker*)

The Lang Plan soon splits the Labor Party itself. E. G. Theodore, one of its towering figures, brands the Premier a charlatan.

No bones about it: the conservative media claims Lang's moratorium on interest payments would be madness, destroying Australia's good name abroad.

Jock Garden, powerful trade union boss, backs Lang. An ex-communist, he embarrasses the Premier by declaring him greater than Lenin.

(Fairfax Photos)

The newly elected Prime Minister, Joseph Lyons, will prove the Big Fella's most formidable enemy. The Federal Government introduces draconian new laws to seize New South Wales tax revenue in lieu of unpaid interest. (NewsPix)

Lyons's remarkable brood of eleven children, seen here with his wife Enid on the lawn of the Lodge, doesn't quite match his image as a ruthless political assassin. (National Library of Australia)

LIEUT. JACKA V.C

JOIN TOGETHER
TRAIN TOGETHER
EMBARK TOGETHER
FIGHT TOGETHER

Enlist in the Sportsmen's Thousand

SHOW THE ENEMY WHAT
AUSTRALIAN SPORTING MEN CAN DO.

World War I veterans will play a key role in the political crisis of 1932: many see Lang as a tool of the communists. This famous poster featuring Victoria Cross hero Albert Jacka lured thousands to enlist. (Australian War Memorial. ARTV00026)

Right-wing militants from among the veterans will go on to form the New Guard. Their leader, Lt. Colonel Eric Campbell, gives this ominously familiar straight-armed salute during a patriotic rally at Sydney Town Hall. (NewsPix)

The New Guard boasts an astounding 100,000 members. Some are seen here supporting Campbell during his court appearance for publicly insulting Lang. Worse than mere insults, the Guard plots Lang's overthrow.

down before anyone had a chance to walk on it – an image that had Game and his aides-de-camp almost in tears.

'Imagine it – how many rounds is that? Almost eighty,' an assistant chortled. 'Oh dear, I can't bear to think of it. They'd have to have four guns firing ten rounds a minute, and what with the noise and the smoke and the dogs barking (because you know they always do) everyone will be quite deafened.'

Rosemary Game had been listening intently.

'Eighty guns! Micky'd hate it,' she shrilled in mock horror, rushing over to give the family pet a comforting hug.

The Games enjoyed an even bigger belly laugh when Sir Philip read out part of a letter from the royal salute bureaucrat describing what would happen after the artillery finally fell silent, the smoke had cleared and people had recovered enough to open their eyes and pull their fingers from their ears.

'The Governor-General will then cross the bridge and arrive informally on the North Shore side,' he proposed, in a generous concession to the hoi polloi.

Informally? Sir Philip took a good few minutes before he could steady his voice enough to read on.

By the day before the opening, however, the Games's sense of humour had begun to wear thin. Government House took on the appearance of a kind of blue-blooded backpackers' hostel with fourteen guests arriving to stay. They included the Governor-General, Sir Isaac Isaacs and Lady Isaacs, the Governor of South Australia, Sir Alexander Hore-Ruthven and Lady Hore-Ruthven, the Lieutenant Governor of Victoria, Sir William Irvine and Lady Irvine, and their assorted aides-de-camp and attendants. Lady Game had planned a gala garden party for that Friday in the late afternoon, but was badly tricked by the weather. It had rained heavily the day before and the caterers warned that if she didn't cancel with at least 24 hours' notice, the government would be stuck for the bill.

She made the prudent choice to cancel, but the next day turned out to be perfect weather. The newspapers rubbed salt in her wounds by hinting the function had to be called off because of a massive snub by hundreds refusing to attend.

To add to her woes, she had to deal with an unexpected guest, a senior aide to the Governor-General of New Zealand who happened to be passing through Sydney on his way back to England. With every bedroom taken, she turned the ballroom into a dormitory for the single men. Amid so much fuss, Lady Game may well have forgotten her commitment to throw open the Government House gardens for public inspection as a lunchtime fundraiser for the Bush Nursing Association. A twittering plague of middle-aged ladies swarmed everywhere. Bypassing the camellias and rhododendrons, they made a beeline for the ballroom windows, though no nook or cranny of the crowded mansion was safe from prying eyes.

'The poor G.G. was standing in the hall when, to his horror, he saw curious faces peering at him through one of the windows,' Gwendolen recounted. 'I had to explain exactly what was happening, and his *horror* was really too funny, as he asked by whose wish this was done. When I feebly confessed that it was mine, he was as usual most courteous, but I'm afraid his opinion of me has gone down by yards, especially as I told him he would be safe in the billiards room. I heard afterwards that people had climbed up and looked in those windows, too.'

One of the more enterprising aides-de-camp had decided to pitch a tent off the corner of a veranda. He was inside about to slip on his trousers when he heard female voices asking, 'I wonder what's in here?'

'He wrapped a towel around him and waited,' Lady Game reported. 'When they opened the flap of the tent to take a peep, he stood like the Statue of Liberty and roared: "I am, if you want to know."' His surprise had the desired effect, sending the infiltrators scooting off 'uttering tiny little shrieks' as they ran.

That Friday night, over brandy and cigars, the discussion between Sir Philip and his vice-regal colleagues turned inevitably to the dismissal of Jack Lang. Both the Governor of South Australia and the Lieutenant Governor of Victoria 'came up here red hot to have the man sacked', Gwendolen later revealed. 'But when they had talked it over and heard all sides, they entirely changed their views and said Philip was absolutely right and could have done nothing else but what he has done at the moment.'

She made no mention of the Governor-General joining in such a discussion. Sir Isaac, apart from being the King's chief representative in Australia, was a former High Court judge and eminent scholar with special interest in Biblical history. His opinion about Lang was the one Game desired above all others, believing it would be the fairest he could ever hope to come across. Sir Isaac had the honour of being selected as the first Australian-born nominee to serve as governor-general, all the more remarkable for the fact he was a Jew in a society where anti-Semitism still prevailed at all levels. His appointment could only have been possible because of his immaculate reputation. Precisely because of that, Sir Philip sounded him out on several occasions, eager for his counsel. Sir Isaac, though, was well into his seventies by that time and had apparently decided to spend his time in office studiously avoiding trouble. Whenever the New South Wales Governor mentioned Lang to him he always found a way to change the subject, usually by being reminded of some obscure curiosity of ancient history – perhaps the interesting number of times quadrupeds were mentioned in the Bible or the fact that Babylon, in Greek, meant Gate of God.

'How frightened they are of doing anything that might be

criticised,' Lady Game sadly observed after a visit to the Isaacs at Yarralumla. 'It is an odd contrast to Philip.'

⌘

By 9.30 am, when the pageant began its colourful procession, Bob McWilliams still hadn't sold a single sandwich. He was all the more miserable for spotting a saveloy vendor serving a customer at Queen's Square and he couldn't help noticing that icecream sellers were enjoying a roaring trade. It was becoming an oppressively hot day and he could almost hear the heap of sliced bread in his two boxes desiccating into stale crusts. Instead of trying to push his way through the crowds lining the route of the parade, he decided to get as close to the bridge as fast as he could. That meant going in the opposite direction of the marchers, who were following a circuitous route south down College Street, then turning west along Park Street and past the Town Hall before heading north on York Street toward the bridge.

At a trot, he made his way five blocks north to Grosvenor Street, hurrying up the hill there to join the throng pressing against police barricades at the corner of Grosvenor and York streets. That intersection marked the last public access before the bridge itself, which was reserved at its southern approach for VIPs and their special guests. All eyes were fixed on the Governor-General's Guard of Honour, an impressive troop of Light Horse, which was just then turning right to follow the vice-regal limousine to the official dais. Bob got there only in time to see the flicking tales of the last rank of cavalry, but his eyes strayed to a lone rider following by 10 yards or so behind the main body. As little as he knew about horses, his nasty experience with his own nag had taught him to eye each and every specimen with deep suspicion. This one looked strange indeed compared to the fine animals that normally featured in military parades. Its neck seemed too thin and its rump too ample, its gut bulged beneath shrunken flanks and its mane and tail were scraggly. The rider was in an officer's uniform, but the tunic seemed oversized for his frail frame and for some reason he carried his sword tucked through his Sam Browne belt. At any Anzac Day parade Bob McWilliams had attended, the swords were always attached to the saddles.

The grim-faced officer noticed him staring and gave a curt nod before spurring his mount on to catch up with the others. Only when Bob read the newspaper next day would he recognise the man as Captain Francis de Groot.

⁂

Sir Philip and Lady Game had left Government House five minutes before the Isaacs accompanied by an escort of mounted police. They were greeted warmly by Premier Lang and his wife Hilda and stood chatting amiably enough despite the starkest of contrast in styles. The Governor looked like a prince plucked from a Viennese operetta, his snug-fitting Air Vice-Marshal's uniform aglitter with medals and decorations, its unique rounded helmet strapped tight to his chin and topped with a feathered plume. The Big Fella had showed up in a well-worn dark business suit and grey felt hat. He turned to chat to Gwendolen, who was elegantly dressed in cocoa-brown silk crepe with a hat of matching colour and a delicately patterned parasol which she twirled in her right hand. Hilda Lang could only have suffered by comparison, her squat frame looking even bulkier draped in navy georgette. Gwendolen Game had every reason to detest Lang for all the tense moments he had caused her husband, but the truth was, though they met only on rare occasions, she had come to respect and even admire him as a sensitive and caring man.

'He certainly left me with the feeling that whatever he does, and whatever mistakes he makes, he has a genuine and most sincere desire to do the best he possibly can for this State,' she confided in one of her letters. As the two exchanged small talk, waiting for Sir Isaac to arrive, the Premier slipped into a more serious mood, confiding his one concern about the forthcoming ceremony. The remark could be taken as somewhat indiscreet, directed, as it was, to the Governor's wife.

'That's the only thing I'm afraid of – the Governor-General coming in – it's our show, not his. It's a State thing.' She later described his tone of voice as cross and even childish.

Lady Game's parasol would soon land her in big trouble. A newspaper photograph published next day showed her seeming to hold it above Lang's head in an apparent attempt to shield him from the broiling sun. It was only the angle that created the illusion of proximity but that didn't stop the hate mail over the next few days. Someone sent her a copy of the press photo with an angry scribble across it: 'You should be ashamed of yourself.' It was signed, 'Englishman'.

The Governor-General duly arrived but quickly settled into his place on the dais without any of the undue attention Lang feared. He obviously saw Sir Isaac as a symbol of the federal power that was about to be turned so forcibly against him with the threatened seizure of state revenues. The Prime Minister, Joe Lyons, was also in the VIP stand, though seated further back. He had arrived to a smattering of polite applause, but nothing compared to the ovation received earlier by Lang. The two antagonists studiously ignored each other.

Sir Philip was first to speak. The previous month he had expressed his concern to Lang at the lengthy list of speakers; ten altogether, ranging from state politicians to the mayor of North Sydney and several of the bridge builders. The Premier insisted on allowing everyone to have his due place in the limelight so

Game was determined to be as brief as possible. His job was to unveil the tablet proclaiming the name of the span as the Sydney Harbour Bridge – hardly as simple a choice as it might seem. During the nine years of its making, there had been lively public debate over alternative titles, including the North Shore Bridge, the Australia Bridge, even the Canberra Bridge, as a goodwill gesture to the nation's capital. A pub favourite was the Ned Kelly Bridge, in recognition of its tollbooths.

The Governor, after his own few words, then read a rather innocuous message from the King expressing his 'earnest hope' that the bridge should increase the prosperity and welfare not only of the people of Sydney but of all the citizens of New South Wales. Later that year George V would address his loyal subjects throughout the world in a broadcast marking Empire Day, so the technology was certainly available for him to open the bridge himself via radio if he felt so strongly about the issue. At that stage, though, no one was willing to risk the embarrassment of a transmission failure.

As it turned out, the one aspect of the ceremony that was to make the monarch most upset was Lang's casual attire. He was flabbergasted that the Labor Premier should show such blatant disregard for propriety as to forgo the traditional shiny top hat and black frock coat worn by so many others around him. It wouldn't be long into the morning's events, however, before His Majesty would be treated to an occurrence much more to his liking. First, though, the Big Fella had a speech to make.

13
A blue-ribbon occasion: Part II

When Jack Lang rose to walk to the microphone, his supporters and enemies alike would have crossed their fingers and held their breaths. Was he going to behave himself or would he take advantage of this once-in-a-lifetime opportunity to state his case to the world? All heads turned as if watching a tennis match back and forth from Lang to Joe Lyons, searching for any hint of hostile intent. The Premier, though, for all of his aggressive instincts, knew the moment belonged to the people, not to him.

Any number of politicians from both sides of the House deserved a share of credit for making the Sydney Harbour Bridge a reality but Lang had been inspired by a much broader vision than most. Over the years he insisted that the project could only be viable if tied to the development of an extensive electrified suburban rail network, culminating in a metropolitan underground. The enormous costs of so grand a scheme put him under almost unbearable strain during his first term as premier and treasurer, but he held firm knowing that each pound spent then could only multiply beyond belief to present a priceless gift to future generations.

At the podium, under the spotlight of history, he had every right to think of the structure as a testament to all that he stood for. He was determined, however, that the day be dedicated to reconciliation, not self-justification or recrimination. Despite his looming showdown with the Commonwealth Government, Lang's speech proved to be a simple, yet moving tribute to Federation.

> The achievement of this bridge is symbolic of the things Australians strive for but have not yet achieved. Just as Sydney has completed this material bridge which will unite her people, so will Australia ultimately perfect the bridge which it commenced just over 30 years ago. The statesmen of that period set out to build a bridge of common understanding that would serve the whole of the people of our great continent. That bridge, unlike this, is still building. The builders of that bridge, as the builders of this, meet with disappointments which make the task difficult sometimes – often delicate. But that bridge of understanding among the Australian people will yet be built.

At that point in the ceremony the Premier was not being asked to cut a ribbon but merely to push a button which unveiled another tablet declaring the bridge open for traffic. He did so to cheers and applause and then took his seat to hear out the other speakers. The Minister for Public Works, Mark Davidson, stepped before the microphones. He was of the old school of public speaker, the superlatives spewing forth like smoke from a steam locomotive and nothing lent itself to hyperbole like the Sydney Harbour Bridge: the largest single-arch bridge on earth, boasting 6 million rivets, a world record of 598 tons of steel erected in one day, 500 cubic yards of reinforced cement laid in one day . . .

'This giant structure of steel and stone, with its simplicity, beauty, and utility, stands not only as a feat of modern engineering,' Davidson intoned, 'but as an imperishable monument to Australian skill and workmanship. The Australian artisan, wherever his place of activity may be, is without a peer in the world. I base this claim . . .'

Davidson bravely rambled on though he could see his audience was paying no heed to him whatsoever. Instead they had turned in amazement to a scene unfolding a few metres further north along the bridge where a blue ribbon stretched across the roadway shimmering in the mid-morning sun. An army officer astride a skinny chestnut horse had moved out past a Movietone News camera position, where he had stationed himself at the start of the ceremony. He somehow managed to inch his way through police lines, and then goaded the baulking animal forward to the point where he could start slashing at the ribbon with his sabre. He failed with one upward stroke. He failed with another. Flustered but intent on his mission, he grabbed up the ribbon in his hand and furiously began to saw at it with the hilt end of his sword until it finally parted, the separate sections fluttering to the roadway.

'In the name of the loyal and decent citizens of New South Wales, I declare this bridge open,' he shouted victoriously, holding his weapon high. When a police inspector rushed up to grab the reins, he warned imperiously: 'You can't touch me, I'm wearing the King's uniform.' But those were the last words Francis de Groot would say in public that day. Superintendent Billy Mackay had reached the scene as de Groot started wheeling his mount around in semicircles and waving his sabre in an attempt to fend off police. Without a second thought, the big cop rushed hard against the horse's right flank, cupped his hand under de Groot's stirrup and with a powerful thrust, hurled him out of his saddle and into the air. With his other foot still caught in the left stirrup, the rider flipped over and crashed to the ground on his back, his horse stepping on him for good measure. He lay there stunned and helpless, his foot still dangling from the stirrup before several constables, acting on Mackay's orders, lifted him up and frogmarched him away to a nearby police hut adjacent to the tollbooths.

'I do not like a man waving a sword at me,' the superintendent muttered as he followed after de Groot to decide what to do with him. A young detective had had his hand slightly cut by the sword and Mackay could have brought quite serious charges, including assault with a deadly weapon, carrying a possible prison sentence. Instead, he decided to treat this New Guard hero with the kind of cold contempt that would send a pointed message to all of his colleagues.

'I deem this man to be insane,' he announced loudly as he walked into the small station where de Groot was being held. 'He's not fit to go to the cells. Take him to the Reception House for a proper examination.'

On the official dais that morning, only one person would have looked upon de Groot's antics and realised how close the ceremony had come to a complete disaster. Dr John Crew Bradfield, the engineer-in-chief for the bridge, was a man renowned for his remarkable foresight. His plan for uniting the two shores of the harbour was capable of serving double the population of the 1,235,000 who lived in Sydney in 1932. Though the idea of a crossing had been discussed since early colonial days, Bradfield was the first to argue for a comprehensive network of roadways and railways to feed into the span. It was his brilliant intellect and sheer enthusiasm that ultimately convinced Jack Lang to share his dream.

'He had a tremendous faith in his own ability,' Lang would later remark. 'Least of all did he regard finance as an obstacle. It was the Government's job to find the money. All he had to do was set it out on his drafting board.'

Bradfield's foresight fortunately didn't stop with the completion of the span. Before the ceremony that morning he had had a word with one of his technicians. Concealed in the shiny blue ribbon was an electrical wire. When cut, the circuit was designed to send a pulse to an explosive device mounted atop a pylon. The eruption would launch a shower of streamers – the signal for the artillery battery at Bennelong Point to begin its 21-gun salute. At the first cannon's roar a squadron of aircraft would swoop down from the skies over the top of the arch and an armada of passenger ships – some from foreign countries – would cross beneath, sirens blasting. All that commotion could have occurred a full half-hour before the Premier was scheduled to step up to the ribbon. Bradfield, though, had ordered that the wire not be hooked up until the technician actually saw Lang approach with his gilded scissors.

'I had a premonition something might happen,' he explained later.

Only after all ten of the speeches were read did Lang walk over to complete the historic snip. With the press cameras flashing, he made sure to stand a good distance away from the bulging knot that tied the severed ribbon together again.

The official party still had more formalities to go through, hopping into their limousines to drive to a mini ribbon-cutting at the northern end. The Premier and the Governor shared a back seat, but an obviously annoyed Prime Minister was left to wander about alone for some minutes with no apparent transport lined up for him.

'Why not hop a lift with Lang in the Premier's car?' a reporter cheekily suggested.

Joe Lyons merely bit his lip and said not a word. Mercifully, he was soon rescued by one of the publicity officers. On the brief trip north his ears may well have been burning with Lang's pious words about the need to bridge differences within the nation.

With all rituals finally completed it was time for the celebration, the pageant taking 50 minutes to cross the bridge from head to tail. Hundreds of schoolchildren marched in the lead, some wearing the medals of fathers they had never known, lost in the Great War. Directly behind them was a proud company of 100 men who stirred emotions even higher. They represented the more than one thousand workers who actually built the bridge – sixteen of them paying the ultimate price. The stories of their deaths had become part of the folklore surrounding the awesome structure.

'Jim Campbell, the rigger, that was bloody awful – I saw that,' one of them recalled. 'He fell from the top of the pylon, hit the corner stone coming down, then hit the lighting arm. His head got chopped off.' But there was also an extraordinary escape: one workman plunging 150 feet into the water and surviving with only two ribs broken and a pair of boots he would never wear again. They were split wide open by the impact and pushed up around his thighs. He received a gold watch for his trouble.

The parade was immediately followed by an incredible surge of ordinary spectators pressing shoulder to shoulder, filling every square inch of the span, roadway, tracks and footpath. Sir Philip and Lady Game had made a point of staying on to review the full pageant – the Governor-General had left long before –

and they were almost trapped in the crush before police managed to clear a way for them.

Their adventures, though, were only just starting. That evening they arranged for their guests to go out on the harbour aboard the Government House launch. They were able to enjoy the magnificent spectacle of the bridge lit up and a display of fireworks all the more dazzling for the fact that it almost didn't happen. The Lang Government had fretted about the expense but decided to go ahead at the last minute hoping to give an extra boost to public morale. It was when the launch returned to the Man o' War Steps that the vice-regal party of twenty realised it was in big trouble. The shoreline was packed solid with onlookers blocking the path they planned to take back to Government House. Luckily someone found two sturdy policemen to walk ahead and try to clear a passage but at every step the crowd still pressed around them.

'Philip told me he found himself clasping Lady Isaacs (an ample figure) to his heart,' Gwendolen later reported in a letter describing the melee. 'And I held like a vice to the two Rosemarys [the other was the young daughter of a senior staff member] who were shrieking with laughter and delight. Suddenly we lost Lady Isaacs in the seething mob. She was unfortunately wearing evening dress with diamonds, and we found she had stopped to take off her earrings, fearing they'd be snatched.'

The group decided to change course towards a side of the mansion where the crowd wasn't so thick but as soon as they reached the gate they ran into another obstacle.

'An irate member of the staff who saw our hilarious figures appearing in a mass at the back entrance shouted "Get along with you!"' He was preparing to shut the gate in their faces when he shined his light on Lady Game and hurriedly vanished.

The vice-regal stragglers finally made it safely through the kitchen door, another source of great amusement to them, though nothing could have been funnier than the remark made by a kindly middle-aged woman who saw them struggling up the hill with the two constables in the lead.

'Isn't it a shame the police have got them,' she sympathised aloud.

Francis de Groot was destined to spend the rest of the weekend listening to the screams and ranting of the other inmates at the Reception House, basically an emergency psychiatric ward set up to deal with those who came to the attention of police for their bizarre behaviour. As prescribed by law he was duly examined by two qualified medical experts who readily agreed he was not insane; but he still had to wait until Monday morning for a magistrate to verify the doctors' judgement. Then he would be arrested again and charged with destroying public property, to wit, a ribbon. Billy Mackay could not have planned it better. If he had brought a criminal charge to begin with, de Groot would have been set free on bail immediately. This way the New Guard swordsman at least had to sweat it out in custody for a short time.

Of course, de Groot felt nothing but elation as he relived each step of his exploit. The idea first came to him a few days before when he saw a cartoon in *Smith's Weekly* showing a man eagerly racing Jack Lang to the ribbon to cut it first. It was captioned, 'The man who beat Jack Lang to the tape.' The New Guard officer went to his leader, Eric Campbell, to discuss the possibility of attempting such a stunt. He knew that certain militant members were considering far more aggressive action to stop Lang ever reaching the bridge and he hoped his ribbon-cutting plan would be seen as an honourable alternative to violence.

'As the big day drew near, a number of young hotheads were not satisfied with vague promises and I began to hear all kinds of harebrained schemes such as plots to kidnap Mr. Lang,' de Groot later explained, 'and some of those boys were quite capable of doing it, too. I would not have given much for his chances of survival if they had laid hands on him.'

Campbell readily gave permission for de Groot to undertake the mission. However, as late as 5 pm Friday it looked as if the plan might have to be called off for lack of a horse. Campbell's wife, who was a keen amateur equestrian, managed to find an animal at the last minute. Her gardener rode the horse next morning to the Bennelong tram sheds, where de Groot took charge. He led it up Macquarie Street, waited until the Light Horse escort had left Government House, then followed at a safe distance. The members of the Honour Guard, of course, had their eyes rigidly locked straight ahead and no one could have noticed him trailing behind. At the corner of Bridge and George streets, a helpful constable even held back traffic so the lone officer could catch up with his troop. Despite his strange horse, misplaced sword and oversized uniform (the tunic borrowed from Campbell) the police simply assumed he was from some special military detachment they hadn't been informed about. Francis de Groot, to his delight, had discovered the truth of the military maxim: *who dares wins*.

Bob McWilliams was just one of 750,000 people who descended on Sydney Harbour on Saturday, 19 March 1932 to watch history being made. The story of his ordeal as a street vendor that day is set down here pretty much as his wife Daisy recorded it in a touching memoir, altered only by a few creative guesses as to what else he might have been thinking or seeing. Despite the huge crowds surging around him, despite the fact that other street vendors were besieged by famished customers after the bridge opened, Bob McWilliams still did not manage to sell a single sandwich. That is, until 2 pm, when he finally got lucky.

'He changed his stand many times,' Daisy wrote, 'and yelled himself hoarse. He was feeling a hatred of the sandwiches, which were rapidly getting drier and staler. Suddenly a rush of people swooped down upon him, and in about ten minutes every one was bought up. He said it was like the relief of Mafeking to see them go. We made 25 shillings on the sale of these. It was a great day for us. If they had not been sold it would have meant disaster as we had borrowed the money to start the sandwich business.'

Jack Lang, interviewed years later, couldn't remember what he did after the most fulfilling moment of his life. Did he and Hilda go out on the harbour to see the bridge bathed in light? Did they attend any balls, like the Governor and his wife had done, or have a great celebration?

'Oh no, nothing like that,' he replied, almost shocked at the idea.

More than likely he simply went home, had a quiet meal and an early night. Lang never owned or wore a dinner suit and apart from important political functions, rarely accepted a social invitation. Though he had no objection to others partying the night away, he couldn't bring himself to do so while so many were in such a state of need.

Thanks to the wireless, Australians in every part of the nation got their chance to share in the historic festivities and the sensational news of the ribbon-cutting incident would have been the subject of endless, excited discussion. In pubs or sly grog establishments like the Fifty-Fifty, there were bound to be heated arguments as gamblers attempted to settle a popular bet leading up to the great event. Did the New Guard succeed or fail in following through on its much publicised vow? Who actually opened the Sydney Harbour Bridge on that memorable Saturday, 19 March – Jack Lang or Francis de Groot?

14
The Swindell saga: A morality tale

The day after the Harbour Bridge festivities, Phar Lap gave Australians something more to celebrate. The 1930 Melbourne Cup champion proved itself among the most exciting racehorses in the world by winning the high-stakes Agua Caliente Handicap, watched by a grandstand packed full of movie stars, mobsters, millionaires and grifters – the best and worst of what prohibition-era America had to offer. The course was strategically located just inside the Mexican border so as to be able to serve liquor legally. It had become a major part of the US racing circuit and sporting writers promptly declared the new import to be the best thing to happen to their thoroughbred industry since the depression set in. 'Australia's lightning bolt Phar Lap has blazed a rainbow over the American turf,' gushed one dazzled commentator. Hollywood studios even vied to make a movie about the wonder horse from down-under.

On the surface it was hard to understand why this one

animal – born in New Zealand, owned by an American, with a Sinhalese name meaning 'lightning' – should go on to become such an Australian icon. Perhaps the simplest answer was that, in the hardest of hard economic times, Phar Lap constantly delivered for the small punters who put their few bob on it each way. On the rare occasions he didn't, he all but broke his huge heart trying. When the horse's owner, Dave Davis, an expatriate Yank, decided to send the great thoroughbred off to the United States, adoring fans were shattered. Even more concerned, though, was the powerful band of knights who controlled thoroughbred racing at tracks like Flemington and Randwick. They soon saw crowd numbers, already diminished by heavy unemployment, slump disastrously through lack of interest.

Ironically, though, a new form of racing – the tin hares – was booming. More modest entrance fees and lower betting minimums at the greyhound track allowed ordinary battlers to enjoy a pleasant evening's entertainment. Yet those who tried to deride the dogs as a 'poor man's sport' were well off the mark. In Sydney, a night at the dogs was pronounced by *Smith's Weekly* to be 'the latest social craze' among the sophisticated younger set. Well-known gay blades and their fashionable flappers clamoured to place bets with Jack Shaw, the dapper society bookmaker known as the Beau Brummell of racing.

No matter how lucky the punters, though, they could never hope to match the fortune being rapidly piled up by the rather mysterious syndicate which had backed the tin hares venture to begin with. The investors, their names hidden behind complex corporate structures, were raking in dividends of 280 per cent. But buried somewhere deep in the story of their success lay the seeds of a scandal that could not have had a grander cast – a colourful con man, a fabulously wealthy merchant prince and the most controversial politician in the land.

The Swindell saga: A morality tale

The introduction of greyhound racing at Sydney's Harold Park, in December, 1931, sparked widespread allegations of political corruption – predictable enough in view of the strong protests from church groups, backed by the conservative Opposition. By mid-February, however, the dark mutterings rose to a crescendo of indignant outcries when the same syndicate that controlled Harold Park was granted a second licence for another dog track at Kensington, giving it a lucrative monopoly over the hugely popular new sport. Adding to suspicions of favouritism, the Labor government was reported to have rushed through approval for the application on the very day it was lodged, 17 February, ignoring a rival bid from a reputable company that had spent months preparing a track and grandstands at Mascot. In parliament, the Opposition wasted no time in digging up as much dirt as possible about the shady American entrepreneur, Judge Frederick Shaver Swindell, who had somehow emerged with total power over the greyhound racing industry in New South Wales.

Around the crystal-laden dinner tables in the grand mansions of Woollahra, however, it was not Swindell who set high society tongues furiously wagging. One of the establishment's very own was about to be caught up in the controversy, exposed not only as Swindell's main financial backer but as a secret supporter of the despised Lang Government. That ordinarily would have been enough to brand him a pariah and traitor to his class; yet in every other respect Anthony Hordern stood out as the perfect symbol of the eastern suburbs social elite. His entanglement in the tin hares saga would provide an intriguing glimpse into the mores and lifestyles of the super-rich at the time of the Great Depression.

Hordern, known to his inner circle as Tony, was the 43-year-old heir to a department store dynasty. For cashed-up families like his – with fortunes founded on the bedrock industries of retailing, banking, newspaper publishing, clothing and food manufacture – the worldwide crash actually had its advantages. Not only did it offer lucrative bargains in property and other investments, it brought drastic reductions in the price of cars, furs, jewels and other luxury goods. As a side benefit it also resulted in the wages of domestic servants and tradesmen being slashed by 20 per cent or more. Of course, widespread unemployment would have cost the Hordern emporium at Brickfield Hill, a few blocks south of the Town Hall, a good percentage of its regular custom; but the impact on sales could be offset at least to some degree by the tidal wave of bankruptcies eliminating small competitors. With fewer outlets to supply, wholesalers had no choice but to accept whatever margins the big department store dictated to them, allowing it to offer rock-bottom prices. Meanwhile, Hordern's management had the virtually unfettered ability to impose wage cuts or order dismissals among its 3000 employees without fear of union resistance.

In such ways did most of the wealthier businessmen manage to cope with the downturn, suffering only superficial hardship if at all. Their sons still attended expensive private schools, with the headmaster of Cranbrook, Iven Mackay, pronouncing himself 'astonished' at the number of boys who arrived each morning in chauffeur-driven cars. Their daughters were still sent off to England to be presented at Court, one young debutante summing up her fairytale adventure at Buckingham Palace in these breathless terms: 'But of course, we all had to wear feathers in our hair, and a train, curtseying to the King and to the Queen as we moved backwards, backwards. Oh, it was a marvellous experience!'

Throughout the depression years, development applications in Woollahra Council – embracing such upper-crust suburbs as Double Bay, Darling Point, Point Piper and Bellevue Hill – showed a continuing enthusiasm for home improvements, new garages, even the building of miniature golf courses, which were a fad at the time. David Jones, of the famous retailing family, sought approval to spend £4000 – or $280,000 – for alterations to his house and garage in Bellevue Hill. His Victoria Street neighbour, newspaper proprietor Warwick Fairfax, went well beyond keeping up with the Joneses. He lashed out on additions to his residence, Ginagulla, amounting to £30,000, or $2.1 million.

The jewel in the crown of this privileged area, gleaming in its very heart like a giant emerald, was the Royal Sydney Golf Club. In 1932, despite a few resignations from among the hard-pressed landed gentry, the club still listed 2473 members willing to pay its hefty fees, not that much different to membership in the boom times. On some mornings, before the first foursomes hit off, the New Guard took over the lush fairways for its military training exercises, free from the threat of police interference. On a per capita basis Woollahra may well have had more supporters for the anti-Lang militia than almost any other district in the city.

In all of the eastern suburbs no residence was more imposing than Retford Hall, the famous Hordern family estate set in 3 acres of gardens in Darling Point. It was here that Tony Hordern presided when he was not overseeing the development of Milton Park, his exquisite stud property in the southern highlands. He had thrown all his energies into that project after the sudden death of his wife of eighteen years, the former Viola Bingham of Melbourne. If the department store boss entered 1932 as the most eligible of widowers, however, the gossip columns were soon bubbling over with news about his new romance with the beautiful socialite Mary Bullmore. In February he bought her a Packard roadster as an engagement present. His income at the time – even after absorbing an appropriate reduction in salary in recognition of the difficult trading conditions – was still estimated at £100,000 a year, or $7 million dollars in today's equivalent value.

Though the ultra-wealthy could cite any number of reasons for detesting Jack Lang, one would have been enough: the fact that his was the highest-taxing government in the land. During the glittering parties at Retford Hall, Tony Hordern no doubt joined his guests in raising champagne toasts to the imminent downfall of the Premier. Yet buried among the stubs in the back of his chequebook was evidence of just how eager he appeared to be to keep the Big Fella in power. Four cheques, totalling £6000 or $420,000, were made out in ways to disguise their purpose, but all ended up as cash in the hands of Judge Frederick Swindell. He, in turn, quietly paid out the money in the form of 'donations' to cover election advertising for the Lang Labor Party of New South Wales.

The exact details of these transactions would not be fully disclosed until a royal commission began sitting in June but by the end of March various bits and pieces of gossip were starting to fit together like a jigsaw puzzle, painting Hordern in a not very flattering light. His involvement with Swindell and the tin hares could be traced back over a number of years. The American, with his infectious southern charm, arrived in Australia aboard the liner *Tahiti* in September, 1926. He claimed to be from Virginia, where – as he happily confessed – almost anyone with a law degree was accorded the honorary title of 'Judge'. Indeed, one of his endearing traits was to appear so willing to admit his little foibles that he immediately won the confidence of strangers. By his own account, he had decided to leave the United States after making and losing a fortune as a real estate speculator in the short-lived Florida land boom. His fellow passengers would no doubt have sat entranced as he told them story after story of alligator-infested swamps transformed overnight into multi-million-dollar residential developments.

Most likely, though, he never bothered to mention that the Florida boom was also notorious for attracting swarms of con men who made huge killings by selling the same property ten times over in a day. The cleverer ones managed to flee just ahead of the sheriff and before the inevitable bust that left thousands bankrupt by the middle of 1926.

One of the passengers listening in fascination to Swindell's colourful tales happened to be the prominent Sydney retailer Hugh Foy. He was associated with a group of sportsmen who spent their Saturday afternoons betting on live hare coursing at Rooty Hill on the western outskirts of the city. Recently, though, animal welfare groups had been making life difficult by staging protests against the bloody spectacle of greyhounds tearing apart terrified rabbits. Foy and his friends were keen to find out more about the introduction of mechanical coursing in Britain and the United States.

'That is why I am going to Australia!' Swindell immediately proclaimed. 'I am going to establish tin hare racing.'

Apparently no one was more surprised at the announcement than Judge Swindell's wife. She later confided she had never before heard her husband mention such an idea.

Through his chance meeting with Foy, Swindell went on to make other valuable contacts, including Felix Booth, a leading publican who was Tony Hordern's uncle and most trusted financial adviser. The effusive stranger soon found himself at the head of a well-funded consortium trying to get political backing to set up the first greyhound track at Epping, on Sydney's north-western outskirts. Only a Labor government would have considered the idea. Night-time betting on the dogs was recognised as a threat both to thoroughbred racing and the big movie chains; and in each case the business magnates concerned enjoyed considerable influence within the Nationalist Party (forerunner of the UAP).

The Lang Government quickly approved the Swindell syndicate's application, enabling the new form of racing to get under way on 28 May 1927. The Epping venture was destined to be short-lived, with the conservatives returning to power less than seven months later and promptly declaring tin hares gambling to be illegal. Even in that brief period, however, Swindell's company had netted nearly £50,000 or $3.5 million in profits and seen its shares shoot up by 1000 per cent. Labor's defeat would soon enough make them as worthless as pricked balloons.

In an earlier era Swindell might have been among the soldiers of fortune who descended on Australia during its great gold rush days. His natural instinct, though, was to prospect for the gold where it was easiest to get at, which was in somebody's pocket rather than buried in the ground. Once he spotted the right opportunity, he set out to exploit it from every possible angle. He easily could have arranged to import some expert from the United States to advise on the technical requirements for sending a mechanical hare racing around a track at just the right speed to keep out of reach of snapping jaws. Instead he presented his financial backers with what he claimed to be his very own patented design for the basic tin hare mechanism, which he licensed to them in return for thousands of free shares. He also came up with his own design for the night lighting, which earned him thousands more.

Confronted by a hostile government in power at the end of 1927, Swindell decided to sail off to South Africa with a pack of 80 greyhounds to start up a tin hares venture there. In interviews with the Cape Town press, obviously aimed at impressing local investors, he insisted that greyhound racing was still booming in Australia and painted a glowing picture of the profits to be made.

'I made a fortune of £40,000 [$2.8 million] in Australia,' he told reporters, 'and I hold Australian greyhound rights worth £100,000 [$7 million].'

His intention, as he announced it, was to start dog tracks in Cape Town, Durban and Johannesburg; but in a land where lions still roamed free, metallic bunnies held little public interest. While he was able to coax some trusting souls to put their money into his new company – he had given himself 25,000 free shares as the price of his patents – provincial authorities soon killed off any hope of success by prohibiting betting on the dogs. Swindell's South African adventure proved such a financial debacle that he was actually placed under arrest to stop him from boarding a ship back to Australia until he paid back at least some of his debts. He was only allowed to leave the country after handing over a sizeable security bond.

'I consented to the judgement against me only to avoid delaying my departure,' he blithely explained to the Australian press upon his return. The truth was he had squandered much of the money made during his first stay in Sydney and was struggling to keep up appearances as a prosperous entrepreneur. Still, Frederick Swindell had never gone down without finding a way to bounce back up, and with the return of Jack Lang to power he set out to hitch a ride on a whirlwind.

At his persuasive best Swindell was almost impossible to say no to, his personal magnetism reinforced by the powerful chemistry of unbridled greed. He soon convinced his old associates that the profits they had raked in from the Epping track during the previous Lang administration were nothing compared to the bonanza that awaited them once Swindell managed to get a few key political contacts on side to approve racing at Harold Park, much closer to the Sydney CBD. Tony Hordern, urged on by his adviser, Felix Booth, would emerge as the major player in this comeback bid. Booth was convinced immense riches were there for the taking, though success obviously depended on Swindell doing whatever was necessary to get a new tin hares bill passed through the New South Wales Parliament.

If the American had shown himself eager to milk the old consortium for all he could get out of it, he proved himself absolutely voracious now. He demanded – and was granted – effective control of the new Harold Park company by being allowed to stack its board with his own three straw-man nominees. More important in terms of the drama which would later engulf Tony Hordern, Swindell was quietly provided with a slush fund of 5000 free shares worth some £5000 ($350,000), to dispose of as he wished. Their purpose was made clear enough when he later faced cross-examination before the Royal Commission on Greyhound Racing, presided over by Justice Percival Halse Rogers.

> *Commissioner:* It was a tacit understanding that you were to get the legislation through?
> *Swindell:* Yes. They never asked me what my methods would be.

Swindell not only had his own company's 5000 shares to use for buying political favours. The new bill that he hoped to push through called for not one but two tin hare licences in the Sydney metropolitan area, the first to be granted upon passage and the second three months later. With remarkable cheek, he struck a deal to also represent a rival company hoping to establish a dog track in the inner city suburb of Mascot. For that task he was given 12,000 Mascot shares, then about half the value of Harold Park stock, to aid in his shadowy lobbying activities. As the royal commissioner would later conclude:

> The companies made the shares available to Swindell, and put themselves unreservedly in his hands, on the

understanding that no questions were to be asked; they were not to bother about his methods, and he was going to use every endeavour to get the legislation through. It seems to me apparent that the shares were to be used for that purpose, whether the money derived from them was to be given to party funds, or they were to be used in some other way.

Political corruption is notoriously hard to pin down, especially when a good case can be made for the legislation being in the public interest. To the Big Fella the tin hares represented a valuable source of extra revenue for a badly depleted state treasury. During his first term in office the dog track at Epping had brought in a healthy flow of taxes from betting and entrance fees. The proposed new venue at Harold Park, with its more favourable location, promised even more.

Yet there would still be many unanswered questions about the preferential treatment which the Lang Government accorded Swindell. Lang would always insist that he had never once met the greyhound promoter. However, his chief political adviser and daily luncheon companion, Harold McCauley, certainly had. McCauley would tell the royal commission that he conferred with the American on several occasions, including just before the government first presented its tin hares legislation to the parliament in September, 1931. He swore they did not discuss any of the provisions contained in the bill but acknowledged that Swindell had stressed how much money the Lang Government could expect from having two Sydney dog tracks as well as others in larger regional centres.

'Mr. Swindell produced figures to show that dog racing would bring in additional revenue to the extent of £200,000 [$14 million] a year,' McCauley testified. 'I told him I never thought there could be so much in it.'

Whether or not Swindell had a hand in drafting the legislation, it turned out to be tailor-made to his interests. It called for two metropolitan licences, the second to be issued a few months later, just as he wanted, with a number of other permits for outlying centres like Wollongong, Lithgow, Newcastle and elsewhere. While he had agreed to put in a good word for the Mascot company, there could be little doubt that he set out from the start to undermine its chances. The American was believed to be the primary source of poisonous rumours suggesting that Jack Lang's most hated enemy – New Guard chief Eric Campbell – had joined the Mascot consortium as a silent partner. The smear was all the more effective for having a grain of truth – Campbell's law firm did do occasional work for the rival tin hares company, though there was no evidence of his ever having sought a major financial interest.

From that point on, however, whatever other inducements Swindell might have to promise, he knew he was in the driver's seat. As anxious as the Lang Government was to reap the maximum amount from tin hare taxes, there was no way it would ever grant a racing permit to the Mascot syndicate so long as it carried the taint of a New Guard connection. The wily southerner set his sights on forming a dummy company to grab the second licence for himself and his Harold Park associates. First, though, he had to contend with an unexpected setback.

The tin hares bill easily passed through the Lower House in late September, but after lengthy debate was shelved indefinitely in the Upper House just before a two-month parliamentary recess. Swindell found himself staring bankruptcy in the face with his own cash reserves running low and some of his backers threatening to cut their losses and pull out if the licence issue was not quickly resolved.

On Saturday, 21 November 1931, however, the entrepreneur's plummeting prospects rebounded once again. It was announced that Sir Philip Game had finally agreed to appoint 25 new Labor members to the Upper House in the following week, assuring quick passage for a number of stalled bills, including the tin hares. Swindell could be confident of securing the Harold Park permit because of his syndicate's previous experience running the races at Epping in 1927 but he was now playing for much higher stakes. He needed to act quickly to seal a deal with his government contacts that would guarantee him the second Sydney dog track as well.

The subsequent royal commission – faced with hours of evasive and conflicting testimony – never came close to establishing the true sequence of events but it may well have proceeded along these lines. At some point over that weekend Judge Swindell learned a most valuable piece of inside information from one of his political sources, possibly Harold McCauley who was in charge of publicity for the New South Wales Labor Party. The Lang Labor representatives in Canberra were about to make a move to bring down the Scullin Government and set the stage for a federal election. The Big Fella hoped to take over as many seats as possible from the rival federal Labor faction but his party's coffers were empty and there was no money for election advertising. If Swindell and his wealthy backers wanted to show how deserving they were, they had no better way to prove it than by making an immediate and substantial contribution to the Lang Party campaign fund.

On 24 November 1931, the day before the tin hares bill was to be revived in the Upper House, Swindell met with Felix Booth, explaining that he urgently needed to swap his secret cache of shares for ready cash. The quickest way to do that was for Tony Hordern, already a shareholder, to open his chequebook to buy some more. Swindell may or may not have told Booth exactly where the money was going but the elaborate methods used to disguise the transaction certainly raised deep suspicion in the eyes of the barrister representing the royal commission.

'The proper inference,' he suggested, 'is that Booth and Hordern, or at any rate Booth, knew that the money was required for some improper purpose and that the methods employed were intended to cloak the real transaction.'

Swindell would continue to insist under intensive grilling that his contribution to the Lang campaign was totally spontaneous and without conditions of any kind. He claimed he only thought of it a day or so after the fall of the Scullin Government upon hearing from a friend in the advertising industry that the New South Wales Labor Party had no money for election ads. His donations would end up totalling more than £6000 – $420,000 – starting with an initial pledge of £4000, or $280,000.

> *Commission:* Was this the first occasion you had had a request to pay for political advertising?
> *Swindell:* I have never had any request and this was not a request. I asked Mr. Cruickshank [his advertising friend] how the election outlook was. He said it was pretty bad – that the state Labor Party did not have any money.
> *Commission:* You made a voluntary offer to pay £4000?
> *Swindell:* Yes.
> *Commission:* Do you want to make any explanation why you were contributing £4000 in this way?
> *Swindell:* I had a company which was headed for the rocks and me with it. Without the passage of this [tin hares] legislation it would never have been possible for me to have made any profit. I saw only disaster ahead. I certainly have some gratitude.
> *Commission:* It was gratitude was it?
> *Swindell:* Absolutely.

Commission: You realised perfectly well that you would be making application for a licence under the new Act?
Swindell: Yes.
Commission: Do you say the realisation of that fact had no bearing in any way on your giving £4000?
Swindell: Not in the slightest.

Lacking lie detectors or truth serum the tin hares royal commission was never likely to shake the testimony of such a cagey witness. On several occasions Swindell coolly shrugged off stern warnings about the consequences of perjury. The one indisputable fact is that his 'voluntary' contribution to the Lang Party certainly did him no harm. Not only did he obtain the first licence for Harold Park but the dummy company he had envisaged did indeed go on to be awarded the second metropolitan permit on the same day it applied, Wednesday 17 February. Known as the Greyhound Racing Club, it boasted Anthony Hordern himself on its board of directors in an attempt to make it look more legitimate. Control of the Sydney greyhounds, however, was only a start. The royal commission would interview a number of witnesses from New South Wales country centres who all told the same story. When attempting to apply for a dog track licence from the appropriate government agency, they were advised to speak first to Judge Swindell. He invariably demanded a cash payment or a share of the business to help speed the application through.

Typical of the testimony was that given by Frederick Ford Cowdroy, managing director of a Wollongong syndicate. He reported this exchange with the American when they met to discuss his bid for a tin hares permit.

Swindell: Have you got any money?
Cowdroy: Not much.

Swindell: You will want some money to get a licence.
Cowdroy: How about £500 [$35,000]?
Swindell: That is not enough. How about £1000 [$70,000]?
Cowdroy: That is pretty hot. It is a lot of money but I will try to get it.

Ultimately, the tin hares royal commission could find no firm grounds for prosecution though Justice Halse Rogers would single out Frederick Swindell for a reprimand so scathing as to be a virtual death sentence in terms of his ability to do any further deals in Australia. He was, in the judge's cutting words 'a taker of toll – a schemer and devisor of crooked stratagems, a man of personality but unprincipled and unscrupulous, a sinister figure in any community'. While bribery could not be proved, it was clear that the American's fortunes had completely turned around following his donation to the Lang Party and whatever other inducements he may have offered to any individuals.

'From financial embarrassment he passed to affluence and became a power, a Czar as it were in the dog racing world,' the commissioner continued. 'It was intolerable that any man in the community could be in such a position that he could demand money from people who wish to obtain the consideration of a claim to which they were entitled by law. Yet the evidence established that Swindell did occupy that position. The inquiry revealed a widely held opinion that to get things done bribery must be employed and a readiness of people to subscribe money to be used for bribery.'

Yet if Swindell would end up in total disgrace, he was, after all, a foreigner who could soon sail off to his next dubious adventure. The inquiry would prove even more damning in terms of the lingering shadow it cast on the ethical conduct of some of Sydney's wealthiest and most respected businessmen. The tallest poppy of them all – Tony Hordern – was destined to suffer gross humiliation on the witness stand. Though he had allowed his name to be used as a director of the newly formed Greyhound Racing Club, he would claim to know absolutely nothing about its operations, including the fact that Swindell had been handed a secret swag of shares in someone else's name to hide his involvement.

Commission: Was there any agreement between the directors as to whether or not shares should be sold?
Hordern: I do not know.
Commission: Were you told at a certain point in time that Swindell had come along and wanted shares handed over to him?
Hordern: No, I was not told that. I did not know he had shares.
Commission: You have never known he has had shares?
Hordern: No. I did not know Mr. Swindell was in the company.
Commission: Do you know one thing about the management of the company since it started?
Hordern: No, nothing.
Commission: Have you made a single inquiry into the affairs of the company since it started?
Hordern: No.

Justice Halse Rogers, in his summing-up of Hordern's testimony, would barely conceal his contempt.

'It is not proved that he was knowingly a party to any improper transaction,' he conceded, 'but I think it is highly unsatisfactory that a man in his position should have to set up the plea that he was ignorant of what was going on. The company, of which he was a director and whilst he was a director, carried into effect an agreement tainted with corruption.'

Yet nothing the royal commissioner had to say could come close to condemning the Darling Point multi-millionaire as effectively as his own words during perhaps the most memorable exchange of the entire inquiry. Ordinary citizens, reading their *Sydney Morning Herald* next day, would be treated to a rare close-up of what a high society figure really looks like when suddenly stripped bare of the last shred of dignity.

> *Commission:* I do not know whether you realise that practically every answer you have given this afternoon has been that you do not know?
> *Hordern:* I do not know.

Jack Lang would always contend that the allegations leading to a tin hares royal commission were blown out of all proportion: part of a smear campaign set in motion by the conservatives in the first months of 1932 following his defiant refusal to pay further interest. Speaking in parliament in late February he launched a stinging counterattack, denouncing the hypocrisy of his accusers.

'How is it that racecourses are bad when dogs do the racing but are good and respectable when horses compete?' he challenged. 'Is it that depraved people patronise dog racing, while the patrons of the pony course belong to the elite? If ever there was a humbugging, hypocritical attitude adopted by the Press and the Politicians it is over this question of dog racing. If racing is wrong, let all of it go.'

He reserved his sharpest rebuke for Bertram Stevens, who had just taken over from Tom Bavin as Leader of the Opposition in the New South Wales Lower House. Stevens, the day before, had described the profits being made by the Harold

Park syndicate as 'outrageous'. Lang set out to make him regret the word.

'Are we to take from that that the Nationalist party in this House favours the principle of the limitation of profits?' he chided. 'If it does then the Government will quickly oblige the Opposition with legislation to prevent any investment earning prodigious profits, including banks, insurances and money lending offices.'

Yet the issue remained: was the Big Fella himself knowingly involved in any corrupt deal to give Swindell so much influence? The answer to that had to be yes, though not within the usual meaning of corruption in the sense of illicit personal gain. The royal commission turned up convincing evidence that the Premier had personally and improperly intervened to veto the Mascot application, presumably for no other reason than its alleged connection to New Guard leader Eric Campbell. While all tin hare matters were ostensibly resolved by 'Cabinet', one senior minister after another – including the Chief Secretary, Mark Gosling, who was nominally in charge of racing permits – admitted under oath that they had had no say whatsoever in awarding Swindell's connections both metropolitan licences and Mascot none. At the crucial 17 February 'Cabinet' meeting – as it was portrayed to the press – the Big Fella was the only cabinet minister listed as present, apart from the relatively junior Minister for Health, Bill Ely, and Gosling, who conceded that he merely recorded the decision.

> *Commission:* Really, you did not confer on the matter at all?
> *Gosling:* That is so.

'As regards matters with which Swindell was concerned, I do not think there ever was a Cabinet decision in the proper sense,' the royal commissioner concluded. 'The application of the Mascot company was improperly passed over. Swindell's interests determined the fate of the [decision].'

Lang himself exercised his right not to testify at the inquiry and publicly dismissed any suggestion of his improper involvement. In the end, even if he did misuse his power, the state would still benefit from the same amount of dog track revenues. If that meant making Frederick Shaver Swindell and his greedy little band of capitalists all the richer while denying the New Guard bastard Eric Campbell and his friends a quick bonanza, wasn't that what politics was all about? Once the Sydney licences were disposed of, the Big Fella promptly lost all interest.

The tin hares royal commission would not release its formal report until early November, well after Lang's downfall. Judge Swindell, who had by then been stripped of all connection to the greyhound industry, was philosophical about the corrosive findings against him.

'Sinister figure!' he picked up on Justice Halse Rogers's description. 'What's sinister about me? I've never done a dirty thing in my life.'

But then he added what was probably the one truthful thing he ever said during his highly eventful stay in Australia.

'I was just made the goat so they could get at Lang, that's all.'

15
Getting physical

Lay the proud usurpers low! Tyrants fall in every foe! Liberty's in every blow! Let us do or die! Superintendent Billy Mackay may well have remembered the words of his favourite poet as he surveyed the seething mass of demonstrators gathering thick as locusts outside Central Criminal Court. Nearly 3000 fighting fit New Guardsmen had been called in from all parts of the city to stage a daunting show of force before the trial of Francis de Groot. Mackay had only 300 white-helmeted policemen to disperse them but he would send them marching into battle to the drumbeat of oratory no less inspiring than that of Robbie Burns.

'Lang is Premier,' he rumbled in his gruff Scottish brogue. 'It was his bounden duty to cut the ribbon and officially open the Harbour Bridge and he was prevented from doing this by the man I locked up. De Groot has got to come before the court and be dealt with according to the law and it is your duty to see that no one interferes with the normal procedures of the court. So whether you believe in the New Guard, the Nationalists, the

Labor Party or the Communist Party, go out there and belt their bloody heads off!'

The only thing missing that memorable Friday morning, the first day of April, was the bagpipes.

Guard leaders would later claim that their intentions were entirely peaceable – they had assembled merely to cheer their hero's arrival. Far from posing any threat, they had been ready to assist police in case 'communists' in the crowd should try to make trouble. The truth was, however, it wouldn't have mattered how well the militiamen behaved that morning – Mackay was determined to teach them a painful lesson. He was still boiling mad over de Groot's cheeky exploit, but even angrier with himself for failing to live up to the faith Jack Lang had put in him. He had concentrated so much on protecting the Premier from physical harm that he had ignored the possibility of some ridiculous publicity stunt.

Yet for all the personal embarrassment the incident caused him, it also opened his experienced detective's eyes to a glaring weakness in the Guard's basic structure. Clearly the militia was not the tightly disciplined military machine it purported to be. The relative freedom given to neighbourhood commando units allowed room for all sorts of self-deluded fanatics to take matters into their own hands. If that was the case, the superintendent decided, it was time to throw away the rule book. Why wait around trying to guess his opponent's next moves? He already had a well-established network of informers inside the militia, including one who had risen to high rank within the New Guard central command. What if these double agents, rather than just passing on key intelligence, started actively organising a few special missions of their own – the kind of impulsive derring-do that would prove appealing to the militia's extremist fringe? The police would be in a position to make arrests in just the right circumstances to shatter the organisation's credibility among its own more moderate supporters as well as the public at large.

That kind of black espionage, however, would take time to produce a result. At this moment, Mackay had more practical matters to deal with. He was about to show a bunch of arrogant bastards the fist-end of the long arm of the law. At 9.50 am he spotted the excuse he had been waiting for. At the Liverpool Street entrance to the court, both footpaths were clogged with ranks of athletically built Guardsmen in their grey felt hats and neatly pressed suits, standing ramrod straight and shoulder to shoulder so that no bystander had a chance to squeeze through. They were just starting to put on their armbands in anticipation of de Groot's appearance. That was all the provocation Mackay needed and with a prearranged signal he set the assault in motion. The first company of 100 policemen strode smartly four abreast up Liverpool Street from the corner of George Street, halting in front of the court. Two columns wheeled a snappy right face, two columns turned to the left to confront the crowds packed solidly on either side of the street. With no further warning the officers sprang to the attack, seizing people by the shoulders and wrestling them out of their way or using their bare knuckles to hammer a dent in any line that failed to yield. Some of those in the front rows tried to fight back and were punched to the ground, the blood from smashed noses flowing freely into the gutter. Others turned to flee but could make no headway against the crush behind them. At the shrill blast of a police whistle, Mackay called in his reinforcements – another hundred hidden within the court precincts and a third company hurrying down from the Pitt Street end – to drive home the advantage. The superintendent himself was seen grappling with a powerfully built man whose khaki and blue armband identified him as a senior officer of the Guard's elite mobile brigade. He had been shouting orders, trying to make himself heard above the din, when the big cop grabbed him and ripped the band from his suit sleeve.

'You have no right to wear this here,' Mackay barked. 'It is only an incitement to riot.'

The shaken militiaman meekly allowed himself to be led away by a constable to become one of eleven arrested that day. Another twenty or so were left lying dazed in the street, though no serious injuries would be reported on either side. By the time Francis de Groot showed up for his ten o'clock appearance before a magistrate, the entrance to the court building was relatively clear save for a couple of crushed Akubras and the odd puddle of blood. Mackay and his gallant 300 – as Jack Lang later summed up with glee – had 'kicked the Guard's backsides from Liverpool Street right down to George Street'.

When it came to the Guardsmen, though, Lang's sense of humour obviously had its limits. Under order of the New South Wales Government, the newsreel film showing de Groot cutting the ribbon was quickly banned from cinemas throughout the state. The step was taken under an old statute 'for the preservation of good manners and decorum' after cabinet members noticed audiences breaking into spontaneous applause and roaring with laughter as the scene flicked by on the screen.

'The eagerness of the Government to suppress the film is a source of satisfaction to me,' de Groot gloated in the press. 'The camera had recorded too faithfully the rueful look on the Premier's face as he gazed on the ribbon which he was only second to sever.'

Meanwhile, though, de Groot would find his trial a big disappointment. He had hoped to convert the proceedings into a platform for spouting New Guard propaganda but got no further than his first response. Asked if he admitted to behaving in an offensive manner, he replied: 'No. It may have been offensive to Mr. Lang and some of his Communist friends, but . . .'

The magistrate immediately cut him short and warned any further such outbursts would not be tolerated.

Superintendent Mackay would feature almost as prominently within the court case as he did in the melee before it. The New Guard's aggressive barrister, Ernest Lamb, KC, called him to the witness stand for lengthy cross-examination, obviously seeking retribution for the humiliating way he had treated de Groot, first throwing him from his horse and then sending him off to spend an uncomfortable weekend with lunatics.

> *Lamb:* Did you warn your detectives to keep an eye on people who might prevent Mr. Lang from cutting the ribbon?
> *Mackay:* No.
> *Lamb:* You did not anticipate it?
> *Mackay:* No. That is right.
> *Lamb*: Have you been on holidays?
> *Mackay:* No. I have been on other work. If I had anticipated that the New Guard intended by such trivial methods to make it appear that Mr. Lang did not open the bridge, it would have been my object to stop them. I never thought anybody would be so silly and childish to think he could open the bridge by cutting a ribbon.
> *Lamb:* Mr. Lang was there to do that. Do you think he was silly?
> *Mackay:* He was there in his proper position of Premier of the state, not by subterfuge. I thought what he did was a sacred thing.
> *Lamb:* Do you still believe the defendant is insane?
> *Mackay:* No, not now in view of the medical testimony.

The superintendent was shown a newspaper photo of de Groot hanging upside down, one foot still caught in the stirrup just after Mackay had unsaddled him.

Lamb: Is that the usual way to arrest a man?
Mackay: Yes, quite common in such circumstances. If I hadn't pulled him down he could have ridden off and slashed other ribbons. In his state of mind he might have slashed at me with his sword. He held his sword at me and waved it and shouted: 'I am a King's officer; stand back, don't interfere with me'. His words were uttered in a menacing way.

Mackay's dark, craggy looks and lumbering build were intimidating enough in any circumstances, but he triggered anxious gasps throughout the courtroom when he was handed de Groot's sword and began waving it around like a drunken samurai to show how the New Guardsman had supposedly handled it. When next he spoke his eyes were set squarely on his inquisitor.

Mackay: This is a dangerous weapon. A blow from it could kill a man easily, could cut a man's head off. It could even cut Mr. Lamb's finger off.
Lamb: Please don't try in this court.

Lamb managed to persuade the magistrate to drop a charge of offensive behaviour. Instead de Groot would be found guilty of maliciously damaging government property – in the form of one blue ribbon – and fined £5 ($350). That, however, proved to be mild punishment indeed compared to what was meted out to him as he returned to the hearing after lunch. He looked up the courthouse steps to see a quivering bundle of female fury wrapped in fox fur and waggling a bejewelled middle finger in his direction. Tilly Devine was back in court – though this time she had promised her solicitor to be on her best behaviour. Devine, it turned out, was in the process of lodging an appeal against a six-month prison sentence handed down to her in early March for consorting with known criminals. Upon her conviction she had raised an even bigger stink than during her notorious crayfish caper. 'You don't give a woman a chance!' she had screamed, loud enough to be heard through the entire Central Court precinct. 'You're all against me. You don't give a woman a fair go!' Today, though, she was out to impress the judge, determined to show what a refined lady she could be – of the most genteel manner and temperament. But that, of course, was before she spotted the austere, gaunt-faced gentleman coming up the steps. Newspapers of the time would never dream of quoting her tirade verbatim but this is undoubtedly the way it came out.

'Are you that fucking de Groot?' she shrieked.

He stopped in his tracks and nodded.

'You ought to be fucking well denounced,' she pressed on, much to the amusement of bystanders and junior court officials enjoying their lunch break in the April sun. 'You are the New Guard–Nationalist basher gang. You were got to cut the fucking ribbon so that Lang couldn't.'

The flustered de Groot continued up the steps, trying to maintain a dignified pace while making sure not to come within the radius of a swinging handbag. For a moment Devine turned her wrath on the crowd that had gathered around staring at her.

'You wait 'till the fucking Nationalists get back. You'll starve then. They would not give a starving man a fucking feed.'

Then, she managed to get in one last jibe at the New Guard captain just before he ducked inside the door.

'I wish that your fucking wife was here, I'd give her a fucking go, too!'

Perhaps her judge was one of the rare examples of a Lang sympathiser among the judiciary. That afternoon he obligingly granted Devine the right to appeal her sentence and let her go free on bail.

Francis de Groot would become an instant celebrity, dining out on his exploit for years to come. His appearance as guest of honour at a Sydney Arts Club luncheon was typical of the jubilant receptions accorded him – greeted with a standing ovation as he was introduced by the president in these rousing terms: 'Everyone is going around killing Mr. Lang with their tongues, but only one has risen to the occasion by killing him with ridicule.'

His fame wasn't confined to Australia. He even seems to have become something of a tourist attraction for members of the British aristocracy travelling to the Antipodes. Lady Angela St Clair Erskine, as blue-blooded as they come with a family line dating back to Charles II and Nell Gwyn, boasted of arranging to meet de Groot during her brief stop in Sydney aboard the liner *Orama*.

'For about ten minutes I became an object of general interest on the *Orama*,' she wrote in a memoir of her travels. 'De Groot had got my message after all and had come down to the ship to see me off. The news spread like wildfire and everyone produced a Kodak!'

Their conversation doesn't appear to have been all that exciting, though Lady Erskine obviously treasured every word as a highlight of her trip.

'The situation was so tense in Sydney that people's nerves were on edge,' she observed. 'Revolution was being spoken of as more than a possibility. I mentioned this to de Groot. "Will there be any fighting?" I asked. "Not if we can help it, but we are ready," was de Groot's reply, which tallied with everything I heard about the New Guard.'

Lady Erskine was invited to dinner at Government House and had a chance to speak to Sir Philip Game privately not long after the ribbon-cutting incident. She would abuse his trust by later publishing an account of how he reacted. He told her de Groot's exploit, combined with all the previous New Guard antics, had simply stiffened his resolve not to sack Lang without the clearest of provocations.

'If he talked like this to everyone,' Lady Erskine suggested, 'it is not surprising that he was called "Red Game."' That remark was to raise such a furore when her book *Fore and Aft* appeared in London that her publishers agreed to have it deleted from later editions.

Francis de Groot would discover that he had an even more ardent English fan. Some weeks after the bridge opening, he received a letter from a friend telling of the scene in Buckingham Palace when King George V first heard of the ribbon-slashing. His Majesty was said to have slapped his royal thigh in sheer delight and exclaimed: 'Good enough! Well done, de Groot!'

༄

Billy Mackay was not about to ease up on his crusade against the New Guard but he also looked like facing more pressing problems from an entirely different direction. Under the federal government's Financial Agreements Enforcement Act, the time was fast approaching when Commonwealth law officers could be expected to start confiscating various sources of New South Wales revenue. Once Jack Lang gave the word, it would be up to Mackay and his constabulary to confront and arrest them.

'The state employs me and the people are my masters,' the Scotsman told a reporter. 'I am bound by my oath and the law to do my duty irrespective of governments. I must do my duty and I must serve the state.'

The federal government's first move, however, would cleverly avoid any chance of a physical confrontation. It came in the form of a decree ordering the various commercial banks to seize all New South Wales Government accounts and immediately transfer the deposits to Canberra. Lang's senior bureaucrats had to scramble to find an answer. On Saturday morning, 12 March – just before noon – a New South Wales Government car screeched to a halt in front of the headquarters of the Bank of New South Wales. Treasury officials – accompanied by a police guard – rushed in to withdraw £750,000 ($52.5 million) in notes of small denomination. A similar scene at the Commercial Bank saw another £400,000 ($28 million) whisked away. The action was reportedly timed to within five minutes of when the Governor-General was due to sign the bill into law.

'It would seem,' the Prime Minister fumed, 'that Mr. Lang had sufficient money in the banks after all with which he could have paid his interest had he desired to do so. He is deluding himself if he thinks that his action is a means of evading the effective weapon that has been forged by the Commonwealth Government to compel him to meet his undertakings.'

Lang, for his part, accused Lyons of purposely setting out 'to provoke disorder' by trying to prevent government cheques from being used to pay the state's civil servants.

'This Enforcement Act will not enable the Commonwealth Government to collect one penny piece from this state and the Commonwealth knows it,' the Premier insisted. 'If the law is not to obtain money – and I say it is not – why was it passed other than to try to create turmoil and conflict during which the State Government would be deposed?'

The Premier went on to warn against any further escalation of Commonwealth tactics.

'It is an invalid law passed for a nefarious purpose and is certain to be declared invalid the first time an Australian judicial bench has a chance of making a pronouncement of it,' he predicted.

At least the two political warriors would be able to agree on one point – that there should be a cease-fire through the rest of March pending the New South Wales challenge to the law being heard by the High Court. Lang had 'counted the numbers' within the High Court in the same way he might normally assess votes in parliament. He was confident that with the known progressive members on the six-man Bench the verdict would just tip his way. Two of them, Justices E. A. McTiernan and H. V. Evatt, were prominent former Labor parliamentarians who had actually served for a time under Lang's leadership.

The Big Fella, though, wasn't just fighting against an intrusive piece of federal legislation. He was trying to hold back the march of time.

16
Phar Lap: Myth and reality

Sixteen days after the race that made him the talk of America, Phar Lap was dead – cruelly struck down by a sudden and mysterious illness. On Monday 4 April, the headline-grabbing Australian import had paraded happily in front of hundreds of gawking fans who gathered at the picturesque Menlo Park stud, outside San Francisco, to watch him performing a light workout coaxed along by his devoted assistant trainer, Tommy Woodcock. Almost always gentle and good-natured, the big thoroughbred didn't even seem to mind when children ran up to souvenir a few hairs from his tail.

By the next morning, though, he was lying on his side writhing in agony, his stomach aflame and horribly distended. Woodcock looked on helplessly, tears streaming down his face, as the horse's eyes seemed to glaze over in shocked disbelief. Horse and trainer had been virtually inseparable from the time the chestnut galloper was but an awkward yearling and Woodcock an eager young stable-hand, often sleeping next to the animal's stall at night to make sure he was safe and always ready at an insistent nudge to hand over a rewarding lump of sugar. The horse's final paroxysm soaked his grieving handler in a hot gush of blood – that's how close they were at the end and had always been for three of the most momentous years in the history of horseracing.

Poisoning – whether accidental or deliberate – was naturally suspected but a series of autopsies conducted by pre-eminent scientific experts failed to establish a conclusive cause of death. Some minute traces of arsenic found in vital organs may well have come from an agricultural pesticide sprayed in a nearby orchard but the quantity was far from lethal. Horses did occasionally succumb to colic from some contamination of their normal feed – grain too damp or alfalfa too green. Yet few experienced vets had ever seen an attack as catastrophic as this. One theory that gained prominence for a time was that 'the Red Terror' was already a very sick animal before he was shipped off to the United States, riddled with stomach ulcers – just as a human might have been – from the stress of having too much expected of him. That was just one hypothesis among many, though, with no way of proving it since the violent seizure had left the stomach lining too badly lacerated for a definite post-mortem diagnosis.

No one, then, would ever know why Phar Lap should die in such tragic circumstances though most Australians instinctively guessed the ultimate cause. It was surely human greed that had plucked the horse from his rightful destiny, putting him in the wrong place at the wrong time. The depression-weary population was already upset enough over their idol being sent overseas. Their one consolation was that they could at least look forward to watching newsreels of him beating the world's best. Instead they woke up on the morning of Wednesday 6 April to radio flashes announcing that the revered champion would race no more.

Some were quick to dismiss the report as a hoax. It was almost as if, by refusing to believe, they could make it not so. By that afternoon, however, the news had brought the nation to a standstill as surely as the Melbourne Cup itself. People from all walks of life went into deep mourning – heads bent in silent prayer, flags flown at half-mast, loving death notices posted in the newspapers. And of course, it would not be long before the man in the street found someone to blame. Dark tales could be heard in every pub telling of a conspiracy to do the poor animal in before he had a chance to take on mob-owned competitors.

Plain commonsense should have told them just the opposite. From the moment Phar Lap showed his magic at Agua Caliente – performing in front of some of the Prohibition era's most powerful racketeers – it could only have been a matter of time before he ended up as a prized Mafia asset. The feelers were already out to the horse's owner, Dave Davis, to sell off a controlling share.

The sad truth, in terms of the great Phar Lap's enduring reputation, is that in all probability he died not a moment too soon. Somewhere along the way, the national icon had been transformed from a stirring symbol of the competitive spirit in motion to a cynically manipulated money machine, no longer allowed to race on his merits. That didn't imply anything so crude as being doped or pulled up – but it did mean more and more occasions when the animal was made to gallop when he was clearly unfit, or scratched for no apparent reason other than to pull off a sensational betting coup.

With only a handful of other horses in Australia considered fast enough to be worthy rivals, it was relatively easy for their owners to come to secret agreements on when to race and when not in order to obtain the most favourable betting odds. So it was that Phar Lap's famous victory in the 1930 Melbourne Cup could well be described as 'rigged'. Long before the big race, Dave Davis was rumoured to have set up a major sting against unsuspecting bookmakers by entering a pact with the connections of Amounis, Phar Lap's most formidable rival. Davis would make sure his champion pulled out of the Caulfield Cup at the last minute – clearing the way for Amounis to win – in exchange for Amounis dropping out of the Melbourne Cup. Betting weeks in advance on a Caulfield Cup–Melbourne Cup double and using commission agents to hide his identity, Davis was able to back his horse at an unheard-of twenty to one compared to the miserably short odds of eight to eleven that mug punters were offered on the day. He would reap millions when Phar Lap easily romped home ahead of inferior opposition but his plunge could well have cost the gelding his life at the hands of those who had most to lose. On the Saturday before the Cup, returning with Woodcock from early morning track work, the favourite was fired upon from a speeding car. Two shotgun blasts narrowly missed him, the pellets pounding into a nearby tree. Whether the assailants meant to kill or simply to scare the horse's connections into scratching, it was clear that Phar Lap's career had taken on a dangerous new dimension. The betting frenzy surrounding him had reached the point where his life had to be considered on the line at every major race.

But it was not just the gamblers who were eager to exploit him. Each new success saw zealous racing officials encumbering Phar Lap with ever more difficult handicaps. Their aim might seem reasonable enough, to try to keep his races competitive and encourage more punters to the track. Pushed to logical extremes, however, it meant that the harder the animal tried the more he would be punished until the weight on his back simply became too much to bear. For the 1931 Melbourne Cup, the Victorian Racing Club decreed a handicap denounced by some commentators as bordering on animal cruelty – 10 stone 10, or 150 pounds, a full 25 per cent heavier than the average weight carried by the rest of the field. It was a burden so onerous as to give the champion little chance of winning. Worse than that, however, if the powerful animal stayed true to form and gave his all over the gruelling two miles, he would be carrying a load big enough to cripple or even kill. Harry Telford, Phar Lap's chief trainer and, by that time, part-owner, warned that he would rather pull the horse from the big race than risk his breaking down in mid-stride. What the public never knew was that Phar Lap probably should have been scratched from the 1931 Cup whatever the handicap, because his condition was in grave doubt. On the Saturday before, running in the Melbourne Stakes, he had barely eked out a win in what was supposed to have been an easy warm-up for him. Nearing the finish he appeared wobbly, losing his footing. That night Woodcock judged him to be burnt out from over-racing. The champion gulped his feed ravenously and kicked up a fury when his handler would give him no more. It was this episode that would later lead to speculation about stomach ulcers – but by then Phar Lap's welfare was no longer the primary issue.

Harry Telford's complaints about the enormous handicap were widely reported in the press, leading to intense speculation about whether the horse would be allowed to start. A nabob of the VRC is said to have responded by calling Dave Davis to a secret meeting in which he laid out the position in the most menacing of terms. The beloved champion's failure to appear at Flemington that Tuesday would be a serious blow to public morale, not to mention the gate takings. If Davis hoped to stay on the right side of the powers that be in Victorian racing, he would make sure his horse ran, whatever the circumstances.

Even with his crushing handicap, Phar Lap still entered the 1931 Cup a three to one favourite backed by tens of thousands of small punters who continued to put all their faith in him. They would get their fingers badly burnt when he finished eighth in a field of fourteen, the first time he had been unplaced in his last 41 starts. Davis had already tipped his friends not to waste their money. The American may well have ended up making another small fortune by backing a long shot named White Nose. It flashed first past the post carrying a third of Phar Lap's handicap weight.

After his disappointing run Phar Lap trotted back to his stables to only a polite ripple of applause. It should have been a memorable ovation, but the 82,000 at Flemington that day had no way of knowing this was to be his last Australian race. Davis had quietly arranged to ship him off later that month, first to New Zealand for toning up and then to the United States. The Cup had been the final straw, making him realise that his four-legged treasure could only become worthless remaining where it was: caught in a squeeze between the bookies, with their prohibitively short odds, and the racing clubs with their punitive handicaps. No matter how much Australia claimed to love Phar Lap, its rigid racing regulations and conservative attitudes were basically forcing the horse into exile. America, at its best, had much more imaginative ways of dealing with a great champion: high-stake match races, movie contracts, huge exhibition fees. And America, at its worst, offered other ways to exploit a big name galloper for all it was worth, especially when it reached a stage in its career when – with the right bet – a surprise loss could end up paying many times more than a win. The shockingly high number of race-fixing scandals in the United States during the Prohibition years was testament to that.

As it was, Phar Lap repaid the trust that ordinary punters put in him many times over. In 51 races he delivered an outstanding 37 wins, along with five second or third placings. During the last race, at Agua Caliente, his courage was tested as never before when he suffered a badly cracked hoof during a training workout just a couple of weeks before the big event. It was an injury that would have left many another horse too sore-footed to run, let alone come first in record time. The metaphor that was constantly applied to his performances – of a *big-hearted* animal giving its all – proved no exaggeration. When his heart was removed, to be sent back to Australia, it was found to be more than twice the size of an average cavalry charger's.

Will Rogers, the well-loved American humorist and social commentator, offered perhaps the most moving tribute of all the condolences flowing back to the Antipodes.

'It's too bad, Australia,' he lamented. 'Phar Lap was just a horse, but he brought you honour and represented you nobly. For you never saw a good horse grow where a good man didn't grow.'

Had Phar Lap lived another six months he almost certainly would have become the biggest money-winning thoroughbred of his time. Then again, the longer he stayed in the United States, the less likelihood there would have been of his being remembered as a proud Australian legend.

17
The battle of the decrees

The death of Phar Lap was an omen of nasty surprises to come. On Friday, 8 April, the citizens of New South Wales woke up to find a startling announcement in their morning newspapers. It was the first shot in the battle of the decrees – the war of attrition that would serve to redefine the Commonwealth of Australia.

> **Financial Agreements Enforcement Act, 1932**
> **Payment of New South Wales Income Tax**
> It is hereby notified that **Income Tax** payable under the law of New South Wales is now payable to the **Commonwealth** and is not payable to the State.
> Payment of any such tax, in accordance with the undermentioned directions, is a good and effective discharge of the taxpayer's liability to the State in respect of that tax. Payment of the tax to the State is not only no discharge of the taxpayer's liability to pay the tax, but also involves him in liability to heavy penalties.

Until then income tax had been regarded as a prerogative largely left to the six states. Canberra took only a minor share, drawing most of its receipts from customs and excise. Now, though, the federal government seemed to be demanding that responsible citizens do the unthinkable: break the law as it had been drummed into their conscience all their adult lives, thumb their noses at the New South Wales tax man and hand over what they owed to some nameless teller at the Commonwealth Bank. Filing a return could be unnerving enough in the days when there was no withholding tax and the amounts to be accounted for seemed daunting in the best of circumstances; but this sudden twist made it positively alarming. What guarantee did New South Welshmen have that at some stage down the line they wouldn't face prosecution for evasion? Yet as the proclamation warned, anyone who hesitated faced enormous fines, even a jail sentence.

Joe Lyons and his advisers had hit upon the perfect way to seize the revenue they required without risking a direct physical showdown with New South Wales officials. They would simply turn their legislative blowtorch on the soft underbelly of the average law-abiding citizen instead. The Commonwealth Bank arranged for special tellers to process returns and the anti-Lang tabloids did their utmost to encourage compliance with a hallelujah chorus of quotes attributed to enthusiastic taxpayers.

From a city businessman: 'I am happy this is not going into Mr. Lang's bag. I have never before seen people so eager to pay taxes and I have never been so pleased myself.'

From a Macquarie Street medical specialist: 'I am glad of the opportunity to help Mr. Lyons and show Mr. Lang what we think of him.'

And from someone described as a 'leader of the Italian community', this almost evangelical exaltation: 'It is a miracle. Everybody is delighted.'

Perhaps there was a grain of truth in such reportage but many families would spend long hours agonising over whether their first loyalty should be to their state or to a Canberra-based regime that remained something of a mystery to them. The federal government would later admit that it only managed to collect about £1 in every ten outstanding. Income tax, however, was merely the opening round of a month-long onslaught: a bewildering series of tit-for-tat skirmishes in which innocent civilians would inevitably end up as the main casualties.

On the same night the federal government's income tax decree took effect, Jack Lang ordered a bureaucratic counter-attack. A team of senior public servants worked into the early hours sealing off three full floors of the Tax Department. This was no spur-of-the-moment operation. The doors had been carefully reinforced and refitted with special heavy-duty locks so that unauthorised entry could only be gained by a full-scale assault using sledgehammers and oxyacetylene torches. Inside those closed-off rooms were endless rows of filing cabinets containing the records of more than a million taxpayers. They were not only essential for processing New South Wales returns but the federal government's as well since Canberra had traditionally relied on state agencies to collect its relatively limited share of Commonwealth tax on certain categories of earnings. That morning 200 clerical workers were astonished to report for duty only to find that their offices on the fifth, sixth and eighth floors no longer existed. Almost all of them were put on immediate leave. The issuing of any further assessment notices, state or federal, had effectively been brought to a dead stop.

To Jack Lang the shutdown was nothing more than a tactical ploy to gain some leverage in future negotiations. To Joe Lyons it was simply a cue to introduce further legislation forcing those closed doors back open through the threat of a court injunction. But for a wool buyer named George Ayrton it was a full-blown nightmare that meant missing the boat, quite literally, on an important business deal. Under existing regulations Australians travelling overseas needed to obtain a certificate showing they had no taxes owing before they could pick up their tickets. As embarrassed New South Wales officials tried to explain to Ayrton – and hundreds of others like him – it was currently impossible to access the files needed to provide the necessary clearances. They hoped the matter might be straightened out within a week or so but by that time the liner on which the distraught Ayrton had booked passage would have been well on its way to England.

The income tax proclamation – and other even more disruptive measures to follow – had been set in motion earlier that week by a momentous judgement of the High Court. In a majority decision of four against two, the justices found the Financial Agreements Enforcement Act to be constitutionally valid, rejecting the appeal lodged by the New South Wales Government in mid-March.

Lang's intuition had been correct in singling out two of the judges he expected to win over to his side. In his view the Irish-born Chief Justice, Frank Gavan Duffy, 'retained a very fair streak of rebel instincts'. Duffy, indeed, would strongly condemn the act's impact on ordinary citizens. As the Chief Justice noted, the legislation was supposedly aimed at making state governments stand by their contractual obligations to the Loan Council, yet it actually went much further than that. It allowed any money owed to be obtained directly 'from taxpayers, who are no parties to the agreement'.

Justice Herbert V. Evatt also lived up to Lang's expectations, insisting that the act destroyed a basic principle of Federation by giving the Commonwealth the power to pass what in effect was a discriminatory law aimed at one state only. The result, he warned, was that 'irreparable damage may be sustained by the

State and the exercise of its legislative and executive capacities may be completely paralysed'.

Lang felt sure he could count on Evatt as someone well known for his progressive beliefs but he badly miscalculated when it came to pinning his hopes on another former Labor parliamentarian, Justice Edward A. McTiernan, who had once served under him as Attorney-General. To McTiernan, and the three more conservative-minded judges with whom he sided, there was only one issue that mattered. Under the relevant section of the Constitution, 105A, the Commonwealth had the right to 'carry out' various financial agreements with the states and that must necessarily mean the capability to enforce those agreements by whatever means necessary. The clause in question was a relative latecomer to the Constitution – an amendment added in 1929 after being approved by referendum – but as McTiernan would argue with some passion, 'it pulses with the vitality of the Constitution itself and imbues any agreement to which it applies with the force of a fundamental law'. Enough force, he further suggested, to push aside all that came before it.

'The State is under an obligation – regardless of anything contained in the Constitution or any law of the State – to perform its undertaking to pay money to the Commonwealth,' McTiernan concluded.

Up to that point the 31-year relationship between the six states and the Commonwealth had remained poised in delicate equilibrium. Each government surrendered a precious fraction of its sovereignty to form the Federation but no single entity was assumed to carry any greater or lesser weight within the protective framework of the Constitution. The High Court judgement of 6 April 1932 was tantamount to dropping a brick on a finely balanced gold scale. The federal government catapulted into an ascendancy never before envisaged in all of the pre-Federation debates. From that moment on, Canberra had the power to bypass or override state parliaments by tapping directly into the day-by-day flow of their revenues. Evatt used the stinging term *invasion of State revenues* in denouncing the unprecedented repercussions of the new law. Some indignant critics went even further, warning that the Commonwealth would from then on have 'the power to destroy the states as political entities one by one'.

The decision would come to be regarded as one of the High Court's more clouded judgements – a verdict tainted by the toxic political atmosphere and the near-hysteria surrounding Jack Lang himself. Then again, if the judicial reasoning was suspect, the practical results would soon enough prove to be most definitely in Australia's best interests. Without that giant leap towards centralised control, the nation would have found itself in an infinitely more vulnerable position as it plunged into World War II.

Lang might therefore be credited with being the prime – if unwitting – catalyst in a crucial phase of the Federation's evolution. Typically, though, he dismissed the High Court opinion as not so much muddy legal thinking as dirty politics: an extension of a right-wing plot to bring down his government by any means. He turned his full wrath on McTiernan, making a startling claim under parliamentary privilege about a certain unnamed Justice who 'had so much difficulty in making up his own mind that it had to be made up for him'. He went on:

> When the legislation was first mooted this particular judge and the Prime Minister had dinner at the home of a mutual friend. The process of making up the judge's mind was begun there. On the Saturday night preceding the announcement of the judgement, a leading Sydney KC was able to assure Mr. Lyons and his colleagues that the vote of this particular judge would be in favour of the

Commonwealth. The reason why the KC had been able to give such a confident assurance was because he himself had written out the judge's judgement for him.

'What is this judge's name?' a member of the Opposition challenged.

'Everybody knows his name,' Lang responded. He left it to Labor Party interjectors to complete the smear by jeering, 'McTiernan! McTiernan!'

When it came to weaving tales of conspiracy, the New South Wales Premier had an almost Shakespearean flair. In a whisper thick with portent, he described the six judges sombrely setting out from their Sydney chambers on a rainy morning to deliver their verdict before a packed courtroom. 'The Chief Justice,' he intoned, 'opened his umbrella with a grim look at the dark sky overhead and was heard to say: "Come, gentlemen, we have a dirty day for a dirty deed."'

Regardless of how it came about, the High Court loss hit the Big Fella much harder than he was prepared to admit in any of his public pronouncements. He was now like a general under siege, his enemies pressing in from every direction, methodically cutting off all possible channels of relief. His one comfort was that his 'common folk' still believed in him with all their hearts. His one hope was that time would prove to be on his side. The longer he could hold on, the more chance there was that the cyclical nature of boom and bust would see the economy begin to show encouraging glimmers of recovery. He had even asked the New South Wales Agent-General in London to quietly try to make peace with the British bondholders, offering better returns in the future if they would only give their official blessing to a year-long suspension of interest. They had turned him down cold, but who knew what might happen if wheat or wool prices began to pick up again?

Meanwhile, he still had another crucial court decision pending that could change his political fortunes overnight. He had been elected to government in late 1930 on a platform that included abolishing the state's Upper House, the Legislative Council, altogether so that New South Wales would have only one parliamentary chamber, like Queensland. The bill he introduced to that effect had been challenged by his opponents, who insisted a full referendum was required. The legal arguments were currently being considered by the Privy Council in London and its decision could come down at any moment. Even with its additional Labor appointees, the Upper House remained a worry for him as long as it was in a position to challenge the emergency revenue-raising measures he so desperately needed. But a favourable Privy Council decision would sweep away all legislative obstacles once and for all.

On the Monday following the High Court setback, Lang went on radio to appeal to his supporters to keep the faith and stay firm.

'Although this fight is now at its most intensive point, it is also nearing its conclusion,' he reassured them in a butterscotch baritone overflowing with confidence. 'You can win if you keep fighting. Your Government won't weaken. Don't you.'

Lyons's response was to issue a flurry of new decrees targeting more sources of revenue for confiscation. Racecourses throughout the state were still providing the New South Wales Treasury with a lucrative flow of betting and admission taxes. In the final quarter of the financial year alone, April to June, the potential receipts were estimated at £200,000, or $14 million. By the latest proclamation, however, race club officials and bookmakers faced fines of up to £500 ($35,000) or prison sentences of from six months to two years if they failed to divert these payments to the Commonwealth. The professional bookmakers were left in a particularly precarious situation since under state regulations they had to settle their tax accounts each week in order to obtain the official logbooks needed to continue dealing with the public. Some simply gritted their teeth and paid twice to appease both governments. Others found themselves laughed out of the room when they attempted to renew their New South Wales betting book by producing a Commonwealth tax receipt.

No federal edict was to have more chaotic repercussions than the instant freeze on New South Wales Government bank accounts. That drastic measure had first been introduced in March but then temporarily suspended pending Lang's appeal to the High Court. As a pre-emptive move, just before the decree was to take effect, state officials had hurriedly withdrawn well over £1 million in cash reserves. But there were still numerous deposits scattered among a half a dozen or so institutions. Under the decree all bank balances held on behalf of the state were to be transferred immediately to the Commonwealth. The loose wording, however, meant there was no clear distinction between accounts linked to the Lang Government's revenue-raising activities and those used by independent statutory bodies like the State Superannuation Board or Public Trustee to distribute funds earmarked for specific public benefits.

Lyons did promise that any moneys later found to be exempt would be paid back but that was hardly enough to prevent a near-disastrous breakdown in day-to-day administration. The court system was one of the first to feel the pinch, as evidenced by the petulant outburst of Mr. Justice Langer Owen, chief judge of the divorce court, when he was asked to expedite an alimony payment which had been lodged with the court's registrar several weeks earlier.

'How can I order that money to be paid out?' Judge Owen protested. 'The court has been officially informed that the money is not there. Even though it has already been paid into the Supreme Court and belongs to individuals, it is no longer there!'

'Could his honour at least make an order that the money be paid out when available?' pleaded the barrister representing the aggrieved ex-spouse.

'How can I make such a direction when the court knows that the money is not there?' Owen rebuked him. 'Moneys paid into the court for the benefit of wives, children, lunatics, invalids – they're all in exactly the same position.'

Among the worst-hit by the subsequent fallout were 4000 retired civil servants destined to receive a devastating notice in the mail.

> The State Superannuation Board direct me to inform you that, owing to the fact that for the time being they are without banking facilities, arrangements cannot be made to pay you your pension on 1 May Next. The Board desire me to express their regret for the inconvenience and assure you that immediately they are in a position to do so, they will arrange a cheque to be forwarded.

These retirees were by no means the 'fat cats' of the public service but rather those at the middling levels who for 30 years or more had diligently wielded their rubber stamps with the dream of a secure retirement to spur them on. Despite the added taxes and cuts to their pensions inflicted by the depression they had somehow been managing to get through. Now, though, by the cruellest of ironies, they had fallen victim to a monstrous bureaucratic bungle dwarfing any they might have contributed to in their lives. Both governments immediately blamed each other for the retirees' predicament: Lang accusing Lyons of impounding the super funds out of sheer spite,

Lyons accusing Lang of draining them dry during his lightning withdrawals in mid-March. The banks, meanwhile, insisted they were merely following standard procedure, automatically stamping every state cheque, regardless of origin, 'refer to drawer' because the relevant accounts had been proclaimed extinct.

The former civil servants were all the more frantic for knowing the missing pension funds needed to save them from a month of starvation could almost certainly be traced to one pigeonhole or another. They publicly appealed for someone – whether federal or state – to stop the buck-passing and cut the red tape. Sadly, as they should have been the first to know, that wasn't very likely to happen.

With New South Wales Government cheques bouncing around his ears – including those for widow's pensions and child endowment – the Big Fella decided to issue a decree of his own. The state, from that point on, would not only cease to issue cheques but it would also refuse to accept any tendered by members of the public as payment for government services. Water bills, stamp duties, death duties, licence and transfer fees, charges for rail freight, even crown land leases and purchases henceforth had to be paid in cash. The reason was simple enough. Each such cheque could only be made good upon presentation to a bank and under the proclamation, the amount to be drawn would then automatically be credited not to New South Wales but to the federal government. Lang's retaliatory policy was spelt out in what may well stand as one of the most extraordinary public service directives ever issued.

12 April 1932
The Treasury, New South Wales
Subject: Collections and expenditure – Procedure to be followed.

Will you please instruct your departmental officers and officers of your sub-departments, and other collecting officers, to –
(1) Refrain from meeting any Governmental expenditure by the drawing of cheques until further advised.
(2) Hold all moneys collected coming under their control until forwarded as mentioned hereunder.
(3) Under no circumstances to pay receipts into any bank.
(4) All collections to be made in cash or, if in any case it is necessary to take a cheque, such cheques must be 'bearer' cheques made payable to 'cash'. Cheques with specific crossings must not be accepted. On no account must a cheque be officially marked either by stamp or otherwise.
(5) All cash and cheques collected to be delivered to the Treasury. Banks must not be used for this purpose, but safe and suitable arrangements should be made for forwarding. For this purpose it is suggested it may be possible to use the organisation of the railways.
C.R. Champion
Under-Secretary

The circular was to produce a truly wondrous sight. Just on dusk near the close of business each day, lorry after lorry pulled up to the Treasury offices in Macquarie Street to discharge their precious cargoes. Anxious, pale-faced public servants could be seen stumbling up to the door lugging heavy bags full of coins and pound notes, much like leprechauns secreting their pots of gold. In such a manner, over the next month, did the giant steel vault in the bowels of the stately sandstone building come to be stuffed with over £2 million, or $140 million, flowing in from every corner of the state.

The sudden transition to a cash economy tested bureaucratic ingenuity to its limits. Lang's first priority was to cover the fortnightly salaries of police, schoolteachers, nurses and other civil servants. He and his advisers hit upon the idea of making the payments, where possible, through the relative unions. Each trade organisation was given an appropriate lump sum from the Treasury to deposit into its own bank account. Meanwhile, members of parliament, including cabinet ministers, suffered the indignity of having to line up in the basement of the Treasury building to be handed a wad of bills and coinage.

Despite the apparent pandemonium, Treasury officers would later be credited with accounting for all moneys right down to the last threepence. Still, the state of New South Wales was much too large to be served for long by such makeshift antics and cases of hardship and injustice mounted alarmingly. Small country grocers who provided dole rations to unemployed drifters would find themselves pushed to the brink of ruin. The cheques they received had proved worthless, yet the amounts due to them – often ranging up to £1000 – were deemed too large to be settled in cash. Thus they waited weeks without reimbursement.

If the Big Fella's troubles were mounting, though, Joe Lyons soon realised he had a tiger by the tail.

18

Descent into chaos

The Prime Minister was under no illusion. The law might be on his side but New South Wales still had all the trappings of power: more people, more money and by far the biggest share of the basic assets that had allowed Australia to prosper as a nation. Each new confiscatory decree that Lyons unleashed against the Lang Government had the potential to seriously disrupt the revenue source at which it was aimed and thus inflict long-term damage both to the state's economy and indirectly, to the national economy as well. Meanwhile, tens of thousands of ordinary people were inevitably going to end up hurt and angry, threatening a political backlash of untold consequences for his newly established United Australia Party. The longer this war of attrition was allowed to stretch on, the more likely Lyons's backers in the world of business and high finance would begin to panic and demand some face-saving compromise.

Canberra's most immediate problem was that Lang's unpaid interest bills were accumulating at a far faster rate than the revenues seized to pay for them. Toward the end of April the balance stood at only £1 collected for every £8 owed. To try to minimise the adverse political fallout from his Enforcement Act the Prime Minister had agreed – for the moment at least – to exempt two major streams of taxation. Unemployment relief in New South Wales was being financed by a special surcharge on income tax worth millions of pounds a year. The state also imposed a levy on larger corporations to cover its child endowment scheme. Lyons recognised that both programs were too sensitive to risk tampering with. Still, he needed to make up the difference somewhere before the Commonwealth itself was dragged under by the dead weight of its largest state.

The New South Wales railways and trams generated a huge daily cash flow which represented the most tempting of targets. Any move to confiscate such takings, though, raised the spectre of outright violence – federal and state law enforcers physically grappling for the ticket money in front of horrified passengers. That kind of nose-to-nose confrontation was exactly what the federal government had set out to avoid in its initial debt recovery strategy. However, as April dragged on with little sign of the Lang administration either surrendering or crumbling, the Lyons Government decided to push a notch higher the powers bestowed upon it by the High Court. An amendment to the Enforcement Act was rushed through federal parliament, giving Canberra the right not only to confiscate various sources of revenue but to direct New South Wales Government employees to make sure the money was paid. With the issuing of an appropriate decree, senior public servants and even cabinet ministers would be obliged to hand over all receipts from their departments, as well as the accounting records needed to confirm the amounts in question. Anyone failing to comply risked up to three years in prison.

In this way Lyons effectively put himself in a position to seize control of the New South Wales public transport system at the moment of his choosing. The same procedure could be extended – if and when the need arose – to expropriating a wide range of other revenue sources such as motor registration fees, liquor licences and even proceeds from the lease or sale of crown land. With masterful foresight, the Lyons Government backed up these drastic measures with a decree stating that all New South Wales public servants who agreed to cooperate would be protected from any form of punitive action by their superiors.

Jack Lang prided himself on being able to thrive in times of crisis – his inner strength soaring with the adrenaline rush, his instincts sharpened in grinding adversity. Yet in this relentless tug-of-war with Lyons he found himself dragged from the political arena he knew so well and cleverly manoeuvred into a legalistic spiderweb that entangled him all the more he struggled. Even so, Joe Lyons might well have seemed the lesser of two evils facing him at this moment. Amid the high drama surrounding the Enforcement Act, the New Guard was shouting anew for his blood. Eric Campbell had sent a provocative telegram to the Prime Minister pledging the use of his militiamen to meet any sign of resistance from Lang supporters.

'In case of emergency the New Guard will unreservedly place its entire resources at the disposal and under the control of the Commonwealth Government,' he advised. 'Any number of thoroughly trustworthy, reliable men, highly organised in units under known commanders, will be ready on two hours' notice day or night.'

Hotheads within the Trades Hall predictably responded in kind, calling for the formation of a labour movement defence corps – quickly dubbed 'the Red Army' by the hostile conservative press. This left-wing militia was to be spearheaded by ex-servicemen, very much like the New Guard, and bolstered by 'all workers who are prepared to take their place in the fight which is impending'.

'We call upon unions to place their organisations at the disposal of the Government either on the industrial field or on any field where it may be necessary to meet the attacks of the Fascist forces arrayed behind the Federal Government,' declared a resolution of the New South Wales Labor Council. A spokesman accused Lyons of forcing people 'at the point of a bayonet' to hand over their meagre savings to the overseas bondholders.

The Prime Minister, considering the string of successes he had enjoyed so far, might have been expected to take the lead in trying to soothe frayed tempers on all sides. Even if he had the will to do so, though, Joe Lyons lacked the rhetoric. Instead, his equivocal reply to Campbell's offer only succeeded in contributing an extra gust of hot air to the inflammatory atmosphere.

'While we welcome at all times the co-operation of all sections of the community in maintaining law and order,' he droned, 'we deprecate the suggestion that an emergency is likely to arise that will require intervention by the Commonwealth and the use of organised forces to this end.'

Lang, though, had good reason to treat this latest threat of New Guard intervention more seriously than ever before. He was already nervous enough about the large amounts of cash being shifted around the state with minimal security. On some days, a country train might be rattling along with as much as £100,000 worth of notes and coinage stashed away in its guard's van. Campbell's militia included units experienced in sabotage and guerrilla warfare and fully capable of launching a wave of robberies designed to cause the government maximum disruption and embarrassment. As good as Superintendent Billy Mackay was, he simply didn't have enough men to ride shotgun everywhere they were needed. In his worst dreams, Lang could imagine squads of armed militia stealthily moving against the Treasury itself. He also worried about the vulnerability of the Tax Department should the Guard, perhaps in support of Commonwealth bailiffs, make a grab for the valuable records sealed off under lock and key. Though he would officially deny it at the time, he quietly arranged for the Timber Workers' Union to select 30 of its toughest members to mount a 24-hour watch.

Joe Lyons may well have had similarly bad dreams in which the Red Army featured prominently – perhaps smashing its way into Parliament House in Canberra or worse yet, looting the Commonwealth Bank headquarters at Martin Place in Sydney while Lang's police looked the other way. The federal government, up to that time, had barely a dozen uniformed constables in Canberra and perhaps twice that many specially appointed auxiliaries to call upon in an emergency. Before the crisis was over, the number of Commonwealth 'peace officers' would swell to close to 200, though Lyons refused to confirm exactly how many, where they were posted and what duties they might be expected to perform in case of an outbreak of civil unrest. In a full-scale emergency he could have called in the army, though at that time it was a greatly depleted force joked about as having more officers then men. It was not beyond the realms of possibility – as Lang later acknowledged in his memoirs – that the Prime Minister might choose to appeal directly to King George V for a supportive show of British force.

The Big Fella decided his best chance to survive these next few weeks was in staging his own show of force, a clear demonstration to his adversaries that he still enjoyed the support of the silent majority. Lyons might have the writs but Lang had the words. He set out to prove that the Enforcement Act was aimed at nothing less than a total restructuring of the Federation: stripping New South Wales of the last vestiges of its sovereignty to allow a chosen few to reign supreme. He would hardly be the first New South Wales leader to suspect a jealous clique of power-hungry Victorians of trying to organise a coup.

'The Commonwealth move is not intended to get money,' he reiterated in speech after speech. 'By this legislation the Commonwealth Parliament hopes to transfer from you, the electors of New South Wales, to a little anti-Australian coterie domiciled in Melbourne, the power to make and unmake your Governments. It is an indirect way of robbing the people of New South Wales of their franchise.'

The injustice was all the greater, he contended, for its ostensible cause – the payment of interest bills at a time when many other nations of the world were doing exactly what New South Wales had done. 'Australia alone in practically the whole world is the only one which is harassing its people to make these impossible payments,' the Premier asserted.

On Thursday, 21 April, 50,000 people converged on the Sydney Town Hall and its surrounding streets for a rally set amid giant banners and stirring chants. When the Premier strode to the podium, the crowd broke into a tumultuous ovation, climaxed by a heartfelt chorus of 'For he's a jolly good fellow'. For Lang it must have been one of the most intensely emotional moments of his life. He had been born 56 years earlier in a well-appointed house on George Street at fashionable Brickfield Hill just two blocks from where he was standing now. By the age of fourteen he was still living only a short walk further south on Liverpool Street but in greatly reduced circumstances following his father's extended illness. Either way, he would have been close enough to the Town Hall during his childhood to hear these thrilling cheers and wonder what manner of man could possibly have inspired them. He did not often dwell on his accomplishments but this was one occasion when he had every reason to feel enormous pride. From a barefoot newspaper boy he had risen to lead the most powerful state in

Australia; and that was the way he intended it to remain. He spoke with his usual forcefulness on the themes he had stressed so often before but nothing he said at this meeting would trigger such a thunderous roar as the reading of the resolution framed in his honour.

> This mass meeting of citizens of New South Wales pledges itself to stand solidly behind the Premier and declares that in his determination to place men before money, LANG IS RIGHT!

Perhaps so, perhaps not. In the end, that would be a matter to be resolved by a single judgement. As Sir Philip Game walked with his dog Micky through the Domain earlier that brisk April evening he carried a crumpled piece of paper that he had brooded over for many long hours. It was a copy of the New South Wales Treasury directive of 12 April ordering all public servants – indeed, even the Governor's own official secretary, Harry Budge – to immediately refrain from transferring any further receipts to the bank. Game realised that such an instruction was in direct violation of the state's own Audit Act which required public moneys to be banked into an appropriate account at the first opportunity. His Premier, then, had apparently committed a breach of the law, though it might be regarded as a mere technical breach. Even the Auditor-General – in reporting on the matter to parliament – would acknowledge that the mountain of cash in the Treasury basement was being well looked after with meticulous bookkeeping. Nevertheless, of all the many possible reasons Sir Philip had been urged to consider as grounds for dismissing Lang, the issue of illegality loomed largest in his mind. He was so deeply concerned that he sent off a secret cable to the Dominions Office in London warning that matters were quickly coming to a head.

'I feel it is far better that the Commonwealth and State Governments should decide the quarrel without my intervention,' he wrote, 'but my hand may be forced by the issue of the legality of the Ministers' actions. I feel quite clear I cannot dismiss Ministers because their actions offend my own and other people's sense of public integrity. I am not so sure, however, as to whether I can do so on the grounds of the illegality of administrative acts which do not require my signature, or whether by doing so I should usurp the functions of the courts.'

That last sentence summed up in a nutshell the complex decision facing Game. Was it up to the King's representative to determine if his elected ministers were breaking the law or was that an issue best left to a qualified judge? So long as he himself wasn't being asked to sign some illegal measure, why should he feel the need to intervene? While he pondered those questions and waited on advice from London, he was subjected to a lobbying campaign more virulent than any he had known.

'The Press barrage is very intense in its efforts to galvanise a supine and feeble Governor into action,' he wryly noted in a letter home, 'and it is backed up by the individual and collective efforts of a great many well-meaning people whose intelligence is blinded by fear, outraged feelings, and other considerations good and bad. But hard words break no bones and if I can only keep in subjection the natural masculine joy of a good old scrap, I have some slight hope of pulling through.'

He added as an insightful postscript. 'By the way, all you get in England is the case as it appears to the die-hard anti-Labor element; an entirely one-sided view, so don't let anything you see in the papers worry you. I am satisfied that I have the bulk of sensible and unprejudiced opinion behind me and that it would be criminal folly to bow to the outcry.'

While the Governor pondered his next move, the situation was becoming more chaotic every day in small ways and large. Students at an agricultural high school outside Sydney served as a sorry example of how petty-minded the combatants could be. They woke up to discover the modest allowances deposited on their behalf by their parents confiscated from a Department of Education account. At the other extreme, 60,000 mothers dependent on fortnightly child endowment cheques found themselves cut off from benefits while the warring governments cynically exploited their plight for propaganda purposes.

'Mr. Lang should be in a better position than ever to pay these pensions,' Lyons huffed, noting that the state was saving millions of pounds by refusing to honour its interest commitments. 'He apparently has no difficulty paying the wages and salaries of members of Parliament and Public Servants. The Premier's policy is quite clear. By withholding, without any justification, payments to widows and others least able to bear the loss he seeks to bring these people to a state of desperation which he can then turn to his own political advantage.'

What Lyons refused to acknowledge was that further bank deposits made on behalf of the mothers still would have been automatically expropriated. Under the letter of the Enforcement law, the federal government lacked the authority to allow the funds to be used for any other purpose than paying back the state's interest debts.

'The Prime Minister's statement that he is anxious to assist the payment of family endowment is absolute humbug,' Lang responded. 'If he is sincere let him instruct the banks to meet the family endowment cheques that have previously been dishonoured. It is sheer hypocrisy on his part to profess to be concerned about future payments of endowment when he himself is holding up the current payments.'

Lang, too, was being less than honest. The endowment

cheques that had previously been stamped 'Refer to drawer' had been rejected not only because the banks froze the relevant account but because there was no balance left after his massive withdrawals in mid-March. If he had so desired, he could have arranged to pay the endowments in cash but his first priority was to meet his public service payrolls.

The end result was that the mothers would have to find a way to survive through six desperate weeks – three fortnightly benefit periods – without assistance that readily could have been given them by one government or the other.

Yet, as always, there were a fortunate few who managed to glide through this most troublesome and turbulent of periods with hardly a care. With May came the glittering highlight of the opera season – a rousing performance of Rossini's *Barber of Seville*. His Majesty's Theatre was filled to capacity, in fact jammed to the point that some enthusiasts could be seen sitting in the aisles. And as a correspondent for the *Sydney Morning Herald* observed with delight:

> As the weather grows colder more luxurious furs are worn and Saturday's audience displayed some exquisite fur coats and wraps, several white ermine coats collared with deep bands of white fox exciting admiring comment. Lovely mink, squirrel and sable wraps were plentiful and velvet coats with lavish fur trimming added to the gala appearance of the theatre.

Most members of the audience, no doubt, would have enjoyed their night at the opera all the more knowing the impact of the latest Enforcement Act decrees. The amusement taxes levied on their expensive seats were now been diverted away from Jack Lang and straight into Joe Lyons's pocket.

19

Vested interests

The Great Depression ticked away impervious to all human remedy, putting another Australian out of work every two minutes, 700 each day; as many a 5000 a week. The month of May, for all its other dramas, would see 20,000 more laid off with worse still to come. At the beginning of 1929 unemployment had hovered around 230,000, or 10 per cent of the work force, considered disastrous enough. By the winter of 1932 the figure would reach a staggering 700,000 – and even that could only be described as an optimistic guess in view of the crude surveying techniques in use at the time. Tens of thousands were to be excluded from official estimates by the stroke of a statistician's pen. Teenage boys and girls desperate for apprenticeships hardly rated a mention. How could they be considered out of work when they never held a job before? Destitute farmers were deemed to be fully occupied so long as they remained on their worthless properties. Idle wharfies or coal miners, intinerant labourers, newly arrived migrants, part-time workers on drastically reduced hours – all could easily miss being counted for want of a clear definition of unemployment compared to chronic underemployment. There were also many salespeople, office managers or small-time entrepreneurs simply too proud to accept the label of jobless when 'self-employed' – if penniless – sounded so much more dignified.

Governments had not only underestimated the extent of the crisis but as it gained momentum were woefully slow to offer assistance to the victims. Initially, private charities or wealthy donors took on the primary role of handing out food and clothing parcels. The stories of their generous deeds filled the newspapers with no end of impressive – if rather meaningless – statistics. A Christmas lunch put on by the Melbourne retailer and philanthropist Sidney Myer was said to have been attended by 11,000 diners gratefully consuming a ton of ham, half a ton of corned beef, 22,000 bread rolls, 33,000 pickled onions and countless servings of peaches, toffee and Christmas cake. And on it went: 10,000 blankets distributed by the Victorian Relief Committee, 8000 free meals served up each week by a Salvation Army soup kitchen, 80 rail trucks full of firewood arriving at Melbourne's Spencer Street Station courtesy of Victorian farmers with their 'wood chop' days. Such accounts were obviously meant to lift the spirits but they also tended to blind the public to the true dimensions of the tidal wave of human misery about to engulf them. Within weeks many of the charities were simply overwhelmed, their resources totally exhausted.

Not until April, 1930, did South Australia introduce the first government-funded food dole for the unemployed. The ration tickets allowed for the purchase of only the barest of subsistence diets, a little more than 5 shillings ($17.50 worth) of food per adult per week, half that for a child. However, the newly elected Labor premier, Lionel Hill, had at least been able to establish an important precedent. Until then the prevailing laissez-faire view was that a dole was 'morally wrong' because it would only encourage laziness. During the depression of the 1890s, that mind-set had contributed to countless deaths from malnutrition or exposure. Nothing so extreme would be allowed to happen again.

Several weeks after Hill's initiative, another newly installed Labor government in Victoria took unemployment relief a step further. Premier Edmond 'Ned' Hogan introduced a compulsory surcharge on income tax to pay for a food allowance which was to be distributed mainly through local councils. The conservative New South Wales government of Tom Bavin would adopt the same principle, and after Jack Lang returned to power in November, 1930, he quadrupled the levy to provide a relief fund of close to £6 million a year, several times larger than Victoria's.

Perhaps it was natural that these first dole programs should focus on sustenance rather than seeking a more comprehensive approach to the plight of the jobless. The bureaucratic mentality could cope with a faceless queue of ration applicants a lot more easily than individual cases with their wide array of special needs. Yet for many a family the most pressing problem was not feeding themselves – they could always share meals with relatives or friends. What they urgently needed was a few extra shillings to keep up with their rents or mortgages. Once cut loose from the security of their own home and forced to seek emergency shelter their difficulties quickly compounded – marital discord, demoralisation, illness – until they sank beyond help like strugglers in quicksand. Jack Lang offered at least some protection with an ejectments postponement act requiring landlords to apply for court permission to evict a defaulting tenant. A family in genuine distress could usually count on three months' grace before being thrown onto the streets. He also introduced a moratorium law which made it much more difficult for a mortgage holder to foreclose on a home-owner no longer able to meet payments.

Yet the Lang administration was as cold-hearted as any when it came to surrounding its relief programs in thickets of red tape. An applicant for a dole chit might have to walk miles to an office in one part of the city to get his book stamped, then traipse miles back to an approved grocery store or supply depot. The typical ration offered little variety beyond the basic stodge: bread, potatoes, pumpkin, onions, sausages, mutton chops; no fruit or vegetables. The best chance of varying the routine was to find a kindly storekeeper willing to bargain by swapping one item for another. Jobless families were constantly being cajoled by public health authorities to plant vegetables; yet if they were too successful they risked running afoul of the dole regulations.

'We had many a laugh over the propaganda for the unemployed to grow vegetables,' noted Daisy McWilliams, the enterprising housewife who had sent her husband Bob off to sell sandwiches at the opening of the Harbour Bridge. In her memoir she recalled a much talked about comedy skit lampooning the image of inner city slum cottages being transformed overnight into gardens of Eden.

It went like this: if the unemployed would only use their initiative, the difficulty of space to grow these vegetables would be overcome. Turn the kitchen table upside down, fill it well with earth. Then there is the water cistern, which is just being wasted. Sow tomatoes, not only having a bright appearance but also useful for shade. But a word of warning. Be sure and notify the nearest dole inspector so he can adjust your dole allowance. Otherwise there is danger of overeating yourself.

The value of the ration ticket was means-tested against other income and a few extra pennies earned on the side might be enough to disqualify the recipient for another fortnight or longer. An overly zealous inspector could interpret the arcane guidelines almost any way he chose and applicants faced the constant risk of being picked at random for a humiliating third degree. Was the wife taking in washing? How much help was being received from relatives? Did that white dust on the boots come from working at a construction site? Some queues were subjected to martial discipline, with dole officers ordering those in line to get their hands out of their pockets, stand straight or stop smoking. Such treatment was all the more offensive since it was well known that many of these petty tyrants owed their jobs to having the right political connections, perhaps a relative in state parliament or crony in Trades Hall.

The most common grievance with the early dole systems was that they made no provision for even a few pennies in cash. A single man might connive to sell his ration ticket at half price to be able to buy a few beers, so long as he was prepared to go hungry or resort to garbage scraps; but families with children had no real choice in the matter. Edna Ryan, a young Sydney mother, well educated but destitute, would later give this account:

> What was worst about being on the dole was having no spare money at all – sometimes not even to buy a needle and thread. Such items had to be borrowed or cadged from friends and relatives. It meant no money to pay the smallest fare. Mostly people walked, for miles and miles. One man we knew had four children and he swore they were not going to be deprived. He discovered the dole days for other suburbs, and registered himself and his family for multiple doles. What irked us was the fact that

because people could not survive on the dole, they had to become dole frauds to stay alive.

Ryan was luckier than many others because she lived in New South Wales where she had the advantage of Lang's child endowment to provide her with a small amount of cash to buy milk and perhaps a packet of arrowroot biscuits. Of the other states, only Western Australia allowed its dole to be taken both in the form of food and cash.

The harshest criticism to be levelled at such rudimentary relief schemes was that they might fill the stomach but starved the spirit. Most people wanted nothing more than the chance to earn their keep. One by one the states began to experiment with their own particular versions of a work-for-the-dole scheme. Recipients were generally sent off to pick-and-shovel projects suited to the use of unskilled part-time labour – road and sewerage construction, park and forestry development or improvements to local council amenities. To help pay for these new schemes, however, funds often had to be diverted from existing public works, resulting in more lay-offs of full-time staff. The net effect was to spread the available work more widely, but at the cost of forcing some unfortunates to sacrifice their weekly wage so that thousands of others could get the chance to earn a day's pay. That, indeed, was the great paradox inherent in so many of these depression-era relief schemes. They actually ended up increasing the number of registered unemployed.

At the start of 1932 ALP governments were in control of New South Wales, Victoria and South Australia. Considering the Labor Party's working-class sympathies they might have been expected to show a high degree of compassion in their treatment of the jobless. All practical evidence – from the strictness of dole regulations to the use of police to break up demonstrations – suggests otherwise. The Lang, Hogan and Hill administrations, as it turned out, were heavily influenced in their dealings with the unemployed by a powerful vested interest group as ruthlessly self-serving as any associated with the conservative alliance.

Trade unions regarded their jobless brethren with a volatile mixture of embarrassment and fear – much like an unwanted relative forever threatening to make a scene. In 1929, Australia had 901,000 card-carrying unionists belonging to 189 trade organisations. By 1932 that membership had shrunk to a little over 740,000, with twenty unions disappearing altogether. Once the dues stopped, so did any pretence of loyalty. Most union leaders, for all their talk of socialist solidarity, were quick to recognise that a mechanic, plumber, or storeman who lost his job was no longer an ex-colleague but a potential scab.

In the first months of the downturn a few of the better-organised unions did at least pay lip-service to the fraternal ideals that had inspired their creation, setting up appeals on behalf of out-of-work members or allowing them to continue to attend meetings, though without the right to vote. Their charity money quickly ran out, however, and so did their patience. Any sympathy that still existed for their stricken mates largely vanished with the introduction of the first work-for-the-dole programs. Trades Hall officials warned such schemes could only lead to a breakdown of award conditions as the jobless grasped at whatever wages they could get. Conservative-led states pressed ahead regardless but when Victoria's Labor government proposed to follow suit, requiring up to two days' labour for a week's dole, its program was promptly declared black and those eager to take part were branded as scabs. With its back-to-work project effectively sabotaged by the union movement, the Hogan administration had little choice but to suspend it indefinitely.

As the apathy and even hostility of their former workmates became increasingly evident, the jobless began setting up their own organisations, with radical agendas openly critical of mainstream unionism. In Melbourne a militant group known as the Unemployed Workers' Movement (UWM) became a force to be reckoned with. Its members marched through the streets with banners proclaiming 'Down with Labor Leaders' and distributed pamphlets accusing both the Hogan regime and the union bureaucracy of abandoning their jobless brothers. The UWM, citing government inaction, launched an aggressive campaign to prevent house evictions, leading to frequent bloody clashes with Melbourne police. Whenever its members got wind of another family about to be thrown out onto the streets, they descended on the neighbourhood to block the bailiffs gaining entry, using fists and fence posts to defend the citadel. If the battle was lost – as it almost always was – they crept surreptitiously back at night to vandalise or set fire to the premises to teach the landlord a bitter lesson. On occasions they directed their anger against the estate agent responsible, smashing his office windows or intimidating the potential tenants he lined up so that there would be no further rentals.

From the start, the UWM had been infiltrated by hard-core communists who saw it as an ideal platform for spreading their revolutionary ideology. At the same time, though, the new group attracted widespread sympathy from many rank-and-file union members who recognised that their leadership had failed in its duty of care to those hardest hit by the slump. The seeds of violent confrontation were sown in mid-1931 when the UWM began demanding the right to take its place within the Melbourne Trades Hall Council as an affiliated union in its own right. To keep their campaign bubbling along, UWM agitators filled the visitors' gallery during council meetings, interjecting and hurling abuse at the official delegates. The council, inevitably, decided to have the visitors' gallery closed altogether. On the evening of 10 September 1931, UWM members showed up anyway, prepared to mount a noisy demonstration and perhaps even force their way through an iron grille erected in front of the entrance. They were surprised by a strong contingent of police beating them back with batons swinging freely. Rumours quickly spread that Trades Hall itself had organised the ambush, arranging for the constabulary to wait in hiding within the building.

Police harassment of the unemployed – whether attacking their protest rallies or arresting them for vagrancy – emerged as one of the most explosive issues within the labour movement during the depression years. Militants had long accused the union hierarchy of failing to use its influence within the Parliamentary Labor Caucus to bring the police into line. Now, the confrontation at Melbourne Trades Hall seemed to confirm the worst. The bosses who controlled the union movement were no better than the capitalists: both were prepared to unleash the loathsome weapon of police repression to keep the hundreds of thousands of jobless from upsetting their comfortable little worlds.

Within the Labor Party itself, a conciliatory few – including Victorian State President Arthur Calwell – were prepared to acknowledge that the protesters had a valid point: they had 'not been given the sympathetic consideration that unemployed workers and their dependants have a right to expect'. However, the gap between the two sides only grew wider. The jobless, ever more desperate, kept escalating their demands for employed workers to support them in street marches and even general strikes to force governments to boost their benefits. The unionists, watching their numbers decrease month by month, were far more concerned with preserving their own wages and conditions. Whatever pressure they chose to put on ALP politicians would be strictly for their own benefit.

The polarisation within the labour movement could not have been demonstrated in more dramatic fashion than during Melbourne's traditional May Day marches. The Victorian Labor Party, along with the Trades Hall Council, had been in the habit of celebrating the occasion on the first Sunday in May. Communists and other factions of the far left preferred to stick to the letter of the law, marching with red flags flying on 1 May whatever day of the week that should be. In 1932, as it happened, 1 May fell on Sunday so for the first time in years the two warring factions – each followed by huge throngs – were destined to meet on the Yarra bank. Tempers quickly got out of hand with the more radical elements storming the official speakers' platform. They threw the President of the Trades Hall Council, F. J. Riley, to the ground and set upon the acting Labor premier, Thomas Tunnecliffe, inflicting a serious head wound.

Tunnecliffe, who had assumed the temporary leadership of the Labor government due to the prolonged illness of Edmund Hogan, had more to endure than a sore head that fateful month of May. Victorian Labor would be swept from office in a snap election brought on, in large part, by the sheer bloody-mindedness of those in control of the union movement. For months Trades Hall had been twisting the screws ever tighter on ALP politicians, demanding that they renounce the wage reductions and other cost-saving measures prescribed by the Premiers' Plan. Unlike Jack Lang, Edmond Hogan had reluctantly agreed to go along with the Plan on the basis that it was the only way for his state to gain access to the bank loans it desperately needed. He did his best to persuade the unions to accept short-term pain for long-term gain. As he warned them, his approach offered the only hope of Labor remaining in power in Victoria, especially since it needed the continued support of several moderate independents. The Victorian labour movement, however, obviously preferred to risk the despised Nationalists returning to power than to allow its own parliamentary wing to defy its wishes. The unions wielded tight control over the selection of ALP candidates and as early as February had warned that any sitting members who continued to support the Premiers' Plan would be expelled from the party. That included Hogan and most of his ministry. His temporary stand-in, Tunnecliffe, began to wither under the political heat, raising so many doubts about his intentions that the independents finally deserted him, setting the stage for a successful vote of no confidence. In the subsequent election it was virtually impossible for traditional Labor voters to know which candidates enjoyed official ALP endorsement and which, like Premier Edmond Hogan himself, had been declared pariahs. The final result was a fiasco. Hogan – recuperating on a visit to London – neatly summed up the consequences in a letter to one of his colleagues.

> The Melbourne Trades Hall atavists have at last done what I often forecast. They not only assassinated the Labor Government. They have reduced the Victorian Parliamentary Labor Party to an insignificant group consisting of a few members representing Melbourne industrial electorates who in future can talk as much flapdoodle as they like but who will be without any influence and will not be taken any notice of by the new Government.

In South Australia, Premier Lionel Hill found himself similarly undermined despite the courage he had shown in bringing in the first large-scale relief program for the state's unemployed. He and 22 of his loyal parliamentary colleagues were subjected to an extraordinary mass expulsion – stripped of their official ALP membership for persevering with the Premiers' Plan in defiance of Adelaide's Trades Hall. Hill, however, managed to cling to power by forging a new parliamentary alliance freeing him from further dependency on union support.

'The people of today care more about good Government than they do about party politics,' he confidently declared. 'The Plan must go on.'

South Australia, under Hill, actually took the lead among all states in meeting its harsh budget-cutting targets. It paid the price in terms of suffering the highest ratio of unemployed.

∽∾∽

Jack Lang's relationship with the unions was no less tempestuous. With the capitalist system in seeming disarray, the socialist left was enjoying an ideological resurgence, hounding him at party conferences to make nationalisation his number one priority. On the right, the powerful Australian Workers' Union, among others, still simmered over his betrayal of Jim Scullin and the federal ALP. Each end of the spectrum worked away like malicious elves, concocting secret plots to replace him. Lang, though, was a much tougher and more resourceful leader than either Hogan or Hill. He was the one national figure most closely identified with the cause of the working man and the struggle to maintain the hard-won Australian standard of living. Thus, when he occasionally bucked Trades Hall by implementing some of the budget cuts called for in the Premiers' Plan, the mainstream of the union movement could still feel sure he had their interests foremost in his mind.

Lang's Daniel-like success in keeping the lions at bay was all the more remarkable considering he had entered parliament with virtually no experience in the labyrinthine world of union politics. His career path had taken him through a placid period of bookkeeping into the real estate business. By temperament, he was actually repulsed by the idea of treating men as if they were all cut of the same cloth, with no encouragement for the more ambitious among them to forge ahead. His commitment to the Labor Party had nothing to do with socialist theories about oppressed masses and the evils of capitalism. He was concerned only with finding practical ways to ease the burden of the poor and allow every child a decent chance to get ahead in life.

'We were not interested in revolutions,' he said firmly, early in his ministerial career. 'All that we wanted was to give our people a brighter, happier life, and particularly a better standard of living, shorter hours and better opportunities.' And later, when militant socialists looked close to seizing control of the New South Wales Labor Party, he silenced them with a single line.

'The revolution *has* come . . . in the way the labour movement always said it would come, by Act of Parliament.'

That one sentence highlights perhaps the greatest paradox in the Big Fella's career. His conservative enemies refused to see that for all of Lang's apparent radicalism, he actually acted as a kind of escape valve, allowing the labour movement to control the explosive build-up of extremist sentiment generated by the Great Depression. If he came across as the most militant political leader in the land, he could still only be described as moderate compared to angry and frustrated workers who may well have chosen a more violent path without his strong voice to speak on their behalf.

The fact was that Lang had nothing but contempt for the communists. He saw them as deluded fanatics and spearheaded a successful campaign in the early 1920s to have them barred from Labor Party membership. In his rise to power, however, he did establish an extraordinary love–hate relationship with one of the left wing's most colourful and controversial union leaders. Scottish-born Jock Garden, as secretary of the Labor Council, was to become the Big Fella's most enthusiastic sponsor during tense Trades Hall debates. A former communist, he was a scrappy terrier of a union boss, constantly in trouble for his off-the-cuff revolutionary rhetoric which the anti-Labor press promptly headlined with delight. His gift for hyperbole would soar to its highest peak during a New South Wales Labor Party conference in which he was reported as declaring: 'Lang is greater than Lenin!' Those weren't exactly his words, but they were close enough to cause his champion added embarrassment at a time when he was wrongly being portrayed as a mere puppet of Moscow.

In the early 1920s Garden had actually been one of the founders of the Australian Communist Party and Lang's anti-communist crusade made the two implacable enemies. In politics, however, a few years can change anything. The irrepressible Garden eventually returned to the Labor fold, recognising the Big Fella — with his strong-willed leadership and powerful oratory — as the workers' best hope. Only through absolute allegiance to Lang, he insisted, could they last out the Great Depression with food in their bellies and a flame still alive in their souls.

Perhaps, then, he wasn't that far over the top when he rose to speak to his union comrades, heaping scorn on the left-wingers who complained so loudly about Lang's failure to launch a full-scale socialist revolution. For the record, this is what Garden actually said, pointing his figure derisively at the radical zealots.

'Our leader is ahead of the god they bow their knees to,' he chided them. 'Our [policy] goes further than the policy advocated by Lenin. Mr. Lang is the greatest leader the country has ever produced.'

The month of May would turn out to be every bit as memorable for Jock Garden as it was for the Big Fella, his one-time enemy and new-found hero.

20
Dirty tricks: The unmaking of the New Guard

Superintendent Billy Mackay was not about to let the New Guard forget the thumping his men meted out to them during the de Groot trial in early April. On the last Friday of that month he rubbed salt into their wounds by ordering a spectacular police parade through the very heart of the Sydney financial district, enemy territory as far as Jack Lang was concerned. Some 1700 officers – almost half of the entire New South Wales force – were called in from all parts of the state to stage an impressive show of force. If the Guard prided itself on its mobile strike force, Mackay showed he could more than match it with fleets of wireless cars and motorcycle units. The overall emphasis, though, was on sheer power with fifteen companies of constabulary marching eight abreast to the stirring chords of a bagpipe band and led by a contingent of war veterans proudly bedecked with their campaign ribbons. The Big Fella stood side by side with Governor Game to take the salute as large crowds shouted 'Lang is right,' 'good old Jack' and other supportive slogans. Despite a drenching rainstorm, the mood was cheerful and even Sir Philip was graciously given a hearty round of applause.

Mackay had personally organised the route to make sure the long line of marchers went past the Stock Exchange and leading business and investment houses as well as the Union Club, Australia Club and other establishment watering holes. 'We are going where the New Guard are to be found,' he confided, when he first informed the Premier of his plans for the unprecedented display. 'We are going to let them see what they are up against if they start any trouble.'

Like Lang, the superintendent was seriously concerned about the capacity of the militiamen to exploit the administrative chaos spawned by the various Enforcement Act decrees. With ready access to high-powered weapons and the training to use them, they were, as one of Mackay's top detectives would later testify in court, 'a body of men superior in strength to the combined military, naval and police forces in the whole of New South Wales'. Mackay, of course, realised that a mere parade could hardly be expected to deter such self-styled patriots for long, but he hoped it would at least buy him the few more days he needed. The crafty cop had a secret plan he was about to set in motion. It was so hush-hush not even the Premier knew anything about it, which was just as well because he could then disown it in all honesty if anything went wrong.

When Mackay returned to headquarters after the march that Friday, he was soaked to the skin but happy enough to allow himself a quiet chuckle. He had noticed Eric Campbell and Francis de Groot among the bystanders. He no doubt kept the image of their smirking faces firmly fixed in his mind as he clamped his meaty fist around a telephone and made the call that would wipe the smiles from their faces once and for all.

∽∘∾

Captain Walter Warneford was exactly the kind of recruit the New Guard was looking for – physically fit, well groomed and outspoken in his contempt for Lang and his gang of red rabble-rousers. He had served as an intelligence officer during the war and was a psychologist by training, which made him ideally suited to join the Guard's propaganda unit at General Headquarters. A major problem facing the militia was to make sure its members remained highly motivated despite long, dull periods of inactivity when it seemed they might never get a chance to strike a real blow against the communist foe. Warneford's expertise allowed him to come up with any number of interesting ideas for keeping a man inspired and dedicated to the cause.

Psychology, in the early 1930s, still carried a whiff of black magic around it – the possibility that just the right word or symbolic action could set off a chain reaction in the human brain that would make a man do anything. Warneford, a frequent visitor to the Guard's head office at Angel Place in the CBD, intrigued his listeners with tales of the instant success to be achieved through the latest techniques in mental manipulation. One of the cases he cited happened to be in the newspapers just around the time he volunteered his services in the autumn of 1932. It involved a war veteran who suffered from debilitating fits triggered by his memory of being buried alive by a shell burst. He had been unconscious at the time of his rescue and the psychiatric team treating him at Caulfield Military Hospital in Melbourne suspected that was the problem: deep in the back of his mind he was still terrified because he had no conscious memory of ever being saved. It was decided to put the patient to sleep under hypnosis, dig a trench in the hospital grounds and once again bury him alive. This time, however, when he was ordered to wake up he would immediately hear his rescuers digging to save him. From that moment on, Warneford boasted, the man was completely cured.

It was little wonder, then, that New Guard headquarters should allow the psychologist free access to its personnel records to see if there might be other cases to benefit from his special attention.

If Captain Warneford exhibited one all-too-obvious character defect, it was his tendency to become overly exuberant after a couple of drinks. That was the case on the Sunday afternoon following the big police parade when he joined a half-dozen of his New Guard colleagues for lunch in a flat at Kings Cross. He eventually pulled one of them aside for a quiet chat.

'Are you a communist?' he challenged.

'That's of no interest to you,' the man snapped, obviously taking umbrage.

'Well I have been told that you are bad friends with Jock Garden and I have a proposition to put to you,' Warneford continued. 'If the New Guard wants to get anywhere, the best thing is to clean up Garden for a start. Will you be in it if we get a team together and go out and clean up Garden altogether?'

'You're drunk,' the other man shrugged him off. In the next few days, however, the psychologist would provoke much more enthusiastic reactions from a number of other men whom he had singled out as keen to see some action. He was helped along by a glaring weakness in the Guard's otherwise tightly disciplined chain of command. Trusted officers were encouraged to use their own initiative in promoting activities in keeping with the organisation's broad strategic goals. While that kind of flexibility might be admirable in itself, it seemed almost foolhardy in view of another extraordinary quirk in the way some militia units chose to launch their operations. As a security precaution, orders were written on a blank sheet of foolscap paper without a signature or even an identification mark.

So it was that a 28-year-old mechanic named William Scott returned to his flat at Underwood Street in Paddington on the evening of Thursday, 5 May, to find a message under his door.

'Pick up car corner of Underwood and William streets between 11 and half-past,' read the simple instruction, written in pencil and unsigned. Scott had received similar notes before and following the standing orders, tore it up as soon as he memorised the contents. So, too, did seven other New Guard stalwarts. They would have had no idea who had actually issued their orders. Perhaps it was only coincidental that the mission came up not long after Captain Warneford was welcomed into the New Guard's upper echelons.

∽∞∽

At 1.45 on the morning of Friday, 6 May, Jock Garden was woken up by a loud knock at the front door of his modest home in the beachside suburb of Maroubra. 'Who's there?' he shouted. 'Police,' came the reply.

As Garden slipped on a robe over his pyjamas, he must have muttered to himself, what a mongrel of a start to a very special day. It happened to be his twenty-fifth wedding anniversary. He and his wife had planned to celebrate later on with their two grown sons and daughter who still lived in the house with them. Instead, he urged his wife to try to get back to sleep and made his way through the dimly lit hallway, opening the door to see four burly men in business suits and fedora hats.

'We are the wireless patrol,' one of them explained. 'We've

had reports of some suspicious characters lurking around here. It might be best if we looked through the house.'

From the outside the Garden home was as ordinary as a suburban Australian residence could be, with its squat Federation style of liver brick and orange-tiled roof. Inside, however, it took on a decidedly international ambience. In his days as a devout communist, Garden had visited Moscow to be granted a coveted audience with Lenin and a place of honour at a meeting of the revolutionary Comintern. He had any number of photographs to show for it, along with other exotic memorabilia which his unexpected guests were able to pick out as they shined a torch into the darkened lounge room. Considering who they were, it is doubtful they would have been all that impressed.

As they reached the back door Garden offered to unleash his guard dog.

'No, don't bother,' he was advised by one of his visitors. 'The dog could get injured.'

What the Labor Council secretary couldn't know was that four other men had already made their way around to the back of his house and were lurking there in the darkness. When he walked outside he was set upon from all directions, starting with a nasty crack from a spanner on the back of his head. Garden was not a big man but he had survived enough all-in brawls to know how to defend himself with fists and elbows pumping away.

'Help, they're on me!' he shouted to his sons. 'Let the dog loose.'

One son, Harcourt, rushed out but was immediately overpowered. When his brother Ian arrived soon after with a large dog flashing its fangs, seven of the attackers called a hasty retreat, fleeing over a fence. The eighth man, William Scott, got bitten on the hand and seemed temporarily flustered. He had been carrying a tyre lever, which one of the sons grabbed from him and used to whack him over the arm. He put up no more resistance and meekly allowed himself to be led off into the house. Mrs Garden and her daughter had both fainted in the excitement. However, when the mother recovered, she proceeded to wash and bandage Scott's injured hand and even give him a cup of tea.

'I'm a mug,' the young man told them. 'What will my family say? I am to be flung into a cell with crooks. This will break my mother's heart.' Scott insisted he had no idea what the mission was about until the very last minute. He found himself in a car with three men he had never seen before, followed by another car carrying four others. They remained silent through two hours of what seemed like aimless driving around. Only when his car pulled up in front of the Maroubra address was he told by a man in the front seat: 'The job is communists. Your job is to quieten the dog.' The man handed him the tyre lever, adding: 'If the dog makes any noise, hit him with this.'

Fortunately for Jock Garden's dog, just like its master it obviously knew how to handle itself in a brawl.

Garden offered to have one of his sons drive Scott back to his apartment in Paddington so long as the militiaman made a pledge of honour to turn up later that day to speak to detectives. That act of kindness would later fuel rumours that the assault was a set-up and Garden himself one of the conspirators. His gesture to Scott, however, was not out of keeping with his character. Before becoming a founding member of the Australian Communist Party he had served as an evangelical pastor. The reason he gave for eventually splitting from the party was its hostility to the Christian religion, with its message of forgiveness.

Colonel Eric Campbell would be quick to publicly deny any responsibility for the attack, which was to be expected, even if he had planned it himself. However, the fact that he went on to issue several different statements on the matter does seem to suggest he was caught on the hop and had no prior knowledge.

'It is ridiculous to try to make a movement of 100,000 men responsible for the independent action of a half a dozen,' he first contended. A day later he seemed to come closer to endorsing the exploit. 'It seems to me,' he told the press, 'that a number of decent and thoroughly loyal New Guardsmen set out to do a job on their own account, and which they considered highly desirable in the public interest. And if the squeals that rent the night air are any criterion, they apparently did it thoroughly.'

Finally, though, he threw himself wholeheartedly behind allegations that the entire episode was a frame-up. 'What first appeared to me to be the mistaken act of a few gay spirits acting independently is now showing itself to be something of a far more sinister nature,' he complained. 'It is unfortunate that some men of good repute were used as tools and were very cleverly tricked.'

William Scott, true to his promise, met with detectives and was the first to be placed under arrest on Friday afternoon. One of the investigators, Detective William Alford, would later tell the court a fascinating story of how he persuaded the Guardsman to break his code of silence and reveal the names of his seven accomplices. As the detective explained it, he didn't have to resort to any heavy-handed third-degree tactics. Instead, he simply set out to make Scott aware of what a dangerous organisation he had joined. For the first time, an outsider was allowed to see some of the alarming police intelligence reports relating to the plot to kidnap Jack Lang.

'We returned to the detective office where I showed him the secret reports,' Alford's sworn testimony began. His interrogation then proceeded along these lines.

'Now look, Scott, I am going to tell you certain things about the New Guard. Did you join to assist the police in maintaining law and order?'

'That's what the New Guard is for,' Scott was said to have replied.

'We know that the New Guard has departed from those principles, that they are themselves breaking the law,' Alford pressed on. 'On the third of March last, the Council of the New Guard decided to take action to throw armed battalions across the main approaches to the city. They intended to isolate Sydney and then to cut off the electric light from Bunnerong [power station] and throw the city into darkness. Then, under cover of darkness they intended to form up other armed forces in the city, overthrow Parliament and the Constitutional Government, take possession of all Government departments and set up a dictatorship.'

'That is what Eric Campbell had in mind,' Alford continued. 'If this plan had been carried into effect the lives of many innocent people would have been lost.'

'Is this all true?' Scott reportedly gasped. 'Are you sure of what you are talking about?'

'I am certain,' Alford assured him. 'We are in a position to prove what we say. And you, Scott, are in a position now to do what you intended to do when you joined the New Guard and that is to assist the police. We want the names of the other men.'

Alford's shock tactics clearly had the desired results. As he told the court, Scott was so stunned that he promptly made a full statement naming the seven others in his assault team, including its leader, John Dynon, a 27-year-old company director.

By Saturday morning all eight had been brought before a magistrate to be charged and released on bail. On Monday they each pleaded guilty and were sentenced to three months in prison. All but Scott were represented by lawyers appointed by the New Guard. By that time he had been denounced as an informer and expelled from the organisation.

If Scott's evidence about the Garden assault wasn't damaging enough, he created a minor sensation by claiming that he was actually a member of an elite cell within the New Guard chosen to perform the most sensitive kinds of cloak-and-dagger missions. This sanctum sanctorum was comprised of just 52 men, who worked under code names corresponding to the denominations of a deck of playing cards. So hush-hush was the group that its members even hid their identities from each other. They wore hoods and gowns like the Ku Klux Klan, except that their hoods were black. Scott was happy to show Alford his own black hood that he used at meetings. The name of this inner core caused as much of a stir as its mystical rituals. According to William Scott's sworn evidence, it was called the Fascist Legion.

The attack on a prominent union leader had given Billy Mackay all the excuse he needed to raid New Guard premises throughout the city, seizing files under a hastily arranged search warrant. The main office at Angel Place was hit early Saturday morning while the organisation's loudly protesting secretary was stripped of his keys and held under arrest. By Tuesday, the superintendent was in a position to release what he described as the first documented confirmation of the kidnap plan. He showed the press diagrams pinpointing a long-disused convict-built prison at Berrima, four hours' drive south of Sydney, as the fortress where Lang and key cabinet colleagues were to be held indefinitely. The historic landmark even had positions marked out for possible machine-gun emplacements to ward off attack from any direction. The confiscated papers also contained numerous references to various defence installations, military munitions depots and other places where rifles and other weapons could be readily obtained.

The Berrima Gaol document contained no reference to the broader coup plot described by Detective Alford but as part of a logical master plan it seemed to fit in perfectly. The kidnappings could be seen as the opening phase in a multi-pronged 'blitzkrieg' creating enough shock and confusion to put the Guard in control of the New South Wales capital. Presumably, it then expected to be able to rally enough public support to convince Sir Philip Game to formally dismiss the Lang Government and call for new elections.

Campbell immediately dismissed the documents as crude fakes and the whole Berrima Gaol scenario as a 'cock and bull story clumsily engineered'. The allegations about the Fascist Legion with its weird rites were probably even more damaging to the New Guard's image – and these he denounced with extra vehemence. Such mumbo jumbo, he insisted, was absolute anathema to any military man, and if the group existed at all, it could only have been part of a lunatic fringe. Allegations would soon appear in the press that Captain Warneford was behind the secret cell and that he had used Scott to help lure other gullible members. By that time, however, the blazing headlines had served to disillusion and alienate many of the New Guard's mainstream supporters.

Campbell was not without loyal allies in the New South Wales Parliament, and within a week of the Garden assault they launched an aggressive counteroffensive to try to salvage the organisation's tattered reputation. In one of the stormiest sessions of the year, they demanded a royal commission into the whole affair, naming Warneford as a highly paid spy in the service of the Lang Government. They also accused William Scott of being an undercover agent.

'This paid agent provocateur [Warneford] has, under Government instructions, set out to incite others to illegal and criminal actions,' claimed the Deputy Opposition Leader,

Reginald Weaver, in a speech that had the Lower House convulsing in uncontrollable uproar. He went on:

> Acting under instructions from the Government he has organised a group known as the Fascist Legion, without any authority from the New Guard. As a result of this agent provocateur's activities, an assault was committed upon Mr. Garden. The names and addresses of the members who would be used in the assault were in the hands of police two days before the assault occurred. It is clear, therefore, that certain police officers and others are guilty of a criminal conspiracy to implicate the leaders of the New Guard in a crime which the Ministers themselves and others inspired.

Lang and his key ministers promptly dismissed the allegations as sheer fantasy, insisting they had never heard of the so-called spies mentioned by Weaver.

'I deny it and my word is better than Reg Weaver's,' Lang interjected to hoots of laughter from his colleagues.

Superintendent Mackay no doubt had a laugh as well when he read of the Premier's remark in the afternoon papers. 'It's probably the one time in his life the sly old bastard was telling them the truth,' he may well have thought. During the course of the debate, no one dared suggest that Mackay himself might have had a hand in instigating any dirty tricks. He was much too popular a figure to have his formidable reputation as the state's best cop sullied in any way.

Undoubtedly the weakest link in the police case against the New Guard involved the testimony of the key witness, William Scott. During his trial on Monday, 9 May, he had sworn under oath that the seven accomplices who accompanied him to Garden's house were total strangers. 'I did not know any of the men and had never seen them before,' he told the magistrate. Yet, if he didn't know the others, how was he able to give Detective Alford their names and addresses on the Friday before the trial? Scott clearly perjured himself, which suggests that he may well have been an undercover agent or at the very least a paid informer, acting in cahoots with Captain Warneford to help lure gullible Guardsmen into what was probably an unauthorised secret cell conceived as a kind of mini-version of the Ku Klux Klan. If so, Detective Alford's testimony must also be considered suspect since he hardly would have needed to pressure the young man into confessing by 'shocking' him with details from confidential police intelligence reports.

As for Warneford himself, the mysterious psychologist would make the briefest of public appearances during a court case in June when those convicted of the Garden assault lodged an appeal against the severity of their three-month prison sentences. At that hearing, a barrister for the New Guard attempted to introduce witnesses prepared to swear that Warneford had tried to persuade them to join the raid on Garden's home. The presiding Judge Adrian Curlewis ruled such evidence to be inadmissible.

'I have heard of audacious defences in my time,' Curlewis reprimanded counsel, 'but never heard it said that a man was entitled to break into a house at 2 o'clock in the morning and commit an assault simply because someone else has suggested it.'

Warneford, however, was still called to the stand by the prosecution to show that he was a man of good character and had never specifically suggested that there should be an assault on Garden. During cross-examination he readily admitted his association with Mackay.

'Were you employed by police?' he was asked.

'Yes, I was on special work under Inspector Mackay.'

'In connection with what?'

'The New Guard Case.'

At this point in the examination, Judge Curlewis stepped in and Warneford would soon feel the sting of his scepticism.

Judge: Did you suggest to Mr. Purcell [a New Guard member] that some of the Reds should be dealt with?
Warneford: Yes.
Judge: How did you want the Reds dealt with?
Warneford: Not physically, mentally.
Judge: You mean you would make faces at them?
Warneford: No, I would deal with the Reds by reasoning with them.
Judge: I don't believe a word of it.

Yet that was the furthest Warneford was ever pressed about exactly what duties he performed for Mackay to earn his considerable fee of £6 ($420) a week from the New South Wales Police. Judge Curlewis cut his interrogation short and proceeded to reject the appeals of all but Scott, whose sentence he reduced by one month.

The episode effectively marked the beginning of the end for the New Guard, transformed in the public eye from a body of noble knights to a bunch of depression-era vigilantes. Did the formidable organisation bring such disgrace on itself or was it given a sneaky push in the wrong direction by Billy Mackay?

Such questions, as intriguing as they might be, were destined to remain unanswered – totally forgotten in the political explosion to follow.

21
The power of one

The besetting sin of the Australian of today is want of moral courage. They have placed physical courage and bodily strength on a pinnacle to the exclusion of moral courage.

So wrote Sir Philip Game in one of the perceptive pen portraits he sent off regularly to King George V. Game set out during his governorship to keep the monarch abreast not only of the latest political developments but to give him a good sense of what Australians were like in everyday life – their special qualities and endearing little foibles. Generally his informal letters to Buckingham Palace were filled with praise but as a trained observer he pulled no punches when he spotted a potential flaw.

The reason for the want of moral fibre is I think that governments of all descriptions have taken or accepted too much of the responsibilities which should rest on the individual. Child endowment, free education up to university, free hospitals, free institutions for troublesome children, in fact state aid of all kinds from birth to death, excellent though they may be in themselves, have so undermined private responsibility that the universal idea of anybody or everybody in trouble is to run to the government for help. So far they have had it. Now they can no longer get it, they neither understand or have the habit or the power to fend for themselves.

Game was usually astute in his assessments but he would soon learn how wrong he was in this particular rush to judgement. His letter was written before he ever heard of Robert Beardsmore, one of the ordinary Australians whose 'moral fibre' would be tested thread by thread in the tug of war between their state and their Commonwealth. On the surface Beardsmore might appear to be the very embodiment of the kind of irresolute character Game described to the King. He was a middle-aged accountant, part of an anonymous ant heap of public servants scribbling away in some obscure corner of a New South Wales Government office, bent over their desks as much to avoid eye contact as to add and subtract their sums, saying as little as possible amid the political storms raging around them lest they offend someone and lose their jobs. If ever a lack of rectitude could be considered excusable it surely must have been during the Great Depression when feeding one's family might easily be deemed a higher virtue than speaking one's mind. Yet Beardsmore would choose this crucial stage of history to stand up for what he believed was right. He would prove the rock of integrity on which the Lang juggernaut was finally to founder, though his story would not emerge until the dramatic finale of the Enforcement Act crisis.

Commonwealth decree number 42 cracked above the Big Fella's head like the horse whip he remembered as a kid – a humiliation too much to bear. Set to take effect on Friday, 6 May, the measure was ostensibly designed to extend the categories of revenue to be confiscated, ranging from drivers' licence fees to crown land sales. Its practical effect, though, was to commandeer the services of hundreds of New South Wales bureaucrats who happened to work in the targeted areas of administration. A bewildered public servant in the Department of Lands, for example, would have found himself trying to decipher a half-dozen lines of legalese that could mean the difference between going home to his family that night or spending the next three years in prison.

> Where any moneys from sale or lease of Crown Lands come into the hands of any officer or employee of the State of New South Wales, that officer or employee shall not pay those moneys to the Colonial Treasurer of the State of New South Wales, or in any other manner to the benefit of the said State, but shall not later than the second banking day of the receipt thereof, pay or transmit those moneys to the Commonwealth Bank of Australia, to the credit of the account called 'the Commonwealth Public Account – Financial Agreements Enforcement'.

The official was still on the New South Wales payroll, yet he now had to answer not to his premier but to the Prime Minister. Decree 42 effectively stripped Jack Lang of control of his state's public service.

The blow to the sovereignty of New South Wales was insult enough but the personal impact on Lang himself would unsettle him as nothing else before. Month after month he had lived with the threat of being summarily removed from power. Now the power was being removed from him. It is not difficult to imagine the frustration he felt – for a moment, perhaps, as overwhelmed as that little boy of long ago, cringing under the whip of the buggy driver, the contemptuous laughter of his persecutors ringing in his ears. Yet, the passing years had hardened him to disappointment and he would not allow himself to surrender to such a feeling of hopelessness for more than an instant. Lang, the boy, had been so consumed by shame and anger that his only escape was to collapse into a catatonic heap. Lang, the man, had long since learned to harness his rage and turn it to his advantage. Or so he liked to believe. The one certainty was that he would never again allow himself to bend to another lash.

How Lang decided upon his next move is a matter of pure speculation but the process may have taken shape much along these lines. He spent that weekend wielding his pen in a cold fury, ripping up draft after draft of a directive to be issued to all government departments as his reply to decree 42. As far as he was concerned, a thousand High Court judgements could never make such a monstrous injustice right. Not only were his public servants being ordered to betray their state but they were effectively robbing themselves of their own salaries by diverting the funds they collected to Canberra. How was he expected to pay them? His final draft was a perfect reflection of his troubled state of mind: 115 rambling words wrapped around the raw seed of a barely rational idea. It read in part:

> As forced labour without payment by the Authority who would use such forced labour, or in other words, slavery, has been abolished in the British Empire for over 100 years and as the first charge on revenue in every civilised community is the payment of those who collect the revenue for the Government, it is the decision of Cabinet for

the guidance of, and as an instruction to, all servants of the State and State Statutory Bodies, in order that the essential and social services of the State of New South Wales may be carried on, that the method of collecting revenue and paying same shall be as outlined in the Treasury Circular of 13 April . . .

And on it went to remind public servants of the strict orders that had been issued to them the previous month. Despite decree 42, they were to continue to refrain from writing or accepting cheques, doing business only in cash; and it remained their sworn duty to transfer such funds not to the Commonwealth but directly to the State Treasury in Macquarie Street.

The Big Fella, in the best of moods, rarely took his parliamentary colleagues into his confidence. In his eyes most of them were nothing more than self-serving connivers, interested only in feathering their nests or saving their skins. The long weeks of confrontation had seen him go further into his shell, refusing to share his thoughts even with his more senior ministers, though he invariably cloaked his personal initiatives in the guise of being Cabinet-approved. If he bothered at all to try to justify such autocratic conduct, it would be on the basis that a period of crisis was no time to be sitting around canvassing opinions or debating options. His job was to make the tough policy decisions, and theirs to follow.

When the Big Fella was at the top of his form, his one-man-band style of leadership worked well enough. No politician could match him in a tense bargaining situation. However, decision-making in such isolation also held inherent dangers. Even small mistakes, left unchecked, could balloon out of all proportion with disastrous consequences. The instruction the Premier drafted that weekend was hardly a *small* mistake. It was a clear incitement to the public servants of New South

Wales to violate the laws of the Commonwealth. Yet when he did show his masterwork to a few trusted advisers on Monday, there would be no one – having seen the smouldering look in his eye – who dared oppose him. Lang's defiant counter-decree would be circulated on Tuesday, 10 May under the signature of the Under-Secretary of the Premier's Department, C. H. Hay. It set him on a course fraught with so much danger that, in retrospect, it could only be described as a political version of Russian roulette.

On the Saturday when Lang first sat down to compose his diatribe, Gwendolen Game was also at her writing desk sending off a letter to her mother in England. As one tends to do when burdened with a heavy heart, she began on a lighter note, referring to the glorious May weather with its powder-blue skies and crisp, invigorating air.

'We rather need anything we can get to cheer us now, as things are pretty bad,' she confided. 'One can't see how they can go on much longer with the Federal Government starving out this State Government slowly. They think in about a fortnight things must come to a head and this will be the time Philip will have to step in.'

A few days earlier, she wrote that her husband had been put on the spot during a visit to the western wheat-belt town of Narromine, confronted by a typical outback bushie who refused to beat about the bush. 'When are you going to do something about this god-awful state of affairs,' he was asked in effect. Sir Philip, in his response, tried to be as straight-shooting as he possibly could.

'I agree that affairs are in a chaotic condition,' he admitted candidly, 'but as the country has had self-government for 75 years and the people have accepted the responsibilities of self-government, it is the duty of the people and not of the State Governor to find a way out of the trouble.'

Met with groans, if not jeers, Sir Philip offered one ray of hope. 'I will help as much as I can, however, to bring about a state of peace.'

Gwendolen worried herself sick about the pressure her husband was under, yet obviously remained proud of the stand he was taking in the crisis, no matter how unpopular. 'The abuse in the Press and the private and public letters written to or about him have been very trying, but still, he has the courage for anything. And he is on the watch for every movement from both sides, to be ready at any moment to step in firmly, and with decision.'

Considering what Jack Lang was up to at that moment, her last line could only be considered prophetic.

After 41 years in the public service and just three months short of his sixtieth birthday, Robert Henry Beardsmore had a right to think he was on the verge of a happy retirement. With his four children fully grown, his one remaining ambition was to do a bit of travelling with his wife, Ethel. Beardsmore considered himself good at his job but he could hardly say he loved it – thirteen years as an accountant in the Lands Department wasn't exactly the most exciting of careers. The uproar over the Enforcement Act was the last thing he needed at this stage of his life. All he wanted was to keep as low a profile as possible until the day the Under-Secretary of the Lands Department, James Herlihy, made a nice speech and waved him goodbye. Perhaps his minister, John Tully, might even deign to drop by for the occasion to present him with his gold watch.

The accountant didn't see it as his place to take sides in the unseemly battle between Jack Lang and Joe Lyons. His role was to balance the books, not to debate the rights or wrongs of how the money should be spent. The directive from Treasury in April requiring all transactions to be carried out in cash created an administrative nightmare for him, but nothing he couldn't handle. The subsequent Commonwealth decree 42 caused an even bigger stir within the department but actually ended up making his job a lot easier because it meant he could start accepting cheques again, though on behalf of a different government. On Tuesday, 10 May, however, Robert Beardsmore's insular world of mathematical certainties was smashed to smithereens by Jack Lang's rebellious proclamation. A man who prided himself on following orders to the letter was now confronted with two conflicting sets. Disobeying one posed the very real threat of instant dismissal and loss of his precious pension. Disobeying the other could land him in jail.

Like so many of his colleagues that fateful afternoon, Beardsmore put the two directives side by side on the top of his desk, reading one and then the other over and over. Their response would be very different to his. They decided en masse that their safest choice was to do absolutely nothing, merely allowing the paperwork to pile up over the next few days while the warring politicians hopefully came up with some solution. Paper-shuffling and pigeonholing were hardly an unknown art within the bureaucracy and in this case they worked wonders. The Lyons Government would later have to admit that a full week after the publication of decree 42, not one extra penny had been received from the New South Wales Public Service as a result.

Beardsmore, though, was not the kind of man to take such an easy way out of a personal dilemma. Though his years in the public service had tamed him considerably, there was still a hidden side to his persona that his workmates could never imagine. He was a war veteran, but of a very special breed of soldier. Already a champion marksman before he entered the service, he was naturally drawn to the most cold-blooded and obsessive of all military pursuits – the role of the sniper. The classic sniper searched out his target knowing all the while that in the exact moment he shoots to kill, he leaves himself exposed and vulnerable. By temperament he was someone prepared to follow his gut instinct and pull the trigger regardless of consequences. In 1916 Beardsmore was awarded the Distinguished Service Order for his 'great coolness and courage' during combat in France. Sixteen years later, in the twilight of his career, he would decide he had no choice but to pull the trigger one more time. When he sent off his note to the Under-Secretary, Mr Herlihy, it might seem that he was acting out of some profound sense of morality. More likely, he was simply following a deep-seated compulsion to call the shots as he saw them and say what needed to be said.

> Placed in a very difficult position, in which loyalty to the State conflicts with my obligation to obey the law, my clear duty, as I conceive it, is to obey that law and pay any moneys in the manner directed by the Proclamation.
> R. H. Beardsmore
> Accountant, 11 May, 1932.

Without waiting for his superior's reply, Beardsmore gave instructions to the department's clerical staff to start processing all relevant revenues in favour of the Commonwealth in accordance with decree 42. His order was immediately countermanded and he was soon called into the Under-Secretary's office. Beardsmore, as a dedicated public servant, would later refuse all comment to the press, but the conversation presumably proceeded along these lines.

Herlihy: Perhaps it's best if you took immediate leave.

Beardsmore: I don't want any leave. I'm quite happy to stay here.
Herlihy: I'm afraid that's not a suggestion, that's an order.
Beardsmore: From whom?
Herlihy: From the Minister, Mr Tully.
Beardsmore: Then let him put it in writing.

When the written confirmation was duly handed to him on Thursday, 12 May, he had no choice but to walk out the door of the building where he had served since returning from the Western Front. He had been wounded in the course of battle there but as his citation read, 'proceeded without waiting to have his wounds dressed' and remained on duty for another ten hours. Any pain he suffered then was nothing compared to what he was faced with now, having to go home to tell Ethel, his wife of 30 years, that he could lose his pension.

Robert Beardsmore, though, wasn't quite finished. He had the Big Fella himself lined up in his crosshairs.

22

The longest day of the year

If Lang's illegal directive was a roar of defiance, he would follow it up a day later by introducing a piece of legislation so outrageous that it could only be considered an Act of Spite rather than a legitimate bill – an attempt to single out and punish his chief tormentors within the business community. Under his proposed law the state would impose a flat tax on all mortgages amounting to 10 per cent of the value of the loan. If that were not shock enough, each mortgagee would have to come up with the money within two weeks or face a doubling of the penalty. A default exposed him to having his rights over the property seized altogether by the Crown.

While the bill theoretically applied to tens of thousands of small investors who might have only a few hundred pounds on loan, discretion was given to the Treasurer – Lang himself – to grant exceptions to their liability. The main targets were clearly the banks and insurance companies which held mortgages totalling in the tens of millions of pounds. By the Premier's own estimate, such institutions would have to cough up some

£7 million, nearly $500 million, within a fortnight. That was enough to pay off all debts and free New South Wales from the 'crippling embargo' of the federal government.

'The bill will effect a remedy for many of our difficulties and meet the unenviable position in which the Mother State of the Commonwealth has been placed by the Federal Financial Agreements Enforcement Act,' Lang told the Lower House amid tumult bordering on bedlam. 'A feature of the tax is that it is not an impost upon industry, but is in the nature of a levy on the wealthiest section of the community . . .'

He paused for a moment, amid angry interjections of 'robbery', to give all the more impact to his next satirical thrust.

'They are a section,' he added, 'which should not hesitate to exhibit a little patriotism by making a reasonable contribution towards the rehabilitation of the State to which they, as mortgagees, are largely indebted for their accumulation of capital. It is not asking much, after all.'

Howls of outrage contended with gales of laughter, like baboons shrieking at hyenas. Lang took great delight in the uproar as a measure of just how much the defenders of big business were hurting. He knew that one of the insurance companies affected derived 60 per cent of its income from the mortgages it held over private property. It alone would have to find a quick £5 million ($350 million) in cash, which almost certainly meant being forced to engage in a massive fire sale of its securities in the depths of the depression.

Indeed, the end result of the Mortgages Taxation Bill, as it was formally known, was likely to be so disruptive that some couldn't believe Lang was really serious about intending to enforce it. Perhaps it was merely a negotiating ploy – an attempt to give such a fright to the nation's most powerful financiers that they would plead with Joe Lyons to back off from his proclamations and work out some sort of honourable compromise. The Premier could count on speeding the bill through the Legislative Assembly – his solid majority would see it passed on the same day it was presented. The chance of it clearing the Upper House, even with the extra Lang appointees, was much less certain. After that hurdle, there was still the question of whether Governor Game would agree to sign it into law.

Lang surely realised the odds were against his measure surviving to produce a penny of new revenue. He may well have seen it more as a symbolic gesture – a rallying cry to his supporters, paving the way for an early election. For the banks and insurance companies the tax bill might be a confiscatory nightmare but for the common people it could easily be portrayed as their one hope of economic salvation. Certainly in the course of presenting the various provisions the Premier spoke as if he were already on the hustings. His bombshell directive of Tuesday, 10 May, turned out to be a mere preamble to the declaration of independence he delivered to parliament on Wednesday in defence of his new legislation – though once again, his reasoning seemed disordered and his analogies far-fetched. For some reason he chose to ramble on about the Franco–Prussian war of 1870–71, hardly of relevance to an Australian audience. It was as if the sulfuric fumes of his suppressed fury distorted a vision that was normally so sharp and clear.

'When the war between Prussia and France ended, the French authorities sent out an appeal to the people to surrender all their gold to the authorities so that the invader whose heel was crushing the nation could be paid out,' he lectured the House. 'Like France, New South Wales has been invaded by neighbouring states. Only one of two courses can be taken with an invader – he must be either paid out or thrown out. I ask Parliament to pass this bill so we may first of all try the method of paying them out.'

Paid out or thrown out. In three months of rapidly escalating tensions, that was the closest Jack Lang himself had ever come to suggesting – by inference – that outright civil war remained a very real option for Australia's most populous state. Even the most rabid of the interjectors fell silent as the Big Fella shook his fist menacingly to return to the theme that had started this conflict in the first place.

'Not all the High Courts in Australia can compel the Government of New South Wales to rob its own people to pay foreign bondholders,' he proclaimed in a voice quivering with indignation.

The pledge brought loud cheers from the ministers seated behind him, but even they must have felt shaken inside. They were as ignorant of Lang's real intentions as the lowliest backbencher. If his rebellious edict or even his diabolical new tax had been mentioned to them at all, it would only have been in the most perfunctory way. Clearly they had no choice but to follow him, right or wrong, but where exactly was he planning to lead them next? To an election? To war? To oblivion?

It would be the longest 48 hours of their political lives. After the Mortgages Taxation Bill was passed by the Lower House, they had to stand by waiting nervously while it was subjected to a predictably fiery debate in the Legislative Council. Through the early morning hours of Friday, 13 May, the Council conservatives fought a bitter rearguard action – as well they might, for some of them actually held directorships of the companies worst affected. This time, though, the conservatives were at a distinct disadvantage. The chamber was well populated with elderly, ill or uncommitted hangers-on in no mood to see in the sunrise. Many of them were easily lulled into thinking their vote didn't really matter all that much since the bill was almost certain to be declared invalid, either by the Governor, the federal government or the courts. At 6.23 am on

Friday, 13 May, the Upper House adjourned with the bill approved by 47 votes to 38, a majority of nine. It was then returned to the Legislative Assembly where Lang stood by, happy to accept a number of minor amendments. The Lower House adjourned at 6.45 am, with the new act ready to be sent on to Government House for royal assent. Lang was too hypertense to bother trying to get some sleep, which was just as well since for him, the fateful day of Friday the thirteenth was still far from over.

Sir Philip Game must also have endured many agonising hours during the course of the mortgage debate and one might reconstruct a scene like this from snippets of later correspondence. It is Thursday, 12 May, and the Governor sits brooding in his study, hoping – perhaps even praying – that the bill will be defeated in the Upper House. If it isn't, then he can only blame himself for having given in and allowed Lang to stack the chamber with his own appointees. Worse still, Game knows that despite his grave misgivings, once the bill lawfully passes through both Houses of the New South Wales Parliament, he really has no choice but to allow the people's representatives to vent their will. He would have to put his signature to the most dreadful piece of legislation he has ever seen.

As the hours tick by he rereads some of the more extreme provisions, his head pounding beyond the relief of an extra pain-killing injection. Under Clause 11, non-payment of the tax within fourteen days meant the state could take over the title deed 'absolutely freed and discharged' from all fees or liabilities. Clause 14 gave the state the right to sell or otherwise assign the confiscated mortgage 'in any manner' it saw fit. If the owners of a mortgage were absent from the state – as could well be the case with major English-owned stock and station agencies like Dalgety's – the attorneys or estate agents representing such interests 'shall be personally responsible for the payment of the tax'. Clause 25 provided the most pernicious power of all.

> Any person authorised by the Colonial Treasurer may enter, by force if such person thinks necessary, and search any place, building, premises, or receptacle which may reasonably be suspected to contain any title or other documents relating to a mortgage or to any property subject thereto, or any evidences of the amount secured by a mortgage, and such person may seize the possession of and remove all such documents and evidences found in any place, building, premises or receptacle.

The new law would not only override the time-honoured principle of protection against search and seizure without specific warrant from the courts but would even make it a crime for a home-owner to try to resist such an intrusion.

> Any person who in any way obstructs or hinders any person acting or purporting to act under this section shall be guilty of an offence and liable on summary conviction to a penalty of not less than £10 [$700] and not more than £1000 [$70,000] and imprisonment for 12 months.

The ultimate irony of the legislation was that many of its more punitive provisions were framed in much the same language as the Enforcement Act itself. Lang, during his speech to parliament, was happy to admit his intention to copy the federal statute that had caused him so much grief.

'The remaining provisions are analogous to those of the

Commonwealth Financial Agreements Enforcement Act and are incorporated in the bill to ensure the carrying out of the various clauses,' he confirmed.

'Imitation is the sincerest form of flattery,' an Opposition member jibed.

'Yes, that is so,' the Premier agreed.

Clause 28 was a perfect model of the pre-emptive mechanism that had allowed the federal government to claim prior right to revenue otherwise due to the state. The tax on mortgages took first priority over all other claims, prohibiting any payments being made to a mortgagee until his tax obligation was fully met. A lender was also prevented from trying to pass on the tax to his mortgagor.

May was a fateful month for Sir Philip. He had arrived in Sydney on the twenty-ninth of May, 1930, and in the nearly two years of his tenure had never faced a more depressing task than to sign this odious levy into law. He had been able to cope with all the abuse and insults people could throw at him but now, for the first time, he was in danger of being crushed by the burden of his own self-doubt. Perhaps his critics were right after all when they attacked him for his indecision. Could it be that he had no true vision of what his duty really was – that all the reasons he gave to himself for his delay in sacking Lang had merely been an excuse for his own moral weakness? Possibly never, in those two turbulent years, had he been so close to cabling to his King and resigning his commission.

Game – so deep in his thoughts – would hardly have noticed Micky nudging him to go out for an afternoon walk. The dog had long ago given up begging and was asleep at his master's feet, his muzzle resting on a shoe. At a quiet knock, though, the animal would have roused itself and looked on as Turner, the butler, slipped into the room and handed the Governor an envelope addressed for his urgent attention.

The letter was from Robert Beardsmore, the one public servant among thousands who had been prepared to stand up and denounce the Lang proclamation of 10 May for what it was – a direct command to disobey Commonwealth laws. Though sent away on enforced leave, his career hanging by a thread, he obviously was not prepared to let the matter rest. His first duty was to follow his conscience – and that led directly to the Governor of New South Wales, the one person who could be trusted to protect the welfare of all the citizens, not just a self-interested few.

For Sir Philip, having the Beardsmore file land on his desk so unexpectedly that gloomy Thursday must have seemed like an answer to a prayer. There were two documents to grab his attention – not only a copy of the public servant's courageous protest, but the subsequent signed directive from his minister ordering him to take immediate involuntary leave. As Game studied one, and then the other, he may well have had to stop Micky from jumping all over him. The dog would have sensed his growing excitement.

23

Legal pornography: Field v Field

'You dirty, bloody slut – get out of this bloody house before I break your bloody neck!'

So began the longest and most expensive divorce case ever heard in an Australian court. The fact that it was played out amid the grinding hardships of the Great Depression is bizarre enough. That it should coincide with the bitter split between the Commonwealth and its premier state is almost high farce – a parody of what can happen when pride prevails over commonsense.

Sidney Field, like Anthony Hordern, was one of the kingpins of the business world, made immensely wealthy through family interests in the meat trade – both wholesale and retail – as well as extensive pastoral holdings. He and his wife Ivy, a svelte brunette, had always been regarded as a standout couple among Sydney's social elite, known for their lively entertaining whether at their mansion near Waverley Park in the eastern suburbs, their holiday cottage at Palm Beach, or their country estate at Bowral in the southern highlands. They were always around to share a champagne toast or two at the more glamorous race meetings, with Ivy wearing the very latest of imported fashion sure to turn heads. She was Sidney's second wife – they had married just before the end of the war – and as far as their friends could see, he positively adored her, showering her with expensive jewels and furs.

Obviously, though, when the last party guest bid them farewell in the early morning hours, unspeakable things transpired. Ivy fled Merrowie, their marital home, on 30 April 1931 – allegedly driven away by her husband's 'dreadful, degrading and humiliating' abuse, a verbatim sample of which begins this chapter. She filed for divorce a few days later, submitting an affidavit to the court filled with sensational allegations. Sidney's violent temper, she claimed, was the least of the indignities she endured over many years. Sometimes she saw him brazenly dancing with their maid Jenny and pawing at her, even around the dinner table. He frequently goaded her about his interest in other women, referring to various parts of their anatomy and speculating about whether they would 'make a good naughty'. Ivy herself had been forced to indulge him in a sexual act so disgusting that it could only be described in whispered French and which even the judge would later agree was 'of such a revolting nature that it is difficult to believe any self-respecting woman would have submitted for so long to it'. The last straw, she claimed, was Sidney's persistent adultery with a woman she named as Clare 'Girlie' Wilson, herself a married woman.

Ivy Gladys Field's divorce action against Sidney John Field rivalled the Enforcement Act saga for its blazing headlines and reached its dramatic conclusion around the same time, almost a full year after it began. Altogether the case consumed 87 days of court hearings, featured 104 witnesses, and piled up legal costs estimated at close to £35,000 ($2.45 million) – enough to keep 1250 men on the dole for a full year. Each party was represented by the most eminent of King's Counsels and in their final summing-up alone, the barristers set all-time records. Richard Windeyer, representing the aggrieved Mrs Field, proved the windiest. As one newspaper noted, either with tongue in cheek or blissful naiveté, he spoke on her behalf for precisely 69 hours.

Divorce proceedings like the Fields' were the legalised pornography of the era, eagerly followed by all sections of the community, each relating in their own vicarious way. Tilly Devine's girls might giggle among themselves, 'Oh, no, she didn't let him do *that* to her, did she?' For shocked north shore matrons the talking point might shift focus to the husband's having the gall to dance with the maid.

A number of factors conspired to make the 1920s and early 1930s the exuberant heyday of divorce court reporting. The divorce laws actively encouraged full-scale combat between estranged partners by requiring that a specific cause be stated and proved in open trial – it was not enough simply to be incompatible or in love with someone else. In the wife's case, the more common grounds were adultery, including incestuous adultery, rape, sodomy or drunken and cruel behaviour. A husband might claim adultery, drunkenness coupled with neglect of domestic duties, or desertion over three years or more. In the case of adultery, the accused lover or lovers could be and often were named to appear as co-respondents and faced the possibility of having to pay a hefty damages award to the injured partner. At the very least they were likely to find themselves hounded by the press and their photos splashed under titillating headlines.

While it would be rash to suggest that couples in this era were any more prone to adulterous affairs, extramarital sex was certainly being discussed more openly than ever before. Women of Ivy Field's age, in the ripeness of their thirties, had been the emancipated young flappers of the free-wheeling 'Roaring Twenties' following on from World War I. If most were eventually happy to settle down again into sedate respectability, there were still plenty who refused to accept the same subservient fate of their mothers, trading independence for security. Instead they continued to see themselves as free spirits even if that should mean nothing more than carrying on a little flirtation here or there to add some spice to their lives. The new wave of American and British talkie films inspired adventurous attitudes toward romantic involvement and in Australia, the upmarket *Smith's Weekly* contributed to the theme with its avant-garde cartoons depicting the modern female as brazenly blasé about her love life.

'What made you divorce your first husband?' a well-dressed flapper is asked. 'My second,' she replies breezily. 'I married for love,' one girlfriend tells another. 'And I'm going to keep on marrying until I get it.' Even children are portrayed as having a more cynical attitude toward the sanctity of marriage. When a primary school class is asked who most benefited under the reign of King Henry VIII a bright spark volunteers: 'The divorce lawyers.'

Such pinpricks, while hardly enough to deflate the pomposity of the reigning prudes, did at least signal the emergence of a rebellious minority prepared to risk scandal for the right to follow their natural impulses. In that they were helped along no end by the advent of the motor car, so easily adapted as a cosy love nest on wheels. 'Were you very thrilled when he invited you to go for a drive in his new car?' one *Smith's Weekly* sophisticate prods her friend. 'Yes, I was carried away.'

Yet if there was a 'fast set' of any significant proportion they certainly had their work cut out for them trying to make headway against the oppressive conformity that still permeated every facet of Australian life. Censorship remained so strict that at one point British movie producers filed a formal protest against the overzealous snipping of their films. The pioneer Australian filmmaker, Charles Chauvel, almost had his *In the Wake of the Bounty* suppressed before it had hardly begun. During 1932 he was filming on location in Tahiti when Australian customs officials declared that the rushes he was sending back for processing were a prohibited import, presumably because of occasional glimpses of bare Polynesian breasts. Chauvel finally convinced them to hold off their censorship until he at least had had a chance to edit his film back in Sydney's Cinesound studios. Just as well he did or his newly discovered leading man – a dashing young yachtsman named Errol Flynn – might never have gone on to Hollywood stardom. The puritanical censorship laws help explain why divorce reports were read with such prurient interest.

Sydney, as might be expected, had by far the highest divorce rate in the country, some 1600 petitions a year, or two and a half times the per capita rate in Melbourne. In 1931 Victoria broke ranks with New South Wales and legislated to ban publication of evidence in divorce cases other than the names of the parties, a concise summary of the reasons for the petition and the judge's summing-up. The move, though it might sound progressive, was highly controversial, with some churchmen warning it could only lead to a sharp increase in marital break-ups. Couples, no longer fearing bad publicity, would take the easy way out and divorce simply because they were unhappy. That, at least, was the argument used in New South Wales to continue allowing the press to exploit cases like the Fields' for all they were worth.

By the time the hearing got under way Sidney Field was already reluctantly paying Ivy £50 a week ($3500) in alimony, equivalent to the weekly allowance she had been receiving before the court action. She demanded twice that much for a permanent settlement, while he was hoping to cut it by half. If the business magnate sat quietly by and allowed her to win her suit, he opened the way for her to be awarded a ruinous punitive verdict. Under the combative divorce laws, a husband in his position had only two possible lines of defence. He could dispute his wife's accusations, trying to establish his innocence, or more aggressively, he could set out to try to prove that she herself was guilty of adulterous conduct, thus nullifying her grounds for damages.

Field's pricey legal team proceeded on the dictum that the best defence was a good offence. They accused Ivy of carrying on affairs with three different lovers whom they subpoenaed to appear as co-respondents. Like Sidney's alleged girlfriend Clare Wilson, the three unfortunate men would also be grilled to a frazzle under cross-examination.

If any single element served to highlight the sheer absurdity of the Divorce Act, it was the ease with which third parties could be dragged into court to find their reputations – if not their own marriages – destroyed in an instant on the basis of wholly unsubstantiated allegations. Those so named often had to go to the trouble and expense of hiring their own lawyers and were subject to having their most intimate secrets exposed to public scrutiny. It was an unjust anomaly under any circumstances but to have one's life so disrupted in the midst of a job-threatening economic slump was nothing short of cruel. The three co-respondents accused by Sidney Field of being his wife's lovers made that clear enough when they wrote to the court pleading – unsuccessfully, as it turned out – to be excused from having to appear to testify.

Hollis Bush, a travelling salesman living in Melbourne, sent this plea to the court through his Sydney lawyer in early February:

> I have a fixed itinerary for my employers and I am certain if this itinerary is broken and I am compelled to come to Sydney, I will lose my position; and as you know, positions are pretty hard to get these days and I have got my wife and mother to think about besides myself. I can't help thinking how extraordinary it is that I should be brought into such a big case and incur so much expense for barristers and solicitors, with all due respect to you, and that there should be such little evidence of an incriminating nature against me.

Victor Bray, an officer with the Commonwealth Navigation Department in Brisbane, similarly tried to beg off appearing.

> I am a man of limited means. At the present time, owing to retrenchments in the Commonwealth Navigation Department, it would be practically impossible to obtain the services of an Examiner of Masters and Mates to relieve me of my duties. The said department would view my absence with strong disfavour and possibly the only course open to me would be to resign from the service and in all probability, in view of the present economic situation, I would not be able to re-enter the service.

Ivy's third alleged lover, Ronald Nott, a leading silk importer, was obviously in much better financial circumstances though he, too, was most anxious to get out of his subpoena. 'I should proceed to Paris as early as possible in order to buy goods for the next Australian winter season,' he explained.

Clare 'Girlie' Wilson, for her part, asked only for a bit of understanding of what a devastating impact the case of Field versus Field was having on her life. 'Since the petition was served on me, I have been suffering from ill health and worry,' she wrote to the court, 'and have not been able to carry on my usual business. I am being put to considerable expense and trouble and the continued delay [in hearings] is affecting the health and business of my husband.'

While the four outsiders would be subjected to withering interrogation, Ivy Field herself went through nothing less than a Spanish Inquisition, a full 120 hours stretched to breaking point on the verbal rack of the witness stand. Apart from her three alleged affairs, her husband accused her of being an 'immoral woman' even before they married. Her background as a product of working-class Redfern was treated almost as proof in itself. Sidney had employed two well-known KCs to take turns in hammering her. The Chief Judge in Divorce, Langer Owen – the same judge who had exploded over the disappearance of alimony money in April due to the Enforcement Act – later went out of his way to praise her coolness under fire just before he delivered his verdict in May. 'A type of woman uncommon to most judges – a woman with an iron nerve,' he observed. That, however, was not a character trait that would necessarily turn out to be in her favour.

It did not go unnoticed that Ivy Field, in the first twenty days of the hearing, showed up in fifteen different dresses, all of them of the most expensive quality. Indeed, the keystone of her petition was to convince the court that as the wife of a prominent and wealthy business executive she had grown used to the most luxurious of lifestyles. It had been her wifely duty to be a showpiece symbolising Sidney Field's successful career and it was only fair that her alimony award be enough to maintain her in the manner to which she was accustomed. To prove her case she submitted a sworn affidavit containing truly extraordinary revelations of how the 'other half' lived in the midst of the Great Depression.

'I have no income from any source whatsoever,' she began,

meaning outside whatever alimony her ex-husband would be required to give. She listed her assets as follows:

- One Dodge motor car valued at £600 [$42,000].
- Furniture at present in my apartment valued at £200 [$14,000].
- Furniture at Palm Beach home to the value of £400 [$28,000].
- House at Palm Beach which is being purchased for £2750 [$192,500].
- Additions to that house worth £600 [$42,000].
- Certain articles of jewellery insured for £1900 [$133,000].

Ivy went on to reveal the kind of money she was used to spending on her wardrobe, in order to meet the high standards Sidney had always required of her. In her affidavit he is referred to as the Respondent.

> It was necessary for me to dress well and the Respondent was quite satisfied for me to pay £75 [$5250] for frocks as it was necessary for the wife of a man in his position to be suitably clad. Each race meeting, with the Respondent's knowledge, I would spend in the vicinity of about £400 [$28,000] at the furriers alone. I always wear the best of American shoes and stockings and would pay up to £8/8 [$588] for shoes.

'I wear the best of underclothing in uniform with the frocks worn by me,' she added, though perhaps that went without saying.

Ivy also noted that Sidney, on his own initiative, might buy her the occasional fur coat valued at £600 ($42,000) or so. In addition to her weekly allowance of £50 ($3500), he frequently topped up her personal bank account on the numerous occasions it was overdrawn. 'The Respondent has deposited to my account in each year (with the exception of when we were abroad) annual amounts varying up to five thousand £5000 [$350,000],' she noted. For all those reasons she felt entitled to 'respectfully ask this honourable Court to make an order for alimony at the rate of £100 [$7000] a week'.

That was exactly four times more than what Sidney Field thought she deserved, so it was little wonder, then, that his lawyers should set out to destroy Ivy Field's credibility in any way they could. As the hearing progressed it became apparent that Judge Owen was less than impressed with their allegations against two of the co-respondents they had cited, the salesman, Hollis Bush, and the navigation officer, Victor Bray. However, they seemed to be on much more fertile ground with the dirt they had on the suave silk merchant, Ronald Nott. He had been accepted into Sidney and Ivy's close circle of friends and was sometimes invited to sleep over at their Palm Beach holiday cottage. The Fields' servants noted that they had once seen Nott sitting in his pyjamas on Ivy's bed having morning tea. Nott's barrister triggered titters through the packed courtroom when he insisted that the incident could only be considered entirely innocent considering where it happened – in one of high society's favourite haunts.

'In regard to this business of seeing a man going in his pyjamas to a woman's bedroom,' the lawyer began, 'one has to remember that people at Palm Beach take a different view of these matters. If that happened in a city hotel you might draw some inference against the parties, but that inference cannot be drawn from people having morning tea in a bedroom with the windows open at Palm Beach. It would be too absurd for words. People do things at Palm Beach they would not do in their own homes.'

That, however, would turn out to be the mere tip of an iceberg in terms of the startling number of assignations which Ivy and Nott were accused of having during a two-year fling that allegedly extended right up to the time she filed for divorce. Details of their adulterous misbehaviour were so specific as to include not only the venue of their lovemaking but in some instances the hour of the day. Ivy clearly had a job on her hands trying to explain away a record of dangerous liaisons as long as this:

> At Merrowie, Birrell Street, Waverley on 3 October 1929, between the hours of 4 pm and 6 pm; as above one Monday morning between 13 October and middle of November, 1929, between the hours of 7:15 am and 8:30 am; as above frequently at various times between 3 February 1930 and 15 March, 1930; at Doctor Bullmore's Palm Beach house on 4 October between 2 pm and 5 pm; as above 13 October 1929, between 2 pm and 6 pm; Portland Street, Rose Bay, frequently between middle September, 1930, and the date of the petition, during the day time and more particularly on or about Monday, 15 December, 1930, during the daytime.

Sidney's lawyers, meticulous as they appeared to be in their investigations, took pains to point out that their client 'does not confine his allegations in any of the above charges to any particular part of the house but especially the bedrooms'.

The Portland Street venue would turn out to be the one that brought Ivy Field and her lover unstuck. Ivy would go there frequently, supposedly to consult with a palm reader. Her fate line, it seems, always predicted the same future and that future always came true. Ronald Nott would be there waiting for her, in a room set aside just for them.

The hearing may have been notable for its exceptional length and expense but it was otherwise quite typical both in terms of the bitterness it engendered and the destructive impact of the sensational press coverage on all concerned. The fact that it reached its conclusion in early May, 1932 – at the height of the worst economic and political crises ever to befall the Federation – serves all the better to keep things in their true perspective. The most truly shocking obscenity exposed by the case of Field versus Field had nothing to do with sex. It was that a fortunate few should wind up with more wealth than they could possibly know what to do with while so many others undeservedly suffered in such desperate need.

In the end Justice Owen would be left to ponder some three million words of testimony. 'I can't see that there is any evidence of adultery as far as Bray and Mrs. Field are concerned,' he concluded. 'The case against Bush appears weaker still.' He dismissed the allegations against them and ordered Sidney Field to pay their court costs. Similarly, he found that Mrs. Field had failed to back up her allegations against Clare 'Girlie' Wilson and would thus be responsible for paying all of Mrs. Wilson's costs.

As for Ivy Field herself, the 'iron nerve' which the judge had noted ultimately worked against her. The calm resolve she had displayed under hours of intensive attack on the witness stand was merely interpreted as suggesting she was something of an actress.

'She is an extravagant woman,' the judge noted, 'but not withstanding Field appeared to be very proud of her.' She was also 'clever' and 'attractive,' though that attractiveness, said the judge, was where the trouble started. Ronald Nott had become a frequent guest at the Field household mainly because of his interest in Ivy and there had been an increasing and dangerous intimacy blossoming between the two of them. When Sidney

Field became aware of it, he had forbidden Nott from visiting his house again. That was when the couple started seeing each other at the convenient trysting place of Portland Street.

'Having taken into consideration the whole of the evidence,' Justice Owen concluded, 'I have no doubt that Mrs. Field and Nott have been proved guilty of adultery at 40 Portland Street between January 7 and April 2, 1931.' He added in a sympathetic gesture to them both, 'If I could have found that they were shown to be innocent of the charge or that the case against them had not been proved, I would have willingly done so, for I realise the grave consequences of my finding.'

Those consequences were, indeed, not just grave but financially catastrophic. Nott would be ordered to pay Sidney Field's full court costs. Mrs. Ivy Field – having been proved an adulteress – actually had the tables reversed on her. It was her husband who would be awarded the decree nisi. She did, however, have the right to a token alimony. It amounted to £15 – or $1050 – a week. That was even less than what Sidney Field, in all of his vindictive assaults on her reputation, considered she deserved.

Still, in the worst of the Great Depression, it didn't really seem that bad at all.

⌞⌝

Jack Lang himself had been dangerously close to becoming a victim of the Divorce Act. On 11 August 1908, his wife Hilda filed a petition seeking legal separation and custody of their four children on grounds that: 'Between the 16th day of November, 1907 and the date of the presentation of this petition your Petitioner's husband committed adultery with and cohabited with Nellie Anderson at Leeton Street Burwood and other places with her as her husband.'

If the scandal had ever been aired in open court it might well have snuffed out a promising political career. Lang, at the time, had just won his first election as an alderman in the outer western suburb of Auburn and was a rising figure in the local Labor Party branch. Suburban voters would not have taken kindly to the idea of an aspiring politician irresponsible enough to desert his family for the arms of some saucy young mistress. Indeed, the stain on his reputation might even have spelled ruin for his highly successful real estate agency. What respectable lady, after all, would allow herself to be shown through a house, especially its bedrooms, by a known lecher?

Fortunately for Lang, he was able to persuade Hilda to withdraw her suit only three days later, well before the press had any chance to get a whiff of it. Why she attempted no further legal action over the next four years of her husband's continuing infidelity is something only she would know – she never bothered to try to explain to anyone. Perhaps she was influenced by her mother's advanced radical-feminist views and came to the conclusion that monogamous love – treating a spouse as one's exclusive property – was ultimately demeaning to both parties and reeked of bourgeois hypocrisy. More likely, she simply decided to do what was best for their children and try to shield them from prying eyes and public ridicule. Nellie's sudden death in September, 1911, would have brought her no pleasure nor even the slightest hint of relief. Just the opposite – by then she was fully reconciled to her husband's overpowering love for another woman. It would be infinitely more difficult learning to cope with his inconsolable sorrow. In later years a hostile press could have made a sensation out of the fact that one Lang child, James Christian, was born to a mistress and another, Nellie Louisa, actually bore the mistress's name. Somehow such dark family secrets never leaked out.

24

The suicide note

After months of wavering, Sir Philip Game now acted with breathtaking decisiveness. Late on the afternoon of Thursday, 12 May, he sent Jack Lang the most threatening letter yet in the history of their combative correspondence. Though he made no specific mention of Robert Beardsmore, the grave misuse of power highlighted by that case was clearly foremost in his mind, his every word bristling with biting indignation.

> Dear Mr. Lang,
> It appears to me that the terms of [your] circular direct public servants to commit a direct breach of the law. I feel it my bounden duty to remind you that you derive your authority from His Majesty, through me, and that I cannot possibly allow the Crown to be placed in the position of breaking the law of the land.
> I must ask you, therefore, either to furnish me with proof that the instructions in the circular are within the

law, or alternatively to withdraw the circular at once. I do not wish to press you unduly, but the matter appears to me to be of an urgency which admits of no delay, and I must ask for a definite reply by 11 am tomorrow, 13 May.
Philip Game
Governor

Those could only be taken as ominous words coming from someone able to dismiss a premier at the stroke of his pen. Under what rules and regulations was Game allowed to exercise such an extreme prerogative? As a professional military man he was well used to backing up his every decision by citing a specific section and subsection from one field manual or another. Incredibly, though, as the King's representative in New South Wales, he had only a single ambiguous sentence to guide him, Clause VI of the Royal Instructions to a Governor, the closest thing to a code of conduct available for an arbiter in his difficult position.

> In the execution of the powers and authorities vested in him, the Governor shall be guided by the advice of the Executive Council [inner circle of cabinet ministers]; but if in any case he shall see sufficient cause to dissent from the opinion of the said Council, he may act in the exercise of his said powers and authorities in opposition to the opinion of the Council.

Was that it, the sole summation of a governor's extraordinary power to destroy a democratically elected government – all based on just two words: *sufficient cause*? A typical training manual would use a hundred times that many to define what constituted a polished boot.

By a strange quirk of Imperial rule, Sir Philip Game had actually ended up with more power than the King himself to intervene in the affairs of parliament. In Britain, it had long been accepted that the monarch no longer had a right to over-rule his elected ministers, but that one brief clause in the Royal Instructions, so clumsily drafted in 1900, allowed his vice-regal representatives to do so – and for no specific reason. Game, after his appointment, naturally sought guidance from the writings of various constitutional experts but he had no legal training to help him and ultimately, the widely varying opinions boiled down to just one stunning conclusion. What constituted due cause to sack a popularly elected premier? It was anybody's guess.

How such an anomaly was allowed to slip through a system filled with so much pomp and ceremony was difficult enough to understand. It was most definitely compounded, however, by the Empire's curious predilection for drawing so many of its vice-regal representatives from the military: the most dictatorial of professions chosen to preside over the most pragmatic and unruly of forums – a parliamentary democracy. It was presumed, of course, that a retired general – or in Game's case, Air Vice-Marshal – could be relied on to exhibit impeccable impartiality, free of any political preference. That, however, was a farcical supposition. Senior British officers were overwhelmingly the product of an upper-class upbringing that virtually guaranteed their affinity – if not their outright allegiance – to the more conservative side of politics. The confidential correspondence from Buckingham Palace to the Governor is filled with snide allusions to both the naiveté and social ineptitude of Lang and his Labor supporters.

There could be no better example of this inherent class snobbery than in comments from Lord Wigram, the King's private secretary, following the Harbour Bridge opening. 'Really,' he wrote in exasperation to Game, 'we all thought that Lang might have been more suitably clad both as regards his garb and headgear.' Wigram made no attempt to hide his concern over what might happen if Lang got his wish to abolish the New South Wales Legislative Council. 'I suppose we may expect a New South Wales under Trade Union dictatorship,' he opined, rather indiscreetly since his views reflected those of his supposedly fair-minded Majesty.

Sir Philip certainly showed some of the same class prejudices in his letters back to the Palace, especially in the fears he expressed over the dire consequences if Lang were allowed to rule unchecked by an Upper House. It is doubtful he would have had that same degree of concern if the Nationalists were in control. Luckily, though, there was one enormous difference between Sir Philip Game and so many of his counterparts. He was keenly aware of his inbuilt biases and tried in every way he could to keep them from influencing his judgement. The tolerance he showed toward Lang's increasingly aggressive behaviour went well beyond what could reasonably be expected from any other royal umpire – including the King himself. His coolness under fire from all directions was worthy of a Victoria Cross.

With no preparation and little practical advice from London, Game had spent eighteen gruelling months caught in the middle of a vicious power struggle between the two houses of the New South Wales Parliament. More recently, the battle between state and Commonwealth had taken him, as vice-regal representative, into wholly uncharted territory. The chaos in public administration had reached the point where even Sir Philip was receiving his salary in cash and his wife, Gwendolen, was being forced to resort to sending out money orders rather than cheques to pay for the daily necessities. A government's inability to govern was certainly one of the more frequent triggers used to invoke the royal prerogative and dismiss a premier or prime minister. Game, however, recognised that such a reason more often than not served as a mere excuse for biased decision-making. Lang's enemies – both in parliament and in business – had conspired to use every nasty trick to starve him of funds. Did he really deserve the sack for that?

Once, during an early row with Lang over the Upper House issue, Sir Philip had actually announced his intention to fire him. However, no sooner had the Premier left Government House than Game realised he had let his anger cloud his better judgement and immediately offered an apology.

'Almost as soon as I was alone, in a position to think quietly, it was borne in upon me that I should be entirely wrong if I were to ask you to surrender your Commission,' he wrote to Lang in late March, 1931. One can only wonder from that incident how many dismissals throughout British history were actually due to nothing more than a mere fit of temper. Game, however, proved a big enough man to admit his error and came out of the fray more determined than ever to act only on the most certain of grounds.

It would be a full year later, at the beginning of the Enforcement Act crisis, before the Governor came close to believing that he might finally have found his 'sufficient cause'. That involved the Premier's blatant violation of the state's Audit Act by failing to bank receipts as required – certainly a technical illegality though, as the Governor quickly decided, hardly the grounds for a public execution. However, the case of Robert Beardsmore was obviously a far more serious and urgent matter. Here was a faithful public servant facing severe retribution – the loss of everything he had worked for – simply for doing his duty to his country. It was a situation so grossly unfair as to make Game almost ill to think that it could be happening under his jurisdiction. He, after all, was effectively

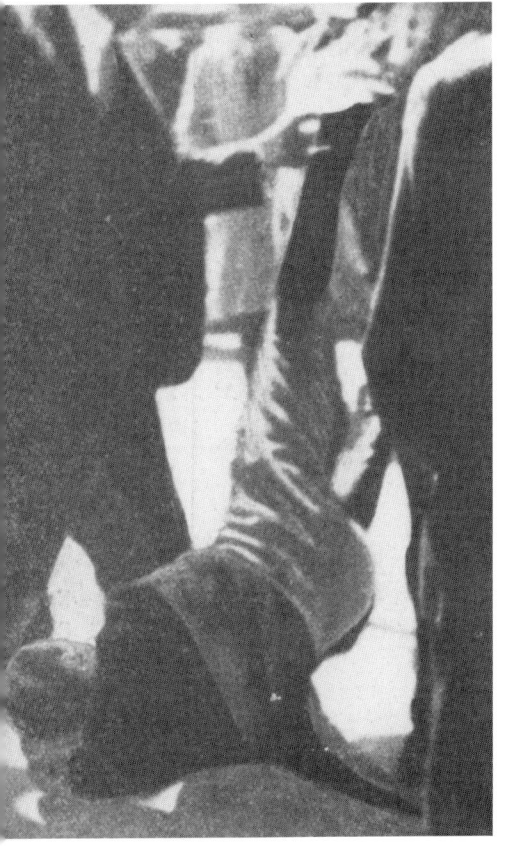

'In the name of the loyal and decent citizens of New South Wales, I declare this bridge open'. New Guardsman Captain Francis de Groot beats Lang to the ribbon in the best-remembered episode from 1932. (NewsPix)

Not such an heroic image: de Groot is unceremoniously dumped from his saddle by Superintendent Billy Mackay. (Fairfax Photos)

For Lang, the bridge celebrations are a highlight of his political career. Here, before the de Groot incident, the Premier chats amiably with Lady Game while Sir Philip – in his air vice-marshal's uniform – charms Lang's wife, Hilda. (Hood Collection, State Library of New South Wales)

The Big Fella still cuts the ribbon for the news cameras, making sure to stand well away from the knot that tied it together again. Lang's casual dress – no top hat or tails – enraged King George V, though he slapped his knee in delight at news of de Groot's brazen stunt. (Hood Collection, State Library of New South Wales)

The colourful pageant draws 750,000 onlookers. Most floats, like this tribute to the nation's agricultural exports, were still quaintly horse-drawn. (Boorowa Productions)

The marching 'lady surf lifesavers' in their eye-catching bathers are considered rather daring for the time. The display behind promotes the St George district, bordering Botany Bay. (Boorowa Productions)

How could there be a parade without Captain Cook aboard his *Endeavour*?
(Boorowa Productions)

In contrast, this impressive fly-past demonstrated just how far Australia had come since colonisation. (Boorowa Productions)

Renowned aviator Charles Kingsford Smith led the bridge fly-past. Two months earlier he caused great excitement when he delivered the Christmas mail from London. (National Archive of Australia: A1200, L96364)

Wireless is another sign of modern times. Radio pioneer Emil Voigt persuades the trade unions to start up 2KY. Broadcasting will enable Jack Lang to break through a solid wall of media bias and speak directly to the people. (Courtesy 2KY)

State-of-the art: the 2BL control room in Sydney. The Australian Broadcasting Commission hits the airwaves on 1 July 1932. (Australian Broadcasting Corporation, ABC Content Sales)

The ABC boasts its own dance band, but a national news service is still some years away. (Australian Broadcasting Corporation. ABC Content Sales)

Radios will prove a special blessing for isolated outback families. That's not an exercise bike – the daughter pedals to generate power for the transmitter. (NewsPix)

Sport has always been a way to lift Aussie spirits, and it booms in the depression years as never before. 1932 will see world-record attendances in cricket and football. (Hood Collection, State Library of New South Wales)

Two Aussie icons get together to shoot the breeze. Walter Lindrum (left) is dubbed the 'Bradman of billiards' after scoring a world record break of 4137. Donald Bradman chalked up his record-breaking fifteenth double century in 1932. (NewsPix)

The fabled Phar Lap in training before his stunning debut in American racing. After the big-hearted gelding wins the prestigious Agua Caliente Cup race, Hollywood wants to put him in the movies. (AAP Images)

The beloved champion nuzzles his devoted trainer, Tommy Woodcock. The horse's mysterious death, not long after this photograph was taken, left many Australians in shock. (NewsPix)

Despite the hard times, race fans – like these onlookers in Brisbane – still enjoy a flutter, not to mention the chance to show off the latest fashions. (John Oxley Library, State Library of Queensland)

Beachwear for both sexes was becoming more adventurous – though still tame by modern standards. The young man with his back turned risked arrest by showing up at Bondi with his upper torso 'indecently' exposed. (Hood Collection, State Library of New South Wales)

At exclusive Palm Beach, an attractive surfer could always get away with more – or, in this case, less.

For members of the social elite, the Great Depression hardly changed a thing except, perhaps, to make hired help cheaper. This cosy group enjoys a bit of après-ski socialising at a hotel near Mount Kosciusko. (Hood Collection, State Library of New South Wales)

It's not exactly women's lib, but Victorian prudery did seem to be giving way on many fronts. Flappers of the era were strongly influenced by Hollywood's emphasis on glamour and romance. (Peter Luck Productions)

Field Divorce

Wife's Rain of Tears in Dread Ordeal

THE OTHER LITTLE WOMAN IGNORES PUBLIC GAZE

The first week of what is destined to be one of the most extraordinary divorce cases in the history of the Southern Hemisphere—the Field cross suits—was packed with colorful, picturesque, and at times, pathetic incidents.

ON two women in this case the searchlight of public attention is focussed—Ivy Gladys Field and Clare Meta Wilson—the former a blonde, the latter a brunette.

Each is fighting for her honor, but the spotlight is unquestionably on Mrs. Field.

She is a somewhat elusive personage, hence the "curiosity brigade" waiting each morning in battalions near the Supreme Court has not been

This great array of counsel, picturesque and powerful, is not at the Bar table for the good of its health.

The case is costing £500 a day —6 2-5d a second; £1/13/4 a minute; £100 an hour!

So each of the K.C.'s and lesser lights may smile complacently that there is such an institution as the Divorce Court, and such an amazingly lucrative case as Field v. Field.

Up in the gallery the crowd, of all forms and phases of humanity, follows incident by incident, the dramatic evidence of Mrs. Field with bated breath. As soon as the Court clears for lunch, it rushes back to the main door of the Supreme Court, and again queues up, again to enter the magic atmosphere.

Mrs. Field's ordeal of the witness box lasted 15 hours.

Like Niobe, she was, at times, the personification of sorrow—all tears!

In a headline-grabbing divorce battle, socialite Ivy Field and her wealthy husband Sidney accused each other of having numerous affairs. The lurid details sparked lively debate over whether 1930s women were becoming too fast and loose. (Fairfax Photos)

"I married for love and I am going to keep on marrying until I get it."

"Is your husband good to you?"
"Yes, he pays his alimony in advance."

The upmarket *Smith's Weekly* raised eyebrows with cartoons like these.

"What made you divorce your first husband?"
"My second."

"My boy and I have no secret from each other."
"Good heavens, then you know!"

In any rogue's gallery from 1932, Judge Frederick Shaver Swindell would be highest on the list. Here with his wife, the American con man attends an inquiry into corruption in dog racing, known then as the 'tin hares'. (Fairfax Photos)

Boss of the notorious Fifty-Fifty Club: Phil 'the Jew' Jeffs. (State Records New South Wales, NRS 2467, No 18946, [3/6108 p.129])

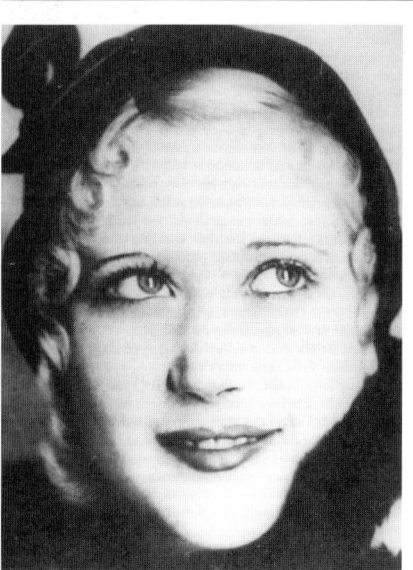

Dulcie Markham: in one night of lovemaking she could earn the equivalent of six months' wages for a top secretary.

Tilly Devine, Sydney's reigning vice queen. (Fairfax Photos)

The big story of 1932, in terms of international interest, was the incredible rescue of German aviators Adolf Klausmann (left) and Hans Bertram, missing in north-west Australia for forty days. The two Aboriginals in the middle, Miaman and Murungnunga, were among the first searchers to find and feed them. (Reg & Mavis Weston collection, Northern Territory Library)

Out of petrol and blown hopelessly off course: the seaplane *Atlantis*, which had been heading from Timor to Darwin. (Western Australian Maritime Museum)

Citizen hero: Robert Beardsmore, the public servant whose defiance of Jack Lang led to the Big Fella's downfall. 1932 would test the courage and resourcefulness of ordinary Australians, men and women, like no other year before or since. (Courtesy Ann Hart and Judy Campbell)

regent of New South Wales charged with the ultimate responsibility of protecting all its citizens. How could he possibly allow his elected ministers to turn Australia's proud founding colony into an outlaw state?

Game's letter reached the Premier at 6 pm Thursday, just as the Legislative Council was about to launch itself into the final stages of the Mortgages Taxation Bill debate. Amid urgent tactical meetings with his Upper House supporters, Lang would have had little time to think through his reply but several quite reasonable responses were open to him. He could, for example, mount a persuasive case that the circular was specially designed to set the stage for another High Court challenge. Though the court had approved the general principle on which the Enforcement Act was based, there were still good arguments to be raised against individual decrees. In particular, Lang might well have had at least an arguable point in suggesting that decree 42 violated natural rights by forcing New South Wales public servants to work without pay. Every penny they collected would be sent off to Canberra, leaving nothing behind for their fortnightly pay cheques. The federal government itself seemed to admit the truth of that argument, judging by the way it framed an earlier proclamation dealing with confiscated revenue from railways and trams. Provision was made to set aside £1 in every £6 specifically for the payment of salaries and other working expenses. Yet no such exception had been allowed for employees like Beardsmore handling stamp duties, estate duties, motor licensing or lands sales.

Since Game had demanded 'proof' that the 10 May circular was legal, Lang could also have agreed to suspend it temporarily pending a review by senior counsel. Ultimately, though, if the Governor persisted in his demand to have the instructions withdrawn altogether, Lang – as a practical-minded politician – would seem to have nothing to lose by giving in and catering to his whim. He could afford to be conciliatory, particularly after the Upper House delivered him a near-miracle – passing the mortgages tax, with its promise of the millions of pounds needed to be rid of the dreaded Enforcement Act.

The next twelve hours, however, would see the Big Fella undergo an extraordinary transformation – a change that appeared to have much more to do with psychology than politics. Somewhere in that time frame he seems to have reached a point where he simply could no longer cope with the chaos he had created around him.

There is nothing in Lang's later writings to explain his actions on that historic Friday, 13 May, but it is possible to imagine the emotional turmoil he may have been going through as he returned to his office from parliament's marathon all-night sitting. The House had adjourned at precisely 6.45 am. Lang must have been totally exhausted, both mentally and physically, and no doubt prone to slipping into the downcast mood that so often follows the adrenaline high of a hyper-tense confrontation.

The passage of the new tax should have been cause for celebration, if nothing else, for giving him a powerful negotiating tool in his ongoing battle with the federal government. More likely, though, it left him flooded with self-doubt, no longer sure whether he had either the strength or the desire to move on to the next stage of this punishing contest. No sooner did he deal with one problem than another cropped up. If it wasn't Lyons hounding him, then it was the English Governor – two outsiders attempting to subdue and humiliate him in the eyes of the people, his 'children', as he called them, those careworn, deserving *faces in the street* he had vowed to serve as a social reformer and maker of dreams. The sad truth, if he was prepared to admit it, was that he had let them down badly during his second term in office. In his prolonged battle

The suicide note

for survival, he had allowed his focus to shift almost entirely from benefiting the needy to futile bickering with his conservative opponents. Perhaps his enemies were right: he was becoming the man they accused him of being, Lang the Wrecker, obsessed with his own ambition regardless of the consequences.

Many theories would later be advanced for the Big Fella's next baffling move. None seems any more valid than the possibility that he was simply swept away by subconscious undercurrents beyond his control. To a newspaper editor who interviewed him at this critical turning point he was like an ice-capped volcano, 'extraordinarily cool . . . but beneath this outward quietude there are fierce and consuming fires raging. He could almost truly be described at the moment as a bombe glace'. Governor Game, who would confront the Premier later that day, likened him to a person possessed. 'I have come to think he is a living Jekyll and Hyde.'

The passing of the mortgage tax legislation had been an unexpected win. Jack Lang now seemed to have every chance to hold on to power. Perhaps, though, some self-destructive inner voice told him he no longer deserved to. Sometime in the morning of 13 May, he penned the virtual suicide note that served as his response to the Governor's demand.

Dear Sir Philip:
I received your letter on the 12th instant at 6 pm and must say that it is hard to understand how you do not wish to press me unduly and yet insist on a definite reply by 11 am on the 13th instant.

The circular of which you do not appear to approve represents the decision of Cabinet and no doubt was arrived at after consideration of the primary duties of maintaining the essential and social services of the State.

The only reply you can be given is that the circular cannot possibly be withdrawn.
John T. Lang.

When the two men came together later in the day, they would never get around to any serious discussion of the Mortgages Taxation Bill. What would be the sense if Jack Lang was no longer premier?

25

Game and Lang: The final showdown

Jack Lang's defiant reply to the Governor boomeranged, as he must have known it would, bringing an instant summons to Government House.

'You will, I'm sure, realise that I cannot allow the matter to rest where it is,' Game wrote back. 'Before considering what further action I may feel bound to take, I should prefer to discuss the whole position with you.'

The Big Fella had another couple of hours to reconsider his position. Indeed, he might well have continued mulling over his options even as he strode up the all-too-familiar steps of the sandstone residence for his 3 pm appointment. If his term was headed for a premature end, he still had every chance of turning the deadlock to his advantage. Instead of waiting to be sacked, he could have stepped in first to tender his resignation, seeking a dissolution of parliament that would leave him in charge of a caretaker government. That would at least mean being able to fight an early election from a position of strength as incumbent premier, with the resources of public office remaining largely at his disposal. The very worst thing he could do would be to walk away from this crucial meeting with nothing resolved, leaving it entirely up to Game to decide the terms of the dismissal. Sir Philip could never agree to Lang staying on as caretaker premier unless he specifically promised not to try to enforce his contentious 10 May edict during the four weeks leading up to the election. Without such a guarantee, the Governor obviously had no choice but to call upon the Leader of the Opposition, Bertram Stevens, to take over.

Earlier that morning, Lang had been beyond caring, physically and emotionally drained by the months of high tension. His curt response to the Governor was tantamount to telling the King to go hell and might just as well have been written in hemlock. Yet, as impetuous and foolhardy as his letter seemed, he would soon enough feel the need to try to rationalise it in a way that made political sense. An early election was a mighty gamble but if he won, it would be as good as having a referendum demanding that the federal government back down or face the risk of New South Wales going its own way. His mortgage tax was the perfect spearhead for a short, hard-hitting electoral campaign focused on the theme of needy workers versus greedy rich. And if the labour movement's most prominent figure showed himself to be the victim of a high-level conspiracy orchestrated by the Governor and his mogul mates, it could only help to mobilise his supporters and increase the sympathy vote.

The Big Fella was too much the politician not to have such ideas buzzing in his head as he walked into the Governor's study. Before their encounter was over, however, he would think of one more possibility – chilling both for its mutinous implications and what it revealed about the agitated state of his mind.

'One thought that occurred to me,' he admitted, 'was that if I was satisfied that the Governor was acting illegally I could have had him arrested.'

No official record exists of their conversation that bleak autumn afternoon, but by comparing their subsequent written accounts, it is possible to get a sense of the highly charged atmosphere of their final confrontation and piece together what might have been said. To Lang, Sir Philip – though normally amiable – seemed 'tense, taut and obviously ill at ease'. Game, for his part, credited the Premier with being 'entirely courteous and personally friendly'. Their handshake, always a firm affirmation of mutual respect, might on this occasion have lingered an added pulse beat.

'I gather you do not dispute my view that the circular in question is a breach of the federal law?' The Governor would have been quick to come to the point.

'Are you prepared to sign the Mortgages Taxation Bill?' Lang saw one question as answering another. 'By doing that all our financial difficulties will be resolved, and the Enforcement Act will no longer be an issue.'

Game, though, was not about to let himself be sidetracked.

'It's not my role to speculate about what might or might not happen in the future. At this moment, it seems to me, my ministers are committing a breach of the federal law. While you don't admit this, you don't deny it either – and it's only fair to advise you, I am now considering asking for your government's resignation.'

'Can I remind you,' Lang could feel justified in rebuking him, 'that my government has just obtained an overwhelming expression of confidence in the Parliament? The Mortgages Taxation Bill has been passed by a majority of twenty in the Legislative Assembly and a majority of nine in the Legislative Council.'

'Then why not withdraw your circular? I can't see how that would possibly queer your pitch.' Game would have meant that as a plea, not an order – an attempt to talk someone he sincerely liked out of making a serious mistake. Lang was not to be moved.

'As a government our first responsibility is to the people who elected us, not to you as a nominee of the Crown.'

Sir Philip Game had proved himself the most patient of men but he could see the dialogue was going nowhere.

'If you do not withdraw your circular, I have no alternative but to dismiss you from office.'

There it was – what Jack Lang would later describe as 'the assassin's dagger' – raised to strike. His gut reaction would normally have been to hit back immediately with a threat of his own. *Then let the people make their judgement between us and when they do, it will be I who dismisses you from office*! Such fulminations, though, were better left for his forthcoming campaign speeches and he managed to hold his temper in check.

'I find it unthinkable that you should become the instrument for the destruction of responsible government in this state,' the Big Fella would tell the Governor before he left. Bitter as such words might appear in cold print, they would have been spoken calmly and without rancour. If fate had cast the two as enemies, Lang could never have wished for a more fair or honourable foe. They were, after all, both in their own ways victims of a historical accident – a paradox that allowed the voice of 1.3 million Australian voters to be silenced at the stamp of a royal seal.

Game agreed to forward his decision in writing later that afternoon but meanwhile, was left to shake his head in wonder.

'I cannot follow the workings of his mind when the crisis came,' he mused. 'He knew that at any former time [before the dispute over the circular] I should have felt it my duty to grant him a dissolution had he asked for it. Having got his mortgage bill through both Houses of Parliament, I fully anticipated he would have yielded to my request and would have withdrawn the instructions. He is a difficult man to understand and I don't pretend to understand him.'

What Jack Lang would never acknowledge, in all the 43 years that remained of his life, was that it was he who put the blade in his assassin's grasp.

∽∾∽

If the climactic scene in the study was played out with supreme understatement, the rest of Government House crackled like a tinderbox about to spontaneously combust. Gwendolen Game had returned from a busy round of official engagements to learn that Lang and her husband were in the midst of their showdown behind locked doors. The official secretary, Harry Budge, paced nervously in the hallway.

'Everything depends on the next few minutes,' he told her.

No one had suffered more through the torturous war of nerves than Lady Game. She had seen the tension surrounding her husband stretched to the point where it threatened to rebound on the entire family like a broken spring. Their eldest son Bill, then nearing his twenty-first birthday, had suffered a worrying spell of illness that could well have been traced to the stress of never quite knowing where the next public insult was coming from. Attending a charity ball, he could only stand in embarrassed silence as a speaker exhorted all young men of good character to join the New Guard, presumably to do the job the Governor of New South Wales was failing to do. His younger brother David, a shy and awkward teenager, protected himself by withdrawing into his shell. On his rare outings to the theatre he could be seen staring straight ahead, never glancing left or right or making any attempt to socialise. Only Rosemary, by then thirteen, retained her natural ebullience, speaking cheerfully to everyone she met. Yet, she, too, sensed the jagged edges of anxiety intruding into her secure little world, especially the added sharpness in her mother's voice.

The past 24 hours had been the worst Lady Game had known in Australia, with the hostility toward the Governor slipping beyond the pale into outright incitement. The *Bulletin* magazine – enraged by his refusal to act – had published a vicious cartoon depicting him as Pilate washing his hands. Inflammatory media placards were posted around Sydney proclaiming 'Does Governor Game want Revolution?'

'I will send you all the papers, so you will see exactly what happened,' Gwendolen would write to her mother, 'but what you won't see is the crisis coming nearer and nearer and looking blacker and blacker as the mortgage bill went through Parliament and was passed against all our hopes. This would have come up for Philip's assent and after a night of thinking and discussing it with [New South Wales Chief Justice] Sir Philip Street they both regretfully came up with the conclusion that he couldn't refuse. This alone would have produced a storm of such vitriolic abuse that one dreaded it for Philip.'

Her husband, of course, had told her the day before about receiving the damning documents from Beardsmore and his intention to call the Premier to task for his illegal directive. At that time, though, it still seemed inconceivable to him that Lang would refuse to withdraw it.

Gwendolen stood just around the corner from the study waiting out the end of the meeting, her heart pounding so loudly she was afraid nearby staff members could hear it. In a few minutes she was due for another appointment and couldn't bear the thought of leaving the house again without knowing the outcome.

'But before the time was up we heard voices and Philip's

door open. To avoid Lang we fled into the Aide-de-camp's room just in time to see him pass the window.' To Lady Game he looked 'a completely defeated man in his old grey hat – very grey himself, too, for he had been up all night'.

Harry Budge raced in to tell them the news.

'It's all over! He's gone! He'll never come back!' His wild excitement punched through Government House's shroud of gloom like a burst of sunshine.

'I couldn't believe it,' Gwendolen rejoiced. 'We went into Philip together, and found him writing the official letter. He told us they had had a perfectly friendly but quite determined (on both sides) interview, and that Lang had left saying he entertained a high personal regard for him. They shook hands and parted on the best of terms. Mr. Budge and I on each side of Philip put our heads over his shoulder and suggested alterations and improvements and he didn't even seem to mind, and even accepted some from each of us. I think we were all three so excited we hardly knew what we were doing.'

There would actually be another flurry of correspondence before the matter was finally settled. The Governor's first letter reached the Premier shortly after 3.30 pm.

Dear Mr. Lang,
At our interview this afternoon you requested me to communicate my views by letter.

Your case, as I understand it, is that Ministers are determined on their action in order to carry on the essential services of the State.

Into aspects of justification it is not, as I conceive it, my province to inquire. My position is that if my Ministers are unable to carry on essential services without breaking the law, my plain duty is to endeavour to obtain Ministers who feel able to do so.

As I have already pointed out to you in my letter of the 12th instant, it is impossible for me to put the Crown in the position of being party to an illegal action.

If Ministers are not prepared to abide by the law, then I must state without hesitation that it is their bounden duty, under the law and practice of the Constitution, to tender their resignations.

I await an early reply, as I am sure you will agree that the present position cannot be allowed to extend over the weekend.

Philip Game
Governor

If Game really believed that he and the Premier had parted on the best of terms, he would be set straight soon enough. The Jekyll-and-Hyde analogy he used to describe Lang was perfectly true in the sense of the Big Fella having two conflicting personalities: the courteous and considerate gentleman one moment, the ruthless opportunist the next. Lang, the politician, wrote back immediately, letting Sir Philip feel the lash of his scorn. 'If your letter of today's date means that you are requesting the resignation of Ministers, you are hereby informed that your request is refused.'

By 4.30 pm the Governor's final letter was back on Lang's desk, this time leaving no room for the slightest ambiguity.

Dear Mr. Lang,

Your letter informing me that Ministers are not prepared to tender their resignations has just reached me. In view of this and your refusal to withdraw the circular, I feel it my bounden duty to inform you that I cannot retain my

present Ministers in office, and that I am seeking other advisers. I must ask you to regard this as final.
Philip Game
Governor

In years to come Lang would concoct any number of disingenuous theories for why the Governor finally acted against him. He made much of the fact that on the Friday before he was called to Government House, Sir Philip had met there with a delegation representing powerful British business interests in control of the state's largest banks, insurance companies and investment houses. Their purpose – as they openly admitted – was to petition Game to withhold his assent to the Mortgages Taxation Bill pending a further study of the damage it was likely to cause to British business interests within the Empire as a whole. While Lang acknowledged that they might not have specifically asked for his dismissal, he insisted their true intent was 'to precipitate a constitutional crisis between the Government and the Governor'. He went even further, though, inferring that 'authorities in London' had stepped in to take direct control of the situation, keeping in hourly contact with Sir Philip. Thus, when the Governor finally moved against him, he was – in Lang's contorted reconstruction of events – 'acting under specific instructions'.

'Throughout the interview,' Lang summed up, 'he gave me the impression of being a man forced to do a job for which he had no relish. I have never seen a more ill-at-ease man, as if what he was doing was contrary to his own will.'

Yet on the afternoon of his dismissal Lang gave no hint that he felt himself the victim of some grand conspiracy. Just the opposite, his behaviour gives the impression of someone who has just had a crushing burden lifted from his shoulders. A *Sydney Morning Herald* reporter who spoke to him at the

Premier's Department before his sudden departure found his office in a whirl of activity, with aides rushing back and forth carrying boxes of personal files to a waiting car. In sharp contrast to the frantic scene, the Big Fella himself seemed almost serene.

'Well, I am sacked, I am dismissed from office,' he told the pressman. 'I have attempted to do my duty, but now I must be going. I am no longer Premier, but a free man.'

With that, John Thomas Lang slipped on his overcoat and battered grey hat, picked up his attaché case and walked slowly down the stairs to the front door. A number of faithful staff members had lined up to bid him farewell. He stopped by each in turn – whether senior official, secretary or mere office boy – fixing each in his grateful gaze and shaking hands with great feeling, all the more poignant for his silence.

It was a moving end to the Premier's crisis-plagued reign but it was also marred by a peculiarly Langian twist that left most of his parliamentary colleagues totally gobsmacked.

'Mr. Lang himself anticipated the Governor's move and was not surprised when it came,' Sydney's *Telegraph* reported next day, 'but the members of his ministry were taken completely off their guard. It was characteristic of Mr. Lang that his Ministers learned of the fall of the Government only when they bought their evening papers.'

Similarly, senior executives within the ALP and Trades Hall had been left completely in the dark, unaware that a constitutional crisis had blown up overnight because of something as seemingly trivial as a public service memo. In subsequent statements all elements of the party hierarchy – politicians and unionists alike – would make a strong show of support for Lang's stand. 'There was no indication of resentment on the part of members of the Labor caucus,' one political report suggested, 'and no post mortem was held. The general opinion was that in the circumstances, the ex-Premier could not have acted differently without loss of caste and damage to the labour movement.' Privately, though, many of the party faithful were outraged by their leader's stubbornness in refusing to withdraw the circular, and even more so by his almost contemptuous failure to alert them to what was happening.

'Lang played for defeat,' one of his critics bitterly observed.

26
Unanswered questions

Could Jack Lang possibly have been serious when he said he actually considered arresting Sir Philip Game? It certainly appears so, judging from the elaborate scenario he spells out in his last book, *The Turbulent Years*, written when he was well into his nineties. One gets the impression that for a moment or two he was truly toying with the idea of sending Superintendent Billy Mackay over to Government House to batter down the doors.

'There it was,' he writes, referring to the Governor's final letter, 'and I had to face up to the question as to whether I would accept the notice of dismissal or not.'

While I had no doubt that members of the New South Wales Police Force would carry out their orders, at the same time I realised that it would bring about a clash with the armed forces of the Commonwealth. We had information that the Commonwealth, fearing that such a clash might take place, had placed all arms of the service in

Sydney in a state of alert. Arms and ammunition had been distributed to the troops at Victoria Barracks, at Middle Head and at Liverpool, to the naval ratings at Garden Island and Air Force at Richmond. The Commonwealth had also recruited peace officers to supplement the Commonwealth Police Force.

While I was satisfied in my own mind that there would be hundreds of thousands of people in the State who would rally to the defence of their elected Government, I was not prepared to risk the creation of a situation resulting in bloodshed, particularly as the Commonwealth would have its forces fully armed and our supporters would largely be the unemployed, without weapons of any kind.

If we defied the authority of the Governor, we would be denying the authority of the King, whose representative he was. This might be accepted as an open invitation to the intervention of the British Navy and end in the arrival of British warships off Sydney Heads to shell the city. So, rather than risk civil war and have bloodshed in the streets of Sydney, I decided to accept the dismissal.

Nearly four decades after the event, then, Jack Lang still seemed to believe that he would have been perfectly justified in refusing to relinquish his premiership and was deterred only by the desire to save innocent lives. The truth was, however, that he could have challenged the legality of the Governor's decision without going to the extreme of placing him under arrest; and his refusal to accept dismissal – shocking as it might seem – would not automatically have triggered an armed conflict.

While the authority vested in a governor-general had become clearly defined over many decades of Imperial rule, the lawful powers of a governor of one of the newly created Australian states remained very much a mystery. There were few precedents dealing with the dismissal issue on a state or provincial level and none appeared to have any direct relevance to the situation in New South Wales in 1932. Long before Game came along, the Royal Instructions handed on to his predecessors had been criticised by constitutional scholars as hopelessly outdated and even illegal inasmuch as they contradicted modern concepts of the right to self-rule. Any direct challenge to Game's authority would have had to be treated most seriously if made through the New South Wales Parliament. Lang still had the controlling numbers there and could have passed an emergency resolution asking King George V for the Governor's recall on grounds that he had acted unconstitutionally. Such a tactic would have been guaranteed to spark an international legal debate stormy enough to engulf Buckingham Palace itself. At the very least, the resulting confusion would have made the use of federal troops highly unlikely for some time to come.

While the Big Fella might therefore be accused of exaggerating his fears of a bloodbath, the fact was that many thousands of his supporters were prepared to go to the barricades with him, doing whatever they could to prevent his forcible removal from office. Indeed, some of them had already volunteered to join the labour defence corps proposed as a counter to the New Guard. If there was genuine risk of civil strife, it was more likely to come from violent clashes between pro-Lang and anti-Lang militias rather than any armed conflict between uniformed soldiers and police.

Lang's more militant followers fully expected him to stand up to Game as he had stood up to the wage-slashing conservatives under Joe Lyons and before that, to the powerful British banks. Here was the one leader able to lift their hopes with his inspiring message of *people before money*. In their eyes that wasn't just some demagogue's meaningless slogan, it was a genuine formula for recovery that made more sense than all the economic experts' voodoo incantations about balanced budgets. Start with one man. Give him a job and enough pay to take care of his family and – just like priming a well pump – the money was sure to flow. In the blackest hours of their lives, such true believers had trusted the Premier to show the way, buoyed by their faith that *Lang is Right*. It was heartbreaking enough to see their great idol so easily shattered. How could they ever have forgiven him if they once suspected that he had set himself up for the fall?

Whatever the sense of loss suffered by Lang supporters on that Friday afternoon, their stunned disappointment was no match for the spontaneous outbursts of joy that erupted across Sydney and quickly spread throughout the nation. Short of church bells ringing, the news was received with a rapture that could almost be likened to Armistice Day. Office workers rushed into the streets to read the latest newspaper posters and thousands more huddled by their radios. In city cafes diners broke into cheers or stood up to sing whatever came to mind, from 'God Save the King' to 'Happy Days are Here Again'. Those of a conservative political bent were predictably jubilant, but even for the less committed mainstream there was instant relief – the feeling that whatever the rights or wrongs of the stand-off, it had become far too explosive to be allowed to continue.

The Fifty-Fifty Club that night would have been no place for the faint-hearted. The contrast in moods from one table to the next must have been something akin to rival football fans drinking shoulder to shoulder after a match narrowly decided on a referee's disputed call. Many guests no doubt found good cause to celebrate and, if their conversation reflected the kind of remarks overheard on Sydney streets earlier that day, it was easy to see why.

'Here's to my just having saved £1000 [$70,000],' a well-dressed businessman boasted, toasting good riddance to Lang and his hated mortgage tax.

He and his friends would have been well advised to avoid eye contact with the heavyset brute sitting glum-faced just a few feet away, angrily mumbling into his beer. 'I say Jack Lang was the best premier the workers ever had and I'll take on anyone who says otherwise.'

Phil Jeffs, ever the considerate host, might wisely have rushed a couple of his prettiest girls over to try to quickly change the subject before a fight broke out.

Within the next day or so, though, the volatile atmosphere dissipated like fog in a fresh breeze. Ordinary citizens, it seems, had had more than their fill of excitement and were happy to enjoy a brief respite before the start of what promised to be a high-voltage election campaign. Sundays in Sydney's Domain, the traditional gathering place for stirrers and radicals of all description, were always a good measure of the political temperature. On that first Sunday after Lang's dismissal, police found 'the soapbox oratory the mildest for many weeks,' Governor Game was relieved to report to his King.

One of the tantalising ironies of Game's intervention was that it would leave forever unanswered the crucial question that inspired it. Could Jack Lang have held on against the Lyons Government's punishing edicts, and if so, for how much longer? His state's social welfare services had already ground to a halt, with tens of thousands of mothers and widows going weeks without their pensions. Of 90,500 civil servants on the public payroll it looked as if at least half would have to miss out on their next fortnightly salaries. Whatever revenue was still accessible to the Treasury was coming in dribs and drabs and entire departments were barely scraping by. Yet, looking around the world there was many another government struggling along month after month in borderline bankruptcy, often with far fewer resources to call upon than New South Wales. Essential services remained largely intact and Lang still had the support of the more powerful industrial unions, whose organisations could serve as a useful back-up for day-to-day administration.

The biggest question mark hung over the mortgage tax. Could it really have saved the day for the Big Fella? Several hours before Lang's demise, Joe Lyons had rushed through a highly controversial piece of legislation specifically aimed at nullifying the New South Wales statute. The new 'Financial Emergency Act' prohibited any attempt to tax the capital value of mortgages held by banks or insurance companies. It was based on the dubious assumption that since the Commonwealth Government had the right to raise taxes, it also had the right to prevent any state from passing laws which might leave a large corporation financially unable to meet its federal tax commitments. Lang might well have won a High Court challenge in this case, but at the very least he would have faced a lengthy delay before he could start collecting a penny of extra revenue. Could he still have managed to carry on until then?

In the end, even without the dismissal, the gruelling struggle might not have turned out all that differently: decided not so much by this or that High Court judgement or act of parliament but the more basic issue of how much longer Jack Lang's iron will could stand up to the blowtorch heat of the disruptive forces he had set loose. In that sense, when Sir Philip finally stepped in, he acted not so much as assassin as mercy killer.

Even so, there would be another ironic twist to Game's momentous decision. The one ground on which he felt justified in sacking Jack Lang – illegal conduct – would turn out to be most questionable of all in the eyes of many constitutional experts. As one acidly observed: the case boiled down to 'an untrained lawyer claiming the right to determine whether or not the law has been broken'. Game could easily have left it to the Australian court system to decide if the 10 May circular was indeed a violation of federal law and if so, what means were available to the Lyons Government to force Lang to withdraw it. In London, the Dominions Office had just finished drafting a cable to that effect, advising Game that the matter might best be handled by a judge. By then, though, the Governor had already made his fateful decision. The cable was never sent.

Still, if Sir Philip ended up choosing the wrong reason for dismissing Lang, he had other grounds that would have served him even better.

'It is the bounden duty of a governor to dismiss his ministers if he believes their policy to be injurious to the public interests, or their conduct to be such, in their official capacity, that he could no longer act with them harmoniously for the public good.' So wrote Alpheus Todd, a nineteenth-century authority on British constitutional law who Game had obviously read and admired. The phrase 'bounden duty' is one the Governor chose to use in his final letter notifying Lang that he was no longer Premier of New South Wales.

Ultimately, it was impossible to determine whether Sir Philip was right or wrong because all of British history had failed to produce a clear-cut, legal definition of the constitutionally 'correct' grounds for dismissing a democratically elected government. Game, however, would be saved from any serious criticism by the mood of the times. On that history-making Friday, 13 May 1932, there were few who would bother to quibble with him and their faint protests hardly registered amid the thunderous roar of approval. The business establishment, the professional elite and especially the media – all rushed to praise the gentle, long-suffering governor with the same passion with which they had condemned him, only hours before, as the most despicable of cowards and a traitor to his class.

'I feel sure that the nation tonight – not only the people of New South Wales but the nation as a whole – will heave a sigh of relief,' the Prime Minister declared, thanking Sir Philip in an Australia-wide radio broadcast.

The King himself would be quick to sing Game's praise, his sentiments passed on in a letter from his private secretary, Lord Wigram, bubbling over with royal delight.

'We are enchanted with your triumph over Lang,' Wigram enthused, 'and despite the New Guard, Old Guard and Red Guard, you have come into your own. From being the villain of the piece you have been exalted to the hero of the day. The King has fully realised the difficult position in which you have been placed for so long [and] with what patience you have faced each stage of the situation. Now you must be delighted to reap the fruits of your untiring efforts; and the King trusts that a fresh era of prosperity, contentment and happiness is in store for New South Wales.'

For Philip and Gwendolen Game, there would be one precious moment that more than made up for all the months of abuse they had endured. On Wednesday, 18 May, the couple went to Her Majesty's to see a performance of *Tosca*. As they walked into their box in the packed theatre, the entire audience rose as one, bursting into wild cheers and sustained applause. The ovation lasted for several minutes, leaving them bathed in its healing warmth. Gwendolen could feel the tears welling in her eyes as they had so many times before but this time she made no attempt to hold them back, nor could she if she tried. Her joy overwhelmed her as her sadness never could.

As for the Governor, he smiled graciously and eventually manoeuvred his stiff leg into a position where he could slowly sink into his seat. As always he sat ramrod straight, showing no further sign of emotion except, perhaps, for a slight, involuntary heaving of his shoulders. They had carried so heavy a burden for so very long. Now, they shuddered with deep-felt relief.

27

The search for *Atlantis*: Part I

The seaplane *Atlantis* left a sequinned trail twinkling in the waters of the Timor coast as it lifted off at the stroke of midnight, 14 May 1932, on a flight that should have seen it reach Darwin by first light. Instead, it could just as well have been a time machine, whisking its two-man crew back to the dawn of an earlier aeon. Not long after take-off the single-engine Junkers was swallowed up in a mighty thunderstorm and spat out god knows where. By mid-morning Hans Bertram, the 26-year-old German pilot, and his mechanic, Adolf Klausmann, found themselves stranded in an unknown cove, surrounded by a lunar landscape, struggling to make themselves understood to a naked, Stone Age man.

If Bertram had recognised the lone figure wading towards him as an Australian Aboriginal – his grey-whiskered face painted in lime and ash, his tall, muscular frame grooved with tribal scars – the Aboriginal had no such assurance that he was dealing with another human being. He had seen other white men before; but these creatures who beckoned him bore the frightening appearance of a Jimy, a ghost. The airmen, in an effort to ward off the flies swarming around, still wore their leather flight helmets and goggles. The goggles were the problem, too much like the wide, empty eyes of powerful spirits staring out from ancient rock paintings of the Dreamtime.

The Aboriginal's name, as would be learned much later, was Jim Bali-bali. He had been hunting alone along the shore when *Atlantis*, nearly out of fuel, splashed down nearby in a spray of tiny rainbows. It took all his courage to climb onto one of its floats and poke his head into the narrow cockpit. Bertram, though fluent in English, spoke far too quickly in his excited state and any signs he tried to make for directions to the nearest town came out as an incomprehensible babble. The German never paused long enough to give the native a chance to respond, but then, Jim Bali-bali was well used to such rudeness. Whatever these strangers were – white men or ghosts – why would they be interested in what a blackfella had to say? He listened politely in respectful silence, then – at the first break in the meaningless jabber – hopped back into the water to go about his business again. Hans Bertram and Adolf Klausmann were left on their own to confront the saw-toothed savagery of the Kimberley coast. They would not meet another human for 40 days.

※

Hans Bertram was one of a glamorous new breed of winged adventurers driven to test their bravery and endurance on the cutting edge of modern technology. Their holy grail was to fly faster or farther or along more hazardous or otherwise unusual routes than ever attempted by anyone before them. For obvious reasons, the island continent at the bottom of the world beckoned as their promised land. Despite the economic slump, the year brought a steady stream of airborne explorers: some determined to leave their mark on aviation history, others content just to discover their own innermost horizons.

A few weeks before Bertram's ill-fated venture, another German pilot – a young woman named Elly Beinhorn – flew into Darwin to complete a remarkable solo flight from Berlin. It had taken her nearly four months, with enough adventures to fill several lifetimes, including a forced landing in the Syrian desert during a blinding sandstorm and a spine-tingling close-up of Mt Everest flying at an altitude of 15,000 feet. In Burma she ran out of fuel, crash-landing in a paddy field, and while trying to relax on a Bali beach saw a swimmer killed by a shark. The outbreak of war between China and Japan dashed her hopes of flying on to Tokyo but she chose Sydney as an alternative after a chance meeting in Calcutta with her aviation idol, Charles Kingsford Smith. Once in Australia, the 24-year-old Fraulein Beinhorn was treated as a national celebrity and proceeded to enchant everyone she met. A newspaper report after her arrival in Brisbane described the type of woman prepared to take such breathtaking risks to taste the freedom of the skies.

'When the engine had stopped,' the *Brisbane Courier* noted, 'the aviatrix removed her flying helmet and goggles and replaced them with a close-fitting beret, which matched her striped travelling skirt, lit a cigarette and smiled at the cheering crowd over a big bouquet of roses. Distinctly feminine and charming, she was at the same time cool and perfectly self-possessed, showing no sign of the strain of travel beyond a coat of tan on her face.'

Beinhorn's skills as a pilot were more than equalled by her soaring abilities as a public speaker and wherever she went in Australia her lectures were always packed. Nothing, she said, though, could match a priceless moment in Sydney. In her enthusiasm to make a point, she drew dangerously close to the edge of the speaker's platform, prompting someone in the front row to shout a warning lest she topple off.

'Oh, that doesn't matter,' she exclaimed, without missing a beat. 'I can fly!'

Kingsford Smith, who had previously introduced her, could only shake his head in admiration and join the prolonged applause.

Some flyers who reached Australia in 1932 didn't show quite the same degree of dedication. Lady Chaytor of Witton Castle in Durham made the trip packing a ukulele as part of her precious luggage allowance.

'If we get lost and come down in the desert, at least it will be a means of passing the time until we are found,' explained the mother of four who, apart from aviation, listed fashion, dancing, and musical comedy among her interests. Fortunately, she travelled in a two-seater Gypsy Moth and was content to leave most of the flying to her male companion, a far more experienced pilot.

From the very start Australians had embraced aviation with an enthusiasm matched by few other populations and pilots arriving from overseas were impressed with the surprisingly sophisticated infrastructure set up to service the new form of transport. By 1932 the country could boast as many as 60 aerodromes and more than 120 emergency landing grounds scattered along the main outback routes. Though the number of pilot licences might appear relatively small – less than 600 – during the year planes still carried 82,500 passengers and accounted for 1,363,636 kilograms of freight. Enthusiastic amateurs like Beinhorn pronounced themselves amazed at the warm receptions they received at every landing point, not just from the well-organised network of aero clubs but from the general public as well. When a famous professional pilot flew in on some record-breaking run, the crowds could easily swell into the many thousands.

Apart from Kingsford Smith's historic airmail flight in January, the most widely hailed achievement of 1932 belonged to the British pilot, C. W. A. Scott. At the end of April he flew into Darwin to establish a new London–Australia speed mark of eight days, twenty hours and 45 minutes, clipping 40 minutes off the old time. Scott had previously worked in Queensland as a flight instructor and had crossed Australia's northern coast several times going back and forth to England. Yet even he admitted nearly coming unstuck on what was widely considered to be the most dangerous leg of the Europe–Australia flight – the daunting 500-mile run across the Timor Sea from Koepang in Indonesia. It was a notoriously unpredictable stretch of water frequently plagued by strong headwinds, if not sudden tropical storms. Though Scott travelled in broad daylight, he still hit Australia's northern coast to find no sign of Darwin.

'I had made a very bad landfall and had to trust to my memory of the coastline to tell me whether to turn left or right,' he told reporters after touching down. 'Fortunately I guessed right.'

Hans Bertram was not to be so lucky. He was flying in the days when it was still possible to get lost, seriously lost, in ways that legends are made of. Radios were unreliable and often judged too heavy to carry on long-distance flights, which is why he chose not to have one. A compass setting was only valid on a given line from take-off to landing and in violent crosswinds the fragile aircraft of the period were vulnerable to being blown well beyond sensible calculation. That was exactly what happened to *Atlantis*, ending up 280 miles (450 kilometres) to the south-west of its destination. Bertram, experienced as he was, wrongly guessed that he might be somewhere to the east – a misjudgement that could only aggravate his predicament. From then on his mind-set sensed salvation in the opposite direction from where it really lay.

Following a bout of adverse weather, pilots were often forced to resort to local road maps to try to re-establish their position. The far north of Australia, though, remained pretty much a blank. Bertram and Klausmann decided to use their last few drops of petrol to make an aerial reconnaissance, hoping to spot a trace of civilisation. After a futile ten minutes *Atlantis* sputtered down on empty to a landing 35 kilometres farther to the west, in a spot even less favourable to their survival. The airmen didn't realise it, but Jim Bali-bali actually understood their gesture indicating thirst. Before leaving, he had tried to point them in the direction of a nearby freshwater pool.

Throughout the ordeal to come, as the Germans exhausted themselves in an ever more desperate search for food and water, other Aboriginals observed their movements from hidden vantage points. They could see the two were slowly dying but were too afraid to offer help: warned off by those unblinking ghost eyes.

The epic search for the missing *Atlantis* was to become one of the most dramatic news stories of 1932, overshadowing the sacking of Jack Lang in its international interest. As the weeks passed there seemed no rational hope of finding its crew alive, yet daily press reports continued to hold Australians in thrall. In a curious way they may have sensed they shared the lost aviators' plight: blown off course by forces beyond their control, feeling hopelessly lost and forgotten by the outside world, wondering how much longer they could battle on with no prospect of rescue in sight.

28
The big smear

**PREPARATIONS FOR CIVIL WAR
POST-ELECTION METHODS OF
SOVIETISING N.S.W.
DOCUMENT SUGGESTS HOW LANG GUARDS
HOPE TO OBTAIN CONTROL OF THE STATE**

Daily Telegraph front page, Thursday, 9 June 1932

Jack Lang's dismissal would unleash the dirtiest election campaign in Australian history – a veritable mudslide of smears and lies. Up to that point the conservative press, for all its open hostility towards the New South Wales Labor leader, had continued to observe at least a token regard for fair and responsible reporting. Now, though, even the more respectable broadsheets were set loose like attack dogs, freed from the leash of any ethical restraints. They savaged the Big Fella with a ferocity born of panic that he might somehow still manage to recast his spell over the electorate, creating an unforeseen backlash that could sweep him back to office more powerful than ever before.

The techniques used to discredit the deposed premier included all the classic tools of black propaganda – his speeches misquoted or buried in the back pages, his every action portrayed as corrupt or communist-inspired; and when his accusers looked like running short of ammunition, they didn't hesitate to involve him in crudely fabricated plots woven from synthetic threads of evidence. Never before had public opinion been manipulated so ruthlessly, if skillfully; yet such shameless abuse of the power of the press would also prove to be the last hurrah for newspapers as the dominant influence in Australian life. The exciting new medium of radio was about to take over as a more trusted source of news and information – and looking at some of the more outrageous examples of gutter journalism leading up to the poll of 11 June 1932, it is easy to see why.

Sydney's *Daily Telegraph* led the pack with its blazing headlines announcing the discovery of a secret manifesto detailing plans for a Langist dictatorship. By way of proof, its front page featured the photo of a single typewritten sheet of paper looking suitably tattered and thumbed-over, as if snatched that very morning from a conspirator's sweat-stained notebook. Though the incendiary document bore no letterhead or signature, its authenticity seemed clear enough to the paper's editors: 'found in rooms at Parliament House occupied by sitting members of the Lang Party'. Not a moment too soon, considering the insidiously subversive content.

'On our return to power on June 11 with a definite mandate from the people to govern for the people and carry out the Lang Plan, we must press on to our objective and do it quickly,' the anonymous memorandum began. It then proceeded to spell out, point by point, the supposed priorities for a new hard-line leftist regime. The list began with what must surely have been the two most frightening words in the conservative vocabulary.

> *Socialisation and Confiscation.*
> *State Governor to be peremptorily deposed.*
> *Federal Government must be given 24 hours to quit N.S.W.*
> *All Federal property not removed within 24 hours to be confiscated and vested in the N.S.W. Government.*
> *Exodus of men and money to other states must cease. All persons in N.S.W. on June 11 to be compelled to remain in N.S.W., except on obtaining a passport to leave.*
> *No person travelling on N.S.W. passport to be allowed to take cash in excess of £10 [$700] over border.*
> *Lang guard from Workers' Defence Army to be stationed at all vital border points to hold up transport.*

Sealing off the borders of a secessionist New South Wales would be no small task considering the state covered an area roughly equal to a third of the entire Dixie confederacy. Assuming such a feat could be achieved, however, under the measures outlined in the 'manifesto' the unfortunate residents were about to find themselves trapped in an Antipodean gulag having to cope with post-election measures like these:

> *Rigid Press censorship to be enforced.*
> *Lang Guards to take precedence over civil police, to have power to arrest any person disobeying their orders and to be billeted on civil populace when away from residence.*
> *Lang Treasury to seize and control all banking. All Government payments to be made in debenture notes, which will be proclaimed legal tender at face value.*

If it was not an oxymoron to have a blueprint for a Red dictatorship then this surely was it – but could voters possibly have taken such a scenario seriously? The *Daily Telegraph* edition of Thursday 9 June stands as a testament to the fact that they obviously could and did amid the rampant paranoia of the time. The paper's regular subscribers tended to be from solid middle-class backgrounds, fiercely loyal to King and Empire. They were well used to a daily litany of Langite atrocities, but it is hard to understand how even they could miss the telltale signs of a grotesque hoax, especially evident in the curious instruction with which the sinister diktat concluded.

'If Lang should, by any mischance, be defeated for Auburn, he to be [sic] appointed State Governor.' Considering the document began with an optimistic prediction of a sweeping victory for the Lang Labor Party, it wasn't easy to see why its namesake should be in any danger of losing his own ultra-safe seat. Even if he did, how could it possibly matter if he was about to preside over a Soviet-style police state? The answer, one suspects, is that there could be no surer way to enrage a gullible royalist than to raise the spectre of an unscrupulous cad like Jack Lang usurping the revered title of governor.

What made the *Telegraph*'s fanciful beat-up all the more extraordinary was that – within the context of the overall election coverage – it wasn't extraordinary at all. Every newspaper served up its own poisonous blend of distorted fact and one-eyed opinion. The *Sun*, Sydney's most popular afternoon paper, specialised in sensational crime reporting so its readers would not have been too surprised to find a prominently displayed double-column spread laid out in the form of a trial transcript. It purported to show a prosecutor in the 'Court of Public Opinion' cross-examining Jack Lang about broken promises from the previous 1930 election. It takes only a couple of brief exchanges to get the drift.

Prosecutor: What did you do to inspire the confidence of investors?
Mr. Lang: Well, shortly after the election I told the world that I intended to stop paying interest on money borrowed in the past.
Prosecutor: Did that inspire confidence?
Mr. Lang: It is hard to answer that question definitely, but shortly after I made my announcement, the Government Savings Bank of NSW – one of the biggest institutions of its kind in the world – had to close its doors because people would insist upon taking their money out.
Prosecutor: Did you also say 'every effort will be made to assist and stimulate industry?' What effort did you make?
Mr. Lang: Well, I introduced an amendment of the Arbitration Act which, if carried, would have placed the control of industry in the hands of the chaps called the [ALP] Inner Group – I forget the Russian equivalent – who have been closely studying the Moscow model.
Prosecutor: Was not the effect of that measure more or less to paralyse all industry?
Mr. Lang: For the time being, perhaps, but people would have got used to it. I'm told that even an eel gets used to being skinned.

For a major metropolitan daily to taint its news pages with fiction was questionable enough but the punchline was yet to come. The *Sun*'s bizarre parody turned out to be specially designed to fit into the theme of a full-page election advertisement for the United Australia Party scheduled to appear a week later. The ad featured a drawing of the Big Fella as a surly prisoner sitting in the dock of the same 'Court of Public Opinion', with sledgehammer copy lines that read in part:

Guilty! On all counts

Lang Rule has been convicted of a number of the worst political acts in the history of the Commonwealth. Lang Rule is the rule of the 'Push' – a Rule of Terrorism and Strife as a smokescreen to cover up its objective – a Dictatorship of New South Wales by 'Red' Revolutionaries of the Trades Hall. It subsidised Communist newspapers with Government money and its administration shrieked of Bribery and Corruption. Lang made the name of New South Wales hated throughout Australia and despised throughout the world. Being convicted on all these counts, Lang Rule must go.

Even the grand dame of Australian journalism, the century-old *Sydney Morning Herald*, threw discretion to the wind and joined the anti-Lang crusade tooth and claw. The paper was normally impeccable in keeping its strong editorial views insulated from its newspage coverage, but as the tense campaign progressed it dropped all pretence of objectivity, most notably in its coverage of the various Lang election rallies. The huge turnouts were beginning to cause the conservative camp grave concern but in two scornful lines the *SMH* managed to dismiss the enthusiastic crowds as mere automatons.

'They wildly applauded or hooted with something suggestive of demoniac fury. Like puppets, they moved to the strings pulled by their leader.'

As always, though, the journalistic bias showed itself first and foremost in the selection and placement of the day's news. Throughout the campaign the balance of coverage was to swing constantly between sordid corruption allegations and Red Bogy alarms. The new conservative caretaker premier, Bertram Stevens, made sure there was an abundance of scandals in either category to keep the presses rolling.

By tradition a caretaker government was expected to refrain from introducing any major new policy initiatives until after the election. Stevens, though, was quick to announce three different royal commissions to investigate fraudulent misconduct within the previous administration: the tin hare inquiry, a separate probe into illicit kickbacks from fruit machines, and a third panel to interrogate a Lang-appointed transport commissioner suspected of taking bribes. Damning leaks began to appear in the press almost immediately.

Stevens was a devoted churchgoer and lay preacher with puritanical views about the evils of gambling; yet his focus on corruption had less to do with religious scruples than hard-headed politics. He instinctively saw the issue as crucial to undermining his opponent's credibility within his own working-class constituency. Among regular ALP voters, there were undoubtedly many who – though concerned about Lang's more impulsive judgements – had tended to forgive him as a sincere idealist with their welfare foremost in his mind. Such supporters would be shocked to the core if they once began to believe their idol to be just another venal, self-serving politician. It was these potential conscience voters whom Stevens cleverly targeted in feeding a steady stream of top-level corruption claims to his allies in the press.

The one allegation that ended up causing the biggest stir had nothing to do with high-profile cases like that of the notorious Judge Swindell. Instead, it boiled down to the relatively mundane issue of 'jobs for the boys'. The previous Labor regime was accused of diverting thousands of pounds in relief funds to put more than 250 union officials and party hacks on the government payroll as commissioners or inspectors, some at salaries ranging up to 50 per cent above the basic wage. It was hardly unknown for political parties of any persuasion to reward their backroom boys with minor positions – but this was in the midst of the Great Depression when a job was the most precious of gifts and such favouritism was bound to cause deep resentments. For those who had always put Jack Lang on a pedestal – above the grubby wheeling and dealing of a Tammany Hall – it was a sad awakening. They could not escape the fact that their hero almost certainly had to be personally involved in approving the names of those on the gravy train. Among them, after all, was his staunchest Trades Hall ally, Jock Garden. The *Sun* was quick to sum up the effective cost of such petty graft in what may well have been the single most damaging headline of the campaign.

Enough To Pay 20,000 Men Fortnight's Wages

Still, when it came to appealing to the public at large, conservative politicians invariably turned to their most tried and true tactic: fanning the flames of the anti-communist hysteria that had gripped Australia since the early 1920s. In this they were well-served by the Labor Party's own 'loony left' with its open devotion to Moscow and constant talk of forced nationalisation within Australia itself. Such ideological rantings offered the perfect launching pad for stories and editorials likening Jack Lang to a Lenin down-under. The *Sydney Morning Herald* sneeringly referred to him as leader of the 'Socialisation Party', a theme that was reiterated by quality broadsheets across the country, including the normally sober Melbourne *Argus*. 'Mr. Lang and Mr. Garden have drunk at the fountain of Russian Bolshevism,' the *Argus* warned, waxing poetical. 'They see in themselves pocket editions of Lenin and Stalin, exercising in the name of democracy a cruel and ignorant tyranny.'

Any astute political reporter or industrial roundsman would have been well aware of Lang's personal disdain for the extremist ideologues within his party and his constant battles to stamp out communist infiltration. Never once would those efforts be acknowledged in the many learned 'commentaries' during the course of the campaign. At best, the Big Fella was demeaned as a mere puppet of the Red conspiracy if not actually a communist himself.

'Vainly do Mr. Lang and his docile henchmen disclaim Communistic attachments,' the *SMH* lectured its readers a week before the poll. 'Actions speak more loudly than words, and both the personnel of his party and the courses he has adopted prove that Langism is hastening at top speed along "the Red Road." The actors responsible for the drift of Communism in Australia during the past decade are of two types. There are the fanatics who relentlessly pursue their aims with a satanic passion. These are, at any rate, avowed enemies of the social order. There are others who, by callow enthusiasm or personal ambition, are seduced into paths the ends of which they do not clearly foresee. It is difficult to say which type is more dangerous.'

Such an intellectual analysis might appeal to the *Herald*'s better educated subscribers but when it came to scaring the wits out of ordinary voters nothing was more effective than a story about how the Reds were trying to indoctrinate their children. Bertram Stevens reaped a lush harvest of outraged headlines when he revealed that the Labor Party's so-called Socialisation Units had been allowed to use the state's public schools as the venues for their regular lectures and discussion groups.

'The Socialisation Units of the ALP are the official spearhead of the Revolution,' he reminded worried parents. 'It was never intended that these centres of learning should be turned into centres for revolutionary propaganda aimed at the overthrow of constituted authority.'

Stevens released a list of more than 30 school buildings which the previous administration had made available to the socialists for their weekly or fortnightly meetings. To drive home the potential danger to young minds, he cited a kindergarten booklet already known to be in circulation in some union libraries enticingly entitled 'Moscow Has a Plan'. It was a volume of nursery rhymes to help smaller children understand the benefits of the Soviet Union's latest five-year plan.

'You will be told during this election that the Socialisation Units are only a wing of the ALP but they are a most powerful wing,' Stevens stressed. 'My Government resents school buildings being put to this use and I am confident that the electors will also express their detestation of such disloyalty.'

The blanket coverage given to the conservative leader's shocking revelation neglected to mention one small point that might normally have been considered relevant. The seminars on socialism were part of a neighbourhood adult education program and were only convened in the local classrooms after the children had long gone home.

The Big Fella was well used to fighting his way through a thick fog of disinformation at every election. Despite his opponent's Red scare tactics he had shown his ability in 1925 and especially in 1930 to win the trust of a sizeable body of uncommitted voters beyond the usual reach of the ALP. Never before, however, had he confronted such a solid wall of press bias blocking his access to the mainstream of public opinion. He had only one newspaper – the *Labor Daily* – at his disposal to respond to the worst of the allegations made against him. His rallies would draw the largest crowds ever assembled; but at the end of the day they only allowed him to preach to the converted. He needed a way to get up and over the wall, beyond the distortion and outright censorship of hostile newspaper managements, and for that he would have to harness the power of the wireless, riding into battle on its magical electromagnetic waves.

29

Radio days: The birth of the ABC

The Big Fella was a natural for radio and he could sense that from the very beginning. He did more than any other politician of the time to try to transform the new medium into a basic tool of parliamentary democracy. In so doing it could even be said that he played a significant – if indirect – role in paving the way for the most momentous development in the cultural life of the nation, the creation of the Australian Broadcasting Commission.

Radio, as a reliable source of information and entertainment, had come relatively late to Australia compared to the United States or Britain. There was certainly no lack of experimentation in the early stages and the Victorian Police could claim in 1922 to be the first such force in the world to adopt the wireless for its mobile communications. However, the federal government proceeded to stifle the natural progress of the medium through zealous over-regulation, starting with what must rank as one of the silliest ideas in the history of broadcasting. In 1923 the Commonwealth Postmaster-General proclaimed that each purchaser of a new wireless would be required to nominate the particular station he intended to listen to and then pay a given annual fee to access that frequency and that frequency only. His receiver was mechanically modified to block out all other signals, though – as the geniuses who dreamed up the 'sealed set' system soon found out – a clever child could quickly learn to alter the wiring to pick up more stations. The nonsensical rule was to slow sales of new sets to a near standstill for a full year, with only 1400 licences issued in 1923–1924. It was not until 1925 that Australians could truly be said to have unfettered access to their own fully fledged broadcasting industry. By then a more sensible approach allowed them to tune in as they wished to a new two-tiered system of A-class stations, supported by licence fees, or B-class stations, catering to more popular tastes and surviving on paid advertisements.

Jack Lang would feature in one of the world's first broadcasts of an actual parliamentary debate. On 24 March 1925, in his role as opposition leader, he led the attack against a controversial amendment to the New South Wales Marriage Act proposed by the conservative government of Sir George Fuller. At issue was a recent Vatican decree that seemed to suggest that children born of civil marriage could not be considered legitimate unless the union also had the blessing of the church. Fuller's drastic new bill went so far as to make it a crime punishable by twelve months in prison for any clergyman to publicly cast doubt on the validity of a civil certificate.

Lang quite rightly saw the measure as a cynical attempt to stir up anti-Catholic bigotry before a forthcoming election – its ultimate aim being to call attention to the Labor Party's relatively high number of Irish Catholics, himself included. The government, for its part, was so convinced its bill would be a vote-winner that it had arranged for radio station 2FC, an A-class station, to broadcast the proceedings. Lang – with his distinctively commanding voice and plain-speaking delivery – managed to turn the event into a public relations disaster for the Nationalists.

'I have always held,' he began, 'that people's religion is a matter between their conscience and their God and is not one for members of Parliament to legislate upon. When anything is sacred to us, or held very dear by us, the very last place in which it should be talked about is in Parliament – in the mire and dirt associated with politics. The Government has deliberately set out to throw the bone of contention before the public in the hope that in the heat of anger and the passion of prejudice, its political shortcomings will be clouded and smothered. The Labor Party has no religion and does not belong to any particular Church. We are a political party and we are here to look after the interests of the people of this State. I am not prepared to allow the Church to interfere in State affairs but at the same time I believe that members of religious bodies should have freedom of conscience.'

The 2FC audience would have been no more than a few thousand listeners at the time – small but highly influential – and Lang's stirring performance succeeded in winning over the very people the government had hoped to enlist into its anti-Catholic crusade. Influential Anglican and Presbyterian churchmen immediately joined in denouncing the bill as a threat to the right of all religions to practise their beliefs and conduct their sacraments without political interference. The government was soon forced to accept amendments that watered down the bill to the point where it was virtually meaningless. In the election that followed two months later, Lang continued to make good use of radio, broadcasting his opening campaign speech. Against long odds, he went on to overcome the widespread prejudice against both Rome and the Reds to win a bare two-seat majority.

Lang's early successful experimentation with the airwaves was to make him an instant convert, convinced that electronic communication was the way of the future in winning hearts and minds. He was in the fortunate position of being able to call on the wisdom of one of the foremost pioneers of Australian broadcasting, Emil Voigt, an English-born engineer and committed socialist intellectual who had joined the New South Wales Labor Council as a senior researcher and adviser. Voigt studied the evolution of the wireless in the United States and became convinced that it could not be long before the same conservative interests who controlled newspapers would seek to impose a similar monopoly over the younger medium. His philosophy was summed up in a few impactful words: 'non-Labor is anti-Labor.' Only by operating their own station could those on the left of the political spectrum guarantee direct access to a mass Australian audience, allowing ordinary citizens to form views untainted by the prevailing bias of the press. Voigt set out to persuade the state's union bosses to invest in a new B-class commercial licence; and though he at first met stubborn resistance from the Luddites among them, 2KY took to the air at the end of October, 1925.

By 1932, with Voigt as its innovative chairman, the station had become the second most popular in Sydney after 2GB, offering a lively mix of original made-for-radio drama, music and sport. For its Trades Hall backers, though, the icing on the cake was 2KY's strong emphasis on talk, much of it aimed at pushing the Labor view on issues in the news like industrial disputes or social reform legislation. There was no indication of listeners being put off by such serious fare. Just the opposite: the Big Fella proved a star attraction on the occasions when the station carried one of his major speeches.

To Voigt, though, 2KY was just the start. He opened Lang's mind to a much bigger picture – the possibility of New South Wales establishing its own comprehensive network of state-owned broadcasting stations, with relays set up in key regional areas to reach the remotest country town. The Queensland Government was already operating its own A-class station, devoted mostly to music and entertainment. In sharp contrast, 'Station Lang', as opponents immediately branded the concept, would be designed to fill special needs across the entire spectrum of government services. The Education Department would produce its own programs, with a radio supplied to every school. So, too, the Agriculture Department could serve up useful information like market reports to those on the land. Police, Railways, Health, and other agencies would all gain their own frequencies to communicate either to their own outlying offices or to the public at large. When the network wasn't being used for official transmissions, it could be freed up to relay entertainment programs with the promise of much clearer reception. Voigt's grand vision saw state government radio as the primary means of reaching out to isolated country listeners who were otherwise likely to be neglected by profit-driven broadcasters. To Lang's detractors, of course, the real purpose was far more sinister.

'The plan to provide country centres with broadcasting stations might seem worthy of consideration,' the influential *Wireless Weekly* editorialised, 'but for the obvious fact that it is intended as a blind for the far more important and insidious scheme of making the public pay for a means of propaganda by which the present Government may be kept in office.'

Both Lang and his mentor, Voigt, openly acknowledged the possibility of misusing such a network for political propaganda. That, ironically, turned out to be one reason why the New

South Wales Premier had initially hesitated in proposing it. 'Governments come and Governments go;' Lang was on record as warning, 'and what might be to our advantage today might be to our disadvantage tomorrow.' Voigt, for his part, foresaw a time when every cabinet minister could have a radio microphone 'comfortably installed at his elbow as means of lightning communication and publicity'. He admitted the implications deeply worried him, but ultimately he came to believe that with the proper regulatory controls in force, the many benefits of a state-owned system far outweighed the risks. The average city listener, at any rate, would not be worse off because he would still have his choice of flourishing B-class entertainment stations to tune in to and he might even end up paying much less in licence fees. Perhaps Voigt allowed himself to be swayed by his socialist ideals, but his concept certainly deserved better than the vicious attack launched upon Lang and him by the *Wireless Weekly*.

'The idea of using radio to pass such information along savours too much of the system which is in use in Russia,' the periodical chided. 'Mr. Lang's State Wireless Scheme, if it is allowed to be put into effect, will prove the most serious setback that the science of wireless in Australia has ever experienced.'

'Station Lang' had to be shelved after the Labor leader lost the 1927 election but the concept undoubtedly helped spur the creation of the Australian Broadcasting Commission. That esteemed institution would begin broadcasting on 1 July 1932, too late for the New South Wales election; yet it was inspired at least in part by some of the pivotal issues raised by Lang and Voigt years earlier. All parties – conservative as well as Labor – came to accept that some sort of government intervention would be needed to spread the benefits of the wireless to more remote areas. Then, too, there was increasing acknowledgement that commercial interests had badly abused their monopoly over the media, churning out so much biased and inflammatory misinformation as to threaten the very fabric of Australian society. If Jack Lang happened to be the current target, the ultimate victim must inevitably be the ordinary citizen, robbed of the precious gift of enlightened democratic choice. Even within the United Australia Party, then, respected figures such as the former prime minister, William Morris Hughes, began calling for the creation of a publicly owned network that could be trusted by all. 'I am entirely opposed to the political control of broadcasting and I want to see a Commission established which will be entirely independent of such control, so that no political party will be able to use this great instrumentality for its own purposes,' he told his fellow federal parliamentarians. 'We all, I think, want this.'

It would be Hughes, more eloquently, perhaps, than anyone else, who summed up the potential of the wireless in shaping the nation's destiny. 'Broadcasting will be more potent in reaching out to the distant parts of this great country and in exerting an influence for good or evil than any other agency, including our educational system and our universities.'

The one question still to be settled, though, was whether public broadcasting need automatically be left to the Commonwealth alone. Lang accepted that the federal government had the exclusive authority to allocate frequencies but he argued that such technical control didn't necessarily extend to putting out actual programs. Under the Constitution, he contended, each state still had a right to start up its own version of a publicly funded network so long as it didn't compete directly with any pre-existing Commonwealth-owned broadcaster. In Canberra the federal ALP, under Jim Scullin, was just as anxious as the conservatives to kill off any chance of 'Station Lang'. Scullin was first to draft an ABC bill in 1931 and after his defeat the succeeding UAP Government of Joe Lyons was quick to adopt the legislation almost in its entirety. It was a rare instance of full cooperation among all the major parties and only two issues sparked any degree of factional wrangling. The ALP was keen to allow the national broadcaster to accept advertising, perhaps more as a punishment to its arch-enemies within the commercial media than a means of making extra money. The government offered the compromise of 'sponsorships', but even that possibility was withdrawn as Lyons's powerful newspaper allies raised an almighty stink. The conservatives, for their part, tried to give the Postmaster-General extensive veto powers over all ABC programming. After a general howl of protest, that measure, too, was modified to allow for the PMG to intervene only on rare occasions 'in the public interest'.

As it finally took shape the ABC was an amalgamation of the twelve previous A-class stations, eight city-based and four in the country, broadcasting to 370,000 licensed receivers across Australia. Perhaps three times that many listeners were able to tune in on crystal sets or other unauthorised devices. The commission's founding chairman was the prominent Sydney retail magnate and art lover, Charles Lloyd Jones. Its first program began promptly at 8 pm, Friday, 1 July, beginning with the sound of the bells ringing the hour from the Sydney General Post Office, very much in the tradition established by the revered BBC. 'This is the Australian Broadcasting Commission,' the announcer intoned in impeccable BBC English. Joe Lyons pronounced the national network duly inaugurated. Then Charles Lloyd Jones humbly implored the audience not to expect too much too quickly.

London is the Mecca of all artists of outstanding ability, whereas in Australia, although we have many fine artists, the field is limited. When listeners take into consideration that every day, with the exception of Sunday, the service begins at 7 am continuing without intermission until 11:30 pm and during the greater portion of this time in some cases two stations are operating simultaneously – they will understand the enormous difficulty of presenting programmes of a high standard of merit every day of the week, every week of the year. That they can and will be improved we do not doubt. We intend to give every encouragement to local talent; we will also from time to time engage visiting artists of distinction. We would ask the public not to expect too rapid a change. The service now belongs to you. We are your trustees.

It was a timid start to what in truth was a monumental achievement considering the highly volatile temper of the times. The Australian Broadcasting Commission had somehow emerged from the normally corrosive and corrupting processes of hard-line party politics as pure as the driven snow. Much of the credit for that, in a curious way, could well be traced back to the daunting spectre of the Big Fella hovering menacingly in the background.

The ABC would slowly but steadily succeed in remoulding some of the uglier features of 1930s-style Australian journalism, leading by example and allowing the public to cross-check distorted print coverage against the unbiased reality. That transformation would come much too late, however, to assist Jack Lang in reaching beyond his town hall meetings to the broadest possible audience. The Lyons Government – taking advantage of its last few months of absolute control over the outgoing system of privately owned A-class stations – had even barred the New South Wales Premier from appearing on 2FC despite that station being made freely available to the Prime

Minister for a highly partisan speech on the evils of Langism.

Lang naturally turned to 2KY as a means of counterattack, but he used it in far more imaginative ways than simply for speechmaking. Remembering his success during the 1925 Marriage Act broadcast, he arranged in late February to transmit an entire session of Parliament, not just a single debate. Lang and his key ministers exploited the opportunity for all it was worth, calling attention day after day to various examples of misreporting in the daily newspapers. This typical excerpt is taken from Question Time, Tuesday, 23 February 1932, when the Opposition attempted to needle Lang's Chief Secretary, Mark Gosling, about a current press campaign blaming the government for the state's allegedly high crime rate.

Sir Daniel Levy: May I ask the Chief Secretary if he has given consideration to the serious question of amending the law relating to the use of firearms?
Mr. Gosling: A daily newspaper for a considerable time has been featuring a small picture of a gun and a few words. The committal of crimes is not confined to periods when a Labor Government is in office. Crimes were committed during the regime of the last Government, of which the honourable member was a supporter.
Interjector: Point of order! The Minister was asked a question, and he is making a statement which is not an answer to the question at all!
Mr. Gosling: I had anticipated that some honourable member would carry on the propaganda of the newspaper and ask a question here and I am now giving my version of the story. Although the previous Government was in power for three years, it thought fit to slumber on this question without amending the Gun Act, about which it now makes so great a to-do.

Lang himself used his parliamentary air time to disclose some of the secret discussions which went on at one of the Premiers' Conferences, including an extraordinary direct quote from the Premier of Western Australia, Sir James Mitchell. According to Lang, even the arch-conservative Mitchell had allegedly challenged Joe Lyons by demanding to know: 'Who is going to pay our interest and feed our unemployed?' The revelation stirred Lang's opponents into a fury, with a swarm of interjections insisting that it violated the confidentiality rules applying to a premiers' forum.

'The honourable member asked me if this is confidential,' Lang jibed, playing to the microphone. 'How can it be? I am not abusing any parliamentary privilege.'

'Was it from the records of the conference?' another interjector angrily demanded.

'It was a secret conference, held in secret against my protest,' Lang boomed. 'I wanted the newspapers to be there, and the public, also. They said "no".'

Such parliamentary fireworks made for exciting listening and to avoid any hint of a 2KY monopoly, Lang authorised Voigt to share the broadcasts on alternative days with another popular and innovative station, 2UW. However, a more creative use of the new medium for political campaign purposes was yet to come. A brilliant young radio actor and scriptwriter of the day, John Pickard, happened to be a fervent believer in Jack Lang. He proposed that the Labor Party sponsor a series of Sunday night made-for-wireless dramas built upon overtly political themes, such as a battling family's desperate dependency on child endowment or an evicted tenant's last-minute rescue by the Lang moratorium laws. They were called 'Plays of the People' and as Lang fondly recalls in his memoirs, they were to have an instant impact on the listening public – though producing far more howls of anger than rave reviews.

'The night the first play was broadcast, everyone must have been listening in,' he recalled. 'The phone never stopped ringing. The station was abused by everyone who hated Lang – at the time that was no insignificant number of people.'

Pickard, who would soon go on to become a famous radio writer in the United States, suffered from all the predictable side effects of precocious genius, the foremost of which was a tendency to be so late with his scripts that they were often frantically pounded out while the actors hovered in mid-sentence. For the last drama of the series the young playwright had persuaded the Big Fella to appear as himself, answering questions put to him by cast members playing the roles of concerned voter, impoverished widow and so on. He, too, found himself waiting in front of the mike to go live to air with Pickard nowhere in sight.

'As the hour of the broadcast approached, our playwright was caught up in the emotion of the occasion and was unable to finish the script,' Lang remembered. 'There was mild panic. Eventually, when everyone was preparing to cancel, John suddenly charged into the room, grabbed a typewriter and finished the script just in time for us to go to air.'

There was no mention of these plays in the mainstream press or even the specialist periodicals like *Wireless Weekly* or *Broadcasting Monthly*, such was the determination of the print media to keep Lang from scoring a trick during the 1932 election campaign. The *Sun* even stopped listing 2KY in its daily rundown of wireless programming schedules. No matter how effectively Lang used the station, though, it was still only one voice raised against a crescendo of denunciations.

Ironically, of all the techniques used by the conservative media to try to ensure the Big Fella's defeat – the unceasing lies, smears, distortions and hate-mongering – nothing was to prove more effective in the end than *truth*, or at least, a gilded version of it. Every newspaper, day after day, besotted the public with glowing tales of an almost miraculous upswing in the economy since Lang's dismissal. On an item-by-item basis most of these recovery reports drew on at least a semblance of fact, although together they tended to paint far too optimistic a picture, especially since unemployment was actually still worsening. Nevertheless, the 'good news' campaign, combined with incessant allegations of corruption and communist conspiracy, must have exerted a powerful influence over the relatively small but critical mass of undecided voters. In pushing this type of 'white' propaganda, the *Sydney Morning Herald* led the way.

SINCE THE DISMISSAL
Signs of Improvement

There are many concrete examples to show how the downfall of the Lang Government has cleared the way for more prosperous times. Within an hour, almost, of Mr. Lang's dismissal, people began to show signs of returning confidence, and in less than a week there have been striking improvements in every kind of business. In Sydney many stocks immediately gained 10 per cent. The announcement in London was the signal for almost meteoric rises in Australian stocks. Real estate has shared in the general reaction. In two days after Mr. Lang's dismissal, one real estate company sold more than £50,000 [$3.5 million]. A trust company in Sydney has been holding up the erection of a £43,000 [$3,010,000] building for the past 12 months. It was announced yesterday the premises would be built immediately the Stevens Government returned to power. The Commonwealth has allotted £600,000 [$42 million] for relief work in New

South Wales. The new Ministry's assurance that it will adhere to the Premiers' Plan will probably mean another grant of £600,000.

Sydney Morning Herald, Thursday, 19 May

With such mighty forces arrayed against him, Jack Lang might have seemed to stand hardly any chance at all. All that was left to him was his voice and his magnetic persona. Heading into the last week of the campaign, they would prove enough to give his opponents the fright of their lives.

30

The last hurrah!

I wonder would the apathy of wealthy men endure
Were all their windows level with the faces of the Poor?

His brother-in-law's poem must surely have come to mind once more as Jack Lang stepped up to the speaker's platform on the afternoon of Sunday, 5 June, to gaze upon the greatest sea of faces ever recorded at an outdoor political rally in Australia. As many as 250,000 people converged on Moore Park, close to the Sydney Cricket Ground, to hear him launch the final week of his campaign. Even with the media's overwhelmingly anti-Lang bias, enough colour shines through in the various press reports of the day to paint a vivid picture of a truly memorable occasion. The massive turnout could only have left the Big Fella's conservative enemies quaking, much as described by Henry Lawson in his prescient verse.

> Ah! Mammon's slaves, your knees shall knock, your
>   hearts in terror beat,
> When God demands a reason for the sorrows of the
>   street,
>   The wrong things and the bad things
>   And the sad things that we meet
> In the filthy lane and alley, and the cruel, heartless street.

Not since the opening of the Harbour Bridge had the city seen such lively and good-natured throngs flocking in from every direction, many marching under banners proclaiming the suburbs they were from and spurred on by brass bands playing the latest jazz hits. Lang Party and union officials had worked out elaborate flow charts to coordinate the marchers but apart from the obvious organisational links there was no possible way to distinguish the crowds as pro-Labor or even particularly 'working class'. They were from all ages – bemedalled war veterans, grannies in wheelchairs, hip-swinging flappers with their hopeful young swains and rough-housing kids in bare feet. Most were jauntily dressed in their Sunday finest, though scattered through the assembly here and there were telltale glimpses of an old military greatcoat or threadbare suit jacket denoting the uniform of the unemployed.

The roar of five SCGs at the crack of a Bradman six could hardly have been greater than the ovation that greeted the first sight of the Big Fella. Altogether, those attending accounted for 20 per cent of Sydney's entire population. Lang, in relative terms, would have been speaking to today's equivalent of more than 800,000 people.

If the ex-Premier had begun to regret the reckless judgements that had led him into this unwanted early poll, what he saw before him now filled him with a surge of confidence powerful enough to set every nerve tingling. He may have lost himself for a moment – giving way to his self-destructive mood swings – but he had not lost his 'Langites', the ordinary folk who still hung on his every word. Their presence in such vast numbers suggested to him that the single campaign issue he had instinctively chosen to focus upon was beginning to show results. From the very start he had set out to make 11 June a 'him or me' election. The 'him' had little to do with his UAP opponent, Bertram Stevens, or even his federal nemesis, Joe Lyons. Instead, an English governor had thwarted the will of 55 per cent of the New South Wales electorate, more than 700,000 people who had voted for Labor less than two years earlier. Now Sir Philip Game would have to answer to them.

'This magnificent demonstration is a fitting answer to those who are attempting to set up a despotic rule in this state,' Lang exulted. 'By the illegal and arbitrary use of the Governor's position, they have driven the people's representatives out of Parliament.'

'Deport him,' one female interjector screamed in a voice shrill enough to slice through the general clamour. 'Show him the way to go home,' yelled another, to roars of scornful laughter.

All of Lang's major campaign speeches would serve to reinforce the same theme, making Game synonymous with arch-conservatism and its autocratic assumption of the right to rule for the benefit of a privileged few. Sir Philip – if the Big Fella could manage it – was to become the dividing line in this election: between the past and the future, between outdated colonial subservience and an Australia young and free.

'The opposition we met was tremendous,' Lang reminded the crowds again and again. 'Arrayed against us were the whole of the newspapers of Australia; all the other governments of Australia; corrupt courts – not in the sense that their decisions were guided by monetary considerations, but that they were prepared at all times to twist the law to the benefit of the financial institutions and the detriment of the people.'

> Despite these overwhelming odds, your 55 Labor representatives stood shoulder to shoulder fighting every inch of the way. When the Mortgages Taxation Bill passed the Legislative Council, our long fight had been won. In our hands was the weapon which would have compelled the financial institutions to make available the necessary finance for the rehabilitation of the state. We had beaten the newspapers; we had beaten the Commonwealth Government; but as we reached out to take for the people the fruits of their victory, the hand of the assassin struck, swift and unerring, and the people's freedom, so hardly gained, has been momentarily taken from them.

At that point the jeers and catcalls could be counted on to carry all the way to Government House. Lang, who sometimes spoke for two to three hours at a time, would use the uproar to full advantage, allowing his voice a welcome rest while building up the dramatic tension for his final thrust.

'On the 11th of June,' he promised, 'the dagger will be taken from the hand of the assassin. The only authority will come from Parliament.'

Sir Philip, by that time, should have been well used to insults being hurled at him from every direction. He had, after all, already endured months of criticism as a coward or idiot for his steadfast refusal to sack Lang. As a man of honour, he was fully prepared to pay such a high personal price if that was what it took to stick to his principles and follow the dictates of his conscience. He could at least take some comfort from knowing that most of the previous anti-Game diatribes were inspired by various factions out to serve their own ambitions and hardly reflective of mainstream opinion.

The Labor leader's line of attack, however, was both more subtle and more subversive – painting him as a mere pawn of powerful vested interests – and it unsettled him like nothing before. What surprised and distressed him most were the spontaneous interjections, the contemptuous shouts and gestures of the crowd. He could not bear the thought that his action in dismissing Lang might cause ordinary citizens to lose respect not only for him but for the office of governor itself and the monarchy it represented. A triumph for the ousted premier – and Moore Park made that a real possibility – would mean Sir Philip's instant recall; but weighing on his mind much more than that, it would mean he had betrayed his King.

'I should not be surprised to see Labor come back,' Game confided to a family friend.

At the start of the campaign, the Governor had encouraged Gwendolen to go off to their southern highlands retreat with Rosemary and David to avoid any chance of getting caught up in a demonstration or other nasty incident. Lang's political organisers – including Jock Garden and some of the more militant members from Trades Hall – had originally demanded they be allowed to stage the 5 June rally at the Domain but were refused the necessary permit. The official explanation was that such a large gathering would unfairly disrupt the traditional Sunday speeches there. Police, however, were clearly concerned at the possibility of a portion of the huge crowd getting worked up enough to stage a protest march on Government House, just a stone's throw away.

'Outwardly all is very quiet here,' Game noted, 'but I suppose we cannot hope to get through the election without a great deal of heat, though I hope it will be confined to talk and pen and eschew gas pipes.'

Up to this point, the Governor had shown remarkable even-handedness, resisting any temptation to involve himself directly in party politics. During the campaign, however, he was finally to yield to his inner turmoil and initiate secret negotiations so partisan in nature as to threaten the most explosive repercussions should they ever have leaked out.

If a Labor landslide was on the cards, there was nothing Game could do about it. He was seriously concerned, however, about the more likely prospect of Lang creeping back to power with the barest of majorities, exploiting factional strife among the conservatives. Relations between the Nationalists (later to become the UAP) and the Country Party (later, the United Country Party) were continually strained by divisive issues such as tariffs and transport and they often ended up fighting each other for key rural seats, to the benefit of Labor. Sir Philip took it upon himself to play peacemaker, personally pleading with Country Party leader Michael Bruxner to join with the UAP in a makeshift coalition. Bruxner knew that he risked enraging many of his party's more independent-minded members by consenting to Game's request, but he went ahead anyway without seeking prior approval.

'Without time to consult the constituencies I made a decision which I considered was in keeping with my duty,' he explained at the time. 'I know it requires some sacrifice on the part of our supporters. I ask them to help not only me but the whole of the people of this state and Australia.'

In his public statements, the Country Party leader never mentioned his private meeting with Sir Philip and only years later was he willing to discuss the Governor's behind-the-scenes role in forging his electoral pact with Bertram Stevens.

'That we resolved our differences in 24 hours was due to the fact that Sir Philip asked me, personally, to help him,' Bruxner admitted in Bethia Foott's book about the dismissal published in 1968. 'I fell afoul of my own executive [but] my defence was that Sir Philip had made a personal appeal which overshadowed everything else.'

Ironically, according to Bruxner, it was his party's unswerving loyalty to the Governor that had strained relations between the two conservative factions in the first place.

'One of the main reasons of the friction between the Nationalist and Country parties was that the latter was wholly opposed to any pressures being put on Sir Philip to dismiss Lang until there was a definite overt act on his part,' Bruxner recounted. 'The Country Party had to publicly dissociate itself from the attempt by [the Nationalists] to have a petition signed which requested his excellency to take immediate action.'

Game was his own worst critic and surely realised that he was misusing his influence in a way that he himself would have found unthinkable only a few weeks earlier. Perhaps he was able to rationalise his indiscretion by arguing that dissension between the main conservative parties could only contribute to further instability in the Parliament. The truth, though, was that his intervention shattered all pretence of impartiality, threatening Lang's control of fifteen country electorates.

Game's months under the battering ram had finally taken their toll, inflicting the hairline crack in an otherwise flawless image. Lady Game, in one of her letters home, gave an inkling of the terrible pressures her husband and the whole family must have been feeling as the election campaign rumbled on toward its uncertain climax.

'Of course, we realise that we are not yet out of the wood. I hardly dare think of it. Anyhow, Philip will never have Mr. Lang back unless he gives a guarantee to keep the law – but even so one daren't think of it.'

On the hustings the battle between the major parties would have been destined under any circumstances to be among the fiercest ever fought, but personal animosity between Lang and Stevens added a white-hot intensity all its own. Their mutual contempt dated back to 1925 when Lang first won office, becoming Treasurer as well as Premier. Stevens, at the time, had been an influential financial adviser to the previous conservative government, known for his tough anti-union views. The Big Fella, typically, proceeded to send him to Coventry, refusing to say a single word to him even though Stevens – then in his mid-thirties – was one of the state's highest-ranking public servants. Eventually, the younger man took the hint and resigned before Lang could find a way to fire him. He went on to open a highly successful accountancy practice, attracting the attention of the city's leading business magnates who urged him to run for parliament as a future conservative leader. Defeating the man who nearly ruined his brilliant career would be sweet revenge indeed. For Lang it was particularly galling to think of this cold-blooded Scrooge sitting in his chair.

The two had hardly begun sniping at each other on the campaign trail before Stevens issued Lang with a £5000 ($350,000) writ for defamation, embarrassed by revelations that his personal chauffeur was being paid for by the owner of a bus company seeking government contracts. Lang, typically, used the writ as a prop in his Moore Park speech, producing gales of laughter by reading the pompous lawyers' letter demanding he cease and desist from inferring that his rival was corrupt. 'If Mr. Stevens' solicitors believe there's an imputation of impropriety and dishonesty against their client, then it is they who are making the statement, not I.'

To which an interjector shouted: 'You are still ahead of them, Jack!'

Compared to Lang's full-blooded oratory, Stevens sounded positively anaemic. Even the *Sydney Morning Herald*, otherwise awash with superlatives in its coverage of his campaign launch, was reduced to describing his lacklustre style as 'a plain story told in a plain way – an appeal not to the heart but to the mind'. Yet his monotone delivery was still packed with some of the scariest language ever heard in an Australian election.

'Continuation of the outlaw policy of the Lang administration in its defiance of the Commonwealth law would create in Australia a position similar to that which culminated in civil war in the United States many years ago,' Stevens solemnly warned. 'That civil strife caused the loss of thousand of lives. Remember that under a Lang Government, Australia would be face to face with civil war and the break-up of the Federal Union. Before the prospect of such a calamity, every other consideration fades into insignificance.'

Such inflammatory words were music to the ears of Eric Campbell and what remained of his right-wing militia, stirring them into action once again. The organisation, by June, was clearly on the wane, having lost thousands of supporters over the fallout from the Jock Garden episode and subsequent bad publicity about its secret coup plans and fascist leanings. The dismissal of Jack Lang had also made the threat of a Red takeover seem far less imminent, though Campbell could still count on his 'Ironsides' to jump to his orders. 'The New Guard threw in all its strength behind the UAP,' he later acknowledged. 'Some 20,000 New Guardsmen were actively associated with the elections and we mustered around 4000 cars to assist UAP voters.' The militants also patrolled conservative party rally venues to make sure that 'candidates got a fair hearing' and any 'hooligan tactics' were quickly suppressed.

Nevertheless, Campbell maintained a fair degree of scepticism toward UAP politicians. He still felt betrayed by Joe Lyons's refusal to publicly recognise the role played by the New Guard in supporting his election the previous December.

Following Lang's dismissal he personally confronted Stevens, demanding to know whether he agreed with the New Guard's anti-communist policies. The newly appointed Premier readily assured him of his full and active support. Stevens no doubt had New Guard votes in mind when he spoke of the pernicious aims of the 'Red Army' supposedly poised to spearhead Lang's plans for a 'rebel' state taking orders directly from Moscow.

'The Lang outlaw Cabinet forgot that we are a community 99 per cent British,' he scoffed. 'We have no time for these Red wreckers and will not rest one moment until we have swept them away and undone the evil which they have done.'

Apart from the New Guard, Stevens could count on the heavy-handed antics of any number of bosses prepared to misuse their positions to intimidate their employees. 'If Lang gets in, you're out,' was the stark warning passed on from work place to work place. The *Sydney Morning Herald* seemed to give such intimidatory tactics its official blessing in one of its most hysterical editorials yet, appearing on the Monday after the Moore Park rally. Should Lang be returned, the paper predicted ominously, 'there will be no money to pay wages. If the electors vote for him they will be voting for revolution and civil war and general savagery.'

What Stevens's campaign depended upon most, though, were the emergency funds diverted to his immediate use by Prime Minister Lyons and the federal government. Within a few days of taking office he was able to make good on the tens of thousands of delayed welfare payments, as well as put as many as 10 per cent of the registered unemployed into part-time work The state's cash-starved economy received £6 million ($420 million) in one lump sum with another £6 million promised after the election.

Joe Lyons himself – obviously concerned by the giant turnout at Moore Park – cast aside his natural distaste for pandering to the mob and came up with one of the most impassioned speeches of his career.

'If I never do anything else in the national parliament,' he told a jubilant UAP meeting at Sydney Town Hall, 'I shall look back with the greatest pride to the fact that it was my pleasure and honour to introduce the Enforcement Acts [against Lang]. When we passed that legislation we drew a cordon tighter and tighter around him. If by any unhappy chance he should get into office again, we will tie him up again as we tied him up before. Whatever your verdict, ladies and gentlemen, the Federal Government is going on with the job.'

The Prime Minister, buoyed by the enthusiastic applause, even allowed himself to indulge in a rare bit of showmanship.

'New South Wales, you have to make your choice: are you going to live up with the other decent, honest governments in Australia' – he paused for the screams of 'yes' to die down – 'or are you going to adopt the spurious policy of repudiation given to you by Mr. Lang and his followers?' A more polished orator would have reversed the two questions knowing the 'yeses' were bound to reverberate much longer than the 'noes'. Still, for the ex-schoolteacher from Tasmania it was one hell of a speech.

Jack Lang knew that to win office a Labor leader needed to reach beyond his own working-class constituency and find ways of appealing to the uncommitted mainstream. He achieved that in 1925 with the promise of major social and industrial reform – a pledge which, to his credit, he largely fulfilled. In 1930 he reaped a landslide by promising to defend the standard of living against the prevailing economic dogma calling for balanced budgets and massive wage cuts. By 1932, however, the Big Fella had simply run out of promises. While his opponent was able to point to the actual transfer of cash into state coffers, Lang could only ask voters to imagine the rivers of gold that might flow from his mortgage tax, and even then, there was the question of whether the High Court would allow the controversial measure to stand. The issue was, indeed, so shrouded in doubt that the Labor leader was forced to dream up a far-fetched alternative by which a new Lang administration might obtain the funds it needed to carry on. His plan – immediately ridiculed by the press – was for the state to issue its own promissory notes, more than £21 million worth, secured by the special income tax surcharges for unemployment relief that were already in place. The theory was that within three years the accumulated tax receipts would be enough to honour all borrowings in full. Meanwhile the holder of a state-issued £100 paper note could treat it as actual currency, for example to pay his rates or motor vehicle registration fee. Unfortunately for Lang, that scheme – which was tantamount to New South Wales having its own form of currency – had even less chance than the mortgage tax of surviving the scrutiny of the High Court. It only served to give the press more excuses to mock and discredit him.

Lang, ultimately, was forced to fall back on an entirely negative campaign, trying to frighten voters about the conservatives' real intentions. He warned of secret plans to dismantle the welfare schemes he had set in place, in particular the legislation to protect destitute families from eviction or foreclosure until they had a chance to plead their case in court. He also raised the spectre of savage cuts to the basic wage under Stevens's new hard-line regime. The Premier shrugged off such allegations as a sign of his opponent's growing desperation, and in the case of Labor's sky-is-falling alarm about a 35 per cent reduction in the basic wage, he seemed well justified.

To add to Lang's woes during the campaign, word came through from London that the Privy Council had upheld the appeal against his bill to abolish the Upper House. That meant that even if he was returned to power, he was likely to encounter the same obstructionist tactics.

Against such formidable facts, Lang could only hope that the people would vote with their hearts – their love for their state above the still vague concept of a larger commonweal, their love of freedom beyond the manipulation of an English governor, their love of a leader who – right or wrong – was willing to put their welfare above the dubious, budget-balancing theories spouted by the bankers and economists. Such a reservoir of affection certainly existed, though it had dried up considerably since the 1930 triumph, when Lang's appeal extended into middle-class suburbia. The massive rally at Moore Park just a week before the election reassured him he might yet have enough loyal followers to scrape through, even if he couldn't share the wild optimism of a key adviser who boldly proclaimed: 'The fight is over – not only will Labor retain all its seats, but will increase its majority!' As absurd as that prediction might sound, here before them was tangible evidence that the Big Fella still had the power to mesmerise the masses. Two hundred and fifty thousand faces couldn't lie. Or could they?

31

11 June:
The people's verdict

In 1932 Dr Gallup was still a few years away from perfecting his scientific opinion polls. Straw polls conducted by the one-eyed media were totally unreliable, so politicians – apart from their instincts – really had no credible way of predicting an election outcome. The Fifty-Fifty Club, with its yeasty mix of high and low life, would have been as good a place as any to get a feel for the mood of the electorate leading up to 11 June. Phil Jeffs had a grapevine that stretched from eastern suburbs society gossip to the nightly titbits picked up by Tilly Devine's ubiquitous whores. He may well have used such intelligence to set the odds for a lucrative sideline in election bets, though no indicator seemed more significant than what was showing up in his own nightly sales of sly grog.

Ever since Lang's dismissal, Jeffs was no doubt delighted to find his business booming – a phenomenon experienced in almost every other category of retailing. One might have expected to see a boost at the toff end of Fifty-Fifty's clientele – the champagne and cognac set – but the biggest increase was coming from sales of beer and sherry ordered by ordinary suburban types, many of them identified by Jeffs as first-time customers.

The most intriguing aspect of this sudden spending spree was that it certainly wasn't based on any change in employment levels, which were still hovering near rock-bottom at the beginning of June. Instead, it could only be coming from secret hoards of pound notes which people had been squirrelling away under their beds or in wall cavities in fear of worse times to come. With Lang's downfall, they obviously started feeling relaxed enough to risk a little splurge. Jeffs was no economist, but he couldn't help thinking how many jobs might have been saved if all that extra cash – tens of millions of pounds' worth, as it turned out – had been spread around earlier in the year instead of being hidden away out of circulation. Still, to Phil the Jew it was a sure sign of where the election was probably headed.

Jeffs also would have had Tilly Devine's Whores' Poll to rely on. Her girls, after all, engaged in nightly random sampling of men from all walks of life; and up to that point it had mainly been the male vote that mattered since women tended to follow the lead of their husbands or fathers. If Tilly's girls really had their finger on the pulse, they would have detected a common reaction among a surprising number of those who had witnessed that memorable Lang rally.

'Saw the Big Fella out at Moore Park the other day.'
'So you gunna vote for him?'
'Nah, don't think so.'
'Then why did you bother?'
'To tell the truth, I was sure he was going to say or do something to save this election for him – you know, like pull a bloody rabbit out of a hat. I just wanted to be there to be able to say I saw it happen.'

'But he didn't?'

'Nah, he's still quite a bloke but I guess he's lost his magic.'

⁂

Radio came into its own that election night, bringing Australians together as never before. From coast to coast perhaps a third of the population – more than two million people – huddled around a wireless to find out whether the Commonwealth of Australia would still be the same next morning. Not all of them necessarily hoped that it would. Western Australia boasted a thriving secessionist movement. As much as those involved might loathe Jack Lang, they saw his possible return as extra incentive for their isolated state to declare its independence from the Federation. For similar reasons, breakaway groups in the New England and Riverina regions of New South Wales were ready to use Lang's re-election as the trigger for referendums demanding recognition as separate states.

In Queensland, meanwhile, listeners had their own state election hanging in the balance that evening, including two seats contested by candidates running under the banner of the Lang Party. While they accepted they had little chance of winning, they hoped their showing would be big enough to reveal a potential groundswell of Langite support outside New South Wales. The outcome, as it happened, would prove especially encouraging for the official ALP after six months of sheer disaster, including the fall of the Scullin Government and the debacle in Victoria. Voters demonstrated that they were still prepared to welcome in a Labor administration, provided it was moderate enough to accept the overall framework of the Premiers' Plan and shun radical unionism. The incoming premier, William Forgan Smith, secured a narrow victory over the conservatives by pledging an imaginative new approach to emergency relief, including public works schemes to be financed by private investment as well as taxes. The two Langite hopefuls – reflecting what was about to happen to Lang himself south of the border – polled just 559 votes between them.

In New South Wales, amid the celebration or lament, one listener remained glued to his set throughout the evening, showing not the slightest glimmer of emotion. Sir Philip Game – if he was true to form – would have taken no pleasure whatsoever from what he was hearing. Certainly he was relieved when it became clear, an hour or so into the broadcast, that his King would not suffer the embarrassment of having to recall him in disgrace; but Lang's brutal metaphor still preyed on his mind – his hands would be forever stained with blood.

'In spite of the popular endorsement of my assassin's stroke, I am still wondering if I did right,' Sir Philip mused. 'I still believe that Lang has a great deal of right on his side, that a lot of what he advocates will have come to pass, and that the extremists on the other side are a greater danger than extreme Labor. But he seemed to have put himself in an impossible position. With all his faults of omission and commission, I had and still have a personal liking for Lang and a great deal of sympathy for his ideals, and I did not at all relish being forced to dismiss him.'

Game's gnawing self-doubt could only have been compounded when he opened the *Sydney Morning Herald* to read an editorial hailing his supposed vindication 'by the ultimate tribunal in the land, the electorate'. As the paper went on to assure its readers: 'A Governor is not concerned with party politics; it is a matter of indifference to him who is in power; he is prompted only by solicitude for the public interest.'

One might imagine Micky – always a sounding board to his gentle master's vibrations – sensing it wise at that moment to escape from the study.

In the early stages of the election count it looked as if Lang might be defeated in his own electorate of Auburn. His personal vote plunged from 76 per cent to just over 50 per cent. His party lost more than half of its 55 seats, including all fifteen of those it had previously held in the country electorates that figured so prominently in Governor Game's secret talks with Michael Bruxner. It marked the first time since the founding of the New South Wales Labor Party that it had failed to secure a single rural seat outside the mining belt.

The showing in metropolitan electorates was even worse, with sixteen seats falling to the conservatives. Some were merely returning to their normal voting patterns after the 1930 landslide, but a significant number represented traditional Labor strongholds. Within these, the losses were spearheaded by a large-scale defection of women voters. In most elections up to this point, Australian women had been happy to stick to a solid tradition of voting the way their menfolk did. In the case of Labor-supporting families, the men no doubt gave their wives repeated pep talks assuring them that Jack Lang was the only politician who had their true interests at heart, that he was prepared to battle on for as long as it took to hold the line on the standard of living. No doubt many women fully agreed with the slogan that *Lang is Right* – in every way that counted, except one.

Many, it seems, had made up their minds that the time had come to stop all this political nonsense and let people get on with their lives as best they could. Giving in to the conservatives – no matter what kind of bastards they turned out to be – couldn't be worse than what they had gone through during the chaos of the Enforcement Act fiasco when 100,000 mothers and widows missed up to three fortnightly welfare payments. They felt sorry, really, deeply sorry that the Big Fella had sacrificed so much to try to make their lives a little easier. But of all the fears they would carry into the polling booths with them, it was now Jack Lang they feared the most.

'The election showed a far greater swing against Mr. Lang and his policy than I had anticipated,' Sir Philip later reported to King George V. 'From all I can hear, it was the women's vote which decided the outcome in the industrial districts. The mothers, I fancy, turned to the Nationalists out of despair at the unemployment of their sons and daughters and in a great many cases voted quietly the opposite way of their husbands.'

Apart from Jack Lang, there was one other big loser from 11 June. Eric Campbell and his fascist-saluting New Guard would vanish like fruit bats at daybreak, leaving only the ludicrous image of Captain de Groot on the Harbour Bridge to remember them by. Campbell claims that immediately after the poll he was approached by an emissary from Bertram Stevens offering some vague promise of a reward for all his good effort. He turned it down cold, perhaps anticipating that Stevens, like Lyons, would soon find it convenient to deny all knowledge of New Guard assistance.

'I do not know Eric Campbell,' the Premier later lied, ignoring their previous meetings, including a dinner party attended by other witnesses, 'but if he or anyone else talks about ruling this country by Fascism, or by Communism, I will deal with him.'

The Big Fella, while continuing in politics, could never hope to recover personally from such a comprehensive defeat. The overall swing against him was 15 per cent. In the sixteen months since he had formed his own breakaway faction of the ALP, his Lang Party had clearly frittered away a sizeable hunk of its bedrock blue-collar support.

'The people have given their judgement upon the case as they saw it,' Lang graciously acknowledged, 'and because we believe that the people alone shall govern we accept their verdict.

I sincerely hope that the amount of suffering to be borne along the road that the people have chosen to go will not be as great as I fear it will be.' But perhaps his truer feelings were revealed during an exchange with a hostile interjector who had accosted him a few days earlier, demanding: 'So, how will you end up on election day?'

'Some people ask what will happen to me on June 11,' Lang shot back. 'What should concern you is what will happen to you if anything happens to me.'

The final irony of the election was that for all the dire predictions of violence – clashes between the New Guard and Red Army, rioting, arson and other acts of sabotage – it actually wound up without a single reported casualty. The spontaneous outbursts after the dismissal a month earlier seemed to have acted as a useful escape valve for pent-up emotions. Or perhaps people were simply fed up with all the drama.

'The prophets foresaw a bitter fight but the reverse happened,' Sir Philip noted. 'Police reports indicate the election was one of the most orderly for many years past.'

32

The search for *Atlantis*: Part II

There were some Australians who couldn't care less about the downfall of Jack Lang or the future of the Federation. They might not have even heard of the Great Depression. The state of Western Australia estimated that as of 1932 it still had 10,000 Aboriginals living 'outside the influence of civilisation', carrying on with the day-to-day business of survival pretty much as they had done for the previous 50,000 years. Similar pockets were known to exist in the Northern Territory and Queensland Gulf country but the sprawling Kimberley region in the country's north-west was still largely unexplored and thus an ideal sanctuary for the last of the nomadic tribes. The oven-hot westerlies which blew through its countless canyons and gorges whispered of primordial mysteries beyond anything outside darkest Africa.

As it happened, Tarzan-style adventure tales were all the rage in 1932 with their spine-tingling theme of lost travellers crashing into the jungle to find themselves at the mercy of bloodthirsty savages. For urban Australians clinging to a narrow, fertile crescent on the fringe of a hostile wilderness that nightmare seemed a good deal more real than anywhere else in the industrialised world. Even at that late stage of development there were still the odd reports of 'trouble with the natives,' adding to the sorry record of attacks and brutal reprisals stretching back to early convict days. For every actual incident, the public was bombarded with a thousand unfounded rumours about some supposed new Aboriginal atrocity, with cannibalism featuring high on the list of unspeakable horrors. 'Numerous natives roam in their wild state and travellers have to exercise every care to avoid treachery,' the *West Australian* newspaper warned in a report reflecting the mood of the day.

Paradoxically, the depression years would turn out to be something of a blessing for the free-ranging Aboriginals. The collapse in primary exports provided a brief respite from the steady encroachment of livestock herds on their hunting grounds. Meanwhile, the exaggerated tales of their fearsomeness gained them a begrudging respect that had been lacking through much of post-settlement history. Up to then, indigenous people of the deep outback had widely been regarded as something less than human, vermin more than noble beast. But in 1932 they were portrayed as cunning and dangerous warriors, wild men who would spear a stray white as soon as look him. Those 10,000 'untamed' Aboriginals – for all the myths that surrounded them – could well have been extras in Australia's own real-life version of Tarzan of the Apes. Some of them would go on to teach the white population a new definition of what it means to be 'civilised'.

The search for *Atlantis*: Part II

Jim Bali-bali never thought of telling anyone about his brief time aboard the *Atlantis*. He had decided soon enough that the two begoggled figures who confronted him were humans, not spirits, but he had no reason to suspect that they were seriously lost. Otherwise, why would they have flown off so quickly again without bothering to replenish their supplies at the freshwater pool he had pointed out to them? Like most other Kimberley nomads, Bali-bali could spend months at a stretch without ever crossing the path of a white man. He occasionally drifted in and out of the two mission stations in the area – at Drysdale River and Forrest River – and knew some of the Aboriginals who camped there in the wet season, taking scripture lessons in return for a regular feed. A week or so after his own encounter with Bertram and Klausmann he met several of these mission natives – Monarra, Donganga and Burgeye – who said they, too, had watched the strangers struggling along the rocky shoreline but were too afraid to approach.

'It is only an aeroplane man,' he assured them, but the others had seen those frighteningly wide blank eyes for themselves and refused to believe him.

'This is not the man you've seen but another one,' Burgeye insisted. 'He doesn't look like a man at all. He must be a Jimy.'

After Bali-bali had left them, though, the three sat by their fire that night discussing whether what the older man told them could possibly be true. They remembered that even though the creatures had the faces of spirits, their legs were scratched and bleeding. They stumbled along like wounded wallabies but the Aboriginals still thought it was wiser to remain out of sight until they passed by.

Later, while continuing on to hunt along the coast, the three had come across two strange objects half-buried in the muddy bank of an inlet. One was a thin, shiny metal container and the other a square piece of woven white cloth. Burgeye had picked them up not quite knowing what to do with them, tucking them into his dillybag in case they might come in handy. He didn't mention the discovery to Jim Bali-bali, embarrassed that he might chastise them further; but now Burgeye and his friends decided the right thing to do was to show the items to Father Cubero at Drysdale River, a hard four-day trek away. They were reluctant to go back themselves for fear of being accused of stealing. Instead, they handed the souvenired items over to another young tribesman who was known at the mission by his Christian name, Gregory, and would be better trusted.

One of the objects turned out to be an empty cigarette case engraved with the initials H.B., the other a handkerchief. Along with a faint shoeprint detected by Gregory on his way back, they constituted the first tangible evidence that the crew of the seaplane *Atlantis* had actually set foot in Australia. Until then, with every passing day without a sighting, it looked more and more as if the plane had crashed soon after its midnight take-off, in the early hours of 15 May, and been swallowed up in the Timor Sea. What young Gregory handed over to Father Cubero on Wednesday, 1 June, would make news to reverberate around the world. Yet 'news' in the sparsely populated Kimberley spread only as fast as a human stride. It would be another twelve days – Monday, 13 June – before word reached Wyndham, 220 kilometres (140 miles) to the south-east. Meanwhile, on 6 June, the German Consul-General in Sydney had sent a cable home officially announcing the episode closed, another chapter in the history of early aviation ending in tragedy.

SEARCH FOR BERTRAM AND KLAUSMANN SUSPENDED. STOP. ALL POSITIONS OF AUTHORITY CONSIDER FURTHER EFFORTS USELESS. STOP.

The German press duly published obituaries filled with tributes to the two brave fliers. Bertram's mother, interviewed in his home town of Remscheid, near Düsseldorf, was among the very few who insisted there could still be hope. It was she, after all, who had given the pioneer pilot a neckerchief for good luck embroidered with the inscription: 'May God watch over you, my son.'

Her faith was rewarded when Wyndham police received Cubero's exciting message a week later and immediately relayed it to Perth to be flashed around the globe.

'Runners from Drysdale Mission brought letter from Father Cubero dated 1 June,' the telegraph read in part. 'Found cigarette case, initials H. B. and handkerchief. Presume from May 26. Two footprints about two miles northwest of Eric and Elsie Islands, one hundred miles northwest of Wyndham, leading south. Natives lost track in rocky area.'

Until then, it seemed almost impossible that the fliers could have ended up so far west of Darwin. Search parties were immediately reinstated and sent by land, sea and air in the new direction indicated. Within another day the mail plane servicing Wyndham had been able to locate the *Atlantis*. It was sitting beached and abandoned in the cove where Bertram had landed after impetuously flying on from his encounter with Jim Bali-bali. Yet, even this first faint ray of hope was quickly overshadowed by dire predictions of the kind of treatment the two aviators could expect should they be so unlucky as to fall into Aboriginal hands.

'That natives would have little hesitation in killing and eating the men if they encountered them is claimed by many experienced in the ruthless, wild ways of the Aborigines around the area north-west of Wyndham,' the *West Australian* reported. 'Five white men have been murdered by blacks in the past 13 years.'

'If the natives lost the tracks, then they lost them because they wanted to,' warned another bush-wise white settler. 'And if so, the men are dead.'

Even if the Aboriginals didn't kill the Germans, readers were told, it was highly unlikely they would ever admit discovering their bodies. 'If the men were discovered dead by the natives, they would be more likely to "go bush" and not speak of the dead men, particularly to any questioning party.'

Perhaps harking back to early colonial days, when shipwreck victims like Mrs Eliza Fraser were infamously enslaved, some accounts suggested the two Germans could end up 'having been taken prisoner by the natives,' a fate presumably worse than death. The balance of speculation, though, tended to tip toward the most gruesome of possibilities, expressed in the simplest of terms.

'Kill 'em with sticks and eat 'em . . .' read a headlined quote neatly summing up a bush rumour circulating at the Forrest River Mission. To which the *West Australian* helpfully added a bit of background commentary: 'There are not any concrete instances of natives eating white men,' the paper conceded, 'but several instances have been recalled of the blacks killing and eating other natives and native children.'

Authorities obviously took such rumours seriously. Within a week of Father Cubero's letter reaching Wyndham, a search party led by Police Constable Marshall had nine murder suspects under arrest and in chains. Among them were Monarra, Donganga and Burgeye.

The first ground party to reach the *Atlantis* found it in excellent condition, though missing its port-side pontoon. A note on its windscreen explained: 'May 27. Have left the plane in a float, using it as a boat.' Bertram had set off with his colleague Klausmann once again to seek rescue where it was least likely to occur, to the west. By the time that note was found in mid-June, the airmen had already been missing a month. What was to follow for them was not so much a battle for survival as – in Bertram's words – a search for 'a peaceful place to die'.

~~~

Lying in a cave on a rocky promontory above the sea, too weak to carry on a step further, Hans Bertram still managed to keep recording his impressions in his battered diary. One day he hoped it would be found and returned to his mother along with the precious neckerchief he tugged at for comfort as he wrote. God, he was sure, was indeed watching over him at this moment, though perhaps not quite as his mother had prayed for: no longer to save his shrunken body but to ease his suffering and prepare his soul.

'The waves crashing sound like the tolling of bells,' he thought. 'We are in a church, a cathedral where we can await death with peace and ceremony. It is indescribably beautiful. Warm and dry now, but dying and knowing it, I rest in the firelight and ask myself what I must have done wrong to be stuck here now. I have done everything wrong, from beginning to end.'

Of all the days in a man's life, the ones he knows to be his last must surely be the longest. They are, after all, the closest to eternity. Hans Bertram had more than enough time to ponder his mistakes, beginning with that spur-of-the-moment decision to take off at midnight. A German yachtsman he chanced upon in Timor had put the thought in his head by raving about the beauty of the tropical night skies.

'Why did I take off on a night flight across the Timor Sea? Did it have anything to do with my task? No, it was pure vanity – vanity and adventure. It was supposed to be something special: to land the first German seaplane in Australia at dawn and make the headlines.'

He acknowledged another, more basic blunder.

'Why didn't we stay near the plane?' he asked himself. 'Why didn't we collect wood and dry grass so we could send smoke signals if a ship or plane approached? I was impatient and I didn't want to wait because I was still strong and thought I could extricate us by will alone.'

Yet the pilot was forgetting a more compelling reason why they left the relative security of *Atlantis*. They could not find a source of fresh water anywhere in the vicinity. As Bertram quickly came to realise, he had failed to recognise salvation when it was staring him in the face. Why had he been so quick to send off Jim Bali-bali? Because instead of a potential rescuer he could only see a stinking primitive covered in grease and ash.

'On the first morning after the emergency landing a human being had come aboard the plane and I chased him away because he had brought flies with him,' the lost pilot admitted. 'I had driven away life for which I now wait in vain. It will not come again for my body can't hold on much longer.'

The most crucial error of all, of course, was in flying so far off course and then so badly miscalculating his position. He assumed that the cyclonic winds he encountered during the night had driven him to the north coast of Melville Island, which sits just above the Australian mainland north-east of Darwin. Instead, he had actually touched down 550 kilometres (340 miles) to the south-west of where he thought he was. It was a disastrous deviation considering the unforgiving emptiness into which he was headed.

Even the most experienced pilot of the era, caught up for hours in a violent storm and with only rudimentary navigational instruments to rely on, might well have wound up in a similar predicament. Once the mistake was made, however, the

26-year-old aviator multiplied his problems many times over through a lethal combination of rashness and indecision. No sooner had he guided the *Atlantis* on its last drops of fuel to a second landing than he decided that he and Klausmann should try to return to the spot where they met Jim Bali-bali. That meant trying to make their way back through a 35-kilometre obstacle course strewn with giant boulders and laced with mud thick as glue, with stinging brambles and razor-sharp spinifex tearing at their legs every step of the way. After several days they could hardly expect the Aboriginal to still be there but nothing could prepare them for the terror that was waiting in his place. They had just begun swimming across a murky inlet when Bertram sensed the danger.

> We are about half-way across, Klausmann a few metres ahead of me. Suddenly I feel an ice-cold sensation at the back of my neck. I am almost too scared to turn but force myself. There are ripples on the surface. I can't make them out, but then ... Crocodiles! two – three – more. Swimming toward us.

The two dumped their packs, kicked off their clothes and shoes and raced back to the muddy shore as stark naked as the tribesman who had tried to befriend them. During the four days it took to return to their aircraft they were so tortured by mosquitoes at night that they literally buried themselves in the sand to get away from the incessant stinging. That process, though, left each of them with one arm exposed – the one that was used to do the digging. The two men taunted each other over which of them should be prepared to make the sacrifice by leaving a hand free to splash sand onto the other.

'We can't spend the night bickering like this, so I help Klausmann cover himself,' Bertram wrote. The next morning his mutilated arm did indeed look like a sacrificial offering. He described it as little more than 'raw meat'.

Once safely back at *Atlantis* the two spent several more days relishing the comforts it offered, including a change of fresh clothing and relative freedom from the mosquito menace. At first they only had a few litres of oily water drained from the plane's radiator to quench their thirst but a sudden squall allowed them to store up enough – by Bertram's reckoning – for twenty days more under strict rationing. Yet even then he decided to push on to the west, hoping to reach a dot on his map marked Port Cockburn, which he wrongly assumed to be a Melville Island fishing community.

After their brush with the crocodiles he and Klausmann had no intention of bush-bashing any farther. Instead they dismantled one of the aeroplane's floats to convert into a makeshift canoe and headed out into open water hoping to sail and paddle until they sighted some sign of civilisation. The strong currents, however, quickly took command and they found they had merely switched one kind of desperate plight for another. From being marooned they were now castaways, dragged out beyond the sight of land, with the real possibility of getting swamped and drowned.

But on the second afternoon, a miracle unfolded before their eyes – smoke pluming from a coastal steamer heading in their direction. It was close enough for Bertram to read the name, *Kooinda*, painted on its bow and lifeboats. The two Germans broke into cheers, then delirious laughter. Klausmann stood up waving his shirt. Bertram had taken along five signal flares and he began firing them into the sky – one flare, two, three, four, even the fifth. The ship had by then come to within a distance of only five football fields, yet still it didn't stop. It just kept steaming on.

'My God! Help! What's going on?' There were no ears to hear their shouts just as there were no other eyes to see the last of the flares drifting back down, bright as a tiny sun, until it finally disintegrated like the airmen's hopes. All that was left of it was a faint whiff of smoke to merge with the trail from the vanishing *Kooinda*. It was mid-afternoon in the stifling tropics and the ship's captain had no intention of sending any poor sailor out into the sun to keep watch. The *Kooinda*'s log, though, would record the time the incident was likely to have happened. It was 3.30 pm, Sunday, 29 May. The location, of course, was nowhere near Melville Island but just off Cape Bernier on the western shore of Joseph Bonaparte Gulf, the body of water separating the top ends of Western Australia and the Northern Territory. At that moment too, as Bertram would later record in his own diary, his partner's spirit gave out completely. He simply could take no more. 'Klausmann goes to pieces on the 15th day. The two of us bob around on the waves, but effectively I am alone now.'

Through that most disheartening of nights, with the waves crashing upon their frail craft, only one shrill sound could be heard above their roar. Adolf Klausmann's unending lament. 'I give up. I can't go on. I don't care what you do to me. I give up.'

Yet by morning he did go on. It took them four more days to get to a landfall – hour upon hour of frantic paddling that drained their dwindling reserves of energy far more than they could afford. The extra effort, combined with severe sunburn and the parching salt spray, caused them to use up all of the drinking water they had carefully stored in three empty film canisters – 20 days' supply gone in four. Once ashore again, thirst drove them inland in search of a natural pool. Luckily they found one, and in so doing made their most important discovery so far. On the twenty-third day of their ordeal, 6 June – the same day the German Consul-General was effectively announcing them dead – Bertram mounted a hill to behold what he thought was another endless stretch of sea.

But something is wrong. The sea is grey and motionless, no waves rise and fall on it. And as we squint against the glare, trying to get a proper look, we realise: there is no sea below us. That's not water. That's bush, dead country. So this is what the north of Australia looks like!

For the first time Bertram realised he was gazing upon the merciless sandstone anvil of the Kimberley plateau – an area as large as Germany but more like some distant, lifeless planet. *Where Hell begins,* he shuddered. 'I now understand why there have been no signs of a search for us; nobody would dream we have been blown so far off course.'

Taking out his map, his new orientation allowed him to match its features with the landmarks of the shoreline he had already noted over the past three weeks and re-plot his position with uncanny accuracy. His first landing would have been at the mouth of a river called the Berkeley. From there he flew another 35 kilometres north-west, passing two islands on his right, which must have been Elsie and Eric. Just north of where he made his second landing was another outcrop, marked on his map as Rocky Island. He could even recognise the long, narrow inlet where they encountered the crocodiles on that ill-fated attempt to return to their original landing spot. As for those harrowing five days at sea, he could see that they must have paddled another 20 kilometres north-west, making their landfall just past Cape Bernier, one of the more prominent headlands in the Joseph Bonaparte Gulf. Finally, he was able to pinpoint the hill on which he was now standing, with its incredible overview of their true location.

In other circumstances he might have been proud of his navigational detective work. Instead the results were nothing less than soul-destroying. From where he marked their position, X, it was but 2 centimetres or so on the chart to reverse their direction and travel south-east to Wyndham. Those 2 centimetres, though, translated into an overland hike of 224 kilometres. Since 15 May, he and Klausmann had had nothing more to live on than a small fish and a few tiny lizards and snails. They had finally been reduced to eating leaves. They were dead men in every sense but one: they hadn't quite realised it until that moment.

'Now I know where we have to go,' Bertram told himself, 'but it is too late.'

On the thirty-sixth day they found their way to the cave that would serve as their crypt. It was on a ledge only about 90 metres from Cape Bernier itself. Its stone floor was dotted with ample pools of rainwater.

'The thought pleases us although we'll be beyond the need for water soon enough,' Bertram wrote.

The next day and the next and the next passed, with no other purpose than to allow them to pray and ready themselves to slip away into serene oblivion.

> Day thirty-nine. It is extremely beautiful. The sun is hanging in a cloudless sky, its rays playing with the crests of the waves. Our cave is open to sun and sea. We watch the sun all day and let the fire burn, even though we'll run out of wood tonight. We are sticking to our promise. We will wait as long as the fire keeps burning. Then we want to leave it at that. We are very tired. We want to sleep.

∽∾∼

Bertram was almost annoyed when he awoke next morning to see an intrusive silhouette passing near the mouth of the cave. It was framed in the shimmering red of the rising sun – a gangling stick figure in a ball of flame. How could it not smoulder and burn before his very eyes?

'Am I raving mad? No, no, the silhouette moves, leaps from rock to rock.' In fact, it is about to disappear. Bertram attempts to shout, though the sound is only in his own mind. His vocal chords seem paralysed. But then there is a mighty shriek from behind him, for Klausmann has seen the figure, too. He reaches deep into his psyche to unleash a bloodcurdling primal scream, more animal than human. The stick figure stops and whips around, holds a hand over its eyes a moment to see where such a noise could come from. Then it races to the mouth of the cave and stands motionless there, transformed into a tall, lean naked figure much like Jim Bali-bali, though without the grey whiskers set off against the ebony skin.

His name is Miaman. He is only a young lad of sixteen or so but he carries the gift of life in his hand. He raises his arm to show the two starving white men he is holding a fish. Weak as they are, they pull themselves forward to grab it from him and tear at with their teeth, swallowing it raw in a few noisy gulps.

In the last two weeks or so Bertram has watched Klausmann weaving in and out of insanity, his lucid interludes becoming briefer. Now the pilot, too, feels himself losing all control – just at the very moment that should be bringing him such blessed relief.

> Everything is unclear and blurry. What is happening to me? With every mouthful of food I become more restless. Everything turns dark. The blood has gone to my head, it is aching terribly. Jesus Christ, don't let that happen now. Not now that life has returned. Don't let me lose my mind.

His next memory was of the young Aboriginal kneeling beside him, cradling his head under one arm while using his other hand to scoop up water to moisten his hot face and parched lips. His sunburnt cheek pressed firmly against the cool, naked black skin offers indescribable comfort, whisking him back to a time beyond conscious memory. It is almost as if he were being christened anew.

In a moment, though, Miaman stands up and makes signs that he must leave. Seeing the look of alarm in both men's eyes, he tries to reassure them with soothing sounds, repeatedly waving his hands from them to him and back to demonstrate the bond between them. Then he bounds away, scrambling beyond the coastal rock ledge to the edge of the bush. Soon he has started a fire, sending a stream of smoke high into the air. In a few minutes, another column of smoke rises perhaps two or three kilometres away. Miaman returns to them, a wide grin on his face, and gestures for both men to sit down and wait with him at the cave entrance. In twenty minutes or so three more Aboriginals emerge from the dense underbrush. They carry a canvas bag filled with a kilogram of flour and four tins of meat. Just as important, they carry a crumpled envelope with a letter from the fathers at Drysdale River Mission.

> Dear Friends,
> When this letter reaches you and you are still alive, then a miracle has occurred for which we should thank God our Father out of profound respect. We have been searching for you for weeks. If this letter reaches you, immediately send two Aborigines with the good news to us, informing us of the exact position where you have been found. Be patient for a couple of days. Don't be afraid of the Aborigines. They're your friends and will care for you.

In addition to Miaman, the other blacks to join them that first day were Tanquinia, Taur and Auselm. They immediately set about gathering wood for a fire to bake the bread but they ate nothing themselves – not even a portion of meat from the tins – until they were satisfied the lost fliers had eaten their fill. The two chosen to return to the mission actually took no food at all even though they had a hard 54-mile (86 kilometres) run ahead of them. Over the next five days other Aboriginals, including several women, trickled in from all directions, alerted by signal fires. None of them spoke English but they set about making the two men as comfortable as possible, collecting grass for their beds and bringing gifts of wild honey, fish and a whopping big kangaroo tail.

Though the food was cooked, the Germans had gone so long without eating that their teeth were loose and they could hardly chew. Seeing their difficulty, the Aboriginals carefully chewed each portion of meat for them first, handing them the masticated morsels as they would to an infant.

'All we have to do is swallow,' Bertram recorded.

The two starved fliers gorged themselves far too quickly. Time and time again they threw up most of what they ate but were not about to let that stop them tucking in again, producing howls of good-natured laughter from their benefactors. The biggest laugh of all, though, was sparked by their horrified reaction to the wild honey that had been presented as a special gift. They pushed it away in disgust when they saw the sticky brown mass seething with flies – a huge source of merriment to those who knew it to be such a treat. Patiently, a tribal elder dipped a finger into the tin and licked it with such an exaggerated show of relish – with loud smacking of lips and almost orgasmic gasps of pleasure – that the Germans could no longer resist.

Miaman had found them on the morning of Wednesday, 22 June, but they would not be declared officially rescued until the following Tuesday when Constable Marshall arrived with his overland search party.

'We travelled hard and at 10 am today came to the two men,' Marshall scribbled in a hurried note, dated 28 June, to his superiors in Wyndham. 'They were in a shocking state and were so overjoyed to see us that they broke down completely. All they could say for a time was "Bread, bread, bread, have you got bread." I had bread, and whisky, too. I gave them bread, weak whisky, some biscuits, coffee and tea.'

Marshall was to be acclaimed in the press as a hero for having travelled with his party of blacktrackers through the rugged terrain in such quick time. No Aboriginal would rate a mention by name. In fact, the final report on the search written by the sergeant in charge of the Wyndham police strongly implied that the blacks almost certainly would have murdered the two airmen had Marshall not arrived so soon.

> The forced march of Police Constable Marshall and his search party to the coast was an outstanding performance [and] doubtless saved the lives of the missing men. They were mentally and physically so exhausted that in my opinion they could not have lived much longer. It is also without doubt that the Aborigines knew that the missing persons were still alive. Marshall's swift advance probably intimidated them because although the plane had been plundered, the natives began to bring their booty to Drysdale as soon as they got wind of the police measures. The Boy with the cigarette case has dropped out of sight, however. Captain Bertram stated that he had seen a Black directly after landing in the mouth of the Berkeley. I am convinced that the Aborigines were observing the white men the whole time and that worse was prevented from happening only due to the swiftness of Marshall and the Boys.

At least, though, the nine Aboriginals held in chains would be quickly released.

Marshall's message didn't reach Wyndham until Monday, 4 July. The news would be hailed around the globe as one of the most extraordinary search and rescue dramas of the century. Klausmann for a time was so demented that he had to be physically restrained from banging his head against a tree. He was convinced the blacks had been secretly plotting to fatten him up just to murder and eat him. Bertram recovered almost immediately though, making plans to procure a new float for *Atlantis* and fly it to Perth to begin his long-delayed tour of Australia.

For depression-stricken Australians the moral of the story was unmistakeable: no matter how seemingly desperate their situation, recovery might well be just around the corner. There really could be no such thing as *false* hope. Hope was the breath of the human spirit.

That was a lesson those 10,000 Aboriginals living 'outside the influence of civilisation' would have had no trouble understanding. For them, every day of their lives began with a crisis of survival and ended with a miracle. And so it had been for 50,000 years.

⁓⊙⁓

In areas of closer contact between white and black Australians a long-hidden problem was just beginning to get the attention it deserved, due largely to protests emanating from within the Australian feminist movement. In June, 1932, the West Australian Government released a new set of statistics showing a record 3715 'half-caste' Aboriginals, nearly 50 per cent under the age of twelve, with the number increasing at an alarming rate. The situation was no doubt similar throughout the Northern Territory and eastern states. The birth of mixed-race babies was hardly unknown when one culture intruded on another but field research conducted by activists like the Perth-based writer and missionary teacher Mary Bennett would reveal the particularly tragic fate that awaited such children in Australia. Nowhere else in the industrialised world were they conceived in such exploitative circumstances or abandoned to such bleak futures. Bennett, refusing to be silenced by the prevailing social taboos, branded the harsh reality for what it was – a tacitly sanctioned form of 'black slavery' that saw young Aboriginal women bartered off to whites singly or in wholesale lots for a bit of tobacco. The offspring of such unions were not only shunned by tribal elders but often barred from attending white schools, thus dooming them to virtual damnation.

Bennett had been raised on an outback Queensland property, her father credited with showing great compassion for the local blacks. By the age of 39 she was already well known both in Australia and abroad for her pioneering book, *The Australian Aboriginal as a Human Being*. She not only rallied women's groups across the nation to take up the cause but enlisted the aid of international forums like the British Commonwealth League to pressure the federal and state governments into introducing desperately needed reforms. Her efforts would be rewarded in 1933 when Western Australia agreed to hold a wide-ranging royal commission. The influence of women's activist groups in the inquiry could be seen clearly among a list of advocates that included the Australian Federation of Women Voters, the Women's Service Guilds, the Young Women's Christian Association, the Labour Women's Organisation and the National Council of Women.

Even before the royal commission sat, Perth formed its first citizens' group dedicated to protecting the state's Aboriginal population from 'injustice' and 'cruelty'. The Australian Aborigines' Amelioration Association, as it was known, convened on

10 October 1932 and one of the first issues raised was the treatment of 'half-castes'. Its minutes make reference to a 'pathetic letter' received from a part-Aboriginal who had been lucky enough to receive some education but had obviously paid a heavy price, having to live the rest of his life under a nightmarish bureaucracy. 'The Aborigines' Act does not give us equity or justice,' he complained. 'In many cases, death alone ends our term of duress.'

The new association, for all its good intentions, started off a bit timidly toward its goal of looking after all aspects of Aboriginal welfare.

'Our attention has been drawn to the methods adopted by some permit holders in the recruiting of their native labour,' it noted. 'When this has been done with a gun in the hand we consider that the greatest care should be exercised. The Association proposes going into this matter fully during the coming year.'

At least it was a start. An even more promising beginning was recorded in Melbourne in mid-1932 when 66-year-old Aboriginal activist William Cooper, himself of mixed descent, founded one of the first associations to be under the full control of Aboriginals themselves. Born in country Victoria, Cooper went on to become a shearer and agricultural worker before tiring of the petty bureaucracy of white authorities at the native reserve where he lived. He moved to the Melbourne suburb of Footscray where there was an impoverished black community of perhaps 100 people. In an old rented house with neither gas nor electricity, working late into the night by candlelight, he went on to form the Australian Aborigines' League, an organisation that would stand as a model for the new wave of black activists to come.

Such examples of progress seemed all the more impressive coming in a year of extreme hardship like 1932. The Great

The search for *Atlantis*: Part II

Depression, in opening white eyes to the fickle nature of impoverishment and disadvantage, may well have encouraged a more sympathetic attitude toward the plight of those Australians who happened to be black.

33

1932: A helluva year

You go your way, I'll go mine, It's best that we do; Here's a kiss, I hope that this brings lots of luck to you. The Fifty-Fifty Club had known many a wild time but nothing like the night its manager, Harold 'Snowy' Billington, opened his door to one tipsy couple too many. Before he could slam it shut it again a beefy plainclothes cop appeared out of nowhere and shouldered his way through, followed by a large pack of uniformed constables who had been hiding in a nearby stairwell. As they fanned out through the crowded room, their portly boss, the aptly named Sergeant Harry Ham, loomed up from behind.

'Stay there! Nobody must leave!' he shouted as men cursed, women fainted and dancers froze in mid-stride.

Only Jack, the jaded pianist, as pasty-faced as his ivories, managed to maintain a semblance of cocaine-laced sangfroid. A moment before he had been pounding out a bouncy rendition of 'Please Don't Talk About Me When I'm Gone'. He switched moods in an instant to the convict's lament: *If I had the wings of an angel . . . over these prison walls I would fly.*

During the next three hours, 127 people – some in white tie and tails or backless evening gowns – were bundled off in paddy wagons to be charged with drinking on unlicensed premises and released on £2 ($140) bail. A correspondent for *Smith's Weekly* later reported recognising many prominent faces, including a 'lad well-known at Government House', but added: 'I don't think it quite fair to give their real names as they were not recorded on the police books.' The defendants did, indeed, show impressive ingenuity in the selection of their pseudonyms, with not a Smith or Jones among them. One exceptionally inventive gentleman even attempted to identify himself as 'Sydney Harbour' but had to find an alternative after being warned by the magistrate that he was being asked who he was, not where he came from. The booking procedure had hardly got under way before a mystery man with a large wad of cash showed up to pay the bail for a cell full of pouting young flappers.

The surprise crackdown on the club would establish a new record for the largest number of arrests made at any one time but its symbolic significance went far beyond that. In the first six months of the year Superintendent Billy Mackay had been too preoccupied with the threat of civil war to worry much about the more routine aspects of keeping law and order. Now, though, his instincts told him it was time to turn his formidable attention back on to the underworld. Drugs, prostitution, gambling – all the rackets were starting to boom again and the last thing the top cop needed was a flare-up of the old gang rivalries that had bloodied the back alleys of Kings Cross and Darlinghurst during the roaring 1920s.

In that sense, the sensational police raid might well be seen as a turning point of historic proportions. No one can be sure exactly when Australia began its recovery from the Great Depression but 2 am Sunday, 24 July 1932, seems as likely a time as any. That was the moment Billy Mackay's men burst through the door of Sydney's most notorious nightclub to send reigning vice royalty like Phil Jeffs and Tilly Devine an unmistakeable message. *The good times may be rolling again, but don't get too big for your britches.*

Of course, the effects of a worldwide economic downturn do not just vanish overnight. The painful symptoms, including chronic unemployment, would be felt for years to come. Yet from July on, there were definite signs of revival – some coming from a completely unexpected direction. Remarkably, it would be the nation's manufacturing sector – not wool or wheat exports – that turned out to be the spearhead for the first phase of the recovery. With expensive imports trickling to a virtual halt, local factories began moving in to fill the gap, churning out goods previously dominated by foreign labels. Textiles, clothing, chemicals, iron and steel – all such industries started thriving under the shelter of protective tariffs and a cheap Australian pound. Each new worker hired onto the production lines meant another pay packet to be distributed into retailing and other support services.

'There has been an improvement in the outlook generally,' an analyst was able to report in September. 'A more optimistic tone prevails and more hands are employed. The textile manufacturers showed marked activity – during the last three months they increased the number of their employees by 3000.'

Perhaps by way of celebration, a union representing clothing workers in Melbourne staged a lightning strike to protest their sweatshop conditions. Such stoppages had been a rare occurrence over the previous two years.

The level of joblessness in the various states would fluctuate for some time to come, with one sector still laying off workers while another expanded; but a more heartening statistic involved the families struggling along on bare sustenance.

In June the number of registered food dole recipients was estimated to have reached the peak of 708,000 men, women and children, over 10 per cent of the entire population. From then on, the figure proceeded to decline fortnight by fortnight.

Before Jack Lang's downfall, his conservative enemies had preached a common sermon based on the doctrines of British banking guru Sir Otto Niemeyer. Australia's salvation depended entirely on the prices of primary exports returning to their pre-depression levels. Until then, the country had no choice but to batten down the hatches and ride out the storm. The best the seven governments could do in the meantime was to focus on reducing wages and tidying up their budgets so that production costs would be at a minimum when world trade eventually opened up again.

It should have been obvious that this was not a 'recovery plan' but a *'wait for recovery* plan' and more aggressive steps needed to be taken to get Australians back to work. Ironically, when Lang's conqueror, Bertram Stevens attended his first Premiers' Conference in late June, he proceeded to give Prime Minister Joe Lyons a tongue-lashing equal to anything dished out by his predecessor.

'You are fiddling while Rome burns!' he rebuked Lyons at one point, threatening to walk out of the summit unless the Premiers' Plan was broadened to include more positive ways to stimulate jobs growth. Under constant goading from Stevens and the new Labor Premier of Queensland, Forgan Smith, the other leaders would at least agree to replace the wasteful and demoralising system of food doles with a nationally coordinated scheme for large-scale public works projects to get the unemployed working again. Despite previous dire warnings about unsecured borrowing leading to inflation, the conference agreed to float a special domestic loan-raising of £15 million – more than a billion dollars – over three years, specifically earmarked for job creation. In the first year that would be enough to put perhaps 40,000 men back to work full time or multiples of that in part-time work.

One of the technical terms used to support the new scheme, 'hypothecasion', sounded faintly familiar. As the theory went, a state might impose a special surcharge on income tax to pay for food relief but the money trickling in over any one year was not enough to initiate a labour-intensive project like sewerage or road building. If, however, state governments were allowed to calculate the sums to be collected through unemployment taxes over three years and use that as security for a substantial borrowing, they could replace the thousands of pounds spent each fortnight on the food dole with the millions needed to undertake major public works. 'Hypothecasion' had indeed been the basis of one of Jack Lang's campaign proposals the previous month – an idea that was immediately howled down in the press as ridiculous, if not insane.

The weeks to follow would produce other examples of how the impossible suddenly became possible with the Big Fella effectively gone from the scene. For a start, the banking community somehow found a way to free up the millions of pounds in credit that supposedly was too dangerous to provide before. The incoming New South Wales Premier, Bertram Stevens, was also soon able to announce almost miraculous progress in cutting back the state's alarming budget deficit. Only later did he admit that his success was largely due to big corporations making haste to pay overdue tax instalments which had purposely been delayed in order to embarrass the Lang administration.

The most breathtaking backflip, however, involved the federal government's stand on the very issue that sparked the Lang crisis in the first place: overseas interest. No longer did it seem such an affront to national pride for Australia to seek to reduce its crippling commitments. Instead, in mid-September, the Prime Minister launched an aggressive campaign to get the current London rates slashed by more than 20 per cent. This was portrayed as a 'negotiation' rather than the kind of ultimatum implied in the Lang Plan; but the tactics Joe Lyons adopted in pressing his case could only be described as intimidatory. He even had the hide to refer to Lang in his cables, warning reluctant British financiers that their refusal to cooperate could infuriate the Australian public enough to bring 'Langism' back with a vengeance.

'We feel very strongly that there will undoubtedly be grave and widespread disappointment even in responsible circles if the loan cannot be negotiated on substantially better terms,' the Prime Minister advised Stanley Bruce, who had been sent to London specifically to obtain loan rollovers at much lower interest. 'We have not defaulted, which many of Britain's debtors have.'

Though the cable was supposedly for Bruce's eyes only, its implied threat was clearly intended to be conveyed directly to the British moneylenders.

> There is an impression in the public mind of a willingness on the part of Great Britain to help other countries in financial difficulties, even though some of them have defaulted in their obligations, while Australia, though a dominion, is not extended any material sympathy or recognition. You will appreciate that the political and psychological effect . . . will be used by the reactionary forces in Australia to misrepresent the position.

Within a month of resorting to such pressure tactics the Commonwealth Government had managed to strike a deal destined to save many millions of pounds on loans renewed at substantially reduced interest rates. The conservatives were quick to boast that they had attained through sensible discussion what the Big Fella proposed to do by unilateral action, if necessary. The truth, though, was that in the very act of denouncing Lang they were cleverly invoking the spectre of his strident 'Australia first' nationalism to frighten the British into submission. It was left to the *Sydney Morning Herald* – one of the Big Fella's most rabid critics – to find just the right words to rationalise such blatant hypocrisy. 'What Langism cannot accomplish is not beyond achievement by other means,' the paper ambiguously suggested. 'If Australia will only play the game, the relief she desires from debt burdens will be possible.'

The ultimate irony, then, would see the Big Fella achieve in defeat what he could never have accomplished with all the antagonism that surrounded him in office. He became Joe Lyons's strongest bargaining point, a daunting symbol of the smouldering resentments that could so easily flare up out of control over the issue of unjust treatment by the Mother Country.

In exploiting Lang's image in such a way, his arch-enemies in the conservative camp were effectively acknowledging the role he had come to play as the voice of the Great Depression's dispossessed. Surely his opponents within the Australian Labor Party should have been prepared to concede as much. Instead, for years to come, they would portray him as nothing more than a self-serving party machine boss, the rat who brought down the Scullin Government for no other reason than his jealousy of its Treasurer, E.G. Theodore. The problem with such a one-dimensional view – Lang, the cynical, coldly calculating politician – is that it took no account of the impetuous nature of the man himself, a personality drawn to risky and even self-destructive choices. With or without the Big Fella's intervention, the labour movement had unquestionably been doomed to tear itself to pieces over the Premiers' Plan with its draconian provisions for wholesale sackings. Indeed, without him, the consequences might well have been far more chaotic than they were. Labor supporters who were pro-Plan tended to be comfortably better off and able to fend for themselves. Many of those associated with the party's left wing floundered in insecurity and despair. They welcomed a spokesman of national stature who could call attention to their grievances while steering away from the more violent forms of protest demanded of them by a radical fringe.

If Lang, in the course of his career, had drawn inspiration from Henry Lawson's poetry, he would also have been very critical of some of it. The final verses of 'Faces in the Street', in particular, went against everything he believed in.

> Once I cried: 'Oh, God Almighty! if Thy might doth still
>   endure,
> Now show me in a vision for the wrongs of Earth a cure.'
> And, lo! with shops all shuttered I beheld a city's street,
> And in the warning distance heard the tramp of many
>   feet,
>   Coming near, coming near,
>   To a drum's dull distant beat,
> And soon I saw the army that was marching down the
>   street.

His brother-in-law, in sharp contrast to Lang, preached bloody revolution as the world's only hope:

> But not until a city feels Red Revolution's feet
> Shall its sad people miss awhile the terrors of the street

At the beginning of 1932 there were tens of thousands of disillusioned men and women who could easily have been tempted to take those words to heart, an alienated underclass unlike anything to test the fabric of Australian society before or since. A leader of less passion and forcefulness than Jack Lang might well have found it impossible to keep such a volatile constituency under control. He may not have been 'right' as his loyal followers so fervently believed, but he certainly showed up in history at the right time, serving as a lightning rod to tame the destructive forces of extremism.

'The revolution *has* come without our streets being barricaded, without the accompaniment of firearms, but in the way the labour movement always said it would come, by Act of Parliament.' Those words, more than any other, deserved to stand as the Big Fella's enduring legacy, his pledge of absolute faith in the democratic process. He would leave office in disgrace, branded a demagogue for his simplistic rallying cry of *people before money* – but no one bothered to ask how much worse the Great Depression might have been without him.

By October Australia had plunged into another crisis, though one much more in tune with its national character. Cricketing idol Donald Bradman became locked in a bruising confrontation with the game's ruling control board and was threatening to pull out of the much anticipated test series with England. Bradman's batting brilliance mattered little to the thirteen immutable eminences of the board. Rules were rules and the star's lucrative new contract to write articles for a newspaper chain was deemed to violate regulations preventing players from publicly airing their views during the course of anything so sacred as a test match.

'My ambition is to play in the tests and do my bit to help Australia hold on to the ashes,' Bradman told a reporter, but then went on ominously: 'Whether I shall be in the team or in the press box is problematical. Perhaps the trouble between me and the board is that I'm too ambitious. I made a big monetary sacrifice when I turned down English offers to go over there and play [for Accrington]. I intend to stick to the promise I gave people [publishers of the Melbourne *Herald* and Sydney *Sun*] at this end who made it possible to remain in Australia.'

One could almost hear the clunk of millions of sinking hearts. The deadlock was made all the more difficult for anxious fans to understand due to a strange interpretation of the rules. A fellow batsman like Jack Fingleton was entitled to keep writing his column so long as his occupation was declared to be that of a full-time journalist. Bradman, it seemed, could only claim to be a part-time journalist because his contract also called for him to appear as a radio commentator and as a special adviser to a leading sporting goods retailer.

'The public cannot appreciate the splitting of hairs which enables a player to broadcast and full-time journalists to write, yet debars Bradman from carrying out the only satisfactory job he was able to obtain,' the *Melbourne Herald* protested in a scathing front-page editorial. 'The board's attitude is completely inelastic and apparently it is perfectly unconcerned whether Bradman plays or not.'

The torrid debate effectively consigned all further talk of politics and economics to the back pages.

'I was told when I had the Accrington offer and several others of a tempting nature besides that if I went there I would not be eligible for selection later on the Australian side,' Bradman complained. 'I cancelled my plans and stayed home. Now I'm told I can't play – the joke's on me, too right it is.'

The series would become the most famous in cricketing history because of the controversial 'Bodyline' tactics introduced by the English captain, Douglas Jardine. His powerful fast bowlers fired their cannonballs directly at the Australian batsmen. Their lethal volleys brought howls of rage from local fans, intensified, no doubt, by so many bitter recent memories. Only a few months before, the English had been symbolically bleeding Australia white with their exorbitant interest charges. Now it seemed Jardine had been sent in place of the despised Sir Otto Niemeyer to spill real Aussie blood. 'Is this cricket or war?' one Sydney tabloid demanded to know, summing up the ugly mood after the English XI inflicted a humiliating defeat in the series opener in Sydney.

Bradman could not have played in that first match in any circumstances because of a bout of illness. The question on every tongue was whether he would settle his differences with the control board in time to take the field in Melbourne. The opening day of the second test saw the Melbourne Cricket Ground draw the largest crowd in the history of the game – a new world record of 63,993. The huge turnout seemed to serve as a double portent of better times to come: not only a sure sign of economic recovery but a living symbol of the all-conquering Australian competitive spirit. All that was needed was Bradman to put the English bullyboys in their place. Until 11 am that morning it was anyone's guess whether their hero would actually play. Then the stands began to buzz with whispers of a last-minute back-down paving the way for his selection. It had been the champion to blink first, arranging for his newspaper contract to be temporarily suspended to conform with control board regulations.

At precisely three minutes to three o'clock on the steamy afternoon of Friday, 30 December, Donald Bradman – carrying a bat that always looked far too big for his diminutive frame – strode across the hallowed ground of the MCG to take his place at the wicket. The roar of his fans filled the stadium like the blasts from a thousand steam locomotives, then immediately ceased in hushed expectation. The English bowler, W. E. Bowes, one of the least intimidating of the visiting pacemen, turned around to face his famous adversary and ran up for his first delivery. The ball fell well short and Bradman lunged confidently across the wicket to hook it to the leg-side boundary for an easy four. Instead, he mistimed his shot like the rankest tail-ender, edging the ball back smack into the middle of his own stumps.

Thus, amid a sickening whoosh of air expelled simultaneously from almost 64,000 instantly deflated sets of lungs, Australia's greatest batsman was bowled out first ball for a duck.

It was a helluva finish to one hell of a year. But after 1932, things could only get better.

Epilogue
Winners and losers

In later years Jack Lang would reveal details of an unreported episode in his turbulent career which – if true – might have changed the entire course of events in 1932. He claimed that just before announcing his Lang Plan, in February, 1931, he held a secret meeting with the other Labor leaders attending that Premiers' Conference. They told him he was becoming a serious embarrassment to the party with his outspoken criticism of Britain's Sir Otto Niemeyer. He, in turn, pleaded with them to drop their previous agreement, made in Melbourne before he returned to office, to enforce Niemeyer's odious recommendations for wholesale wage cuts and sackings in the midst of the Great Depression. 'I felt so strongly against that Niemeyer that I said: well, if you'll promise to drop the Melbourne agreement, I'll resign and you can get rid of me.'

What a hole that would have left in history. No more Jack Lang to contend with, no default on interest, no Lang Party to speed the downfall of the Scullin Government, no clash of wills between New South Wales and the Commonwealth, no dismissal crisis; and for that matter, no Francis de Groot to slash the ribbon on the Sydney Harbour Bridge.

'But they wouldn't drop it. No, they wouldn't,' Lang recalled with seemingly genuine regret.

Would the Big Fella truly have been prepared to sacrifice his own career to save the nation from the ravages of the Premiers' Plan? The answer to that really depends on how people prefer to view him. Lang, as a manipulative demagogue, could never have contemplated making such a gesture, at least not seriously. Lang, at his most impetuous, was fully capable of playing the martyr.

'When I was Premier I tried to do the best for the people. My children – d' you understand? That's how I thought of them. They suffered so much. And I suffered, too. By the end of it I had no friends.' That was the way Lang remembered himself looking back on his dismissal from the ripe old age of 90.

After the disastrous June election Lang would continue to serve in parliament for another seventeen years, the last three as a member of the House of Representatives in Canberra. He never came close to regaining the prominence he attained in 1932, but he had time on his side to even old scores, allowing him to see off – one by one – those who had played leading parts in his downfall.

Prime Minister Joe Lyons died in office in 1939 at the age of only 59, his UAP Government disintegrating around him in internecine rivalries.

Air Vice-Marshal Sir Philip Game returned to England to serve his King for ten more years as Commissioner of the Metropolitan Police. He died in 1961, in his mid-eighties. His devoted wife, Gwendolen, spent her last years living with their daughter Rosemary and her family, passing away in 1972.

Lang's own, very forgiving wife, Hilda, died in May, 1964. One of the most touching things to happen in the Big Fella's life in that sad period was the relationship that blossomed between him and Sir Philip Game's oldest son, Bill. After graduating from Sydney University, Bill had returned to England, where he suffered a terrible tragedy in his first marriage, losing both his wife and baby in childbirth. He eventually remarried a Sydney girl, Vera Blackburn, daughter of the chancellor of Sydney University. On visits back to Sydney he made a point of contacting Lang and enjoying several intimate chats about the old times over a friendly cup of tea.

Lang would also outlast the despised upstart who replaced him as premier. Sir Bertram Stevens was lucky enough to ride to power on the waves of economic recovery but within seven years was ruthlessly dumped from office in a party revolt. He died in 1973.

The Big Fella himself hung on another two years, passing away peacefully on 27 September 1975, some three months short of his ninety-ninth birthday.

Other players in the cast of 1932 would go on to considerably mixed fortunes. Robert Beardsmore, the public servant whose defiant stand set the stage for Lang's dismissal, no longer had to worry about the loss of his retirement benefits. Just the opposite: a year later he was promoted by the Stevens Government to a senior position on the state Superannnuation Board at a healthy raise of £50 ($3500) a year. A month after the June election he was personally introduced to the Governor, and Lady Game, who sang his praises in one of her letters home.

'We met the honest Colonel Beardsmore who bearded Lang,' she punned, 'and refused to obey his illegal orders. He was sent on leave and would no doubt have been sacked [by] Lang. He struck me as such a sterling character, as of course he must be, the only one, so far as we heard, who dared to defy him.'

Detective Gilbert Leary, who took on the undercover role of swagman in the manhunt for accused murderer William

Morton, not only received a commendation for that brave exploit but several other similar awards during his twenty more years on the force. He went on to become a senior inspector, officer in charge of the Riverina district, and was no doubt asked many times over to retell his amazing story of two months wandering though the depression era's heart of darkness.

Leary's Scottish-born boss, the redoubtable William 'Billy' Mackay, took over the top position of New South Wales police commissioner in 1936, introducing notable innovations like the Police Rescue Squad, Police Air Wing, and Police Citizens Boys' Clubs. In later years, however, his iron fist began to show signs of rust, with a royal commission on illegal gambling accusing him of 'impetuous and impulsive behaviour'. By the 1940s he had begun to enjoy a few wee drops too many. His health was affected and he died while on sick leave in 1948, when the bravest of brave hearts finally gave way.

Hans Bertram, the rescued German pilot, was hailed as a hero across Australia in a series of jam-packed public speaking appearances. He decided to convert his famous *Atlantis* from a seaplane to wheels and in December, with an Australian to act as his co-pilot, flew off back to Europe. Somehow, in Darwin, he picked up a secret stowaway whose extra weight almost caused him to crash on take-off and later added to his problems in steering his way through another violent storm over the Timor Sea. On Wednesday, 14 December, while attempting an early morning take-off from Surabaya in Java, his heavily laden Junkers hit a ditch and nosedived into the ground, sustaining extensive damage, though no one was hurt.

'With so much bad luck, I definitely will not do any more flying in 1932,' he wisely decided.

Much luckier was James White, the gunman who defended his girlfriend's honour by killing Frederick Roberts in that terrifying rush-hour shoot-out in Kings Cross at the end of

1931. It would later take a jury just seventeen minutes to acquit him on grounds of self-defence. In the kind of emotional scene tailor-made for the tabloid press, the curvaceous flapper Irene Carson raced up in tears to embrace her freed lover. Before the happy couple left the court, though, the prosecutor offered a sobering word of advice.

'I would be inclined to change my address,' he smiled wickedly, reminding them of Frederick Roberts's extensive underworld connections.

As for the Fifty-Fifty Club, with its heady mix of colourful characters, its reputation as Sydney's hottest hangout would rapidly fade as police raids became more frequent and other, trendier nightspots opened in competition. In the later 1930s its astute owner, Phil 'the Jew' Jeffs, quietly sold it and went off to retire in luxury, as wealthy as many of the eastern suburbs moguls he had catered to.

Tilly Devine, eventually driven out of her vice empire by a ruthless new generation of gang lords, took up the sedate life of an old-age pensioner. She succumbed to cancer in 1970, a bit of a folk hero in her own right.

And then, of course, there were the hundreds of thousands of mostly anonymous battlers who together loomed larger than any single personality, forming the composite face of the Great Depression. Some would be forced to struggle on for years to come with no or little work, continuing to stagger from one eviction to another. Daisy McWilliams, the Harbour Bridge sandwich-maker, would shrink to just 39 kilograms before she and her husband Bob were able to fight their way back to a more normal existence. He died in 1951, with that hectic day at the bridge opening remaining one of his fondest memories. Daisy would live on well into the 1970s, like so many others deeply scarred but spiritually strengthened by her time in the cauldron of heartache and despair.

Ultimately, the Great Depression would serve to define the Australian character in more realistic terms than Gallipoli ever could. As a battle fought on the home front it tested the courage and resourcefulness of a much wider cross-section of the population – women as well as men. With the economy collapsing around them, their livelihoods wiped out, their hopes hanging by a thread, Australians still managed to hold the line against the violent extremism sweeping so much of the world. In so doing, they would prove themselves to be a people at their best in the worst of times, blessed with the healing power of their moderation.

Endnotes

Attributions other than daily newspaper reports

Prologue: Judgement day
Page
1   'By the fateful year of 1929': international loan comparisons are from C. B. Schedvin, *Australia and the Great Depression*, p. 100. Schedvin also provides a concise summary of the origins of the crash from a world perspective.

Chapter 1 1931: The prequel
Page
6   'Fred Roberts and James White were too intent': my description of the shootout is drawn from a composite of press reports dealing with the incident, subsequent committal proceedings and eventual trial.
7   'For sheer spectacle the Kings Cross shoot-out': 1931 homicide total from *Yearbook of the Commonwealth of Australia*, 1933, p. 823.
8   'In a population of 6.5 million': my figure of 650,000 living like refugees may well be conservative. Official estimates of the national total on sustenance relief were variously quoted as from 673,840 to 708,000 in June, 1932.

8   'Translated into today's equivalent': currency conversions (1932 £ to 2004 $) are based on a comparison of the consumer price indexes for the relative periods. Although the modern CPI was not introduced until 1948, statisticians accept a rough equivalency to the retail price C-series index which applied in 1932. The current index level is more than 34 times higher than the 1932 level and must then be multiplied by two to convert from pounds to dollars. The convenient formula of £1 = $70 turns out to be particularly relevant to everyday items like food and beverages. A schooner of beer that cost 1 shilling in 1932 would cost $3.50 today.

9   'The widening gap between the well off and hard done by': additional details of the Adelaide Beef Riot are provided in Ray Broomhill, *Unemployed Workers*, pp. 176–9. The Perth Treasury Building Riot is fully covered in Geoffrey Bolton, *A Fine Country to Starve In*, pp. 151–3.

12 'In August, 1930, Sir Otto Niemeyer': Niemeyer's speech and details of the Melbourne Agreement cited by E. O. G. Shann and D. B. Copland, *The Crisis in Australian Finance 1929–1931*, pp. 18–31.

15 ' "Every 100 additional men employed" ' : E. G. Theodore's plan is cited by Shann and Copland, *The Battle of the Plans*, p. 2.

20 ' "If Australia is to surmount her troubles" ': Robert Menzies, March, 1931, speech cited in Michael Cannon, *The Human Face of the Great Depression*, pp. 228–9.

Chapter 2 1932: A leap into the void
Page

23 'Dancing in the Dark': written by Howard Dietz (lyrics) and Arthur Schwartz (music) for the 1931 musical *The Bandwagon*.

23 'For the couples dancing into the dawn': description of Fifty-Fifty Club atmosphere and characters is largely drawn from Larry Writer, *Razor*, pp. 176–81; also Sydney *Truth*, 31 January, 1932 and various other articles.

24 'If nineteen-year-old Dulcie Markham was among the revellers': Dulcie Markham's earnings of £50 a night may well be conservative. 'Dulcie used to say it was easy to get £100 a night [$7000] at a brothel,' quoted in *Razor*, p. 184.

31   'On New Year's Day Albert Jacka lay dying . . .': Jacka's biographical details are taken largely from Ian Grant, *Jacka, V.C.*

Chapter 3 A call to arms
Page
33   '*One can picture the scene*': Albert Jacka as tall, bronzed Colonial from G. A. Leask, *V.C. Heroes of the War*, p. 21.
36   'The New Guard of New South Wales was formed': New Guard organisational details from Eric Campbell, *The Rallying Point*, pp. 50–8. A more comprehensive account of both the New Guard and the League of National Security is provided by Keith Amos, *The New Guard Movement, 1931–1935*.
37   '*We of the New Guard*': the words of the New Guard anthem were reported in *Smith's Weekly*, 20 February 1932. They continue: 'So when we get our orders, we'll make our voices ring, I'm a loyal guardsman, God save our King'.
37   'The rigid salute and patriotic fervour': a concise summary of the ideological conflicts in Europe at the time is provided by Larry Ceplair, *Under the Shadow of War*, pp. 14–30. Also see Martin Gilbert, *History of the Twentieth Century*, pp. 112–17, 174.
39   'Ironically, Jack Lang was one': Lang as 'an astute politician of no mean calibre,' cited by Campbell, *The Rallying Point*, p. 14.
43   'A giant Scotsman with fists like demolition balls': a vivid description of Billy Mackay was provided by his nemesis, Campbell. 'He had a strong but rather ugly face and when he grinned . . . he disclosed the urgent need for expert dental attention.' *The Rallying Point*, p. 106.
43   '"Do you want to be commissioner?"': quotes regarding Mackay's appointment by Lang to 'sort out . . . the New Guard bastards' are drawn from Writer, *Razor*, p. 136 and J. T. Lang, *The Turbulent Years*, p. 122.

Chapter 4 Faces in the street
Page
44   'Charming or challenging, Lang knew instinctively': Lang's childhood, including descent into poverty, described in J. T. Lang, *The Turbulent Years*, pp. 1–4. Bede Nairn in *The 'Big Fella'* offers the most thoroughly researched summary of his early life, as well as later career.

45   'From the age of seven': Lang's combative days as a newspaper boy from J. H. C. Sleeman, *The Life of J. T. Lang*, pp. 65–8. Sleeman worked as Lang's publicist. His book, written in 1933, is a rambling hagiography but some of its more intriguing accounts could only have come from Lang himself.

45   'A particularly painful memory': the buggy whip incident is cited in Nairn, *The 'Big Fella'*, p. 2. Its full emotional impact can only be a matter of speculation, but according to Nairn it was apparent to some of his fellow parliamentarians. The quote 'grouse against society' is attributed to W. F. Morton, one of the few who could claim to know Lang very well. The incident takes on all the more significance when linked to the young Lang's apparent mental breakdown in the same period. 'The boy began to break up. Smash! He had collapsed,' notes Sleeman, p. 68.

46   'Faces in the Street': the version quoted is from *Henry Lawson: Collected Verse*, memorial edition, volume 1, p. 15, edited by Colin Roderick and published by Angus & Robertson, Sydney, 1981.

47   'By a quirk of fate, Lang was to become': the relationship between Lang and his brother-in-law, poet Henry Lawson, is cited in J. T. Lang, *I Remember*, pp. 8–9. Lang mentions 'Faces in the Street' as showing 'how close' Lawson was to the people, but the influence of the poem is purely speculative on my part.

47   'In his early thirties Lang left his wife': Lang's tragic relationship with Nellie Louisa Anderson is referred to in Nairn, *The 'Big Fella'*, pp. 2, 34. Nairn uncovered the story during personal interviews with several of Lang's closest contemporaries.

48   'The choice was cruelly taken out of his hands': details of Anderson's miscarriage and fatal septicaemia as recorded in her death certificate, 1911/009430, New South Wales Registry of Births, Deaths and Marriages.

Chapter 5 Love in the time of the Great Depression
Page

50   'Saturday night theatregoers in Brisbane': The story of the classical violinist, Winifred Donnier, appeared in *Smith's Weekly*, 2 July 1932, p. 3. I have taken creative liberties in describing her feelings and the music she chose.

56 'Either way, patience was definitely no virtue': the story of Ethel Jane Anderson appeared in the *West Australian* on 5 April 1932, p. 15. Again, I tried to imagine what she might have thought and felt as she went on her rampage of destruction.

60 '"Today, the bursting walls of the insane asylums can trace"': the assertion is one of many such contained in a pamphlet entitled *The Dangers of Birth Control* by P. Fennelly, LLD and MBE, 1933.

60 'The sad truth was just the opposite': Daisy McWilliams's rebuttal to people like Fennelly appears in Len Fox (ed), *Depression Down Under*, pp. 18, 19. More extensive insights into the plight of women in the depression and the issue of contraception are offered by Cannon, *The Human Face of the Great Depression*.

61 'Couples preparing to tie the knot': the *Yearbook of the Commonwealth of Australia*, 1933, shows 93,634 marriages in 1932, a rate of 6.6 per thousand, compared to 8.59 per thousand in 1921. This is one of the lowest rates in the industrialised world for that period.

Chapter 6 Surprise attack
Page

63 '"I may express views in which some of you do not concur"': all quotes attributed to Lyons and Lang are drawn from a composite of press reports.

68 'At dusk a gangling young red retriever': Governor Sir Philip Game, his personality and physical appearance, daily routine and walks with Micky, the red retriever, are drawn from numerous references in Bethia Foott, *Dismissal of a Premier*.

71 '"Will you please ask your hubby how much Lang pays him"': this and other protest letters cited in Foott, *Dismissal of a Premier*, pp. 147–50.

71 'Perhaps Gwendolen's most hurtful single moment': public rudeness including Lady Game snubbing incident, in Foott, *Dismissal of a Premier*, p. 153.

72 '"I was glad Micky was in the room ... Lang really has got some hypnotic power"': from Foott, *Dismissal of a Premier*, p. 136.

Chapter 7 Flying high
Page

74 'For 11,172 lucky Australians': In 1931 small amounts of overseas mail had been flown in via experimental relays by KLM and others.

75 '"Efforts to promote the development of civil aviation would be neutralised"': Stanley Bruce quote cited by J. T. Lang, *I Remember*, p. 349.

77 'As for devoted fans of Australian Rules': love of Australian Rules football cited in Janet McCalman, *Struggletown: Public and Private Life in Richmond 1900–1965*, p. 197.

77 'In 1927 the Big Fella met Smithy': Charles Kingsford Smith's relationship with Lang as cited in J. T. Lang, *I Remember*, pp. 344–51.

78 'Four years later, however': Kingsford Smith's support for the New Guard referred to in Campbell, *The Rallying Point*, pp. 49, 100. 'I was very close to both Smithy and Ulm,' Campbell claims.

Chapter 8 Blood sport
Page

82 'A by-election widely seen as an important test': all speeches, statements and interjections are drawn from a composite selection of day-to-day coverage of the East Sydney by-election.

84 'Their furious interjections, however': E. G. Theodore's personality and background are drawn largely from Ross Fitzgerald, *Red Ted: The Life of E. G. Theodore*.

86 '"And what a grand meeting it was"': New Guard support for Joseph Lyons's campaign cited in Campbell, *The Rallying Point*, pp. 140–4.

Chapter 9 The case of the not-so-jolly swagman
Page

90 'When Superintendent Billy Mackay heard': my description of the Paddington murder and much of the subsequent manhunt is based on a composite of press reports dealing with committal hearings and subsequent trial, put together in the style of dramatised documentary.

92 'While police kept a 24-hour watch on the house': Detective Gilbert Leary's background is as recorded in his police records, courtesy of New South Wales Police.

94 '"When I entered the town, I made for the police station"': Bill Kidman in his book *On the Wallaby* offers a vivid picture of life on the road for tens of thousands of depression-era jobless.

98 'For all the indignities endured': the damning series of articles about life in mass labour camps like Myalup appeared in the *West Australian* newspaper in March, 1932. Further background about the grave discontent in that camp and others is drawn from Geoffrey Bolton, *A Fine Country to Starve In*.

100 'Clay-shovellers fracture': cited in Bolton, p. 217.

Chapter 10 The New Guard bares its teeth
Page

104 'Mackay had set out to infiltrate': 'Mackay's first step was to assign some of his men to infiltrate the New Guard,' Lang wrote in *The Turbulent Years*, p. 122. It's unlikely, though, that a canny operator like Mackay would have risked a leak by giving the Premier any details of the undercover operation while it was still under way.

105 'Mackay immediately assigned extra plainclothesmen': was there really a plan to kidnap Jack Lang in late February or early March? Mackay seems to have been genuinely convinced that there was – otherwise why go through the motions of warning the Premier to take secret precautions? Harder to pin down is the issue of whether the kidnap plot was officially authorised by the New Guard high command or the pet project of a few militants.

105 '"When I finished work for the day"': Lang's own account of driving himself home on the day scheduled for the snatch is recorded in J. T. Lang, *The Turbulent Years*, pp. 136–8.

106 '"I know why you are drilling"': Mackay's confrontation with Francis de Groot is described in the de Groot papers, volume 3, pp. 41–2. For further background see Keith Amos, *The New Guard Movement*.

107 '"It is true that had Communism been introduced"': Campbell

reveals his true stand in *The Rallying Point*, pp. 73, 130.
108 'The New Guard had strayed': New Guard defector Major Treloar quoted in Keith Amos, *The New Guard Movement*, pp. 57, 58.
108 '"Mr. Lang was head and shoulders above any of his colleagues"': Eric Campbell, *The Rallying Point*, pp. 125, 126.
109 '"Look, Campbell... you and your New Guard keep out of this"': exchange between Campbell and banker cited in Campbell, *The Rallying Point*, p. 126.

Chapter 11 Off with his head!
Page
113 '"Philip is having dreadful worries over the bridge opening"': Lady Game's letter to an aunt is taken from Philip Game papers held in the Mitchell Library, Sydney, and is cited in Bethia Foott, *Dismissal of a Premier*, p. 179.
115 '"Some bust-up must come soon"': Lady Game's account of her husband's quarrels with Lang and the possibility of leaving Government House to become a Sydney housewife in Foott, pp. 115–16.
116 '"Vested interests are not above attempting"': Lady Game's account of July Domain rally in Foott, p. 115.
117 'The dispute threatened to run out of control': the Governor's round-table proposal, Lang's reply, their correspondence in Foott, pp. 105–10.
122 '"Mr. Lang asked for permission to publish the letters"': the royal honours scandal, including Lady Game's account to her mother in Foott, pp. 110–12.
123 '"He dropped dead five minutes ago"': this amusing incident is referred to by Lady Game in Foott, pp. 111–12.
123 '"On thinking the matter over"': Game's letter to Lang, cited by Foott, p. 113.
124 '"I feel that Philip was almost at the end of his tether"': Lady Game's letter in Foott, p. 114.
124 'If there was one factor above all': Governor Game's generosity to the homeless is described in *Smith's Weekly*, 3 September 1932.
124 'Game was also the first "fat cat"': Game's voluntary pay cut from Foott, *Dismissal of a Premier*, pp. 98, 100.

125 'Before he did, though, he had called his two sons': Game's conversation with sons Bill and David forewarning of his decision to grant Lang's request for Upper House appointees is cited by Foott, p. 145, as told to her by Bill Game in 1965.

126 'Thinking of all the grief Jack Lang had caused him': my reconstruction of Lang's encounter with Game over the Harbour Bridge opening is purely speculative, though it's clear the Premier must have raised some powerful arguments to persuade the Governor to go against the wishes of both his King and his wife.

127 '"I am so thankful to tell you"': Lady Game's extreme anxiety over the issue is best demonstrated in the relief she felt when George V reluctantly agreed to leave the arrangements as they were, Foott, pp. 179, 180. Nevertheless, His Majesty was quick to remind Sir Philip of his displeasure when the two met at a palace garden party two years later, albeit with 'a pleasant twinkle' in his eye.

Chapter 12 A blue-ribbon occasion: Part I
Page

128 'Bob McWilliams left home at 4 am': my story of Bob McWilliams on the day of the Sydney Harbour Bridge opening is based on a memoir written by his wife, Daisy McWilliams, in 1936, later appearing in *Depression Down Under*, a collection of anecdotes edited by Len Fox. I have taken creative liberties in expanding Daisy's account to illustrate what else was happening on the day. I thank the publishers Hale & Iremonger for their kind cooperation.

132 '"I can hardly describe to you the fuss and difficulties"': Bethia Foott, in *Dismissal of a Premier*, quotes not only from Lady Game's letters but also official correspondence and recollections of her father – a senior aide to Governor Game – in describing the hilarious antics leading up to the bridge opening, pp. 165–72, 191, 192.

138 '"He certainly left me feeling that whatever he does"': Lady Game's assessment of Lang in Foott, p. 100.

138 '"That's the only thing I'm afraid of"': Lang's aside to Lady Game at bridge opening in Foott, p. 185.

Chapter 13 A blue-ribbon occasion: Part II
Page
140 'When Jack Lang rose to walk to the microphone': Lang gives a plausible account of his contribution to the building of the Sydney Harbour Bridge in *I Remember*, pp. 259–69.

142 'The largest single arch bridge': the Sydney Harbour Bridge did rank as the largest of its kind in terms of its width. However, at 503 metres it was not the longest, as frequently claimed at the time. New York's Bayonne Bridge, completed a few months before, was a metre longer.

142 '"In the name of the loyal and decent citizens"': my account of the ribbon-slashing incident is drawn from a composite of newspaper reports which tend to vary in certain details. I have attempted to provide a credible resolution of minor discrepancies.

145 '"Jim Campbell, the rigger, that was bloody awful"': bridge labourer's account, from David Ellyard, *The Proud Arch: The Story of the Sydney Harbour Bridge*, p. 56.

146 '"Philip told me he found himself clasping Lady Isaacs"': the Game family's struggle to get back to Government House is described in Foott, *Dismissal of a Premier*, pp. 187, 188.

148 '"As the big day drew near, a number of young hotheads were not satisfied"': de Groot's justification for his exploit is taken from the de Groot papers in the Mitchell Library, Sydney, volume 2, p. 7, as cited in Amos, *The New Guard Movement*, p. 79.

148 'However, as late as 5 pm Friday': the rush to get de Groot a horse and other details of the day is described by Campbell in *The Rallying Point*, pp. 148–59. The New Guard leader himself came up with a rather lame plan to try to get Lang arrested on the morning of the bridge ceremony by charging him with fraud and corruption. He was quick to endorse de Groot's alternative suggestion.

Chapter 14 The Swindell saga: A morality tale
Page
151 'The day after the Harbour Bridge festivities': Phar Lap's history and mystique is explored at length by Michael Wilkinson in *The Phar Lap Story*.

154 '"But of course, we all had to wear feathers in our hair"': the debutante's quote, statistics on Woollahra building applications and other evidence of eastern suburbs affluence is cited in A. R. Cottle, 'Life can be so sweet on the sunny side of the street: A study of the rich of Woollahra during the depression 1928–1934'.

156 'The exact details of these transactions': the story of the Swindell scandal is a composite of newspaper reports and transcripts from the subsequent *Report of Royal Commission on Greyhound Racing and Fruit Machines*, November 1932, New South Wales Parliamentary Papers, 1933, pp. 993–1058.

168 'Jack Lang would always contend': Lang's own account of the scandal appears in *I Remember*, pp. 356–60. In his view, 'Whether Swindell was a go-getter or a far-sighted businessman is now quite immaterial. To the state [through greyhound racing tax revenues] he has been a great benefactor.'

Chapter 15 Getting physical
Page
171 '*Lay the proud usurpers low!*': the verse is from *Scots Wha Hae*, 'Bruce's Address at Bannockburn' by Robert Burns, taken from *The Poetical Works of Robert Burns*, edited by J. Logie Robertson, Oxford University Press, London, 1960, p. 330.

172 '"Go out there and belt their bloody heads off!"': Billy Mackay's speech to police before the Central Court clash with the New Guard is taken from a witness's account quoted by Keith Amos, *The New Guard Movement*, p. 85.

174 '"Kicked the Guard's backsides"': Lang's delighted reaction is quoted by Amos, who interviewed him personally in 1974, as cited in *The New Guard Movement*, p. 84.

178 '"De Groot had got my message"': Lady Angela St Claire Erskine tells of meeting de Groot in *Fore and Aft*, pp. 235, 236, and recalls her talk with Sir Philip (abridged in later editions) pp. 226–8.

179 '"Good enough! Well done, de Groot!"': King George V's thigh-slapping reaction to the ribbon-cutting incident was reported in a letter from London to de Groot, de Groot papers volume 1, p. 41.

180 'Lang's senior bureaucrats had to scramble': apart from several rather colourful press accounts of the sudden withdrawals, a

Nationalist parliamentarian, Milton Jarvie, claimed to have inside information about the actual amounts of cheques cashed. (The *Age*, 17 March 1932.)

Chapter 16 Phar Lap: Myth and reality
Page
184 'The sad truth, in terms of the great Phar Lap's reputation': the controversies surrounding Phar Lap – including details of secret betting plunges and his mysterious death – are solidly documented by Michael Wilkinson, *The Phar Lap Story*. The interpretation put on certain incidents referred to in this chapter is my own.

Chapter 17 The battle of the decrees
Page
192 'Justice Herbert V. Evatt also lived up to Lang's expectations': extracts from the High Court judgement are taken from *Commonwealth Law Reports*, New South Wales v The Common-wealth, no. 1, volume 46, 1932, pp. 171–94.

194 'He turned his full wrath on McTiernan': Lang's vitriolic attack amid stormy interjections was reported in full by the *Sydney Morning Herald* on 12 May. It was made in the course of the Mortgages Taxation Bill debate.

201 'Will you please instruct your departmental officers': despite its extraordinary nature, the Treasury directive of 12 April some how seems to have eluded any attention in the press for a full month after it was issued. The memo was finally made public on 14 May when the *Sydney Morning Herald* published all documents related to Lang's dismissal from office.

Chapter 18 Descent into chaos
Page
209 '"I feel it is far better that the Commonwealth and State Governments should decide"': Game's cable was sent on 23 April 1932 and would have some surprising repercussions. It is analysed by A. S. Morrison in *Journal of the Royal Australian Historical Society*, volume 61, March 1976, pp. 338, 339.

209 '"The Press barrage is very intense"': Game's letter to a relative, showing the intense pressure he felt, is quoted in Foott, *Dismissal of a Premier*, p. 199.

Chapter 19 Vested interests
Page

212 'The Great Depression ticked away impervious': the figure of 700,000 jobless is an arbitrary compromise, given estimates that varied wildly at the time and remain the subject of debate through decades of later academic analysis. The official peak in 1932, based on figures provided by the trade unions, records the national unemployment rate at just under 30 per cent. A comprehensive review of all available statistics carried out by C. Foster in 1988 puts the figure at 35 per cent of all wage and salary earners, as cited in R. G. Gregory and N. G. Butlin (eds), *Recovery from the Depression*, pp. 289–309. The respected social historian Michael Cannon believes the actual peak was 'certainly more than 50%', which would have meant more than a million people out of work, cited in Cannon, *The Human Face of the Great Depression*, p. 16.

213 'A Christmas lunch put on by the Melbourne retailer': the Sidney Myer lunch and other examples of charity are drawn from Cannon, *The Human Face of the Great Depression*, pp. 61–6. Cannon also provides a well-researched summary of the evolution of the various state government dole programs.

215 '"We had many a laugh over the propaganda"': Daisy McWilliams's comment on vegetable-growing is from her memoir in Len Fox (ed.), *Depression Down Under*, pp. 17, 18.

216 '"What was worst about being on the dole was having no spare money"': Edna Ryan's personal account appears in Cannon, *The Human Face of the Great Depression*, pp. 286–9.

218 'In 1929, Australia had 901,000 card-carrying unionists': trade union membership figures cited in L. J. Louis, *Trade Unions and the Depression*, p. 211. Louis also provides a comprehensive overview of the growing antagonism between the unions and unemployed.

220 '"Sympathetic consideration"': quote is cited by L. J. Louis, *Trade Unions and the Depression*, p. 186.

222 'The Melbourne Trades Hall atavists': Hogan sent the angry letter to a Victorian MLC, J. P. Jones, on 16 May. It was published in the Melbourne *Herald* on 27 June.

223 'Jack Lang's relationship with the New South Wales unions': Lang's troubles with the unions, his battle against communist

infiltration and his strange love–hate relationship with Jock Garden are documented throughout Bede Nairn, *The 'Big Fella'*. Lang provides his own colourful portrait of Jock Garden in *I Remember*, pp. 186–92.

224 '"The revolution *has* come"': the line is from Lang's speech at an eight-hour day dinner reported in the *Sydney Morning Herald*, 5 October 1931.

Chapter 20 Dirty tricks: The unmaking of the New Guard
Page

227 '"A body of men superior in strength"': testimony of Detective William Alford.

228 'Captain Walter Warneford was exactly the kind of recruit': Warneford's activities within the New Guard as Mackay's secret agent are, by their nature, shrouded in mystery. My account of how he might have proceeded to win the confidence of the Guardsmen takes creative liberties based on bits and pieces of press coverage. The story of the hypnotised war veteran being buried alive in the grounds of Caulfield Military Hospital is true, reported in May, 1932, by *Smith's Weekly*.

234 '"We know that the New Guard has departed from those principles"': how much of the New Guard 'plotting' was spontaneous and how much was a direct result of double agents like Warneford, and possibly Scott, fanning the flames to discredit the organisation? Even de Groot admits that certain 'hotheads' within the militia were openly threatening to kidnap Lang and he did not dispute Mackay's direct accusation of a New Guard plan to seize Parliament House. The one issue on which there can be little doubt is that Warneford was a major influence, if not the sole instigator, in setting up a 'Fascist Legion' to attract the militia's lunatic fringe. He also played an active role in organising the assault on Jock Garden.

Chapter 21 The power of one
Page

240 'The besetting sin of the Australian of today is want of moral courage': Governor Game's letter to George V from Philip Game papers, 18 March 1931.

242 'Where any moneys from sale or lease': decree 42 proclaimed the right of the federal government to commandeer the services of New South Wales public servants, pending specific instructions to be issued to each department in due course. Decree 43, published the next day, contained the detailed orders which Beardsmore and his colleagues would be required to follow under penalty of imprisonment. Beardsmore would late cite decree 43 as the basis for his actions, but constitutional lawyers generally refer to decree 42, which was the basic enacting measure.

243 'As forced labour without payment': Lang's inflammatory 10 May proclamation contains a curious error, perhaps reflecting the haste in which he acted. In it, he refers back to the date of his previous directive to public servants as 13 April instead of 12 April, the official release date. All documents relative to the dismissal were made public in the 14 May edition of the *Sydney Morning Herald*.

245 '"We rather need anything we can get to cheer us"': Gwendolen Game's letter of 7 May cited in Foott, *Dismissal of a Premier*, p. 204.

246 'After 41 years in the public service': Robert Beardsmore's family background, military citation etc. is drawn from his personal papers and memorabilia kindly loaned to me by his granddaughters, Ann Hart and Judy Campbell.

Chapter 22 The longest day of the year
Page

250 'While the bill theoretically applied': Lang's biographer, Bede Nairn, offers this brutal assessment of the significance of the mortgage tax-ation legislation as an expression of the Big Fella's last gasp. 'It was a sham, betraying the derangement of the government. If [it] had any relevance at all to the dismissal of the premier, it was in its stark portrayal, by its incompetent injustice, of the ultimate failure of Lang to manage the affairs of the state.' From Nairn, *The 'Big Fella'*, pp. 259, 260.

256 'May was a fateful month for Sir Philip': my account of Sir Philip's agonising over the mortgage tax legislation is speculative. None of his letters mention that he ever thought of resigning but there was no doubt he was sick at heart at the thought of having to sign the noxious bill into law.

Chapter 23 Legal pornography: Field v Field
Page
258 'Sidney Field, like Anthony Hordern': Field v Field is listed as case no. 503 of 1931, the Supreme Court of New South Wales, Matrimonial Causes Jurisdiction. Quotations from various parties are taken from sworn affidavits filed on behalf of Ivy Field, Sidney Field or co-respondents, as well as contemporary press reports.
260 'The divorce laws actively encouraged full-scale combat': various grounds for divorce cited by W. K. S. Mackenzie, *The Practice in Divorce (New South Wales)*, pp. xxxiii–xxxv.
261 '"What made you divorce your first husband?"': the various cartoons appeared in *Smith's Weekly* during 1932.
270 'Jack Lang himself had been dangerously close': Hilda Lang's petition for separation is listed as file no. 3K8107; 6506; 1908, in the Supreme Court of New South Wales, Matrimonial Causes Jurisdiction.

Chapter 24 The suicide note
Page
273 'In the execution of the powers and authorities': Royal Instructions to a Governor are cited in *New South Wales Parliamentary Handbook*, 1931 edition, p. 183.
274 'There could be no better example of this inherent class snobbery': in comments made by Lord Clive Wigram, private secretary to King George V, the political bias of Buckingham Palace was clear enough. Excerpts from Wigram's letter to Game dated 11 May 1932. Game's own prejudices were exposed in a letter to the Palace written four months after Lang's return to power. 'To give Mr. Lang his due he is a leader and can carry people with him and does not appear to forfeit their confidence even when he fails to make good his many and rash promises. He seems to have some magnetic power over them which induces them to accept his assertions as true however palpably absurd and false they may be.' From Game's letters to King George V, 18 March 1931. The Governor's correspondence with Buckingham Palace was kept separate from the other Game papers and was not released for public inspection until the 1990s.

276 '"I should be entirely wrong if I were to ask you to surrender your Commission"': Game's apology to Lang in Philip Game papers, 26 March 1931, cited in Foott, *Dismissal of a Premier*, p. 67.

279 'Many theories would later be advanced': Lang's thought processes during his darkest moods can only be imagined but his isolation and brooding nature is well documented by biographer Bede Nairn. 'He probably never had a friend, even among the thousands of followers he swept up from 1927 to 1932,' Nairn observes in *The 'Big Fella'*, p. 2.

279 '"Extraordinary cool . . . but . . . there are fierce and consuming fires raging"': this assessment of Lang on the day before his dismissal was reported by H. Campbell-Jones, a former editor of *Truth*, as cited by Kate White in *A Political Love Story: Joe and Enid Lyons*, p. 155. Campbell-Jones claimed to be acting as a go-between to sound Lang out on the possibility of a compromise with the federal government and passed on his impressions in a private letter to Joe Lyons.

279 '"I have come to think he is a living Jekyll and Hyde"': Game used this stark imagery in a letter to King George V written on 18 May, setting the scene of his dramatic final meeting with Lang before the dismissal.

Chapter 25 Game and Lang: The final showdown
Page

283 '"One thought that occurred to me"': Lang gives his own account of his dismissal in *The Turbulent Years*, pp. 152–8.

283 'No official record exists of their conversation': my version of the likely dialogue between the Governor and Premier is based on a composite of quotations taken from Lang's account in *The Turbulent Years*, Sir Philip's correspondence with Lang and Sir Philip's subsequent letters to the King and others.

285 'No one had suffered more through the torturous war of words': the tensions felt by Lady Game and others at Government House during the historic last meeting between Lang and the Governor are vividly portrayed in her letter to her mother dated 15 May and cited in Foott, *Dismissal of a Premier*, pp. 211–14.

291 '"Lang played for defeat"': the quote is from a contemporary of Lang's in an interview with political scientist Miriam Dixson, *Greater Than Lenin? Lang and Labor 1916–1932*, p. 25.

Chapter 26 Unanswered questions
Page
292 '"There it was," he writes': Lang's reaction to the dismissal from J. T. Lang, *The Turbulent Years*, pp. 152–8.
297 'Even so, there would be another ironic twist': the discussion of Game's rights and powers is drawn largely from Herbert V. Evatt, *The King and His Dominion Governors*, pp. 157–74. His conclusions, pp. 173, 174 are especially noteworthy. 'Was the Governor constitutionally correct in his action? No judgement can be pronounced until what is constitutionally "correct" is defined by competent authority.' But Evatt goes on. '. . . the power of dismissal can hardly be regarded as properly exercised if a Governor justifies it merely by reliance upon the Ministers having broken the law, and it appears that there is available a competent legal tribunal which can determine the question of legality.'

Evatt's view was, indeed, supported by the legal opinion drafted within the Dominions Office in response to Game's cable of 23 April. In essence, it suggested that so long as the Governor himself was not being asked to put his signature to any allegedly illegal action, then 'The courts of law are the proper tribunal to settle whether any particular action of Ministers is or is not a breach of the law.' That opinion became instantly irrelevant when Game sacked Lang on 13 May, and was never sent. The circumstances are cited in A. S. Morrison, 'The constitutional crisis 1930–32', *Journal of the Royal Australian Historical Society*, volume 68, September 1982, pp. 125, 126.

299 '"We are enchanted with your triumph"': the King's hearty congratulations were passed on to Game by Lord Wigram in a letter from Buckingham Palace dated 7 June, from the Philip Game papers.

Chapter 27 The search for *Atlantis*: Part I
Page
301 'The seaplane *Atlantis* left a sequinned trail': the story of the search for *Atlantis* and the two German airmen is drawn largely from Hans Bertram's book *Flight into Hell*, as well as press reports.
304 '"I can fly!"': Beinhorn later described her stay in Australia in glowing terms in her book *Flying Girl*, 1935, pp. 189–200. 'This remark,' she recalled, 'won more applause than all the rest of the lecture.' She adds: 'The aeronautical organisation in this remote continent is amazing.'

Chapter 28 The big smear
Page
308 'Sydney's *Daily Telegraph* led the pack': it appears the *Daily Telegraph*'s editors were themselves taken in by a hoax in splashing the sensational 'scoop' of a post-election coup plot. The story was eventually traced to a man named Davis who had a contract to collect and sort all waste paper from the baskets scattered around Parliament House to pass on to the Salvation Army. Davis occasionally came across items of news interest, which he secretly sold to the *Telegraph* or other newspapers. He claimed to have found the infamous 'manifesto' during one of his cleanups but he had actually forged it, splicing together various scraps of paper. Cited by J. H. C. Sleeman in *The Life of J. T. Lang*, pp. 313, 314.
311 'Court of Public Opinion': appeared in the *Sun*, 25 May.
312 'Guilty! On all counts': the UAP advertisement appeared on 31 May.

Chapter 29 Radio days: The birth of the ABC
Page
317 'Radio, as a reliable source of information': the early history of wireless is drawn from Alan Thomas, *Broadcast and Be Damned*; Clement Semmler, *The ABC: Aunt Sally and Sacred Cow*; Ken Inglis, *This is the ABC*; and other sources.
319 '"I have always held," he began, "that people's religion is a matter"': Lang's speech during the Marital Act broadcast is taken from *New South Wales Parliamentary Debates*

(Hansard) of 24 March 1925. He also refers to the issue in *I Remember*, pp. 181–5.
320 'Lang's early successful experimentation with the airwaves': Emil Voigt's influence in the development of 2KY and his subsequent advocacy of a state-run radio network are discussed at length by Murray Goot in his article, 'Radio Lang', which appears in Heather Radi and Peter Spearritt (eds), *Jack Lang*, pp. 119–37. Goot suggests the Premier lagged considerably behind Voigt, as well as others in the ALP far left, in his genuine commitment to the concept of state-owned broadcasting.
321 '"The plan to provide country centres with broadcasting stations"': the hostile *Wireless Weekly* editorials quoted include volume 10, number 8, 17 June; and number 9, 24 June.
324 'London is the Mecca of all artists': Charles Lloyd Jones's speech is quoted by the *Sydney Morning Herald*, 2 July.
326 'Lang naturally turned to 2KY': Lang's version of the takeover of 2KY and of the innovative pro-Labor radio dramas of John Pickard appears in *I Remember*, pp. 276–82. He entitled the chapter 'How the State missed its big chance in Broadcasting', which suggests he may have been more keen about Voigt's vision than some of his critics give him credit for.

Chapter 30 The last hurrah!

Page
331 'As many as 250,000 people converged': estimates of the actual number at the Moore Park rally vary but Bede Nairn suggests the police guess of 200,000 'on this stirring occasion may have been too low'. Cited in *The 'Big Fella'*, p. 264. Labor sources claimed as many as 300,000.
335 '"I should not be surprised to see Labor come back"': the pressure felt by the Game family during the election campaign is evident in letters quoted in Foott, *Dismissal of a Premier*, pp. 214–19.
336 '"That we resolved our differences"': the Governor's conspiratorial meeting with Country Party leader Michael Bruxner is referred to in Foott, p. 217.
339 '"The New Guard threw all its strength behind the UAP"': Campbell claims to have been a considerable influence in the June election in *The Rallying Point*, p. 146.

Chapter 31 11 June: The people's verdict
Page
345 'Jeffs also would have had Tilly Devine's Whores Poll': my use of the Fifty-Fifty Club and Tilly Devine's 'whores' poll' in relation to the election is, of course, fanciful – though not necessarily far-fetched.
347 '"In spite of the popular endorsement of my assassin's stroke"': Game's self-doubt, even after the massive election swing against Lang, is seen in his letter to a family member, dated 2 July 1932 and cited by Foott, p. 223. His comments on the election results, including the apparent swing of female voters and his relief that the poll was violence-free, feature in a letter to King George V dated 28 June, 1932. Game's frame of mind during the election is a matter of speculation but his soul-searching and ambivalence is plain enough.
348 'In the early stages of the election count': the analysis of voting figures is drawn from Nairn, *The 'Big Fella'*, pp. 265, 266 as well as contemporary press reports.
349 '"I do not know Eric Campbell"': Stevens's later attempt to disassociate himself from Campbell is cited by Keith Amos, *The New Guard Movement*, p. 98, referring to a speech the Premier gave a year after his election.

Chapter 32 The search for *Atlantis*: Part II
Page
351 'There were some Australians': this chapter is based on a compilation of contemporary press reports, as well as Hans Bertram's recollections of his remarkable battle for survival in *Flight into Hell*, translated by Michael J. Hudson from the original German version *Flug in die Holle*. I thank the German publishers, Langen Müller Herbig of Munich, for their kind assistance.
364 'He is only a young lad of sixteen': the names of Aboriginals involved in the search come from a note sent by Father Thomas at Drysdale River Mission to Bertram some weeks after the rescue. It is unclear what role each played at various stages of the rescue and I have attempted to make an educated guess.
367 '"The forced march of Police Constable Marshall"': this report by Sergeant Flinders of Wyndham Police is quoted by Bertram in *Flight into Hell*, p. 89.

368 'In areas of closer contact': the story of the feminist movement's battle to improve the lot of 'half-caste' children is told by Fiona Paisley in *Loving Protection? Australian Feminism and Aboriginal Women's Rights, 1919–1939*.
370 '"Death alone ends our term of duress"': letter cited in the first annual report of the Australian Aborigines' Amelioration Association.
370 'At least it was a start': the story of William Cooper and the Australian Aborigines' League cited in John Harris, *One Blood: Two hundreds years of Aboriginal encounter with Christianity*, pp. 618–21.

Chapter 33 1932: A helluva year
Page
372 'Please Don't Talk About Me When I'm Gone': written by Sidney Clare (lyrics) and Sam H. Stept (Music).
374 'Remarkably, it would be the nation's manufacturing sector': the role of manufacturing, particularly within the textile industry, in spearheading Australia's recovery is cited by Schedvin in *Australia and the Great Depression*, pp. 301–9.
375 'In June the number of registered food dole recipients': the estimated peak of 708,000 on dole relief was reported in the *Sydney Morning Herald*, though the figure most commonly referred to in post-depression studies is 673,840.
377 '"We feel very strongly"': Lyons's aggressive post-Lang campaign to lower overseas interest rates is cited by Schedvin in *Australia and the Great Depression*, pp. 354–8.
379 'Faces in the Street': as cited, from *Henry Lawson: Collected Verse*, volume 1, Angus & Robertson.
380 '"The revolution *has* come"': this is an expanded quote from Lang's speech to an eight-hour day dinner on Saturday 3 October, 1931, as reported by the *Sydney Morning Herald*.

Epilogue: Winners and losers
Page
384 '"I felt so strongly against that Niemeyer"': Lang's claim about his offer to resign is cited by Foott, p. 60.
386 '"We met the honest Colonel Beardsmore"': Lady Game's comment was made in a letter to her mother dated 10 July 1932. It

was uncovered by Bethia Foott during her letters research and sent on to Beardsmore's son, Henry Robert Beardsmore, in January, 1966 by way of thanks for his assistance with her book. 'I am sure you must have thought I had vanished and taken my cuttings with me,' she apologised.

386 'Detective Gilbert Leary, who took on the undercover role': Gilbert Leary's later history is taken from his police records, courtesy of the New South Wales Police.

387 'Leary's Scottish-born boss': the subsequent fates of William Mackay, Phil Jeffs and Tilly Devine are reported in Larry Writer, *Razor*. Len Fox, editor of *Depression Down Under*, traced the later histories of Daisy McWilliams and her husband, Bob.

Bibliography

Amos, Keith, *The New Guard Movement 1931–1935*, Melbourne University Press, Melbourne, 1976.
Beinhorn, Elly, *Flying Girl*, Geoffrey Bles, London, 1935.
Bertram, Hans, (translated by Michael J. Hudson), *Flight into Hell [Flug in die Holle]*, F. A. Herbig Verlagsbuchhandlung, Munich, 1985.
Bolton, G. C., *A Fine Country to Starve In*, University of WA Press, Perth, 1972.
Broomhill, Ray, *Unemployed Workers: A Social History of the Great Depression in Adelaide*, University of Queensland Press, Brisbane, 1978.
Campbell, Eric, *The Rallying Point: My Story of the New Guard*, Melbourne University Press, Melbourne, 1965.
Cannon, Michael, *The Human Face of the Great Depression*, published by the author, 1996.
Ceplair, Larry, *Under the Shadow of War, Fascism, Anti-Fascism, and Marxists, 1918–1939*, Columbia University Press, New York, 1987.
Craven, Gregory, *Secession, the Ultimate States Right*, Melbourne University Press, Melbourne, 1986.
Dixson, Miriam, *Greater than Lenin? Lang and Labor, 1916–1932*, Melbourne University Press, Melbourne, 1976.

Ellyard, David, *The Proud Arch: The Story of the Sydney Harbour Bridge*, Bay Books, Sydney, 1982.
Erskine, Lady Angela St Clair, *Fore and Aft*, Jarrolds, London, 1932.
Evatt, H. V., *The King and His Dominion Governors: A Study of the Reserve Powers of the Crown in Great Britain and the Dominions*, Oxford University Press, Oxford, 1936.
Fennelly, P., *The Dangers of Birth Control*, W. & J. Barr Printers, Melbourne, 1933.
Fitzgerald, Ross, *Red Ted: The Life of E. G. Theodore*, University of Queensland Press, Brisbane, 1994.
Foott, Bethia, *Dismissal of a Premier: The Philip Game Papers*, Morgan, Sydney, 1968.
Fox, Len (ed), *Depression Down Under*, Hale & Iremonger, Sydney, 1989.
Gilbert, Martin, *History of the Twentieth Century*, HarperCollins, London, 2001.
Grant, Ian, *Jacka, V.C., Australia's finest fighting soldier*, The Macmillan Company of Australia, Melbourne, 1989.
Gregory, R. G. and Butlin, N. G. (eds), *Recovery from the Depression: Australia and the World Economy in the 1930s*, University of Cambridge, Cambridge, England, 1988.
Harmar, Rosemary, *Growing up at Government House*, Angus & Robertson, Sydney, 1989.
Harris, John W., *One Blood: Two Hundred Years of Aboriginal Encounter with Christianity*, Albatross Books, Sutherland, NSW, 1994.
Hordern, Leslie, *Children of One Family: The Story of Anthony and Ann Hordern and their Descendants in Australia*, Retford Press, Sydney, 1985.
Inglis, Ken, *This is the ABC: The Australian Broadcasting Commission 1932–1983*, Melbourne University Press, Melbourne, 1983.
Jones, Colin, *Something in the Air: A History of Radio in Australia*, Kangaroo Press, Dural, NSW, 1995.
Kidman, Bill, *On the Wallaby*, Walsh, Sydney, 1974.
Lang, J. T., *I Remember*, Invincible Press, Sydney, 1956.
Lang, J. T., *The Great Bust*, Angus & Robertson, Sydney, 1962.
Lang, J. T., *The Turbulent Years*, Alpha Books, Sydney, 1970.
Leask, G. A., *V.C. Heroes of the War*, George G. Harrap & Company, London, 1916.

Louis, L. J., *Trade Unions and the Depression, A Study of Victoria 1930–1932*, Australian National University Press, Canberra, 1968.

Louis, L. J. and Turner, Ian, *The Depression of the 1930s*, Cassell Australia, Melbourne, 1968.

Lowenstein, Wendy, *Weevils in the Flour*, Hyland House, Melbourne, 1978.

Luck, Peter, *This Fabulous Century*, New Holland Publishers, Sydney, 1999.

Lyons, Enid, *Among the Carrion Crows*, Rigby, Adelaide, 1972.

Lyons, Enid, *So We Take Comfort*, Heinemann, Melbourne, 1965.

McCalman, Janet, *Struggletown: Public and Private Life in Richmond 1900–1965*, Melbourne University Press, Carlton, Victoria, 1984.

Mackenzie, W. K. S., *The Practice in Divorce (New South Wales)*, The Lawbook Company of Australasia Ltd, Sydney, 1935.

Mackinolty, Judith, *Sugar Bag Days: Sydney Workers and the Challenge of the 1930s Depression* (Master of Arts thesis, Macquarie University), November, 1972.

Morris, Edward E., *A Memoir of George Higinbotham: An Australian Politician and Chief Justice of Victoria*, Macmillan, London, 1895.

Nairn, Bede, *The 'Big Fella': Jack Lang and the ALP*, Melbourne University Press, Melbourne, 1986.

Paisley, Fiona, *Loving Protection? Australian Feminism and Aboriginal Women's Rights, 1919–1939*, Melbourne University Press, Carlton, Victoria, 2000.

Radi, Heather and Spearritt, Peter (eds), *Jack Lang*, Hale & Iremonger, Sydney, 1977.

Robertson, J. Logie (ed), *The Poetical Works of Robert Burns*, Oxford University Press, London, 1960.

Roderick, Colin (ed), *Henry Lawson: Collected Verse*, memorial edition, volume 1, Angus & Roberston, Sydney, 1981.

Schedvin, C. B., *Australia and the Great Depression*, Sydney University Press, Sydney, 1970.

Semmler, Clement, *The ABC: Aunt Sally and Sacred Cow*, Melbourne University Press, Melbourne, 1981.

Shann, E. O. G. and Copland, D. B., *The Battle of the Plans*, Angus & Roberston, Sydney, 1931.

Shann, E. O. G. and Copland, D. B., *The Crisis in Australian Finance 1929–1931*, Angus & Robertson, Sydney, 1931.
Shaw, A. G. L., *The Story of Australia*, Faber & Faber, London, 1955.
Sleeman, J. H. C., *The Life of J. T. Lang*, The Alert Printing and Publishing Co. Ltd, Sydney, 1933.
Spencely, G. F. R., *A Bad Smash: Australia in the Depression of the 1930s*, McPhee Gribble, Melbourne, 1990.
Thomas, Alan, *Broadcast and be Damned: The ABC's first two Decades*, Melbourne University Press, Melbourne, 1980.
Todd, Alpheus, *Parliamentary Government in the British Colonies*, Longmans, Green and Co., London, 1880.
White, Kate, *A Political Love Story: Joe and Enid Lyons*, Penguin Books Australia, Melbourne, 1987.
Wilkinson, Michael, *The Phar Lap Story*, Budget Books Pty Ltd for William Collins, Sydney, 1980.
Writer, Larry, *Razor: A True Story of Slashers, Gangsters, Prostitutes and Sly Grog*, Pan Macmillan Australia Pty Ltd, Sydney, 2001.
Ziebura, Gilbert, (translated by Bruce Little), *World Economy and World Politics, 1924–1931: From Reconstruction to Collapse*, Berg, New York, 1990.

Official publications
Commonwealth of Australia Gazette, April, May 1932.
Commonwealth Census, volumes I, II, III, Australian Bureau of Census and Statistics, Government Printer, Canberra, 1933.
Commonwealth Law Reports (High Court Enforcement Act decision) volume 46, 1932.
Commonwealth Parliamentary Debates, various.
New South Wales Parliamentary Debates, various.
New South Wales Parliamentary Handbook, 1931.
New South Wales Police Record of Service and Stations, Gilbert Edward Leary, 1915–1949.
New South Wales Registry of Births, Deaths and Marriages, Death Certificate of Nellie Louisa Anderson, 15 September, 1911.
Official Year Book of New South Wales, Government Printer, Sydney, 1932.
Report of Royal Commission on Greyhound Racing and Fruit Machines, New South Wales Parliamentary Papers, volume 1, second session, Government Printer, Sydney, 1933.

Supreme Court of New South Wales, Matrimonial Causes Jurisdiction, Ivy Gladys Field versus Sidney John Field, 1931–1932.
Supreme Court of New South Wales, Matrimonial Causes Jurisdiction, Hilda A. Lang versus J. T. Lang, 11 August, 1908, cancelled 14 August, 1908.
Yearbook of the Commonwealth of Australia, Commonwealth Government Printer, Canberra, 1929, 1930, 1931, 1932, 1933.

Manuscripts and original documents
Australian Aborigines' Amelioration Association, first annual report, Perth, Western Australia, 1932.
Cottle, A. R., 'Life can be so sweet on the sunny side of the street: A study of the rich of Woollahra during the depression 1928–1934' (unpublished thesis, November, 1976), MS 5383 National Library of Australia, Canberra.
Francis de Groot papers, Mitchell Library, State Library of New South Wales.
Philip Game papers, Mitchell Library, State Library of New South Wales.
Gwendolen Game papers, Mitchell Library, State Library of New South Wales.

Newspapers
Advertiser, Adelaide
Age, Melbourne
Argus, Melbourne
Brisbane Courier (later *Courier-Mail*), Brisbane
Herald, Melbourne
Labor Daily
Smith's Weekly
Sun, Sydney
Sydney Morning Herald
Telegraph, Sydney
Truth, Sydney
West Australian
The World

1932

Periodicals
Bulletin
Journal of the Royal Australian Historical Society
The Nation
New South Wales Police Gazette
Radio Monthly
Wireless Weekly

Index

Aboriginals 351–2, 351-71
Agua Caliente Handicap 151, 184, 187
Albania
  right-wing coup (1924) 37
Alford, Detective William 233–6, 238
Amounis 185
Anderson, Ethel Jane 56–9
Anderson, Nellie Louisa 47–8, 126, 270–1
Angel Place 228, 235
Anzacs 33–4
Argus 314
Atlantis 301–2, 305–6, 353–6, 358–60, 368, 387
Auselm 365
Australia Club 227
Australia Hotel 26
Australian Aborigines' Amelioration Association 369
Australian Aborigines' League 370
Australian Broadcasting Commission 317, 322–5
Australian Communist Party 225, 232
Australian Federation of Women Voters 369
Australian Labor Party 19-20, 65, 81, 223
  by-election 79–87
Australian Rules Football 77
Australian Workers' Union 223
aviation 73–5, 302–6
Ayrton, George 191–2

Bali-bali, Jim 302, 306, 353–5, 358–9, 364

419

bank deposits, decline in 84
Bank of New South Wales 180
Barrie, Alex 88–90, 103–4
  murder investigation 90–103
Barrie, Mary 88–91, 98, 101, 103
Bavarian Soviet Republic 37
Bavin, Tom 77, 119, 122, 168, 214
Beardsmore, Ethel 246, 249
Beardsmore, Robert Henry 241, 246–9, 257, 272, 276–7, 286, 386
Beef Riot 9
Beinhorn, Elly 303–4
Bell, Richard Thomas 121
Belmore Park 42
Bennett, Mary 369
Berkeley, Busby 26
Berrima Gaol 236
Bertram, Hans 301–3, 305–6, 353, 356–68, 387
Big Fella *see* Jack Lang
Billington, Harold 'Snowy' 372
Bingham, Viola 155
birth control 59–61
birth rate
  reduction in 61
Bishop, Sir Henry Rowley 51–2
Blackburn, Vera 386
Blamey, General Thomas 36
Bloody Sunday 11
Boilermakers' Union 39
Booth, Felix 157, 159, 163–4
Bowes, W.E. 383
Bradfield, Dr John Crew 143–4
Bradman, Donald 28, 73, 380–3
Bray, Victor 264, 267, 269
Bredt, Bertha 47

Bredt, Hilda 47
Brisbane Courier 303
British Union of Fascists 38
Broadcasting Monthly 328
Bruce, Stanley 75, 80–1, 86, 377
Brummell, Beau 152
Bruxner, Michael 336–7, 348
Buckingham Palace 122, 127, 154, 179, 240, 274, 294
Budge, Harry 208, 285, 287
Bulgaria
  right-wing coup (1923) 37
Bulletin 286
Bullmore, Mary 155
Burgeye 353, 356
Burns, Robbie 171
Bush, Hollis 263, 267, 269
Bush Nursing Association 134
bushfires 63
buskers 50

Cairns's 'Bloody Sunday' 11
Calwell, Arthur 220
Campbell, Eric 38–43, 85–6, 104, 107–9, 147–8, 162, 169–70, 204–5, 227, 232–4, 236, 339, 349
Campbell, Jim 145
Canberra
  development of 2
Carson, Irene 7, 388
Catherine Hill Bay 102
Catholic families 60
Caulfield Cup 185
Caulfield Military Hospital 228
Central Criminal Court 171
Chauvel, Charles 262
Chaytor, Lady 304
Cinesound studios 262

citizens' armies 36
civil service payroll 84
Clasby, John 81
Collingwood coke 59
Commercial Bank 180
Commonwealth Bank 21, 190
contraceptives 59–61
Cooper, William 370
Council of Action 40
Cowdroy, Frederick Ford 165–6
Cranbrook 115, 154
cricket 28, 380–3
  world-record attendances 77
crime 7
Cubero, Father 354–6
Cunningham, Lucien 81–2, 87
Curlewis, Judge Adrian 238–9

Daily Telegraph 308, 310
Dalwallinu 56–7
dancing 24
Darlinghurst 24, 26
Darnell-Smith, George Percy 121
Davidson, Mark 141–2
Davis, Dave 152, 184–7
de Groot, Francis 107, 137, 142–3, 147–8, 150, 171–9, 226–7, 349, 385
Devine, Tilly 25, 28, 76, 176–7, 260, 344–5, 374, 388
divorce 261
  Field divorce case 8–9, 258–71
  grounds for 260
  proceedings 260–2
  rates 59, 262
dole programs 213–18, 375–6
Domain 69, 296, 335
Donganga 353, 356

Donnier, Emil 51–2
Donnier, Winifred 50–3, 55
Doone school 115
drifters 92–100
  'clay-shoveller's fracture' 100
  'jumping a rattler' 95
  labour 98–9
  meal rations 93
  Myalup camp 99–100
  outbreaks 100
  survival tricks 94
Drysdale River Mission 353–4, 365
Duffy, Chief Justice Frank Gavan 192
Dynon, John 234

Earl of Jersey 23
1893 financial crash 98
election meetings 82–3
Ely, Bill 169
employment
  women, of 61
Enterprise 73
Erskine, Lady Angela St Clair 178–9
Evatt, Justice Herbert V. 181, 192–4
evictions 10, 30, 214, 219

Fairfax, Warwick 155
family endowment of 62, 66, 210–11
farming families 55–6
Fascist Legion 235–7
Federation 8, 141, 192–3
Field divorce case 8–9, 258–71
Field, Ivy Gladys 8, 258–63, 265–70

Field, Sidney 258–9, 262–3, 265–70
Fifty-Fifty Club 23–9, 73, 76, 91, 150, 295, 344–5, 372–3, 388
Financial Agreements Enforcement Act 1932 111, 179, 189, 192–4, 203, 206, 210–11, 227, 246, 251, 255–6, 277–8, 283
financial crash (1893) 98
Financial Emergency Act 297
Fingleton, Jack 381
Fitzsimmons, Arthur 105
flappers 24
Flemington Race Course 152, 186–7
Flynn, Errol 262
Fore and Aft 179
Forgan Smith, William 346, 375
Forrest River Mission 353, 356
Foy, Hugh 157
Fraser, Eliza 356
Freikorps 37
Fuller, Sir George 318
Furner, Harold 30–1

Galik, John 121
Gallipoli 17, 31, 34, 389
Game, David 115, 125, 285, 335
Game, Lady Gwendolen 71–2, 113–16, 122, 124, 127, 132–8, 145–6, 245–6, 275, 285–7, 299, 335, 337, 385–6
Game, Malcolm Philip 'Bill' 115, 125, 285, 386
Game, Rosemary 115, 125, 133, 146, 285, 335, 385

Game, Sir Philip 26–7, 105, 108, 135–6, 163, 178, 227, 236, 240–1, 245–6
epilogue 385
Jack Lang, dismissal of 287–9, 292–4, 296–300
Jack Lang, disputes with 113–20, 122–7, 272–89
Jack Lang re-election campaign 333–7, 347–50
mortgages tax debate 252, 254, 256–7
public treatment of 69–72
revenue confiscation 208–10
Sydney Harbour Bridge opening 126–7, 132–3, 137–9, 144–6, 149
Garden, Harcourt 231
Garden, Ian 231
Garden, Jock 224–5, 229–32, 235–8, 314, 335, 339
Ginagulla 155
Glen Innes 96
Gordon, Berkeley 26
Gosling, Mark 169, 326
Government House 69, 115, 132–3, 146
Government Savings Bank of New South Wales 21
Greece
right-wing coup (1925) 37
greyhound racing 29, 152–3, 157–68
Royal Commission on Greyhound Racing 160, 163–70
Greyhound Racing Club 165, 167
Gwyn, Nell 178

Index

Halse Rogers, Justice Percival 160, 166–7, 170
Ham, Sergeant Harry 372
Hanlon, Grant 121
Happy Valley 8, 29
homeless people 8
Harlow, Jean 24
Harold Park 29, 153, 159–63, 165, 168
Herlihy, James 246, 248–9
Hill, Lionel 213, 218, 222–3
His Majesty's Theatre 211
Hitler, Adolf 38
Hogan, Edmond 214, 218, 221–3
holiday retreats 26
homicide rates 7
Hordern, Anthony 'Tony' 153, 155–6, 159–60, 163–5, 167–8, 258
Hordern emporium 154
Hore-Ruthven, Sir Alexander 133, 135
horse racing 151–2 see also Phar Lap
house evictions 10, 30, 214, 219
Hughes, William Morris 323
Hungary's Socialist Federated Soviet Republic 37

income tax 189–97
infant mortality
decline in 61
Irvine, Sir William 133, 135
Isaacs, Lady 133, 146
Isaacs, Sir Isaac 125, 132–3, 135–8

Jacka, Albert 'Bert' 31–5, 63
funeral 33–4

Jacka, Vera 32
Jardine, Douglas 381–2
Jeffs, Phil 'the Jew' 25, 27, 76, 91–2, 296, 344–5, 374, 388
job losses 3
Jones, Charles Lloyd 324
Jones, David 155
'jumping a rattler' 91, 95

Kessel, William James 121
Keynes, John Maynard 13
Kidman, Bill 94
King Charles II 178
King George V 113–14, 125–7, 132, 139, 179, 206, 240, 294, 299, 349
King Henry VIII 261
Kings Cross shoot-out 6–7, 387
Kingsford Smith, Charles 'Smithy' 73–5, 77–8, 303–5
Klausmann, Adolf 301–2, 306, 353, 356, 359–61, 363–8
Kooinda 360–1

Labor Daily 316
Labour Women's Organisation 369
Lamb, Ernest 175–6
Lands Department 246
Lang, Hilda 47–9, 137, 149, 270–1, 385
Lang, Jack 27–8, 39–40, 42–9, 62, 70–2, 78, 85–7, 135, 156, 171–2, 237
background 45
characteristics of 4–5
Charles Kingsford Smith, grant to 77
dismissal of 287–99, 306

epilogue 384–6
Financial Agreements Enforcement Act 1932 189–95
Francis de Groot 177–8
Henry Lawson, relationship with 47
kidnapping plot 104–6, 108–9, 235
landslide victory of 16
leaders' summit 63–6
marriage 47
media backlash after dismissal 307–16, 329–30
meeting at Paddington Town Hall 79–83
mortgages tax 250–7, 297
Nellie Anderson, relationship with 47–8, 270–1
1931, leadership during 15–22
overseas debts 18–19, 21, 67–9, 110–12, 195, 202–3, 207–8
police parade 226–7
post-dismissal 375–80
radio broadcasts 317–23, 325–8
re-election campaign 331–51
revenue confiscation 179–81, 197–206, 210–11, 242–7
Sir Philip Game, dispute with 116–25
Sir Philip Game, final confrontation with 272, 274–91
Station Lang 321–3
Swindell saga 159, 162–3, 170
Sydney Harbour Bridge opening 113–14, 126, 137–141, 144–5, 147, 149–50, 174

tin hare racing scandal 161, 168–70
unemployment relief 214–15
unions, relationship with 223–5
Lang, James Christian 48, 271
Lang Labor 20, 81, 87, 156
Lang, Nellie Louisa 271
Lang Plan 18–20, 22, 39, 84, 384
Langites 28, 82, 333
Lawson, Henry 46–7, 331, 379
League of National Security 36
Leary, Detective Gilbert 92, 95–7, 100–103, 386
Legislative Council 70, 117, 196, 253
Lenin 225, 231, 314
Levy, Sir Daniel 326
Lightning Ridge 96
Lindbergh, Charles 74
Lindrum, Walter 73
Loan Council 64–5, 67, 192
Lombard, Carole 24
Lyons, Joe 22, 44, 278, 294, 333, 375, 377–8
   epilogue 385
   Financial Agreements Enforcement Act 180, 190–1, 194
   Financial Emergency Act 297
   Jack Lang, confrontations with 63, 65–8, 80–1, 85–7
   Jack Lang re-election campaign 339–41, 349
   overseas debts 110–11
   radio broadcasting 324, 327
   revenue confiscation 196–9, 201–6, 210–11, 246–7, 251

Sydney Harbour Bridge opening 138, 140, 145

McCall, W.V. 86
McCauley, Harold 105, 161, 163
McTiernan, Justice Edward A. 181, 193–5
McWilliams, Bob 128–32, 136–7, 148–9, 215, 388
McWilliams, Daisy 61, 128–30, 148–9, 215, 388
Mackay, Iven 154
Mackay, Superintendent William 'Billy' 25, 112, 179, 292
  Barrie murder investigation 90, 92, 96, 103
  Central Criminal Court arrests 171–4
  epilogue 387
  Fifty-Fifty Club raid 373–4
  Francis de Groot, arrest of 142–3, 147
  Francis de Groot, trial of 175–6
  New Guard 43, 104–7, 109, 205, 235, 237–9
  police parade 226–7
mail service, overseas 74–7
Markham, Dulcie 24, 91
marriage
  decline in 61
  pressures on 59
Marshall, Constable 366–8
May Day marches 221
Melbourne Agreement 14
Melbourne Cricket Ground 382
Melbourne Cup 151, 184–6
Melbourne Herald 381

Menlo Park 182
Menzies, Robert 20
Miaman 364–6
Milton Park 155
Mitchell, Sir James 19, 327
Monarra 353, 356
Monowai 29
Monty, Julius 30–1
Moree 96
Mortgages Taxation Bill 251–7, 277, 283, 289, 297
Morton, William 'Bill' 91–2, 95–7, 100–103, 387
Mosley, Sir Oswald 38
'Mother Country' 17, 74
Mungana Mines 84
Mussolini, Benito 38
Musson, Mrs 69
Myalup camp 99–100
Myer, Sidney 213

Narrabri 96
National Council of Women 369
Nationalist Federal Government 81
Nationalist Party 157, 171
New Guard 83, 85, 104–8, 155, 162, 294, 339–40, 349–50
  arrests outside Central Criminal Court 171–4
  Charles Kingsford Smith's support for 78
  classes of 41
  Council of Action 40
  Eric Campbell, founder of 38–43
  Fascist Legion 235–7
  formation of 36
  Francis de Groot 175–9

Jock Garden attack 233–9
membership 22, 27, 39
philosophy 86
plot to kidnap Jack Lang 104–9, 235
police parade 226–7
revenue confiscation 204–6
Sydney Harbour Bridge opening 126, 143, 147, 150
Walter Warneford 228–30
New South Wales Country Women's Association 71
Niemeyer, Sir Otto 12–16, 20, 65, 375, 382, 384
Ninety Mile Beach (New Zealand) 73
Nott, Ronald 264, 267–70

Orama 178
Orchard, William Arundel 121
overseas debts 2–4, 17–19, 67–8, 110–12, 195, 202–3, 207–8
  defaults 21, 67
  interest charges 18, 21, 376–8
  reductions in 17
overseas mail service 74–7
Owen, Justice Langer 197–8, 265, 267, 269–70

Paddington, Sydney 89
Paddington Town Hall, Sydney 79
Palm Beach 26
Pearson's Fish Café 105, 109
pension
  widow's 62, 66
Phar Lap 29, 151–2, 182–9
Pickard, John 327–8

Poland
  right-wing coup (1926) 37
Police Air Wing 387
Police Citizens Boys' Clubs 387
Police Rescue Squad 387
Portugal
  right-wing coup (1926) 37
pregnancy, unwanted 59
Premiers' Conference 17, 64, 327, 384
Premiers' Plan 16, 20–1, 64, 66, 82–3, 85, 221–3, 375, 378, 385
Pressenda, Gianfrancesco 52
Prosperity Fiesta 26
Public Trustee 197
Purser, Cecil 121

radio, development of 317–30
railway system 84
Randwick Racecourse 152
rations 213–17
Razorhurst 24
Reception House 143, 147
Red Army 204, 206, 350
Retford Hall 155–6
returned servicemen 34–5
revenue confiscation 190–211
  Commonwealth decree number 42
  242–9
  Mortgages Taxation Bill 251–7, 277, 283, 289, 297
Richmond Club 77
Riley, F.J. 221
riots 9–11
  Beef Riot 9
  Bloody Sunday 11
  Treasury Building Riot 9

Roberts, Fred 6–7, 22, 27, 387–8
Rogers, Will 188
Romano's 26
Royal Commission on Greyhound Racing 160, 163–70
Royal Sydney Golf Club 155
rugby league
  world-record attendances 77
Russian Revolution 37
Ryan, Edna 216–17

Salappo, Don Carlos 26
Salvation Army 213
Scott, C.W.A. 305
Scott, William 230–9
Scullin, James 'Jim' 14, 19–20, 22, 65, 67, 223, 323
  government of 15, 65, 67, 81, 110, 163–4, 346, 378
shanty towns 8
Shaw, Jack 152
Skeen, Leslie 101
Smith, Keith 75
Smith, Norman 'Wizard' 73
Smith, Ross 75
Smith's Weekly 147, 152, 261, 373
Socialist Federated Soviet Republic 37
Southern Cross 74, 78
Spain
  right-wing coup (1923)
St Kilda Cemetery 33
Stadium 26
State Superannuation Board 197–8
Stevens, Bertram 168, 282, 312–13, 315–16, 333, 336, 338–40, 342, 349, 375–6, 386
Stock Exchange 227
Street, Sir Philip 286
Sun 310–11, 314, 328
swagmen *see* drifters
Swindell, Judge Frederick Shaver 29, 83, 313
  tin hare racing scandal 153, 156–67, 169–70
Sydney Arts Club 178
Sydney Cricket Ground 28
Sydney Harbour Bridge
  construction of 2
  opening of 27, 104, 113–14, 126, 130–50, 385
Sydney Morning Herald 168, 211, 289, 312, 314–15, 329, 338, 340, 347, 378
Sydney Town Hall 85
Sydney University 115

Tahiti 156
Tanquinia 365
Taur 365
taxation
  mortgages *see* Mortgages Taxation Bill
  rates 84
Telegraph 290
Telford, Harry 186
Tenterfield 96
Theodore, Edward Granville 14–15, 18–20, 22, 65, 82–4, 87, 378
Timber Workers' Union 206
tin hare racing scandal *see* greyhound racing

Tivoli 50
Todd, Alpheus 298
trade unions 218–24
Trades Hall 38, 109, 204, 216, 218, 220–1, 223
Treasury Building Riot 9
Treloar, Major G.D 108
Trethowan, Arthur King 121
Trinity College 51
Tully, John 246
Tunnecliffe, Thomas 221–2
2FC 319, 325
2GB 320
2KY 320–1, 326–8
2UW 327

Ulm, Charles 74, 78
Unemployed Workers' Movement 10, 219–20
unemployment 11, 80–1, 212–13
  dole programs 213–18, 375–6
  recovery from 374–6
  relief 213–17
  trade unions' intervention 218–223
Union Club 70, 122, 227
United Australia Party 65, 80, 82, 85–7, 202, 311, 323–4, 333, 336, 339, 341, 385
United Country Party 336–7
unwanted pregnancies 59

Victoria Cross 31, 33
Victorian Labor Party 221–2
Victorian Racing Club 185–6
Victorian Relief Committee 213

violence 7
Voigt, Emil 320–2, 327

Walgett 96
Wall Street crash 2–3, 51
war debts *see* overseas debts
war veterans
  employment of 34–5
  pensions 17
Ward, Eddie 81, 85, 87
Warneford, Captain Walter 228–30, 236, 238–9
Warwick 96
Watts, Ernest 27
wealthy families 9, 154–5
Weaver, Reginald 237
Wee Waa 96
Wentworth Hotel 26
West Australian 352, 355–6
wheat industry, demise of 2
White Army 36, 38
White, James 6–7, 387
White Nose 187
widows 53
widow's pension 62, 66
Wigram, Lord 274–5, 299
William Street shoot-out *see* Kings Cross shoot-out
Wilson, Clare 'Girlie' 259, 263–4, 269
Windeyer, Richard 260
Wireless Weekly 321–2, 328
women 53–62
Women's Service Guilds 369
Woodcock, Tommy 182–3, 185–6
wool industry, demise of 2

Woollahra, Sydney 153, 155
work-for-the-dole schemes
 217–18
World War I 1, 31, 33, 37

Young Women's Christian
 Association 369
Yugoslavia
 dictatorship system (1929) 37